Property-Liability Insurance Accounting and Finance

Property-Liability Insurance Accounting and Finance

CORMICK L. BRESLIN

Vice President—Finance and Treasurer
CIC Financial Corporation

TERRIE E. TROXEL, Ph.D., CPCU, CLU

Director of Research
National Association of Independent Insurers

First Edition • 1978

AMERICAN INSTITUTE FOR
PROPERTY AND LIABILITY UNDERWRITERS
Providence and Sugartown Roads, Malvern, Pennsylvania 19355

Second Printing • December 1980

Library of Congress Catalog Number 78-67500
International Standard Book Number 0-89463-015-6

Printed in the United States of America

Foreword

The American Institute for Property and Liability Underwriters and the Insurance Institute of America are companion, nonprofit, educational organizations supported by the property-liability insurance industry. Their purpose is to provide quality continuing education programs for insurance personnel.

The Insurance Institute of America offers programs leading to the Certificate in General Insurance, the Associate in Claims (AIC) designation, the Associate in Management (AIM) designation, the Associate in Risk Management (ARM) designation, the Associate in Underwriting (AIU) designation, the Associate in Loss Control Management (ALCM) designation, the Associate in Premium Auditing (APA) designation, and the new Accredited Adviser in Insurance (AAI) designation for agents and brokers. The American Institute develops, maintains, and administers the educational program leading to the Chartered Property Casualty Underwriter (CPCU) professional designation.

Throughout the history of the CPCU program, an annual updating of parts of the course of study took place. But as changes in the insurance industry came about at an increasingly rapid pace and as the world in which insurance operates grew increasingly complex, it became clear that a thorough, fundamental revision of the CPCU curriculum was necessary.

The American Institute began this curriculum revision project by organizing a committee of academicians, industry practitioners, and Institute staff members. This committee was charged with the responsibility of determining and stating those broad goals which should be the educational aims of the CPCU program in contemporary society. With these goals formulated, the curriculum committee began writing specific educational objectives which were designed to achieve the stated goals of the program. This was a time-consuming and difficult task. But this process made certain that the revised CPCU curriculum would be based on a sound and relevant foundation.

Once objectives were at least tentatively set, it was possible to outline a new, totally revised and reorganized curriculum. These outlines were widely circulated and the reactions of more than 1,800 educators and industry leaders were solicited, weighed, and analyzed. These outlines were then revised and ultimately became the structure of the new, ten-course curriculum.

With the curriculum design in hand, it was necessary to seach for study materials which would track with the revised program's objectives and follow its design. At this stage of curriculum development, the Institute reached the conclusion that it would be necessary for the Institute to prepare and publish study materials specifically tailored to the revised program. This conclusion was not reached hastily. After all, for the Institute to publish textbooks and study materials represents a significant broadening of its traditional role as an examining organization. But the unique educational needs of CPCU candidates, combined with the lack of current, suitable material available through commercial publishers for use in some areas of study, made it necessary for the Institute to broaden its scope to include publishing.

Throughout the development of the CPCU text series, it has been—and will continue to be—necessary to draw on the knowledge and skills of Institute staff members. These individuals will receive no royalties on texts sold and their writing responsibilities are seen as an integral part of their professional duties. We have proceeded in this way to avoid any possibility of conflicts of interests.

All Institute textbooks have been—and will continue to be—subjected to an extensive review process. Reviewers are drawn from both industry and academic ranks.

We invite and will welcome any and all criticisms of our publications. It is only with such comments that we can hope to provide high quality educational texts, materials, and programs.

Edwin S. Overman, Ph.D., CPCU
President

Preface

This text is designed to serve as part of the CPCU accounting and finance course. The other texts used in this course provide a generalized collegiate-level treatment of basic accounting and finance principles as they apply to commercial enterprises. This text describes the principles and procedures of accounting and finance that specifically relate to property and liability insurance companies.

Individuals who are familiar with general accounting and finance but unacquainted with technical aspects of the insurance industry too often regard the accounting and finance practices of property and liability insurers to be abstruse. This book attempts to explain how the administrative and quasi-legislative power of state insurance regulatory authorities, acting principally through the National Association of Insurance Commissioners, has been used to develop and impose insurance accounting and finance practices that safeguard the public interest. This traditionally has meant promulgation of accounting rules that encourage continuity of operations. For example, the asset structure and capital structure of property and liability insurance companies are directly affected by NAIC accounting regulations and other legislative and administrative rules. The focus of insurance accounting and finance therefore differs from the more general principles and practices encountered in other businesses. The variations between generally accepted accounting principles and insurance regulatory accounting are identified in the text. This text also examines the rationale that gives rise to the differences.

More specifically, Chapter 1 describes in some detail various financial reports prepared by property and liability insurance companies. Emphasis is placed on an overview of the NAIC annual statement. The origin and scope of GAAP are traced, and a comparison is made between GAAP and regulatory insurance accounting. Chapter 2 discusses asset valuation and the factors that influence the size and composition of a property and liability insurance company's investment portfolio. A theoretical investment policy model is used to demonstrate how asset valuation rules impact on insurance company investment decisions. In Chapter 3 the principal liability accounts of nonlife insurers are identified, and the methods used to estimate or otherwise determine their values are examined. The balance sheet categories used to classify net worth are also described. Attention turns from balance sheet accounts to income statement variables in Chapter 4. Chapter 5 exposes the reader to a compendium of financial ratios useful in analyzing and comparing property and liability insurance companies. Analysis is based on both regulatory insurance accounting data and on financial information adjusted to a more conventional basis. Methods used to detect financial distress and regulatory tools designed to help assure continued company solvency are discussed in Chapter 6. The 1976 NAIC annual statement for fire and casualty insurance companies referred to throughout the text is reproduced in the appendix.

This text is not meant to be a comprehensive handbook on property and liability insurance accounting and finance. A number of very significant issues relating to this general subject area have been intentionally omitted simply because it is felt that these topics are beyond the scope of the CPCU course of study. For instance, whether anticipated investment income should be included in the computation of premium deficiencies is not discussed in this volume, nor is the actuarial certification of loss reserves. Nonetheless, the text is sufficiently detailed to give CPCU candidates a working knowledge of the fundamental aspects of this subject area and to allow them to apply this knowledge to actual situations.

No review exercises or discussion questions appear in this text. These are included in a companion study aid—the CPCU 8 Course Guide. The Course Guide contains educational objectives, outlines of study material, key terms and concepts, review questions, and discussion questions for each weekly assignment.

Preliminary drafts of the six chapters that make up this book benefited from the critical comments and suggestions of reviewers. The authors wish to thank these persons, especially Glenn L. Wood, Ph.D., CPCU, CLU, Professor of Finance and Insurance, California State College at Bakersfield; and Robert A. Zelten, Ph.D., Associate Professor of Insurance, University of Pennsylvania. Ruth E. Salzmann, FCAS, Vice President and Actuary, Sentry Insurance Company, also furnished valuable comments.

We are pleased to acknowledge that important additions to the text were made by the two contributing authors who are listed elsewhere.

Their participation in preparing or revising text material added significantly to the book.

A number of people have worked diligently on the editing, proof reading, and production of this text; we wish to thank them for their work. Because insurance and accounting are dynamic disciplines, changes inevitably will be needed in the text. Constructive comments and suggestions should be communicated to the authors so that the study material's usefulness may be maintained.

Cormick L. Breslin
Terrie E. Troxel

Contributing Authors

The American Institute for Property and Liability Underwriters and the authors acknowledge, with deep appreciation, the work of the following contributing authors:

Dan R. Anderson, Ph.D., CPCU
Associate Professor
Risk Management and Insurance
University of Wisconsin

James E. Bachman, Ph.D.
Controller
The St. Paul Fire & Marine Insurance Co.

Table of Contents

Gains and Losses in Surplus

Insurance Expense Exhibit ～ *Part I—Allocation to Expense Groups; Part II—Allocation to Lines of Business; Part III—Summary of Workers' Compensation Expenses and Ratios to Earned Premiums; Part IV—Exhibit of Workers' Compensation to Earned Premiums and Incurred Losses by States*

Accounting for Reinsurance Transactions ～ *Reinsurance Procedures; Reinsurance Premiums and Commissions; Reinsurance Losses; Reinsurance Recoverable; Reinsurace Accounting Records*

Summary

Introduction

Goals and Objectives of Insurance Companies

Unique Characteristics of Insurance Operations ～ *Basic Operating Statistics; Capacity Statistics; Liquidity; Profitability; Summary of Financial Ratios*

Financial Ratings of Insurance Companies ～ *Companies Subject to Rating; Best's Policyholders' Ratings; Best's Financial Classification; Effect of Company Size; Changes in Ratings*

Summary

Introduction

Establishing Solvency ～ *The Meaning of Solvency; Minimum Net Worth Requirements; Capital and Surplus Expansion*

Methods of Maintaining Solvency ～ *Insurance Department Examinations; NAIC Regulatory Tests*

The Solvency Record ～ *Factors Leading to Insolvency*

Insurance Guaranty Mechanisms ~ *Federal Proposals; The NAIC Model Bill; State Guaranty Laws; Proposed Changes; Some Unresolved Questions; Future of the Solvency Guaranty Mechanism*

Summary

CHAPTER 1

Introduction to
Insurance Accounting and Finance

INTRODUCTION

The purpose of this book is to demonstrate and explain how the principles of accounting and finance are practiced in the property and liability insurance industry. A basic knowledge of elementary accounting and finance is assumed. From this base, the application of accounting and finance principles to property and liability insurers is developed. Chapter 1 gives an overview of insurance accounting. In Chapters 2, 3, and 4 the principal elements of financial accounting—assets, liabilities, revenues, and expenses—for property and liability insurance companies are investigated. Chapter 5 discusses the tools of financial analysis that commonly are applied to nonlife insurers. Methods used to define, establish, and maintain insurer solvency are examined in Chapter 6.

DIVERSE USES OF ACCOUNTING INFORMATION

The underlying objective of any accounting system is to provide information for decision making. Generally, the four major decision-making areas in which accounting information is used involve (1) resource allocations, (2) administrative control, (3) management stewardship, and (4) social equity. A decision to commit scarce resources to a particular purpose is the most fundamental economic choice that can be made. Whether a particular operating or capital expenditure is made depends on an analysis of the revenue and cost data associated with that project. An affirmative decision to invest in a project gives rise to a

1

subsidiary decision-making area—that of administrative direction and control. In this second area, accounting information permits procurement, conservation, and effective utilization of resources. It gives administrators a means of evaluating the effectiveness with which objectives and goals are being achieved. Information produced by the accounting system is used in a third decision-making area to guage management's stewardship of resources employed within an economic unit. Separation of resource ownership and management makes an accounting information system essential in order for external owners to judge management performance. Finally, society has a need for information on which to base decisions concerning equity among various groups. Accounting systems are called upon to provide a basis for society's welfare judgments and therefore must be structured in such a fashion as to have this information available.

Within this context of accounting as an information system, it often is convenient to approach accounting from a utilitarian point of view. That is, the uses made of accounting data serve to define the nature and scope of the accounting system. Security analysts and stockholders therefore are believed to be primarily interested in financial accounting information, especially income and cash flow measurements. A firm's internal management is charged with the task of establishing objectives and goals for the future. Performance of this duty is facilitated by those accounting techniques that deal with the future, such as budgets and pro forma financial statements. Management evaluation and control requires information on cost-volume-profit relationships. Cost accounting systems therefore concentrate on classifying, allocating, and assigning costs incurred in the production process to various segments of that process. Similarly, tax accounting provides information from which compliance with tax laws can be judged. Accounting reports to governmental regulatory agencies furnish information that indicates whether or not regulatory objectives are being met. Because there are multiple audiences addressed by the accounting system, there are various elements to that system. Alternatively, the individual elements of an accounting system may be considered separate and distinct accounting systems, each with its own purposes. There is legitimate reason for an organization to "keep more than one set of books."

A study of insurance accounting requires that the multiplicity of the information system's audiences be kept in mind. Historically, regulatory uses of accounting have defined the nature and scope of insurance accounting. Regulatory accounting remains important today and continues to shape accounting practices within the insurance industry. But in recent years, other users of insurance accounting information have become more precise in formulating and more vocal in stating their needs for information. This has expanded the scope of insurance accounting and further complicated an already complex subject.

ACCOUNTING REPORTS OF PROPERTY AND LIABILITY INSURANCE COMPANIES

Property and liability insurers prepare accounting reports for distribution to a number of distinct audiences. The dominant influence that regulatory accounting practices have on insurance company financial operations explains why an understanding of regulatory reporting requirements is basic to an analysis of insurance companies. Reports to users other than state insurance regulators also are important. These reports may differ materially from the statutory statements because they are intended to satisfy informational needs of stockholders, the Securities and Exchange Commission (SEC), the stock exchanges, and the Internal Revenue Service (IRS). A total of eight accounting reports prepared by property and liability insurance companies will be examined:

1. the National Association of Insurance Commissioners (NAIC) Annual Statement (see Appendix, p. 343),
2. the NAIC Insurance Expense Exhibit,
3. reports to shareholders,
4. reports to stock exchanges,
5. reports to the SEC,
6. reports to policyholders,
7. federal income tax reports, and
8. reports to company management.

While the majority of these reports properly are classified as financial accounting documents, others contain operating, management, and tax accounting information. This book emphasizes the financial accounting aspects of these reports. Initially, the format and content of the NAIC Annual Statement is described, followed by a discussion of other accounting reports prepared by insurers. Interrelationships among the reports should be recognized as the reports are described. Later in this chapter, the accounting principles that underlie financial statements contained in these reports will be examined and compared.

The NAIC Statement

Insurance statutes in all states require that every insurance company authorized to transact business in the state prepare a comprehensive statement reporting its financial position and results of its operations and other supplementary data of a financial nature, verified under oath of a responsible officer of the company. The statement must be filed annually, and in some states quarterly, with the insurance department or other designated state authority. The annual filing presents a statement of the company's condition and affairs at December 31 of each year as required by the insurance regulatory authority. It must be filed on or before March 1 of the following year. Fines of up to $100 a day are imposed on delinquent companies unless special dispensation has been granted by the insurance regulatory authority for a later date. Once filed, these statements are in the public domain and therefore are available for general inspection by any interested party. Information contained in the reports is published in various degrees of detail by a number of financial data services, such as *Best's Insurance Reports: Property-Liability*.

The regulatory reporting form, generally known as the "convention form of annual statement," "convention blank," or "annual statement," has existed for more than 100 years. The National Insurance Convention was established in 1871, and at the Convention's initial meeting a permanent committee on blanks (financial statements) was established and charged with the duty of developing and continually revising uniform financial blanks for insurance companies. This committee has remained an important part of the insurance regulatory group, which changed its name to the National Convention of Insurance Commissioners in 1874 and changed it again in 1936 to the National Association of Insurance Commissioners (NAIC). Except where specific statutes of the various states conflict with the requirements of this form, all annual statements filed by insurance companies with state regulatory bodies must be on the current form recommended by the Blanks Committee and approved by the NAIC. When a conflict exists the individual insurance departments usually require supplementary schedules in addition to the standard form. In this way special statutory filing requirements unique to the state are satisfied.

Preparation of the annual statement is governed by uniform accounting instructions and the examiners' manual which are prepared and supervised by the Blanks Committee and the Committee on Examinations of the NAIC. These uniform instructions and the examiners' manual, in effect, represent a compilation of insurance accounting principles. They not only govern preparation of the annual statement but they also define the basic accounting and recordkeeping system used by insurance companies. While there is no statutory provision or regulation that mandates companies to keep their records in any specific manner, the fact that they all are required to prepare periodic statements of a prescribed form based on uniform principles and standards makes it impractical to maintain the records in any manner other than that which facilitates the preparation of the annual statement. This explains why the books and records of insurance companies are not kept on the same basis as those of other commercial enterprises.

In its current form, the annual statement is an oversized document containing fifty pages of financial statements, exhibits, and schedules. The cover identifies the document, contains the date, names the company and the state in which the form is filed, lists officers, directors or trustees of the company, and shows certain other information dealing with the company's location and history. The statutory balance sheet is contained on the second and third pages. The statement of underwriting and investment income and the statement of capital and surplus are on the fourth page. Thus the financial statements found within the first four pages roughly correspond to the summary financial statements of other businesses. The fact that the annual statement continues for another forty-six pages indicates the degree of financial disclosure required of insurance companies.

The summary financial statements are followed by a series of exhibits, supporting schedules, and a comprehensive questionnaire. These supporting materials break down the premium writings, the loss payments, unearned premium calculations, and loss reserve provisions in detail by line of coverage. They also show detailed calculation of special statutory loss and loss adjustment expense reserves and the development or maturation of loss reserves for the purpose of indicating whether or not proper reserves have been carried by the company in the past. The schedules that deal with assets itemize the investments and show their cost, market value, the income received, and similar data. The general interrogatories cover a variety of subjects; for example, one question asks the maximum retention of the insurer on any single exposure unit, other questions deal with the company's capitalization, and others inquire about reinsurance arrangements. The purpose of the questionnaire is to easily ascertain information that does not conform to presentation in financial exhibits and schedules. In effect, the annual statement is a comprehensive set of working papers which enable the insurance departments to study the financial position of the company and to obtain a fair idea of the authenticity and reliability of the figures presented without making annual field examinations. Careful study of the annual statement by a properly trained examiner can give a reasonably good idea of the company's position and demonstrate whether or not further examination into the company's affairs and records is necessary.

The finished product of the financial accounting process is expressed in a set of summary financial statements that are based on common underlying data and that are fundamentally related to one another. The summary financial statements consist of a statement of financial position, a statement of operating results, an analysis of retained earnings, and a statement of changes in financial position. The balance sheet, or statement of financial position, is the most fundamental accounting statement in the sense that all transactions involving accounting values have an effect on this report. The income statement shows the results of operations during the accounting period, the effects of which impact on the balance sheet and are reconciled therewith through the analysis of changes in net worth. The change in net worth between balance sheets prepared at the beginning and end of an accounting period is fully explained by net income as shown on the income statement plus any capital transactions—such as dividend payments and the sale of stock—as reported in the statement of changes in net worth. The statement of changes in financial position discloses the net flow of funds resulting from all financing and investing activities during the accounting period.

The summary financial statements of insurance companies contained in the first pages of the annual statement have a general structure and appearance the same as those found in the financial statements prepared by other commercial enterprises. This appearance disguises the fact that there are material differences between statutory accounting principles and the rules that underlie statements prepared on the basis of so-called generally accepted accounting principles (GAAP). Before a comparison of the two sets of accounting rules is presented, the most important sections of the annual statement will be reviewed. Note that a statement of changes in financial position is not included.

Balance Sheet Insurance is said to be a business "affected with the public interest." Because of the public nature of the insurance business, regulators impose a higher standard of financial solidity on insurance companies than is expected of other corporations. One way in which the higher standard is imposed is through restricting the assets that are eligible for inclusion on the statutory balance sheet.

Assets. There are two major divisions of assets on page 2 of the annual statement. The first seven lines show the various kinds of "invested" assets. These assets consist of bonds, preferred stock, common stock, mortgages, real estate, collateral loans, cash (including bank deposits), and other invested assets. The distribution of assets among a large number of insurance companies for these investment categories is shown in Table 1-1. The percentages show the relative importance of each category to total assets as of the end of 1976 among 945 stock, 308 mutual, 48 reciprocal, and 26 American Lloyds property and liability insurers.[1] It can be seen that these invested resources comprise the vast majority (76.5 percent) of all assets held by nonlife insurance companies. Chapter 2 of this text discusses the nature and valuation of invested assets in detail.

Lines 8 through 21 of the annual statement list assets other than those that normally are considered investments. These items represent resources of value to the insurance companies even though, for the most part, they do not yield an investment return. The single most important category among the noninvested assets is "Agents' Balances or Uncollected Premiums." This account represents insurance premiums due on policies written within ninety days prior to the statement date, net of agents' commissions and policyholder dividends, plus the net amount due on reinsurance assumed. An asset category closely related to agents' balances is entitled "Bills Receivable, Taken for Premiums." The amount shown on the balance sheet for this account is the aggregate value of promissory notes, signed by the insured, that are used to finance the installment purchase of insurance. Statutory rules dealing with the quality of the notes must be satisfied in order for a particular note to be included as an eligible asset in this category. Although not considered an investment, the notes bear interest. Another important asset in this section of the balance sheet carries the title "Funds Held by or Deposited with Ceding Reinsurers." The title is somewhat misleading. Values in this account represent amounts due but not currently payable from other insurance companies (primary insurers) that have transferred part or all of their directly insured loss exposures to the reinsuring company whose statements are being analyzed. The terms of the reinsurance agreement may (1) allow the primary companies to retain premium balances owed the accepting reinsurer, or (2) require the reinsurance company to make deposits, in advance of a final accounting, with the primary companies for payment of losses. In either case, funds belonging to the reinsurer are held by the primary companies but are allowed to be shown on the reinsurer's balance sheet if certain qualitative standards are met. Another asset category dealing with reinsurance shows a type of receivable due *from* reinsurance companies *to* a primary insurer. This account is accurately described by its title, "Reinsurance Recoverable on Loss Payments."

The amounts shown for each class of assets entered on the balance sheet are calculated in Exhibit 1—Analysis of Assets found on page 11 of the annual statement. This exhibit is the primary working paper used to determine the asset values that can be included in computing an insurer's net worth. In order to understand its function and importance, four asset classifications peculiar to the insurance industry must be introduced: *ledger, nonledger, nonadmitted,* and *admitted.*

Ledger assets are those assets that are recorded in the company's general ledger by way of the normal voucher-to-journal, journal-to-

Table 1-1
Admitted Assets—
Property and Liability Insurance Companies as of December 31, 1976

	945 Stock Companies		308 Mutual Companies		48 Reciprocals		26 American Lloyds	
	($000,000)	Percent	($000,000)	Percent	($000,000)	Percent	($000,000)	Percent
Common Stock								
Railroad	$ 25.2	0.0	$ 5.7	0.0	$ 2.3	0.1	—	—
Utility	1,374.4	1.6	395.1	1.6	26.7	0.6	0.1	0.1
Bank	853.2	1.0	235.1	1.0	21.5	0.5	0.4	0.5
Insurance	228.6	0.3	76.9	0.3	6.9	0.2	0.2	0.2
Miscellaneous	7,900.1	9.5	2,079.6	8.6	248.9	5.7	1.6	1.8
Parents, Subs, Affils	8,969.8	10.7	1,464.1	6.1	137.8	3.2	1.8	1.9
Total Common Stock	19,351.3	23.2	4,256.5	17.6	444.3	10.3	4.1	4.5
Preferred Stock								
Railroad	7.9	0.0	1.2	0.0	0.0	0.0	—	—
Utility	2,186.9	2.6	401.7	1.7	57.6	1.3	0.6	0.6
Bank	19.0	0.0	0.8	0.0	0.0	0.0	—	—
Insurance	52.4	0.1	5.7	0.0	0.0	0.0	—	—
Miscellaneous	437.9	0.5	104.4	0.4	0.2	0.0	0.0	0.0
Parents, Subs, Affils	70.0	0.1	7.9	0.0	3.2	0.1	0.1	0.1
Total Preferred Stock	2,774.1	3.3	521.8	2.1	61.0	1.4	0.7	0.7

		%		%		%		%
Bonds								
U.S. Government	6,809.7	8.1	3,735.8	15.5	458.5	10.5	41.2	45.0
Other Government	335.5	0.4	110.9	0.5	5.2	0.1	—	—
State, Municipal, etc.	10,188.2	12.2	4,006.4	16.7	1,052.2	24.1	3.8	4.2
Special Revenue, etc.	17,559.1	21.0	4,858.9	20.2	740.1	16.9	1.6	1.8
Railroad	238.4	0.3	126.9	0.5	36.4	0.8	—	—
Utility	2,878.8	3.4	1,174.6	4.9	326.4	7.5	1.0	1.1
Miscellaneous	8,096.5	9.7	1,829.9	7.6	330.6	7.6	1.6	1.7
Parents, Subs. Affils	429.9	0.5	78.7	0.3	1.2	0.0	—	—
Total Bonds	46,536.1	55.7	15,922.2	66.2	2,950.6	67.5	49.3	53.9
Other Invested Assets	223.6	0.3	40.6	0.2	2.1	0.0	0.6	0.7
Mortgages	203.6	0.2	64.6	0.3	1.0	0.0	0.1	0.1
Real Estate	898.8	1.1	537.4	2.2	—	—	0.7	0.7
Collateral Loans	38.6	0.0	12.2	0.1	184.2	4.2	0.0	0.0
Cash	1,396.5	1.7	402.9	1.7	84.1	1.9	15.3	16.8
Premium Balances	6,950.7	8.3	1,442.8	6.0	429.2	9.8	10.8	11.8
Other Assets	5,199.3	6.2	855.4	3.6	213.3	4.9	9.9	10.8
Total Other Assets	14,911.1	17.8	3,355.9	14.1	913.9	20.8	37.4	40.9
Total Admitted Assets	$63,572.7	100%	$24,056.4	100%	$4,369.9	100%	$91.5	100%

ledger, double-entry bookkeeping cycle. The assets discussed thus far normally are recorded in the company's general ledger and therefore are classified as ledger assets in Exhibit 1. In addition to the assets discussed previously, some insurers may carry other assets on their books. These are entered on blank lines provided in the annual statement. Some examples of miscellaneous ledger assets shown by some companies include the depreciated value of electronic data processing equipment, equity in assets of joint underwriting associations, and funds due from affiliated corporations.

Nonledger assets are not entered on the books of the insurer but instead are recorded directly in Exhibit 1 by way of a single-entry bookkeeping system. At the time of statement preparation, the values of nonledger assets are determined by itemizing the incompleted transactions from which these assets arise. The two most important nonledger assets are "Interest, Dividends, and Real Estate Income Due and Accrued" and the excess of market or amortized value over the book value of certain invested assets. Due and accrued investment income in the form of interest, dividends, and rent simply indicates the amounts receivable from invested assets at year end. The nature of the excess market value account is explained later in this section.

Nonadmitted assets may be excluded entirely from the balance sheet or may have a portion of their values eliminated as nonadmitted. For example, the value of furniture and equipment (other than large electronic data processing machines) is excluded in its entirety. Furniture and equipment are resources of significant value that will provide service during future accounting periods. Nevertheless, the restrictive rules of asset admissibility completely bar any value being shown on the balance sheet for these items. An asset whose value is only partially nonadmissible is illustrated by a stock whose ledger value exceeds the value determined in accordance with NAIC rules.[2] The excess of ledger over association value is shown in column 3 of Exhibit 1 as a nonadmissible item and only the lower association value is carried forward to the balance sheet.

Admitted assets are the asset values actually shown on an insurer's balance sheet. These values are arrived at in Exhibit 1 by a formula that uses the terms just defined:

Admitted Assets = Ledger Assets + Nonledger Assets − Nonadmitted Assets

The term *gross assets* sometimes is used to mean the sum of ledger and nonledger assets. Gross assets minus nonadmitted assets then are called *net* admitted assets. This latter term appears at the top of column 4 in Exhibit 1.

The distinction between ledger and nonledger assets is fundamentally different from the division of assets on the basis of admissibility.

Ledger and nonledger assets differ only in the way records of their values are kept. If for some reason a company wanted to convert a nonledger asset to a ledger asset it could do so by making the appropriate journal entries and posting the journals to the ledgers. Some accounts that are treated as ledger assets by most insurance companies are treated as nonledger assets by others. The distinction between these two asset classifications does not imply a difference in quality.

On the other hand, nonadmitted assets are deemed to be of lower quality than assets admitted to the balance sheet. Although nonadmitted assets are resources of value that usually would be shown on the financial statements of other corporations, they do not meet the higher standards used by insurance regulators to judge financial solidity. Nonadmitted assets usually are excluded because they lack the degree of liquidity deemed necessary by the insurance regulators. Liquidity is defined as the ability to realize an asset's value in cash, the most liquid of all assets. An asset's liquidity is measured in two dimensions. First, the shorter the time necessary for conversion of the asset to cash, the more liquid the asset. Second, the higher the certainty of the amount realizable upon conversion to cash, the more liquid the asset. Uncertainties in regard to the time required or the amount realizable upon liquidation forces exclusion of certain assets from insurance company balance sheets. Significant assets such as automobiles, leasehold improvements, furniture, certain types of equipment, supplies, and others are eliminated because of their low liquidity characteristics.

In order to illustrate how the formula set forth in Exhibit 1 operates in the determination of admitted asset values, consider the following example. A particular insurer has recorded a total of $30 million as agents' balances due and payable. Of this amount, $5 million consists of balances outstanding beyond the ninetieth day. Because agents' balances are considered overdue and therefore nonadmissible after ninety days, the ledger value for this asset must be reduced to its admitted value. The same insurer also has purchased common stock at a cost of $50 million and recorded this value for the securities in its ledger. During the accounting period the stocks' market values have appreciated and equal $70 million at the statement date. The excess of market value over ledger value is a nonledger asset. Net admitted asset values for the agents' balances and common stock accounts are calculated in Exhibit 1 as shown in Table 1-2. The adjustment involving common stocks allows the insurer to include the securities on the balance sheet at their market value. Maintaining the ledger value at cost permits a comparison to be made of historical and current values. When the securities are sold, the gain or loss will be determined by deducting the cost figure shown in the ledger from the proceeds of the sale. Reducing

Table 1-2

Abbreviated Analysis of Assets

	(1) Ledger Assets	(2) Nonledger Assets	(3) Assets Not Admitted	(4) Net Admitted Assets
Common stocks	$50,000,000	$20,000,000	—	$70,000,000
Agents' balances	$30,000,000	—	$5,000,000	$25,000,000

agents' balances by the amount overdue eliminates the portion of the ledger value considered to be illiquid.

Liabilities. Obligations resulting from past or current transactions that require a company to convey assets or perform services in the future are considered liabilities. This definition fits the obligations of insurance companies but, historically, insurance accounting has used the word "reserves" to describe liabilities. General accounting terminology uses the word "reserve" to describe a portion of surplus earmarked for a specific purpose. Segregating surplus in this manner is meant to communicate the idea that the company may become obligated to convey assets or perform services at some time in the future because of a current or past transaction, but that this potential obligation is not definitely determinable at the statement date. The segregation of surplus thus is used to create an "in between" account, called a reserve, that is classified in the equity section of the balance sheet but, if more information were available, might more properly be considered a liability. Insurance reserves should not be considered allocated surplus; they are liabilities. Unfortunately, a few insurers, particularly mutual companies, use the term "reserve" to designate net worth. Such practices serve to confuse rather than clarify an understanding of insurance company financial statements. The customary insurance terminology which equates liabilities, estimated liabilities, and reserves will be retained here.[3]

There are three general categories of property and liability insurance company reserves. The first category includes liabilities for losses and loss settlement expenses. The second category reflects an obligation of the insurer to provide coverage under insurance contracts for which premiums already have been paid or currently are due but for which a portion of the coverage extends into the next accounting period. All other obligations can be grouped into miscellaneous liabilities. The catch-all category includes liabilities uniquely associated with insurance

Table 1-3

Net Worth Distortion Caused By Reserve Inadequacy

	Original Balance Sheet	Corrected Balance Sheet
Total assets	$100	$100
Liabilities	$ 75	$ 85
Capital and surplus	25	15
Total liabilities and net worth	$100	$100

$$\text{Overstatement} = \frac{\text{Change in Net Worth}}{\text{True Net Worth}} = \frac{\$10}{\$15} = 67\%$$

operations and other miscellaneous obligations common to many businesses.

Reserves for losses and loss related adjustment expenses plus unearned premium reserves offset about two-thirds of a typical property and liability insurance company's net admitted assets. Capital and surplus may be severely distorted, and thus the financial solidity of an insurer materially misjudged, if liabilities are not estimated accurately. For example, assume a particular insurer's balance sheet shows total liabilities equal to 75 percent of assets; further assume that liabilities are understated by $10. As a result the insurer's net worth has been overstated by almost 67 percent of its true value, as shown in Table 1-3.

It is easy to see how inaccurate determination of reserves can distort an insurer's financial position. Moreover, because the changes in certain liabilities between the accounting period's endpoints are involved in calculation of underwriting results, incorrect reserve valuations also prevent meaningful analysis of the company's operating statement.

The composition of a particular insurance company's liabilities depends on the kinds of insurance coverage written, the product mix of policies, and the average policy duration. A brief discussion of the purposes and functions served by insurance company reserves will explain why the major categories of liabilities vary in relative size among different insurers.

RESERVES FOR UNPAID LOSSES AND LOSS SETTLEMENT EXPENSES. State insurance statutes require property and liability insurers to establish and maintain reserves for unpaid losses and loss adjustment expenses. Many insurance claims and the expenses that will be incurred to adjust them are difficult to evaluate prior to ultimate settlement. This is especially true of liability claims, the value of which may be influenced by such things as length of discovery period, economic conditions, inflation, legal jurisdiction, and other factors. Because values are not readily known for many losses at the balance sheet date, statistical techniques, actuarial concepts, and the judgment of claims personnel are employed to estimate loss and loss adjustment expense reserves. The resulting liability is called the insurer's loss and loss expense reserve.

(a.) Unpaid Losses. Estimating reserves requires that both dimensions of losses—frequency and severity—be considered. Frequency data are developed from the company's claims records which must carefully record the incidence of reported losses. This function requires a significant commitment of resources to gather, code, record, and collate loss data. In many respects, an even more difficult and complicated task is encountered in dealing with the losses' severity dimension. Establishing the total liability of the insurer for unpaid losses is accomplished by combining information on the number of claims with estimates of the amount that ultimately will be paid for each loss. Ideally, reserves developed from frequency and severity data will be sufficient to satisfy all losses that have occurred for which the insurer is liable plus the cost of settlement. If reserves are less than adequate, the insurer's current financial condition is misrepresented and the potential exists for serious difficulties to develop as unpaid losses are liquidated at higher than reserved values. On the other hand, material overstatement of loss reserves understates the company's financial condition and damages its performance record. Insurers therefore should endeavor to make adequate but not excessive provision for unpaid losses. Although this ideal may remain unattained, it provides a frame of reference in which loss reserving practices are carried out.

Loss reserves fall into two general categories. First, there are claims that have been adjusted or are in the loss adjustment process. Second, there are losses which already have occurred prior to the cutoff date for balance sheet preparation but which have not been reported to the insurer and recorded in the claims register.

Within the first category, several subdivisions exist: (1) claims approved for payment but not yet paid, (2) pending claims that require further adjustment, and (3) previously closed claims that subsequently will be reopened for additional payments. Approved but not yet paid claims are a relatively small portion of total loss reserves. This also is true of payments on reopened claims. The largest element of loss reserves is for claims in the process of adjustment. Several explanations can be given for the existence of unpaid claims at the end of an accounting period. Some claims may have been recorded just prior to the cutoff date and adjusters have not been able to process them. Other claims in this subdivision may involve disagreements regarding the coverage, the value of the loss, or both. Disagreements ultimately are settled through negotiation, arbitration, litigation, or appraisal. Unreasonably extending the period of time before claims are settled allows unscrupulous insurers to retain larger invested asset balances by reducing cash outflows for loss payments. Evidence of "claims resistance" should be interpreted as a leading indication of financial weakness. Such practices may be the aftermath of inadequate pricing or underreserving. In other instances, management may follow an intentional policy of grudging loss settlements on large claims and at the same time rapidly settle small so-called nuisance claims. The latter practice may be followed in the belief that it will result in lower total loss payments.[4] In this case, slow loss settlement would not necessarily indicate a weakened financial standing. Because more than one reason exists for delayed claims payment, the financial analyst may wish to study the magnitude of an insurer's loss reserves over time in relation to the growth of its premium writings. If the investigation shows an unusual increase in loss reserves, additional analysis of the insurer's financial condition will be required.

The second category of loss reserves reflects the insurer's liability for losses incurred prior to the financial statement cutoff date but reported after that date. Losses in this category usually are called IBNR (incurred but not reported) claims or, simply, unreported claims. Losses reported after the close of the accounting period that are the result of accidents occurring on or before the accounting cutoff date properly are classified as debts owing at the balance sheet date. Company claims personnel study time lags between loss occurrence and loss reporting and then incorporate knowledge of normal time lags with other information to estimate IBNR liabilities. In most insurance lines, standard actuarial procedures are well suited for estimation of unreported claims reserves. Because only historical patterns are available to place a value on unreported claims, statistical and actuarial techniques are used to estimate this portion of the loss reserves.

(b.) Loss Settlement Expenses.   Reserves for unpaid losses usually provide only for loss payments and not for any associated loss adjustment expenses. In addition to the cost of the loss, significant expenses are incurred by insurers in investigating, processing, and paying losses. A reserve is established for anticipated future expense payments required to settle losses that occurred before the close of the current accounting period. This loss settlement expense reserve is included as a separate liability on the statutory balance sheet.

Methods of classifying and quantifying loss adjustment expense reserves differ greatly among insurance companies but two broad classifications typically are used—allocated expenses and unallocated expenses. Allocated loss adjustment expenses are costs associated with processing a particular claim and therefore are identified by claim file. Unallocated loss adjustment expenses are not identified with a particular claim but are expenses associated with the loss settlement function. Unallocated loss adjustment expenses include the claims department's share of general overhead expenses. The allocated and unallocated expense classifications are used in the annual statement's supporting schedules in which loss and loss expense reserves are evaluated and tested.

UNEARNED PREMIUM RESERVES. Loss reserves show the insurer's liability for losses that occurred before the accounting period ended. Because most policyholders pay for their insurance coverage in advance, the insurance company also is liable for losses occurring after the accounting period's close and before expiration of the continuing policies' protection period for which premiums have been collected. Premiums collected in advance will be used to pay losses incurred before the policies expire or are canceled. In the event of policy cancellation, any refund due also will be derived from advance premium deposits. Property and liability insurers therefore do not recognize premiums as being earned when collected. Any unexpired policy in force at the accounting period's end must have a proportionate share of its gross premium available to meet future costs associated with the unexpired protection as if all costs were incurred uniformly throughout the policy period. Advance premiums held for this purpose are shown as a liability on the insurer's balance sheet under the caption, "Unearned Premium Reserves."

To illustrate the concept of unearned premium reserves, assume a one-year fire insurance policy was issued on July 1 at an annual premium of $200. If a set of financial statements was prepared at the close of the business day on which the policy was issued, the entire premium would be shown in the liability section of the balance sheet as unearned. This is true even though the insurance company had to use a portion of the premium revenue immediately to pay for the expenses associated with writing the coverage. The insurer's annual statement is dated December 31. At that time one-half of the protection period has elapsed. One-half of the policy's advance premium, $100, would be included in earned premiums for the year and the remaining half, $100, would remain in the unearned premium reserve. The remaining $100 is the amount that would have to be returned to the policyholder if the coverage was canceled by the insurance company. Another way to interpret the reserve is to consider it as the approximate amount that an insurance company would have to pay a reinsurer to assume its obligation under the contract. This later view of the unearned premium reserve as the amount of premium necessary for portfolio reinsurance of a retiring insurance company's obligations explains why the liability sometimes is called the "reinsurance reserve."

The fact that a disproportionately large part of the total expenses associated with an insurance policy are incurred around the time of issue means that the insurance company pays for expenses before recognizing premiums as revenue. This advance payment of expenses is said to create an "equity in the unearned premium reserve" for the insurer. As the protection period passes, gross premiums are released from the reserve into underwriting revenue while, at the same time, less than proportionate expenses are incurred. Policies issued during one accounting period and expiring in a subsequent period have the effect of increasing liabilities and lowering net worth on the first period's balance sheet but lowering liabilities and increasing net worth in the subsequent period. This peculiarity of statutory insurance accounting will be discussed more fully in a subsequent section.

Valuation of unearned premium reserves can be accomplished with one of several computational methods. The approach set forth in the annual statement calls for a determination of total premiums in force, net of reinsurance at the balance sheet date. The division of in force premiums between earned and unearned components then is accomplished by applying unearned premium factors that reflect the pro rata manner in which premium receipts are realized as revenue. Many insurance companies now have the ability to calculate their unearned premium liability directly from records of premiums written. This approach is more efficient than the annual statement method which was devised prior to electronic data processing. Nevertheless, because insurers are required to comply with the annual statement method, records of premiums in force continue to be maintained. A detailed description of reserve valuation methods is contained in Chapter 3 of this text.

Relationships among the three liability categories for a large number of companies according to their organizational form are displayed in Table 1-4. The composition of a particular company's liabilities may differ from the averages for its particular industry segment. Nevertheless, the table indicates the relative significance of the three liability categories that make up the obligations of property and liability insurance companies. The data also can be used to demonstrate the importance of accurate reserve estimation.

A distinction commonly made between insurance companies writing predominately fire and allied lines and companies writing predominately casualty lines is that the unearned premium reserve is relatively more

Table 1-4

Composition of Liabilities, Capital and Surplus as of December 31, 1976*

	945 Stock Companies		308 Mutual Companies		48 Reciprocals		26 American Lloyds	
	Reserves in Millions	Portion of Total Liabilities	Reserves in Millions	Portion of Total Liabilities	Reserves in Millions	Portion of Total Liabilities	Reserves in Millions	Portion of Total Liabilities
Unearned premium reserves	$18,112.8	29.9%	$ 5,240.6	30.8%	$1,189.2	35.5%	$17.9	31.5%
Loss and loss adjustment expenses	35,041.7	57.9	10,110.9	59.5	1,927.3	57.7	25.5	44.8
Miscellaneous liabilities	7,397.1	12.2	1,652.6	9.7	226.2	6.8	13.5	23.7
Total Liabilities	$60,551.6	100.0%	$17,004.1	100.0%	$3,342.7	100.0%	$56.9	100.0%

	945 Stock Companies		308 Mutual Companies		48 Reciprocals		26 American Lloyds	
	Capital and Surplus in Millions	Portion of Total Surplus	Capital and Surplus in Millions	Portion of Total Surplus	Capital and Surplus in Millions	Portion of Total Surplus	Capital and Surplus in Millions	Portion of Total Surplus
Capital paid-up	$ 2,230.0	9.7%	—	—	—	—	$ 1.0	2.9%
Underwriter's deposits	—	—	—	—	—	—	6.2	17.9
Guaranty funds	4.9	0.0	$ 76.2	1.1%	$ 24.8	2.4%		
Net surplus	19,406.5	84.3	6,406.0	90.8	667.7	65.0	27.0	78.0
Subscriber deposits	—	—	—	—	14.5	1.4		
Voluntary reserves	1,539.9	6.7	570.1	8.1	320.2	31.2	0.4	1.2
Treasury stock	160.4	0.7	—	—	—	—	—	
Total capital and surplus	$23,021.0	100.0%	$ 7,052.3	100.0%	$1,027.2	100.0%	$34.6	100.0%
Total liabilities and net worth	$83,572.7		$24,056.4		$4,369.9		$91.5	
Total Assets	$83,572.7	100.0%	$24,056.4	100.0%	$4,369.9	100.0%	$91.5	100.0%
Total Liabilities/Assets		72.5		70.7		76.5		62.2
Total Capital and Surplus/Assets		27.5		29.3		23.5		37.8

* Reprinted with permission from *Best's Aggregates and Averages: Property-Liability*, 38th annual edition (Morristown, NJ: A. M. Best Company, 1977), pp. 58, 10B, 64B, and 70B.

important for fire insurers while loss reserves are more important for casualty insurers. The advent of multiple-line underwriting has reduced the significance of this comparison but the distinction remains a valid explanation of why a particular insurer's liability composition may be considerably different from the proportions shown in Table 1-4. Loss reserves are larger on casualty insurers' balance sheets because liability claims, by their very nature, require longer periods of adjustment. For example, a New York state study of average claims settlement durations found that automobile physical damage (property insurance) claims took 1.5 months to settle; automobile bodily injury (casualty insurance) claims required more than ten times as long, 15.8 months.[5] Moreover, because liability policies often have a shorter protection period than fire policies the relative size of the unearned premium reserve is decreased.

MISCELLANEOUS LIABILITIES. All liabilities found on a property and liability insurance company's balance sheet other than the loss and loss expense reserves and the unearned premium reserve can be considered miscellaneous liabilities. Normally, the total value of these obligations is small in relation to the aforementioned reserves, varying between 5 and 15 percent of total liabilities. Although relatively small in comparison to the principal insurance liabilities, these miscellaneous items are important and must be handled properly. Several liabilities in this category are peculiar to the insurance business, such as special statutory reserves for particular lines of liability insurance; others are in the nature of unpaid and accrued expenses and deferred costs similar to those shown on the balance sheets of many business organizations.

Capital and Surplus. Conventional accounting terminology states that assets minus liabilities equals net worth. Using insurance accounting terminology, this relationship is expressed as admitted assets minus liabilities equal "policyholders' surplus." The term policyholders' surplus is meant to convey the idea that total balance sheet assets are available primarily for the satisfaction of policyholder claims. In the case of stock insurance companies, the stockholders' claim on assets is subordinated to the claims of policyholders and other creditors. The primacy given satisfaction of obligations to policyholders is reflected in the industry's use of the term policyholders' surplus for the company's net worth.

Several purposes are served by policyholders' surplus. Initial capitalization provides the resources needed by the insurer to begin business. After operations have commenced, policyholders' surplus furnishes a financial cushion to guard the insurer's solvency against fluctuating investment values and underwriting results. In any business the growth of net worth is necessary for expansion. This is especially true for insurance companies because increases in premium volume depress statutory underwriting earnings and hence surplus during the current accounting period because prepaid expenses are not recognized. In addition to these general purposes, policyholders' surplus in many companies is used to fulfill special functions; for instance, a portion of surplus may be set aside to comply with postinsolvency guarantee fund requirements.

The average size of policyholders' surplus for the three primary types of insurance organizations is shown in Table 1-4. Stockholder-owned insurance companies, on the average, show a lower percentage of surplus to assets than mutuals or reciprocals. This should not be interpreted to mean that stock insurance companies are less financially strong than other insurers nor does this mean that stock companies necessarily operate more efficiently than the others. Policyholders' surplus-to-asset ratios vary greatly among companies and over time. Many reasons may be given for the existence of differing ratios; these include the age of the insurers being compared, the types of insurance coverage being written, management philosophy, the presence of affiliated companies, recent profitability, and other factors. The amount of a particular company's net worth must be evaluated carefully. Techniques for the financial analysis of property and liability insurance companies are given a comprehensive treatment in Chapter 5 of this text. It is sufficient for current purposes to note the existence of varying policyholders' surplus relationships among insurers and to understand the composition and purposes of the policyholders' surplus account. The importance of adequate policyholders' surplus in the establishment and maintenance of insurance company solvency is covered in Chapter 6 of this text.

An insurer's legal form determines what account classifications appear in the policyholders' surplus section of the balance sheet. Line 25A on page 3 of the annual statement is used by stock companies to show their initial capitalization and any subsequent change in capitalization. This line is entitled "Capital Paid-Up." It is equivalent, in general accounting terminology, to "Paid-Up Capital" or simply "Capital." The amount shown as capital paid-up is equal to the number of shares of capital stock issued and outstanding multiplied by the par or stated value of each share. Preferred and common stock are combined for balance sheet presentation on this line. They are itemized separately in question 7 of the general interrogatories contained on page 13 of the annual statement. When shares of stock are sold for more than their par or stated value, the excess is classified on line 26A of the balance sheet as "Gross Paid-In Capital" and "Contributed Surplus." Existing stockholders sometimes are requested to contribute additional money to finance expansion or to add strength to the insurer. If this additional financing does not involve an increase in the number of shares outstanding, the source of the money is classified as contributed surplus on line 26A.

Mutual insurance corporations, unincorporated mutual associations, and reciprocal interinsurance exchanges do not issue capital stock and have no stockholders. Therefore, they show no entry for capital paid-up. Instead these organizations begin business with initial policy-holder/subscriber contributions or guarantee funds.[6] This initial capitalization may be furnished by prospective policyholders wishing to purchase insurance from a cooperative organization they helped to establish or the capital may be deposited by an interested party other than the policyholder/subscriber. The amount of guarantee fund contributions is shown on line 25B of the balance sheet's policyholders' surplus section. It is this initial guarantee fund which satisfies state capitalization requirements that must be met prior to commencement of underwriting operations. After the company has generated additional surplus through successful operations, the initial contributions may be paid back, usually with interest, to the company's founders. State laws regulate the permissibility and timing of such repayments.

Regardless of legal form, all insurers show their net retained earnings on line 26B of page 3. This line is captioned "Unassigned Funds (Surplus)" but often is referred to as "free surplus." With the exception of recently organized companies, unassigned surplus represents the largest subdivision of policyholders' surplus on the balance sheets of property and liability insurance companies. Because surplus in this classification is unassigned, it is available for distribution as policyholder or stockholder dividends, or both.

Insurers often segregate a portion of their surplus by assigning funds for special pusposes. The annual statement provides space for earmarking of surplus on line 24 of page 3. Theoretically, an insurer can list an unlimited number of special uses for surplus; realistically, a half-dozen or less categories are most common. Special surplus accounts sometimes are called voluntary reserves, even though they are not liabilities, because management regards them as a source of funds to be called upon should specific contingencies occur. For example, one of the most common special surplus accounts is established to meet fluctuations that may occur in the value of invested assets. Unlike life insurance companies, property and liability insurers are not required to show a security valuation reserve on their balance sheets. The wisdom of requiring such a statutory liability for nonlife insurance companies has been a subject of debate within the industry for years but no such requirement currently exists. However, management often exercises its discretion and provides a voluntary restriction of surplus to provide for fluctuation in investment values. Changes in the market value of preferred and common stocks during an accounting period, therefore, are reflected directly in this surplus account. Provision for the difference between amortized values of bonds shown on the balance sheet and the market value of these bonds, if lower, also may be reflected in the special securities valuation account.

Surplus may be assigned for a number of other reasons: accounts often are established for potential income taxes on unrealized capital gains, policyholder dividends not yet declared, extraordinary underwriting losses that may occur, and contingent assessments by state insolvency guarantee funds.

Income Statement A summary operating report entitled "Underwriting and Investment Exhibit Statement of Income" appears on page 4 of the annual statement. Three separate divisions of income are shown. First, underwriting income is summarized as the excess of premiums earned over underwriting losses and expenses incurred. Not all net premiums written in a particular accounting period are recognized as revenue in that period. Only the portion of premiums written in the current and prior accounting periods that corresponds to the protection services provided in the current year is recognized as earned. Losses and loss adjustment expenses paid during the year plus any increase in reserves for unpaid losses and loss expenses are allocated against the period's underwriting revenues. Revenue and expense recognition rules of accrual accounting thus are used to handle premium revenues and losses. However, the treatment of other underwriting expenses is similar to cash accounting practices. Expenses incurred in underwriting operations are treated as period expenses and recognized currently. Because most expenses associated with writing a new policy are incurred at the time the policy is issued, increases in premiums written result in a disproportionate increase in expenses compared to recognized revenue. With acquisition expenses allocated to periods in which premiums are written and revenues realized in the periods when earned, net underwriting gain is distorted by changes in premium volume.

The gain or loss from investment activities is summarized in two lines on the underwriting and investment exhibit. Net investment income earned for the period consists of interest, dividends, and real estate income collected and accrued less investment expenses and depreciation. Net capital gains or losses realized on the sale or maturity of assets are added to the investment income items. The sum of these two lines equals net gain or loss from investment activities for the year. Capital gains or losses which remain unrealized at year end are not considered income; instead, annual changes therein are reflected as a direct adjustment to surplus.

The third section of the underwriting and investment exhibit shows revenue and expenses from sources other than underwriting and investment operations. There are several standard entries in this section and a variety of miscellaneous entries that are peculiar to individual company operations. For instance, one standard item—usually a negative figure—is entitled "Net Gain or Loss From Agents or Premium Balances Charged Off." This item is used to write off as a loss agent's or premium balances determined to be uncollectible. If amounts charged off in previous periods subsequently become collectible, an income entry for the amount recovered is made. A net gain is recorded as an increment to income for current period collections in excess of charge offs; a net loss is entered if the opposite relationship exists.

The sum of net gains or losses from underwriting and investment operations plus total other income equals net income before policyholder dividends and income taxes. A deduction is taken for policyholder dividends incurred during the year. The dividend deduction includes dividends actually paid during the year less those incurred but unpaid at the beginning of the year plus dividends incurred but unpaid at year end. The income tax deduction includes federal and foreign income taxes incurred. A footnote entry itemizes tax carryover provisions available after the current accounting period. The final entry in the underwriting and investment exhibit is statutory net income.

Capital and Surplus Account   The bottom section of page 4 of the annual statement contains a reconciliation of the policyholders' surplus account. This statement, entitled the "Capital and Surplus Account," corresponds to the statement of retained earnings found among the summary financial statements of other business organizations. As presented in the annual statement, the capital and surplus account appears to be an extension of the income statement. The final line in the underwriting and investment exhibit statement of income is line 20, net income. The first line in the capital and surplus account is line 21, policyholders' surplus at the beginning of the current period. To this beginning balance is added net income, net unrealized capital gains or losses, and other gain or loss items resulting from operations that have not been reflected in income. A charge for the amortization of unfunded supplemental pension liabilities is an example of a cost that affects policyholders' surplus but does not flow through the income statement. Transactions involving capital accounts, such as declaration of a stock dividend or contributions of surplus by the company's founders, are shown on lines 28 and 29. Stockholder cash dividends declared during the current year are deducted from surplus. Line 39 shows the year's change in surplus as regards policyholders. The closing policyholders' surplus figure on line 40 of the capital and surplus account must agree with the corresponding balance sheet entry on line 27, page 3 of the annual statement.

Exhibits and Schedules Detailed information supporting the summary financial statements is presented immediately following the balance sheet, income statement, and capital and surplus account. The underwriting and investment exhibit on pages 5 through 10 itemizes resource and operating data that are presented summarily in the basic statements. Investment income, realized capital gains and losses, and unrealized capital gains and losses are given extended treatment on page 5, Part 1. The net income and the gain and loss items calculated here are transferred to the income statement and the capital and surplus account. Premiums—written, earned, and in force—are enumerated on pages 6 and 7, Part 2. The premium analysis provides information for the balance sheet (unearned premium reserve) and for the income statement (premiums earned). Losses and loss adjustment expenses that were paid and incurred during the year are listed on page 8, Part 3, by line of business. The total incurred loss figure is carried from page 8 to line 2 of the income statement on page 4. Unpaid losses, including IBNR claims, and loss adjustment expenses are displayed by line of business on page 9, Part 3A. Totals from this page are entered as loss and loss expense reserves in the liability section of the balance sheet on page 3. Page 10, Part 4 of the underwriting and investment exhibit sets forth a detailed presentation of loss adjustment expenses, other underwriting expenses, and expenses incurred in connection with investment operations. The first two expense categories shown here appear as deductions in the underwriting section on the income statement. Investment expenses are netted against investment income in Part 1 of the underwriting and investment exhibit on page 5; net investment income is then carried forward to the income statement.

Page 11 of the annual statement contains two exhibits: Exhibit 1, "Analysis of Assets"; and Exhibit 2, "Analysis of Nonadmitted Assets." It is sometimes said that the completion of the annual statement begins on page 11. This is because assets shown on the balance sheet are developed in Exhibit 1. Ledger assets are entered in column 1, nonledger assets are added in column 2, nonadmitted assets are deducted in column 3, leaving net admitted assets in column 4. Exhibit 2 analyzes any change in nonadmitted assets during the year. An increase in nonadmitted assets is shown as a charge against policyholders' surplus in the capital and surplus account; a reduction in nonadmitted assets is a gain in policyholders' surplus.

Page 12, Exhibit 3, "Reconciliation of Ledger Assets," shows increases and decreases in the real and nominal ledger accounts which

Table 1-5

Accounts Used to Reconcile Ledger Assets

Increase Items	Decrease Items
Premiums written	Net losses paid
Gross investment income	Expenses paid
Profit on investments	Taxes paid
Sundry receipts	Loss on investments
Upward adjustment in	Depreciation
ledger asset values	Sundry disbursements
Increases in ledger	Downward adjustment in ledger
liabilities	asset values
Increases in capital and	Decreases in ledger liabilities
surplus	Dividends to policyholders
	Dividends to stockholders

together explain the year's change in ledger assets. Because nonledger accounts are not shown here, the exhibit may be considered an incomplete trial balance. Items appearing on the exhibit can be classified as shown in Table 1-5. It may seem strange that insurance companies publish what is essentially a cash basis trial balance as a supporting document to their financial statements. The usual explanation given for the practice is that the reconciliation of ledger assets is used in the examination process. Some authorities have recommended that this exhibit be replaced with a complete source and application of funds statement.[7] To date, the exhibit remains in the annual statement.

Pages 13 and 13A contain the regulatory questionnaire. Information provided on these pages should be reviewed carefully by anyone attempting to evaluate the company's financial condition and operations. Various interrogatories relating to the company's capitalization, reinsurance arrangements, affiliated companies, dealings with officers, employees, and stockholders, and the territory of its operations must be answered. An affirmation that reserves have been adequately provided also is required.

Page 14, (a separate page for each state) provides statistical detail of premiums written and earned, policyholder dividends, and losses paid and incurred, on direct business (excluding premiums for reinsurance accepted or ceded), by each line of business for which the insurer is licensed. The annual statement's remaining pages are devoted to analytical schedules. The content and purpose of the lettered schedules are summarized as follows:

- Schedule A: Real Estate Owned

There are three parts to this schedule. The information provided includes a description of the real estate, date acquired, name of vendor, method of acquisition, encumbrances, cost, book value, date of sale, name of purchaser, amount received, and profit or loss on sale.

- Schedule B: Mortgages Owned

This schedule shows all mortgages owned at year end and all mortgage loans made, increased, discharged, reduced or disposed of during the year.

- Schedule BA: Other Invested Assets Owned and Acquired

Transportation equipment, timber deeds, mineral rights, and other sundry items held as invested assets at the end of the year are shown in Part 1. Other invested assets acquired during the year are shown in Part 2.

- Schedule C: Collateral Loans

Outstanding loans that have been secured by collateral in case of default are itemized here. These loans are shown on the balance sheet as invested assets. Loans that exceed the market value of the collateral must be reduced to such market value through the nonadmitted process of Exhibit 1. Collateral loans made to company officers or directors are completely nonadmitted.

- Schedule D: Bonds and Stocks Owned

This schedule is divided into six parts and subsections. It itemizes all bonds, common stocks, and preferred stocks owned, acquired, redeemed, or sold during the accounting period. Information is given concerning the securities' cost, book value, market value, interest rate, dividend yield, and maturity date. The final parts of the exhibit ask questions concerning affiliated companies.

- Schedule F: Reinsurance Ceded and Assumed

Reinsurance recoverable on paid and unpaid losses is shown in the initial part of the exhibit. Recoverable reinsurance on paid losses normally is carried as a ledger asset in Exhibit 1 and on the balance sheet. The second part of the exhibit sets forth reinsurance payable on unpaid losses assumed by the reinsurer. Information regarding reinsurance in force, unearned reinsurance premiums, and portfolio reinsurance activity also is shown here.

- Schedule G: Fidelity and Surety Reserves

Loss reserves for reported fidelity and surety claims are presented for the preceding seven calendar years. The development of the reserves is exhibited retrospectively so that increases and decreases in estimated losses can be analyzed.

- Schedule K: Reserve for Credit Losses

This schedule is used to detail the calculation of minimum statutory loss reserves for credit insurance. Because claims adjustment procedures used for credit insurance are unique to this line of business, the schedule is designed to facilitate the unusual timing of loss settlements.

● Schedule H: Accident and Health Insurance Exhibit

Property-liability insurers that write accident and health insurance coverage detail operations for these lines in the schedule. Part 1 details accident and health insurance premiums in force. Part 2 presents the calculation of underwriting gain or loss. Part 3 sets forth the unearned premium (active life) reserves and claims reserve.

● Schedule M: Expense Payments to Others

The purpose of this schedule is to disclose payments that do not represent employee compensation, expense reimbursement, or insurance benefits. Payments in excess of $100 to legislative or other governmental bodies must be listed in Part 1. Payments to officers, directors, or employees that exceed $500 or amount in the aggregate to more than $5,000 during the year are shown in Part 2. Part 3 lists legal expenses greater than $500/$5,000 paid during the year for reasons other than loss and salvage settlements. All payments greater than $1,000 to industry trade associations and service bureaus are itemized in Part 4.

● Schedule N: Deposits in Fiduciaries

It is common for property-liability insurers to maintain a number of bank accounts. Some are used to pay operating expenses while others may be used for loss disbursements or investment purposes. All deposits maintained at any time during the year in banks, trust companies, and savings institutions must be shown in this schedule. Total depository balances on the last day of each month are listed. Balances remaining at the statement date in each institution also are disclosed.

● Schedule O: Development of Loss and Loss Expense Reserves—
  Nonschedule P Lines (first party claims)

The purpose of this schedule and Schedule P is to test retrospectively the accuracy with which liabilities have been established for unpaid losses and loss expenses. Schedule O tests loss reserves for nonschedule P lines that were reported in the previous two annual statements; and tests loss and loss expense reserves on a Schedule P basis.

● Schedule P: Loss and Loss Expense Reserve Detail and Calendar-
  Accident Year Data for Third-party Liability Claims

This schedule has three parts. The first sets forth the dollar detail and ratios of loss and loss expense to premiums earned on a calendar-accident year basis for the past eight years and is used to determine excess statutory reserves as well as loss ratio trends as reported. The second part shows the development of losses incurred on an accident year-inventory basis through five subsequent calendar years. The third part sets forth data by accident year which can be used to evaluate the relative level of adequacy in the estimated liabilities currently being reported.

- Schedule T: Direct Premium and Loss Detail by State and Territory

This schedule allocates by states and territories premiums written and earned along with losses incurred, paid and unpaid. Information contained here can be used to determine loss ratios in each state and to check premium tax calculations. The method of allocating amounts to individual states and territories is disclosed in Part 2. Reinsurance is disregarded.

Insurance Expense Exhibit

As a supplement to the annual statement, insurers also are required to file annually the NAIC's "Insurance Expense Exhibit." It must be filed with the insurance department or other designated public authority of every state in which the insurer is licensed to transact business. The filing date is April 1 of the year following the calendar year covered by the exhibit. Several purposes are served by the document. It develops a complete statement of operating gain or loss before federal income taxes for each line of business. Operating results include statutory underwriting gain or loss, allocated investment income, and policyholder dividends. Results reported in the exhibit can be used to determine the company's profitability on each line of business. The report provides a detailed presentation of all expenses on a uniform basis for each expense classification and each expense function by line of insurance. In addition, the exhibit furnishes aggregate expense data which can be used in rate making to determine appropriate expense levels by line and by function within each line.

The recordkeeping and reporting of expenses in an insurance company, as in other organizations, necessitate the use of a cost accounting system. Such a system records, classifies, and allocates expenses according to a predetermined underlying set of instructions. In property-liability insurance the preordained principles underlying a company's cost accounting system originally were set down in a booklet printed by the NAIC entitled *Instructions for Uniform Classification of Expenses*. These instructions were developed by the New York Insurance Department and became effective as Regulation 30 in New York on January 1, 1949. Other states followed the New York department's lead and have required use of the uniform accounting instructions since 1950. The purpose of the uniform instructions is to establish standards to be followed by all companies in classifying expenses so that meaningful comparisons can be made among companies and over time. Standardized cost accounting instructions are intended to result in consistency among company accounting systems, annual statements, and supplementary reports such as the Insurance Expense Exhibit. Financial examinations conducted by insurance regulatory authorities also benefit from the uniform accounting procedures.

Reports by Stock Insurance Companies

All publicly owned stock property and liability insurance companies issue periodic reports to their owners. A company is considered "publicly owned" if it is subject to regulation by the SEC. A familiarity with reports issued by stock insurance companies to audiences other than state insurance regulators is especially important because the financial statements contained in these reports often require independent certification by a qualified accountant. Such certification usually involves development of financial data unavailable in the NAIC annual statement. Thus while these other financial statements may appear similar to the annual statement, they are intended to serve clearly distinct purposes and may be based on a separate set of accounting principles.

Reports to Shareholders The general purpose of reports to shareholders of publicly owned insurance companies is to provide the owners with information on the company's current financial position and results of its operations during the most recent accounting period. Owners can use this information to evaluate for themselves the effectiveness of management's current policies. On the basis of this information decisions can be made regarding continued investment in the firm, retention of current management, and approval or disapproval of propositions that are subject to the vote of the stockholders.

Shareholder reports include a comprehensive annual report, and often briefer quarterly reports. The content of these reports can be divided into two parts; a general communication to the owners by management and a set of formal financial statements. Management's communications may contain some financial information but it typically is more editorial, or verbal, in nature. This part of the report allows management a chance to discuss events that have affected the company during the past accounting period and to comment on how past and future events are expected to impact on the company. For instance, the effects of natural disasters, political upheaval, or changing social mores may receive attention. These comments customarily are set forth in the president's letter to the shareholders. The letter often discusses the future of the industry and the economy and makes a statement regarding the company's future position in this developing environment. A comment on special problems within the industry and how these problems relate to society at large has become typical. Although the textual portion of the report may be considered nonfinancial, it sets the stage for the formal financial statements. Because of this, the editorial comment usually ends on an optimistic note regardless of the results shown in the financial statements. In fact, there may be a tendency for the optimism to be inversely related to the results of operations and the company's current financial position.

Reports to Stock Exchanges An insurance company whose stock is traded on an organized stock exchange must issue annual and quarterly reports to its shareholders and file a copy with the exchange. Failure to comply with this requirement will result in termination of trading in the company's shares on the exchange. In order for the company's stock to remain listed for trading, the financial statements contained in the shareholder reports must be certified by a qualified accountant to be in compliance with GAAP. Because regulatory insurance accounting differs in several respects from GAAP, insurance company financial statements contained in shareholder reports must be adjusted from the corresponding documents in the NAIC annual statement. The application of GAAP to property-liability insurers is discussed in a later section of this chapter.

Reports to the SEC In addition to the stock exchange requirements, all companies with publicly traded securities must comply with the disclosure requirements of the federal securities laws, primarily the Securities Act of 1933 and the Securities Exchange Act of 1934. Responsibility for enforcement of the federal securities laws rests with the SEC. The disclosure requirements of the 1934 Act apply to all companies with more than 500 shareholders and assets of $1 million or more. Specific disclosure requirements are contained in paragraphs 12, 13, and 14 of the 1934 Act. *Regulation S-X*, "Form and Content of Financial Statements," is the principle body of accounting rules and articles used by the SEC to administer the various federal securities laws. This body of regulations together with occasional "accounting series releases" promulgated by the SEC dictate the form and content of all financial statements and supporting materials filed with the Commission. Most documents filed with the SEC are available upon request to shareholders and the general public.

When a company first has its stock listed on a regulated stock exchange, or when it attains the minimum size and ownership limits, it must register with the SEC by filing Form 10. This form is used only once for the initial registration. In general, the financial statement requirements of Form 10 call for the filing of certified summary financial statements; i.e., a balance sheet for the most current accounting period, an income statement, a sources and applications of funds statement, and a retained earnings statement for the three previous years.

The SEC's Form 10-K is the primary *annual* report of registered companies. Item 10 of Form 10-K contains financial statements of the registrant in comparative columnar form for the previous two years. It must be filed with the SEC within ninety days after the end of the registrant's fiscal year. Form 10-K actually may be of greater use to shareholders interested in making comparisons than the financial statements contained in the reports sent to shareholders. This is because the SEC prescribes a uniform format and terminology to be used in completing the form. Also, Form 10-K contains more detail than normally is provided in the shareholder reports issued by most companies.

Financial statements of property and liability insurers filed with the SEC after December 25, 1975 are required to conform with GAAP. Insurers domiciled in states which prohibit publication of the companies' primary financial documents on any basis other than statutory accounting principles are required to file statutory documents supplemented by GAAP financial statements. Regardless of whether the primary financial statements are based on GAAP or statutory accounting principles, supplementary material reconciling differences between statutory accounting principles and GAAP also must be filed with the SEC. Financial statements filed for mutual insurance companies other than life and title insurance companies and wholly owned stock insurance companies which are subsidiaries of mutual insurance companies may be prepared in accordance with statutory accounting requirements.

A quarterly report on Form 10-Q also must be filed with the SEC for each of the first three quarters of the year. The fourth quarter information is subsumed in the annual report. Form 10-Q is due within forty-five days of the end of the quarter to which it applies. This form is briefer than Form 10-K and, at present, does not require certification. Part A of Form 10-Q summarizes profit and loss information on a year-to-date basis for the current and preceding accounting year. Part B deals with capitalization and stockholders' equity. Part C is used to report any securities sold by the registrant during the period that were not registered under the 1933 Securities Act because of an exemption from registration. Although this form is not certified, it does require management to affirmatively state that the information provided presents a fair statement of the results for the interim period.

Other Accounting and Statistical Reports

The reports discussed thus far primarily are intended for two groups: (1) the NAIC annual statement and the insurance expense exhibit satisfy state insurance department filing requirements; and (2) the reports issued by stock insurers to their shareholders, to stock exchanges, and to the SEC satisfy disclosure requirements of publicly owned companies. Several additional reports are prepared by some or all property and liability companies.

Policyholder Reports   Property and liability insurers that are not considered publicly owned also issue periodic financial reports to their owners. Nonpublicly owned companies include privately held stock companies, mutuals, reciprocals, American Lloyds associations, and captive insurers. Because these insurers do not solicit capital in the public financial markets, they are not required to comply with uniform reporting practices other than those imposed by state insurance regulation. Consequently, the nonregulatory reporting practices of these insurers tend to be quite divergent. It is customary, however, for nonpublicly owned insurers, especially mutuals, to distribute some form of annual financial report to their policyholders. This usually is done by including a brief policyholder report along with premium billings. These reports present a synopsis of the company's current financial position and operating results during the most recent two-year period. Usually this information is taken from the annual statement and is not certified.

Reports to Statistical Agencies   Property and liability insurers file statistical reports with rate-making organizations or directly with state insurance departments as a part of the procedure used to price their products. Several countrywide rating bureaus are active in certain lines of insurance. For instance, the National Council on Compensation Insurance makes rates for workers' compensation insurance in about half the states and serves as an advisor in many others. The Insurance Services Office, which is affiliated with stock insurers, and the Mutual Insurance Rating Bureau provide statistical services for their members and subscribers. Company associations, such as the National Association of Independent Insurers, also receive statistical reports from their members. These statistical reports detail the company's own premium and loss experience so that the statistical organization can aggregate these data with that supplied by other members and use it in rate making. In addition to the economy and efficiency of this collective approach to pricing, combining the premium and loss data from a number of companies increases the statistical credibilty of the resulting pure premiums and expense loadings.

Data for statistical reports are developed from the company's own premium and loss records. The degree of detail and method of classifying this data on the statistical reports depends on the line of business and the procedures followed by a particular bureau. Codes are assigned to identify general characteristics of insurance coverage.

Additional coding is used to classify information pertaining to the line of insurance. For instance, in workers' compensation the premium rate base is per $100 of payroll. To develop a rating structure, insureds are classified by type of industry, by occupation of the employee, or by industrial operation performed. Loss data in each classification is further divided into one of three loss categories: (1) serious disability loss, (2) nonserious disability loss, and (3) medical expense. Thus the statistical agency receives very detailed disaggregated data from contributing companies. It is the agency's responsibility to verify that the premium and loss data supplied in the statistical reports it receives is in agreement with the company's annual statement. Specifically, the statistical data must correspond to the exhibit of premiums and losses on page 14 and the state by state data in Schedule T. It should be noted that ocean marine, aviation, and some inland marine lines of business are not included in reports to statistical agencies. Reinsurance assumed and ceded also is omitted from the reports.

Federal Income Tax Reports Like most other business corporations, property and liability insurance companies are subject to federal income taxation in accordance with provisions of the current Internal Revenue Code (IRC). This was not always the case. Prior to enactment of the 1942 Revenue Act, only stock fire and casualty insurers were taxed under the federal income tax law. Today, all insurers—including stock, mutual, and reciprocal organizations—come under the IRC and must pay tax on their income.

The application of tax laws to any business enterprise is a highly complex subject that requires a thorough understanding of general accounting, the tax code itself, current court decisions relating to tax matters, and rulings and determinations of the Internal Revenue Service. In the case of regulated industries like insurance, some understanding of accounting practices unique to the industry also is required. It is not the purpose here to fully cover income taxation of property and liability insurance companies. Rather, some broad principles of income taxation as applied to nonlife insurers are discussed and related to regulatory insurance accounting.

Basically, insurance companies are subject to general corporate tax rules. In order to deal with the unique nature of insurance company operations, a special section of the IRC specifically treating insurers supersedes certain provisions of the general tax law. Nonetheless, computation of an insurance company's income tax obligation essentially involves the same types of calculations followed by other corporations.

General Rules. Taxable income is found by deducting expenses incurred from revenues recognized during the tax year. In general, statutory net income determined in the annual statement, subject to certain specified modifications, is used to define taxable income for property and liability insurance companies. The tax rates used to compute an insurer's tax bill are the same as those that apply to other corporations. Beginning with 1975, the initial $25,000 of taxable income is taxed at a rate of 20 percent, the second $25,000 at a rate of 22 percent, and taxable income in excess of $50,000 is taxed at a 48 percent rate. Graduation of the tax rate in this manner is intended to give small- and moderate-sized corporations preferential tax treatment. As noted later, an additional preference is granted certain mutual insurance companies that have relatively small taxable income.

ACCOUNTING PERIOD.   Normally a corporation may choose whether its annual accounting period for tax purposes will be a calendar year or a fiscal year ending on the last day of any month other than December. Insurance companies do not have this option. They must figure their taxable income on the basis of the calendar year. This means that their accounting period for tax purposes is the same period covered by the annual statement.

The tax return is due on March 15 after the close of the tax year. Extensions may be granted beyond the due date. Like other corporations, insurers are required to pay one-quarter of their estimated taxes for the current year on April 15, June 15, September 15, and December 15. It is customary to use last year's taxable income as the basis for estimating quarterly tax payments. Adjustments are made if actual income differs from estimated income. Final settlement must be made by April 15 of the following year.

CAPITAL GAINS AND LOSSES.   The sale of a capital asset at more or less than its cost basis for tax purposes gives rise to a gain or loss. Taxation of certain capital gains is more favorable than the tax treatment afforded ordinary income. Whether or not preferential tax treatment is available depends on the length of time during which the capital asset was held. If the asset was held for a period of one year or less, any gain or loss is considered short-term in nature. Capital assets held longer than one year and then sold may create a long-term capital gain or loss. Short-term capital gains less short-term capital losses are included in ordinary income and taxed at the normal rates. Net long-term capital gains (long-term gains less long-term losses) in excess of net short-term capital losses (short-term losses in excess of short-term gains) are subject to ordinary income tax rates unless an election is made to apply the alternate 30 percent capital gains tax rate. This alternative tax treatment would be elected only if the taxpayer's marginal tax rate is above 30 percent with the inclusion of the net long-term gain.

Table 1-6

Federal Income Tax Calculation:
Alternative Capital Gains Treatment

Regular income	$25,000 × 20% = $ 5,000
Regular income	10,000 × 22% = 2,200
Capital gain ($20, 200−$500+$300)	20,000 × 30% = 6,000
Total Tax	$13,200

Table 1-7

Federal Income Tax Calculation:
Capital Gains Treated as Ordinary Income

Regular income	$25,000 × 20% = $ 5,000
Regular income	25,000 × 22% = 5,500
Regular income	5,000 × 48% = 2,400
Total Tax	$12,900

Consider the following example. The Hypothetical Manufacturing Company had ordinary income of $35,000 during the tax year just ended. It experienced short-term capital losses of $500 and short-term capital gains of $300. The sale of an asset held longer than one year created a gain of $20,200. No long-term capital losses were experienced. If the company chooses to have its net long-term capital gain taxed at the alternative capital gain rate, its tax bill would be determined as shown in Table 1-6. Inclusion of the gain in ordinary income would result in a lower tax bill, as shown in Table 1-7. Clearly, in this situation the corporation would elect to include its net long-term capital gain in ordinary income. But if Hypothetical Manufacturing's regular income had been $80,000, then the inclusion of the gain would produce the result shown in Table 1-8. Choice of the alternative capital gains tax in this case would be advisable, as shown in Table 1-9. A corporation may evaluate both methods of reporting a net long-term capital gain and choose the one resulting in the lowest rate. In general, if the corporation's taxable income including the capital gain exceeds $50,000, it is advantageous to use the alternative tax treatment for the capital gain; otherwise, using the regular tax rates for the corporation's entire income results in a lower tax obligation.

DEPRECIATION. Certain portions of the gain realized on the sale of a capital asset may represent a recapture of depreciation and therefore not qualify for favorable tax treatment. Depreciation is an allowable deduction taken against gross income in the determination of taxable income. Normal depreciation rules apply to insurance companies. The

Table 1-8

Federal Income Tax Calculation:
Capital Gains Treated As Ordinary Income

Regular income	$25,000 × 20% = $ 5,000
Regular income	25,000 × 22% = 5,500
Regular income	50,000 × 48% = 24,000
Total Tax	$34,500

Table 1-9

Federal Income Tax Calculation:
Alternative Capital Gains Tax Treatment

Regular income	$25,000 × 20% = $ 5,000
Regular income	25,000 × 22% = 5,500
Regular income	30,000 × 48% = 14,400
Capital gain	20,000 × 30% = 6,000
Total Tax	$30,900

amount deductible for depreciation expense in a particular year may be figured in any way consistent with recognized trade practices. Three methods are specifically listed in the IRC but any other consistent method may be used if it complies with the depreciation rules. In addition to the annual depreciation expense deduction, a special first-year allowance is available for qualifying tangible personal property. Other special rules apply in cases of extraordinary obsolescence and retirement of assets.

Of special significance to insurance companies is the determination of which assets are subject to depreciation. Regulatory insurance accounting requires that certain expenditures must be considered expenses in the current year even though the service potential of the assets acquired will benefit future periods. For instance, expenditures for furniture, office equipment, fixtures, and automobiles will provide service in more than one period. Yet these expenditures are current period expenses for annual statement purposes. They are considered capital outlays for tax purposes however. Insurers carry these items among their nonadmitted assets shown in Exhibit 2 of the annual statement. In determining taxable income, capital assets must be depreciated over their useful lives rather than deducted fully in the year purchased. This is one reason why annual statement income may differ from taxable income.

INTEREST AND DIVIDENDS. Interest payments made by insurance companies on debts it owes to others are tax deductible expenses to the insurer. Dividend payments to stockholders of the insurance company are not deductible; these payments are made out of aftertax income.

Interest received by an insurance company on obligations of others, such as another corporation's bonds, that are owned by the insurer generally is fully includable as ordinary income to the insurer. However, 85 percent of the dividends received by an insurance company on the common or preferred stock of another corporation is tax exempt. This intercorporate dividend exemption is intended to reduce the multiple taxation of corporate income. The dividend exemption may encourage insurers to seek dividend income instead of interest income or to invest in stocks of corporations with high dividend payouts rather than companies that retain larger portions of their earnings and offer the possibility of capital gains.

INVESTMENT TAX CREDIT. A special fiscal tool known as the investment tax credit was devised by Congress in 1962 as a method of stimulating the national economy by encouraging corporations and individuals to invest in certain assets. Since its initial enactment, the credit has been repealed and restored in countercyclical fashion depending on the need for economic stimulation. It last was restored in 1971 and the maximum credit was increased from 7 percent to 10 percent in the Tax Reduction Act of 1975. Insurers, like other taxpayers, are allowed a credit against their current tax obligation equal to 10 percent of the cost of tangible personal property with an estimated life of at least seven years. Capital assets with less than a seven-year life qualify for reduced credit according to the schedule shown in Table 1-10. No credit is allowed for assets with a useful life shorter than three years. The tax credit is a direct offset against taxes in the year the asset is placed into service. It does not reduce the asset's depreciation base. Insurance companies that lease computer equipment may have the investment tax credit otherwise available to the lessor passed on to them if the lessor agrees to do so and files notice of intent with the Internal Revenue Service.

TAX CARRY-OVERS. The tax law recognizes the fact that annual accounting periods may unfairly result in volatile income determinations for tax purposes. To alleviate the inequity resulting when operating gains and losses occur in different tax years, provision is made to carry losses back three years and forward seven years. Losses initially may be carried back to the earliest preceding year; i.e., three years ago for a firm at least four years old or, at the taxpayer's election, losses may be carried forward. An election to carry losses forward would preserve tax losses in prior years; this might be important for insurance

Table 1-10

Investment Tax Credit Schedule

Estimated Life	Investment Tax Credit
7 or more years	10%
5 to 7 years	6.67%
3 to 5 years	3.33%

companies that are candidates for a merger. If losses are carried back and the operating loss in the current year exceeds total taxable income in the previous three years, the remaining loss is carried forward to the next year and thereafter to the fifth succeeding year. Any remaining loss not offset against income during this nine-year span fails to provide tax relief.

Other carry-over provisions relate to capital losses, excess investment tax credits, excess foreign tax credits, and excess charitable contributions deductions. A net capital loss occurs during a year in which capital losses exceed capital gains. Such a loss cannot be deducted from regular income in arriving at taxable income for the year. Instead, the loss must be carried back three years and forward five years. An excess investment tax credit exists in any year when the total tax credit available exceeds the tax obligation otherwise due. This results in what is equivalent to a negative income tax for the year. The credit can be realized by carrying it back three years and forward seven years. A United States corporation that pays taxes to foreign countries as a result of extraterritorial operations may treat foreign taxes as a credit or deduction in computing domestic income tax. However, limits are imposed on the amount of the credit taken in any tax year. If the foreign tax exceeds the limitation, the excess may be carried back two years and carried forward five years and used as a credit or deduction in those years, subject to the limitation for the year. Insurance companies, like other taxpayers, can deduct contributions to qualified charities. Certain limits are placed on the amount deductible in any one year; generally, this limit is 5 percent of the corporation's taxable income. Excess charitable contributions can be carried forward for five years and deducted if total charitable contribution deductions in any year do not exceed the allowable limits.

Special Tax Rules. Determining an insurer's income tax obligation involves certain departures from the tax laws generally applied to corporations. These departures give recognition to the unique operating characteristics of insurance companies and to a large degree are made to accommodate accounting practices mandated by state insurance regulators. Subchapter L, Parts II and III of the IRC contain special tax rules directed toward insurance companies. Some generally applicable tax accounting principles are supplanted by this section of the tax law.

REVENUE AND EXPENSE RECOGNITION. Tax accounting principles recognize revenue only after the occurrence of a critical event which assures that the revenue will, in fact, be received. This typically is the point of sale; the purchaser pays or becomes obligated to pay. Costs associated with a transaction are recognized as expenses when the costs are incurred or as they accrue. Thus, corporations use accrual accounting principles rather than cash-basis accounting to determine taxable income. The calculation matches recognized revenues and expenses rather than cash receipts and disbursements.

The normal tax rules of revenue and expense recognition are not used to calculate an insurer's taxable income. Premiums are received before the insurer fulfills its contractual obligations. Regulatory insurance accounting requires that premium revenues be recognized as income proportionally over the contractual coverage period. Tax rules are modified for insurers to agree with revenue recognition principles inherent in the annual statement. As a result, premium revenues flow into taxable income later than otherwise would be the case.

Similarly, the expense recognition rules used in the annual statement are incorporated in the tax law for insurance companies. Acquisition expenses normally would be allocated against their corresponding revenues as that revenue was recognized into income. Statutory accounting forces the immediate deduction of acquisition expenses when they are incurred but defers recognition of the related premium revenues. Revenues and expenses are "mismatched" by the annual statement recognition rules. Tax rules for insurers also allow this mismatching of revenues and expenses. This has the effect of reducing taxable income during periods of expanding sales because acquisition expenses are being incurred and recognized in advance of the corresponding increase in premium revenues.

Another variance between general tax principles and the tax treatment afforded insurance companies has to do with the recognition of losses. For an insurance company, claims settlement expenses are analogous to the cost of goods sold by a manufacturing or mercantile corporation. Noninsurance business organizations normally recognize costs only after the events creating them are completed and the amount of cost is fully determined. Unpaid losses and loss adjustment expenses in an insurance company are not fully determined at the close of the tax year; they at least partially must be estimated. Nevertheless, because reasonable estimates of aggregate loss and loss settlement expenses can be made, the estimated loss costs are recognized as deductions from revenue before their final value is fully known.

REASONABLENESS OF INSURANCE DEDUCTIONS. During the 1940s, disagreements arose between the property and liability insurance industry and the Treasury Department in regard to the deductibility of certain insurance items. Specifically, the appropriateness of deducting the change in excess loss reserves developed by statutory formula on Schedule P was questioned. Other areas of disagreement concerned the tax treatment of changes in the liability for unauthorized reinsurance, changes in agents' balances over ninety days due, and transactions involving other nonadmitted assets. Prior to 1950 changes in these items were reflected in statutory income, but the IRS resisted their deduction for tax purposes. In 1950 the annual statement was changed by deleting the contentious items from the income statement and showing them as direct adjustments to surplus. The statutory income calculation was in this way brought into conformity with tax accounting rules. Today the statutory income calculation's methodology may be considered compatible with the income tax calculation to the extent that loss costs and expenses are reasonably determined. At the end of 1975 the IRS issued Revenue Procedure 75-76 as a guideline for ascertaining the reasonableness of estimated loss reserves.[8] This guideline is intended for use by revenue agents examining property and liability tax returns. Unfortunately, the clarity of the Revenue Procedure has been questioned due to the subjective standard of reasonableness it imposes. When differences of opinion occur as to the reasonableness of loss reserve estimates, a challenge by the IRS can be expected. Other factors also may cause the statutory income figure to differ from taxable income. Commission expenses and policy dividends are subject to the general tax tests of accruability and although deducted currently on the annual statement, may not be deductible on the current tax form.

SPECIAL RULES FOR MUTUALS. The general corporate tax return, Form 1120 the U.S. Corporation Income Tax Return, is used by stock property and liability insurance companies. Because the tax rules affecting insurers are in general agreement with annual statement accounting methods while Form 1120 primarily is designed for corporations using generally accepted accounting principles, insurance companies may experience some difficulties in completing the form. Problems of this nature are dealt with by reclassifying annual statement information into the prescribed format on the tax return. A copy of the annual statement must accompany the tax form. This is supplemented by specially prepared exhibits that reconcile and explain differences between Form 1120 and the regulatory report.

Mutual and reciprocal insurance companies file a tax form drafted specifically for their use. This is Form 1120M. It too must be accompanied by a copy of the annual statement when filed with the IRS. The mutual tax form differs because of special tax provisions that reflect the unique nature of cooperative insurance organizations. Mutual insurers nevertheless are taxed basically the same as stock insurers. Differences arise from the distinction made in the tax law between "small" and "ordinary" mutuals, from a special income smoothing device called the "Protection Against Loss (PAL) Account," and from a special $6,000 deduction.

A small mutual is one with annual gross income between $150,000 and $500,000. In the absence of an election to be treated as an "ordinary" mutual, a small mutual company is taxed only on investment income. Mutual insurance companies with less than $150,000 annual gross income are exempt from federal income tax altogether; they file an informational return only. Companies with gross income in excess of $500,000 are considered "ordinary" mutuals, and with the exception of the PAL account, are taxed on total income from underwriting and investments.

It can be seen that the tax treatment given a particular insurer depends on its annual gross income. Defining the makeup of gross income therefore is very important. Actually, what is defined to be annual gross income would be described better as annual gross *revenues*. Included are gross premiums plus investment income but not capital gains and losses. No deductions are allowed for losses, reinsurance ceded, commissions, return premiums, policy dividends, discounts on premiums paid in advance, or interest applied on reduction of premiums. Considerations for reinsurance assumed are included in gross premiums; amounts received from reinsurers in settlement of losses are not included. Using these guidelines, a mutual insurer can be classified into one of the three tax categories.

Since small mutuals are taxed only on investment income, the allocation of overall expenses between investment and underwriting functions can have a significant impact on taxes. It would benefit a small mutual to allocate as much of its overall expenses as possible to investment operations and in this way lower its taxable income. Recognizing this, the tax rules place limits on the total amount of expenses that can be deducted from investment revenues. Overall expenses in excess of allowable investment expenses are not deductible since small mutuals are not taxed on their underwriting income. Allocation of expenses between functions also is of significance to an ordinary mutual because of the impact underwriting expenses have on the PAL account deduction.

The PAL account is a tax memorandum account. It allows a mutual to accumulate untaxed income until that income is needed to offset excessive underwriting losses during future years or until the accumulation reaches a maximum limit. For tax purposes, additions to the PAL account are deducted from underwriting income in the year that the additions are made. Annual deductions are limited to the sum of the following three additions: (1) the addition for losses, which equals 1 percent of losses incurred in the current year; (2) the addition for underwriting gain, which equals 25 percent of underwriting gain as shown in the tax form; and (3) a special underwriting gain addition for insurers with highly concentrated writings in windstorm and other volatile insurance lines within limited geographical areas. Balances in the PAL account are taken down during years when underwriting losses are incurred. This produces a normalization of the income tax expense over good and bad years. It should be noted that although mutual insurers are not allowed net operating loss carry-overs, they can deduct "unused losses" from other tax years. The combination of the unused loss deduction and additions to the PAL account cannot create an underwriting loss for the current year. A ceiling equal to 10 percent of net earned premiums less policyholder dividends is set on the aggregate accumulation in the PAL account. Moreover, limits are placed on the duration of time certain additions can remain in the account without being used to offset losses.

Rules governing the workings of the PAL account are very complex and will not be described further. The nature and purpose of this tax equalization mechanism should be recognized from the brief comments that have been made. The provision reflects a congressional understanding of the fact that mutual insurers are operated to provide insurance to their owners at cost. Small underwriting margins can be expected to produce variable operating results. Volatile underwriting income is especially susceptible to inequitable tax treatment in the absence of a device like the PAL account. Moreover, deferral of tax on current underwriting income improves the insurer's liquidity.

Two additional aspects of the tax rules affecting insurance companies deserve mention. The first relates only to mutual insurers. A special deduction of up to $6,000 is allowed for "ordinary" mutual companies with gross income (premiums plus investment income) between $500,000 and $1,100,000. This deduction is largest for companies at the lower end of the gross income range and declines to zero for companies whose gross income equals or exceeds $1.1 million. The deduction "disappears" as gross income increases according to the scale shown in Table 1-11.

Second, it should be noted that policyholder dividends and similar distributions paid by stock and mutual insurance companies are deductions from underwriting revenues in arriving at taxable income. Dividends "incurred" during the tax year are deductible currently. Some

Table 1-11

Special "Disappearing" Tax Deduction For Mutual Insurance
Companies

(1) Gross Income	(2) 1 Percent of Income Above $500,000	(3) Special Deduction ($6,000−Column 2)
$ 500,000	$ 0	$6,000
600,000	1,000	5,000
700,000	2,000	4,000
800,000	3,000	3,000
900,000	4,000	2,000
1,000,000	5,000	1,000
1,100,000	6,000	0

differences may exist between incurred dividends reported on the
annual statement and those reported on the tax return. These
differences are easily reconcilable in the absence of inconsistent dividend
distribution practices. Special rules apply for taxation of factory
mutuals and perpetual mutuals.

Management Information The reports discussed thus far have
been intended for use by persons outside the insurance company. It
repeatedly has been observed that the basic financial accounting system
of an insurer is structured around the statutory annual statement. Other
external reports begin with statutory accounting information and
adjust it for the purposes to be served. To some extent the use of
financial accounting data carries over into management accounting. The
annual statement and stockholder financial reports adjusted to GAAP
obviously are of use to management. Tax consequences, when material,
should enter all management decisions. While these external reports
enter into the management information system, they do not fully define
it. Given the broader range of uses for accounting information within
the company it is not surprising that some segments of the management
information system are independent of the financial accounting process.

Contrasts to Financial Accounting. A company's internal accounting system differs from its financial accounting system in several
respects. Management information is not expressed exclusively in terms
of a monetary unit. This also is true in financial accounting but not to
the extent seen in internal reports. Other units of measure provide
useful information to management. For instance, activity in a particular
service center might be measured in terms of the number of new

policies, renewals, endorsements, cancellations, claims arising, claims closed, drafts issued, checks issued, and so forth. Such data can be used in performance evaluation and resource planning.

Management information often requires projection of future data rather than analysis of historical results. Establishing budgets and making decisions involving alternative choices illustrate the need for projected information. Of course, data used by management do not always come from within the company. Data supplied by industry associations, institutions, and government agencies may be included in management reports. Outside data of this nature can be helpful in making comparative analysis.

Management information also differs from financial accounting in that it is more often used to influence the behavior of employees. This characteristic helps determine the format and use of internal accounting reports.

Use of Management Information. There are three broad uses of management information: communication, planning, and control. Each use can be subdivided and none is independent of the others. Although a more detailed classification system could be discussed, analysis of these broad uses of management information gives an overview of the system's purposes. Communication is vitally important in any business. Of necessity, communication becomes more formalized in larger organizations with diversified functions. Personal involvement of top management in operations is neither feasible nor desirable. Yet management must maintain familiarity with all aspects of operations if it hopes to avoid surprises, especially surprises involving negative results. Blunders can be avoided by identifying and controlling problems as they develop. To do this, management information must serve as an early warning system which detects problems quickly and reports dimensions of the problem accurately. Communication aspects of the information system also are used to inform personnel of operating policies and company goals. This information serves to facilitate daily activities and motivate employees in their work.

The second use of management information is in the area of planning. Planning involves setting goals for the company and mapping how these goals are to be achieved. Strategic goals are a function of the company's operational objectives. For a stock property and liability company the fundamental management objective might be expressed as long-run maximization of stockholder wealth. A mutual insurance company's management might state its primary objective to be minimization of policyholder cost. Other corollary objectives, such as maintenance or expansion of the company's market share, would be coordinated with the fundamental company objective. Management accounting data can be used to set intermediate goals by which the firm's progress toward its objectives may be measured. The planning process is not solely the responsibility of senior management. It requires communication and negotiation among managers at all organizational levels. In this way individual managers are given an opportunity to participate in planning the company's future and their own.

The third use of management information is for control. There are several aspects to the management control process. Seeing that daily tasks are accomplished successfully is operational control. It is performed by front-line supervisory personnel and does not require the attention of senior management. The control process in which senior management does participate directly involves moving the company toward its operational goals. Frequently summary reports from predetermined responsibility centers that facilitate comparison of actual progress to planned performance are used for control purposes.

Management Reports. The exact type and number of reports prepared for internal use varies greatly among insurance companies. A company's size, corporate affiliations, organizational structure, marketing system, the geographical scope of its operations, and other factors determine the types of management reports needed. A close-up view of an insurance company could easily give the impression that the huge volume of information being processed at any one time is uncontrolled. There seems to be a constant tendency for internal reports to multiply. Companies therefore find it necessary to monitor continuously their information systems in order to avoid meaningless proliferation and duplication of reports. In spite of the lack of uniformity among reports prepared for company management, the following examples should illustrate the nature of these reports.

An executive of a large property and liability insurance company operating through independent agents stated that his company prepares 1,100 management reports each year.[9] A great many of these reports contain operating data; five are major summary reports prepared for broad management purposes. A company-wide agency based production report appears three times each year. The report shows premiums written and earned by line of business; these are matched with losses incurred, IBNR claims, and commission expenses. Data are set forth on a year-to-date basis with comparative information from the previous five years. The report is sufficiently detailed so that individual agency evaluation can be made. This illustrates the type of performance report used to monitor agency profitability, loss development, and product mix. Deviation of reported performance from projected standards can be ascertained from the report in a timely fashion. Analysis of the report over several periods gives company management an indication of each agency's progress and future growth potential. The report is distributed to all branches and agencies to provide each service unit with information on its own performance.

The insurer also prepares a monthly performance report that details company underwriting profitability for each responsibility center and line of business. Premiums written and earned, net of reinsurance are matched with losses incurred, IBNR claims, and incurred expenses to determine statutory underwriting results for the year to date. These data are summarized in reported loss ratios, expense ratios, and combined ratios. The responsibility centers are defined by organizational category. For example, the company's personal property underwriting unit includes residential fire, extended coverage, homeowners, yachts, personal effects, jewelry and furs, and related lines. Data are aggregated from individual responsibility centers to the branch office level and then to the company level. Unit, branch, and company management thus are informed monthly on progress toward annual production and profit goals. Underwriting and rate-making policy decisions can be reevaluated monthly using this performance information.

Performance reports are prepared periodically for investment operations also. These reports are at the company level only. They detail recent acquisitions, show the current distribution of portfolio assets, and indicate current investment income. Average yields from the portfolio and from individual investment categories are shown along with rates of return on newly invested funds. Investment results are compared to the corresponding period in the previous year. In addition, the company's performance is compared to a broad based market index, such as the Standard and Poor's Index of 500 Stocks.

Other management reports deal with resource utilization, cost allocation, and planning. Monitoring resource utilization often involves the use of nonmonetary data. For instance, the number of claims settled per employee-hour worked in the claims office can be a useful check on productivity. Count data on the volume of activity in a given service unit also can provide a base for allocating indirect (fixed) costs to that function. A fundamental planning report prepared monthly and at less frequent intervals is the cash budget. Cash budgeting is necessary in both underwriting and investment operations. It facilitates synchronization of cash flows from premium revenues and investment returns, sales, and maturities with disbursements for loss settlements, expense payments, and investment acquisitions. Frequent comparisons of actual to budgeted cash utilization are required in coordinating underwriting and investment operations. Actuarial reports on the development of loss reserves can be used to assist the budgeting process.

These examples are intended to illustrate the types of internal reports used to manage any insurance company. As in any business numerous reports and subsidiary records make up the organization's internal information system. Graphically, the system could be pictured as a pyramid; the base of the pyramid represents the many documents containing detailed operational data and the apex represents a few summary reports prepared for senior management. Turning the picture upside down converts the pyramid to a funnel of information for internal communications, planning, and control.

STATUTORY
INSURANCE ACCOUNTING PRINCIPLES

Statutory insurance accounting principles are those rules of accounting prescribed or permitted by state law or regulatory authorization for use by insurance companies. An understanding of insurance regulatory objectives therefore is beneficial to a comprehension of statutory insurance accounting principles. Various reasons have been given to explain the need for insurance regulation. A broad answer to the question of why insurance is regulated at all was provided in a 1914 case involving the right of the state of Kansas to regulate rates.[10] In that case, the United States Supreme Court declared that the business of insurance was "affected with a public interest" and therefore subject to governmental regulation. In a subsequent case, the court noted that being "affected with a public interest" did not endow upon the insurance industry a cloak of righteousness.[11] It simply implies that industry operations and regulation should seek to fulfill certain public policy objectives. The objectives most frequently discussed seek to (1) preserve and enhance solvency; (2) promote propriety in premium rates; (3) ensure fairness, equity, and reasonableness in insurance markets; and (4) fulfill certain external goals that are not necessarily pertinent to a successful insurance operation. An external regulatory objective might be assuring marginal loss exposures access to insurance coverage at a lower cost than dictated by economic considerations.

Occasionally, the promotion of uniform financial reporting practices is given as an insurance regulatory objective.[12] This is incorrect. Financial reporting requirements are a means to fulfill the first regulatory objective, solvency. Without maintenance of solvency all other regulatory objectives are meaningless. Statutory accounting principles and reporting practices are not an end in themselves but are a means by which solvency can be monitored and the fundamental regulatory objective fulfilled.

While not all insurance laws and regulations are intended to guarantee solvency, many are concerned with the financial health of insurers. Others must be carefully constructed so as not to conflict with this primary goal. Because they seek to assure solvency, statutory accounting principles have concentrated on conservative valuation rules for balance sheet items. Concern over operating results has always been of secondary importance to analysis of financial position. Generally, a liquidation view of the company has been adopted in the formulation of accounting principles. Nevertheless, regulators have demonstrated little aversion to using a going concern view whenever perpetuation of company operations benefited by the switch. What may appear to be unorthodox and inconsistent accounting conventions become more understandable when placed in the context of the solvency goal.

Insurance accounting practices and rules have been derived from regulatory objectives. Some rules clearly are relevant to guaranteeing company solvency and are justified on this basis. A complete theoretical structure, however, has never been built to house statutory accounting. It often shares a common theoretical foundation with general accounting (for example, both postulate a stable monetary unit, both use a specified time period, and so on) but the theoretical structures are different. Most insurance accounting principles can be traced to the pragmatic selection of accounting concepts and techniques useful in achieving regulatory objectives. A general framework of statutory insurance accounting is based on concepts of valuation, continuity, and realization.

Valuation Concepts

Quantification of assets and liabilities in terms of a monetary unit is the valuation process. Valuation rules of statutory accounting have been designed to satisfy the following criteria:

1. Valuation should result in a conservative statement of policyholder surplus.
2. Valuation should, as much as reasonably possible, prevent sharp fluctuations in policyholder surplus.

A conservative measurement of surplus results when the lowest of several possible values is selected for assets and the highest of several possible values is selected for liabilities. Surplus values are stabilized by selecting asset and liability values that experience the least amount of change from period to period. At times, conflicts arise between these two criteria; when this occurs, the interaction of the continuity and realization concepts with valuation must be used to arrive at a choice between alternative values.

Statutory accounting imposes an unusually harsh valuation rule by excluding some assets from the balance sheet altogether. This is equivalent to assigning nonadmitted assets a value of zero. Whether an asset qualifies for balance sheet presentation depends on its liquidity. Items that cannot be readily converted to cash at or near a known amount are not recognized in the determination of current financial position. Included among the nonadmitted assets are furniture, fixtures, equipment, supplies, automobiles, computer software, uncollected premiums over ninety days due, and loans to certain company personnel. Acquisitions of nonadmitted assets are charged directly to policyholder surplus in the current accounting period.

The majority of assets admitted to the balance sheet are monetary items (see Table 1-1). These assets are cash or can be converted to cash quickly at reasonably certain values. Admitted assets are valued according to rules established by the NAIC. Stocks are shown at their association values which usually correspond to year-end market values. Unrealized appreciation or depreciation from the cost of stock as shown on the company's ledger is reflected immediately in policyholders' surplus. This valuation rule, therefore, results in a lower statement of surplus than would be obtained by using ledger values when current market prices fall below original cost. However, the second criterion of the valuation process, stabilization of surplus, is not achieved. Because investing a large portion of portfolio assets in stock exposes surplus to market price fluctuations, the states regulate the relative amount a company can invest in this asset. Constraints vary among the states but their common intent is to force portfolio diversification and prevent excessive investment in equity securities. It should be noted that on several occasions the association values have differed significantly from year-end market prices. The last occurrence was in 1937. For that year companies were authorized to use stabilized values for stock equal to an average of the previous year's month-end market prices. This resulted in an overstatement of surplus according to the usual rule but prevented numerous technical insolvencies due to temporarily depressed market prices. The rationale behind this inconsistent procedure was that insurance companies are ongoing operations that do not actually realize capital losses unless they are forced to liquidate invested assets. Since the depressed stock prices were regarded as a temporary aberration in the market, forced liquidation and capital impairment under the normal valuation rule were not recognized.

The standard rule for the admitted asset value of bonds is to show them at amortized cost. Amortized cost is the price paid for the bond adjusted to the current period in such a way as to eventually equal the

Table 1-12

Streamlined Balance Sheets

	Bonds at Cost	Bonds at Market	Change Due to Market
Assets	$83,573	$69,410	$14,163
Liabilities	60,552	60,552	
Surplus	$23,021	$ 8,858	$14,163

precise sum that is payable at the bond's maturity date. Thus a bond that is purchased above (at a premium) or below (at a discount) par value is written down or up to par value between the date of purchase and the date of maturity. This accomplishes two things. First, bond values based on amortized cost are more stable than values based on market prices. Policyholders' surplus thus is shielded from fluctuations occurring in the bond market due to interest rate changes. Second, a portion of the bond's premium or discount is allocated to investment income proportionally over the period the bond is held. This has a stabilizing effect on income and, consequently, on surplus. Most state laws allow bond discounts or premiums to be amortized either on a straight-line basis or by use of the annuity method. If the annuity method is used, the bonds yield-to-maturity will be equal to the market rate of interest prevailing for the bond at the date it was acquired.

Basing admitted asset values for bonds on amortized cost reflects a particular continuity concept. It recognizes that insurance companies are going concerns. They normally do not have to liquidate securities at depressed prices but can rely on normal cash flow from underwriting and scheduled investment maturities to meet disbursement requirements. This reasoning explains why the first valuation criterion stated above often is violated by the standard bond valuation rule, especially during periods of rising interest rates.

To illustrate the impact that the use of amortized costs have on company valuation, consider the data in Table 1-1. The average stock property and liability insurer at the end of 1976 held 55.7 percent of its assets in bonds. Assume that the bonds were all recently purchased at par, that their coupon or nominal annual interest rate was 6 percent, and that they are fifteen years from maturity. If the values shown in Table 1-1 were based on original cost and the market interest rate for bonds of this type had increased to 10 percent by year-end, the adjustment necessary to bring these bonds to their market value would reduce policyholders' surplus by 61.5 percent. See Table 1-12.

Only bonds "in good standing" are eligible for amortized cost valuation. A bond is considered to be in good standing if it is not in default, has a maturity date, is amply secured, and is among the classes of bonds approved by the NAIC. Other bonds are shown at their market values unless there is reason to believe a lower value would be realized from their disposal.

Property and liability insurers do not invest heavily in mortgages, real estate, or collateral loans. These assets are not considered to possess the degree of liquidity desired for nonlife insurance company operations. Only first lien real estate mortgages are admissible to the balance sheet. Their value is equal to the balance of the unpaid principle. Accrued interest is shown separately. Direct real estate investments are valued at cost adjusted for additions, improvements, and depreciation thereon. Encumberances due to mortgages on company property serve to reduce the balance sheet value of real estate. If the market value exceeds cost, no adjustment is made. However, market values below cost require a downward adjustment of the asset's value to reflect the difference. Thus, real estate values are cost or market, whichever is lower. While this valuation rule appears inconsistent with valuations placed on other assets, especially stocks, the liquidity characteristics of real estate justify the distinction. Since real estate values do not often fall precipitously the stability of surplus valuation is not unduly threatened by this method of valuation. State laws limit the amounts which insurance companies can invest in real estate. Separate limits apply to property held by the company for use and to total real estate investment. Collateral loans are valued at the amount of the unpaid loan or the market value of the pledged collateral whichever is lowest. Loans made to company officers and directors are not admitted to the balance sheet.

Valuation of liabilities also is subject to standards of conservatism. If more than one possible value exists for a liability, the highest value usually is selected. Balance sheet conservatism in the treatment of liabilities may impact on both underwriting income and surplus or on surplus alone. This is explained by the way in which reserve increases enter into income determination and by the imposition of statutory minimum reserves in certain lines of insurance.

The increase in reserves for losses and loss adjustment expenses during an accounting period are included in losses and expenses incurred in determining statutory underwriting income:

$$
\begin{matrix}
\text{Statutory} \\
\text{Underwriting} \quad = \\
\text{Income}
\end{matrix}
$$

$$
\begin{matrix}
\text{Premiums} \\
\text{Earned}
\end{matrix}
-
\left(
\begin{matrix}
\text{Losses} \\
\text{Incurred}
\end{matrix}
+
\begin{matrix}
\text{Loss} \\
\text{Adjustment} \\
\text{Expense}
\end{matrix}
+
\begin{matrix}
\text{Other} \\
\text{Expenses} \\
\text{Incurred}
\end{matrix}
\right)
$$

To the extent that conservative reserve valuations overstate the actual value at which claims are settled, underwriting income is reduced artificially. Overstatement of loss reserves also distorts the company's loss experience record, for insurers that are taxed on underwriting income it may result in deferral of income tax, and it may affect future insurance rates.

Loss reserves for the principal liability lines—for example, automobile bodily injury liability and workers' compensation insurance—are subject to statutory minimums. Basically, loss reserves can be estimated from individual claims files or by aggregating the average value of claims that have been classified into predetermined loss categories. Regardless of whether an individual case or statistical method is used, the resulting estimate must be compared to loss reserves determined by statutory formula. In New York, for example, the minimum loss reserve for workers' compensation is determined by multiplying premiums earned on policies written in the three prior calendar years by 65 percent and subtracting loss and loss expenses already paid:

$$
\begin{matrix}
\text{Formula} \\
\text{Reserve}
\end{matrix}
=
$$

$$
\left(
\begin{matrix}
\text{Premiums} \\
\text{Earned In} \\
\text{Prior 3 Years}
\end{matrix}
\times 65\%
\right)
-
\left(
\begin{matrix}
\text{Loss} \\
\text{Payments}
\end{matrix}
+
\begin{matrix}
\text{Loss Adjustment} \\
\text{Expense}
\end{matrix}
\right)
$$

If the value arrived at by using the formula exceeds reserve values based on claims file estimates, the excess formula value must be added to balance sheet reserves. This is done by a direct adjustment to surplus and does not affect underwriting income for the period. The purpose of requiring minimum reserves is to make sure insurers do not underestimate losses and provide less than an adequate amount for claims settlements. It should be noted that the minimum reserve requirement is applied on a line-by-line basis rather than looking at aggregate loss reserves for all liability lines. The percentage factor (loss ratio) used for liability lines other than workers' compensation is usually 60 percent. For claims that require deferred settlement over a period of three or more years, the minimum loss reserve is the present value of all estimated future payments at 3.5 percent interest.

Continuity Concept

Almost all corporations are organized to operate over an indefinite time period. The ability of a corporation to have an indefinite and presumably infinite life is one of this organizational form's fundamental characteristics. Continuity and the transferability of ownership interest allow the corporation to be treated separately from its owners. General accounting principles assume that the company will continue to operate and financial statements are prepared accordingly. If there is reason to believe that the business will not continue, standard accounting principles are not used and a disclosure of the company's limited life must be made.

Statutory insurance accounting does not employ a consistent continuity concept. Using amortized cost to value bonds assumes that the securities will be held until maturity. In this respect the insurer is being treated as a going concern. On the other hand, the statutory treatment given premium revenues and the costs associated with writing new business is based on a liquidation concept. This will be illustrated later in the discussion of the realization concept. Use of a liquidation view helps assure that if the insurer does not continue in operation long enough to fulfill its existing commitments, it will be able to transfer sufficient funds to another insurer so that the assuming company may carry out the contracts.

Realization Concept

The net worth of an insurance company is affected by revenue and expense flows from normal operations during the accounting period. Gains and losses also affect the company's value.[13] To the extent that these gains or losses are related to investment activities, they may be considered part of an insurer's normal operations. Revenues and gains represent favorable changes in the company's value; expenses and losses are unfavorable. Because value is measured at a discrete point in time and income is measured for a defined time period, rules are used to establish when favorable and unfavorable changes are to be acknowledged in the financial statements. The term "realization" is used to mean the recognition of revenues, expenses, gains, and losses into income measurement and valuation. Statutory accounting's realization

Figure 1-1

Hypothetical Insurance Company Balance Sheet—July 1, 1977

Assets		Liabilities	
Cash	$1,000,000	Reserves	$ 0
		Common stock, paid-up	200,000
		Surplus, paid-in	800,000
Total assets	$1,000,000	Total liabilities and surplus	$1,000,000

concepts reflect the regulatory emphasis placed on liquidity and solvency.

A simplified example using the unearned premium reserve illustrates statutory realization of premium revenues and the related expenses. Assume that the Hypothetical Insurance Company (HIC) recently was authorized to commence operations. HIC is a stock company that intends to write fire and allied lines. Its initial capitalization consists of 100,000 shares of common stock with a stated value of $2 per share. Promoters who organized the company and who will serve as its management sold all the original shares at $10 each. If organizational costs are ignored and certain other simplifying assumptions made, the beginning balance sheet is as shown in Figure 1-1.

Now, assume that on the first day of operations agents bound 1,000 one-year fire insurance policies generating premium revenues of $210,000. Annual premiums were paid in cash and transmitted instantaneously to HIC. Premium revenues are immediately recognized but, because it will be a year before the contract provisions are completed, revenues are not realized into income at this point. Instead, the insurer is required to establish a reserve for unearned premiums. This liability represents its unfulfilled obligation to provide coverage under the contracts. At the close of HIC's first day of operations, the balance sheet is as shown in Figure 1-2. Premium revenues are realized into income on a pro rata basis over the period for which coverage is provided. However, expenses associated with writing the coverage— agents' commissions, policy printing and mailing, inspection reports, premium recording, recordkeeping, and so forth—are charged against income immediately. Assume that the expenses shown in Table 1-13 were paid on the day after the coverage was put in force. Payment of these "front-end" expenses results in the balance sheet shown in Figure 1-3. Realizing expenses immediately while deferring revenue realization produces a decline in surplus as new business is written. This illustrates why a stock insurance company that begins operations with the

Figure 1-2

Hypothetical Insurance Company Balance Sheet—July 2, 1977

Assets		Liabilities	
Cash (includes premium collection)	$1,210,000	Unearned premium reserves	$ 210,000
		Common stock, paid-up	200,000
		Surplus, paid-in	800,000
		Unassigned surplus	0
		Total policyholders' surplus	1,000,000
Total assets	$1,210,000	Total liabilities and surplus	$1,210,000

Table 1-13

Assumed Expense Distribution

Agent commissions (20%)	$42,000
Other issue expenses (18%)	37,800
Premium taxes (2%)	4,200
Total expenses incurred at issue (40%)	$84,000

Figure 1-3

Hypothetical Insurance Company Balance Sheet—July 3, 1977

Assets		Liabilities and Surplus	
Cash	$1,126,000	Unearned premium reserves	$ 210,000
		Common stock, paid-up	200,000
		Surplus, paid-in	800,000
		Unassigned surplus	(84,000)
		Total policyholders' surplus	916,000
Total assets	$1,126,000	Total liabilities and surplus	$1,126,000

minimum statutory capitalization must have paid-in capital in excess of its stock's stated (or par) value before it can write business. Similarly, mutuals require initial contributed surplus in excess of subsequent minimum capitalization. Even after a company has been operating for a number of years, the realization rules used for premium revenues and

Table 1-14

Hypothetical Insurance Company Abbreviated Income
Statement—December 31, 1977

Premiums earned ($210,000 × 0.50)		$105,000
Acquisition expenses incurred	$84,000	
Losses incurred	47,250	
Loss adjustment expenses	5,250	
Other underwriting expenses	7,350	143,850
Statutory underwriting loss		($ 38,850)

acquisition expenses require surplus in order for the company to expand. The level of surplus therefore gives a measure of the company's underwriting capacity.

Balance sheets, of course, are not actually prepared every day. The sequential balance sheets shown here are used only to illustrate the impact of realization rules on the insurer's financial position. A little more realism can be added to the example by computing underwriting results for the years during which the 1,000 original policies are in force. The example assumes that no new business is written after the initial policies and that none of the policies are canceled.

Between July 1 and December 31, 1977, HIC incurred claims of $47,250, claims adjustment expenses equal to $5,250, and $7,350 in additional expenses. Statutory accounting's revenue realization rule allows HIC to release half the premiums received on July 1 from the unearned premium reserve and recognizes them in determining underwriting income for 1977. The statutory underwriting income formula is shown in Table 1-14.

The balance sheet at the end of 1977 is as shown in Figure 1-4. Comparing the year-end balance sheet to the company's financial position on July 3 shows changes in three of the four accounts. Cash has been reduced by $59,850. This equals the sum of payments for losses, loss adjustment expenses, and other underwriting expenses incurred. Since one-half the coverage has expired, a $105,000 reduction is observed in the unearned premium reserve. Note that policyholders' surplus has increased by $45,150 between July 3 and December 31. Overall, HIC's first year in business has produced a $38,850 underwriting loss; this is the difference between the beginning and ending balance of the policyholders' surplus account. In the absence of further increases in new business, the surplus level is being restored as the contracts run their course. This process continues in the next accounting period.

In order to keep the illustration simple, assume that all the policies

Figure 1-4

Hypothetical Insurance Company Balance Sheet—December 31, 1977

Assets		Liabilities and Surplus	
Cash	$1,066,150	Unearned premium reserves	$ 105,000
		Common stock, paid-up	200,000
		Surplus, paid-in	800,000
		Unassigned surplus	(38,850)
		Total policyholders' surplus	961,150
Total assets	$1,066,150	Total liabilities and surplus	$1,066,150

Table 1-15

Hypothetical Insurance Company Abbreviated Income
Statement—December 31, 1978

Premiums earned ($210,000 × 0.50)		$105,000
Losses incurred	$47,250	
Loss adjustment expenses	5,250	
Other underwriting expenses	7,350	59,850
Statutory underwriting income		$ 45,150

continue in force and expire after June 30, 1978. No new policies are issued. Losses, claims settlement costs, and other underwriting expenses are the same as in 1977. An abbreviated income statement for 1978 shows a statutory underwriting profit. See Table 1-15. During this accounting period no new premiums are received and no additional acquisition expenses are incurred. One-half the premiums paid in the previous accounting period are released into income. Costs associated with underwriting are expensed as incurred. At the close of 1978, the balance sheet shows HIC's financial position to be as shown in Figure 1-5. A summary of the revenues and expenses associated with this block of policies reveals some interesting relationships. See Table 1-16. The insurance policies written in 1977 ultimately made a profit for the insurer equal to 3 percent of the premiums earned (and 3 percent of the premiums written, in this case). Accounting for expenses on a cash basis instead of matching them evenly with the related revenues causes an unequal realization of income in the two accounting periods. In 1977 approximately 71 percent of the total costs associated with this block of business was matched with one-half of the premiums received. A $38,850 underwriting loss was incurred. The remaining revenue was realized in

Figure 1-5

Hypothetical Insurance Company Balance Sheet—December 31, 1978

Assets		Liabilities and Surplus	
Cash	$1,006,300	Unearned premium reserves	$ 0
		Common stock, paid-up	200,000
		Surplus, paid-in	800,000
		Unassigned surplus	6,300
		Total policyholders' surplus	1,006,300
Total assets	$1,006,300	Total liabilities and surplus	$1,006,300

Table 1-16

Revenue and Expense Summary

Premiums earned (100%)		$210,000
Acquisition expenses incurred (40%)	$84,000	
Losses incurred (45%)	94,500	
Loss adjustment expenses (5%)	10,500	
Other underwriting expenses (7%)	14,700	203,700
Underwriting income (3%)		$ 6,300

the second period but only about 29 percent of the total expenses was left to be absorbed. The insurer showed a $45,150 underwriting profit. Statutory realization rules in this area of revenue and expense recognition are conservative in the sense that revenue realization is deferred while expense realization is anticipated. This forces the insurer to maintain greater liquidity than would be achieved if it were allowed to hold deferred acquisition costs on the balance sheet as an asset and amortize them against revenue as it was released into income.

Concepts of valuation, continuity, and realization highlight the rules and conventions that make up regulatory insurance accounting. Additional statutory accounting principles will be discussed and amplified throughout the remainder of this text. These principles are designed to meet the informational needs of a particular group—insurance regulators. They also are intended to force insurers to follow certain practices in their operations. Statutory insurance accounting principles are significantly different from the generally accepted principles of accounting normally applied to other business enterprises. The following section discusses some of the most important areas of difference.

DIFFERENCES BETWEEN STATUTORY ACCOUNTING AND GENERALLY ACCEPTED ACCOUNTING PRINCIPLES

In discussing the development of modern accounting principles and practices, Eldon S. Hendriksen observes that in the late 1920s and early 1930s general accounting underwent a fundamental change.[14] Instead of presenting information to management and creditors, accounting was reoriented to provide information for investor decision making. This reorientation manifested itself in a de-emphasis of the balance sheet and an ascendence of the income statement as the primary financial report. Treatment of a business as a going concern rather than on a liquidation basis reshaped accounting procedures. The balance sheet became a repository of account balances between periodic income statements. Income measurement by means of a uniform income concept became recognized as more important than valuation. Greater emphasis was given to full disclosure of relevant financial information, the need for a consistent application of accounting practices was recognized, and footnote information became more frequently used.

Statutory insurance accounting did not share in this realignment of objectives. It has continued to emphasize solvency by use of the balance sheet formula. Income measurement is of secondary importance. If financial statements of insurance companies were not used for nonregulatory purposes, the differences between statutory accounting and GAAP would not be especially troublesome. However, the broad based and increasing public ownership and trading of equity shares in insurance companies has brought about a need to reconcile statutory financial statements to nonregulatory needs.

Origins and Scope of
Generally Accepted Accounting Principles

Accounting principles in the United States generally have developed in the private sector. Governmental influence on accounting rules comes through the SEC in its role as overseer of interstate securities transactions. The SEC is charged with administering the Securities Act of 1933, the Securities Exchange Act of 1934, the Public Utility Holding Company Act of 1935, the Trust Indenture Act of 1939, the Investment Company Act of 1940, the Investment Company Amendments Act of 1970, and related securities laws. The purpose of the SEC is to promote orderly and efficient securities markets. It does this by requiring, among other things, full disclosure of all relevant financial information on a basis that is intended to prevent misrepresentation, deceit, and fraud in the sale of securities. The formal method by which disclosure is achieved is through periodic reports filed with the SEC. Rules pertaining to these filings are taken from the principal accounting regulation of the SEC, *Regulation S-X.* Article 2 of *Regulation S-X* sets forth the SEC's requirement as to certification of financial statements by independent public accountants who meet certain qualification standards. Although empowered to mandate unique accounting rules for statements filed with it, the SEC rarely has exercised this authority. Instead, it usually has relied on generally accepted accounting principles and practices developed by accountants in the private sector.

Prior to 1973, the accounting profession operated through its professional association, the American Institute of Certified Public Accountants (AICPA), to establish a number of committees and boards whose purposes were the development of authoritative accounting principles. Pronouncements of these bodies were issued in the form of *Accounting Terminology Bulletins, Accounting Research Studies, Opinions,* and *Statements.* Between 1959 and 1973 the AICPA's Accounting Principles Board (APB) was the chief rule making body of the profession. Its *Opinions* were officially approved rules of accounting for use in all but exceptional circumstances. In 1973, the APB was superseded by the Financial Accounting Standards Board (FASB) which is not a part of the AICPA. The FASB is a private organization funded by a nonprofit foundation which receives contributions from business enterprises and the accounting profession. The full-time personnel of the FASB promulgate new accounting standards and revise existing rules in cooperation with interested parties in the affected industry. Through its seven-member board, professional staff, and paid consultants the FASB works extensively in Washington and throughout the country for understanding and support of its standards. At the present time standards of the FASB define generally accepted accounting principles.

A logical question, which might follow from a description of the accounting rule-making bodies is, "Just what are generally accepted accounting principles (GAAP)?" Accountants use the term GAAP to encompass the conventions, rules, and procedures developed from experience and believed to be the tools best suited for the purposes intended at a particular time. Thus the term includes not only the broad guidelines of general application, but also detailed practices and procedures needed to establish reliable financial and operating information for business enterprises. They have been compared to principles of commercial law in that they attain substantial authoritative support from practitioners rather than being derived from theoretical experimentation as is the case in natural science.

Businesses are not directly required to use GAAP in preparation of their financial statements. However, in order to receive an unqualified auditor's opinion these principles must be adopted. The privilege of having the company's stock traded on the national securities exchanges necessitates receipt of an unqualified opinion. Because of these indirect pressures, most businesses find it expedient to follow GAAP in preparation of their financial statements.

It is important to understand that GAAP do not necessarily prescribe uniform treatment of similar transactions by different firms. Although uniformity would enhance comparability of financial reports among businesses, more than one procedure may be considered a generally accepted method of dealing with a particular transaction. For example, several alternative rules may be used to recognize revenues generated under long-term construction contracts. Choice of accounting methods within the range defined as GAAP is left to management discretion. It is the auditor's responsibility to render an opinion on whether the accounting rules used by management are within the scope of GAAP, have been applied on a consistent basis, and result in a fair disclosure of all relevant information.

Applying GAAP to Property and Liability Insurers

It long has been recognized that solvency oriented statutory accounting reports are not of greatest use for nonregulatory purposes. Investors making buy, hold, or sell decisions regarding insurance company stocks are more interested in the company's future earnings than in a conservative measurement of its financial position. As early as the 1930s, A.M. Best Company reported "adjusted earnings" for property and liability insurance companies. Adjustments were made to statutory statements for such things as the insurer's equity in the unearned premium reserve that arose from the mismatching of acquisition expenses and premium revenues.

With the increased trading of insurance company stocks that occurred after World War II, the investment community's interest in financial reporting practices of insurance companies grew. Security analysts, the SEC, institutional investors, the AICPA, and some insurance industry spokesmen called for uniformity in the procedures used to adjust statutory accounting statements. In 1957 the AICPA's Committee on Insurance Accounting and Auditing undertook the development of an audit guide for nonlife insurance companies. Nine years later, in 1966, the Committee published a booklet entitled *Audits of Fire and Casualty Insurance Companies* intended as a guide for auditors called upon to render an opinion on insurance company financial statements. A revision of the AICPA audit guide for nonlife insurance companies is being prepared at the time of this writing.

The type of audit opinion given corporate financial statements is determined in accordance with generally accepted auditing standards developed by the accounting profession. These standards are spelled out in considerable detail in AICPA publications. The following excerpt from Chapter 10 of the AICPA's *Statement on Auditing Procedure No. 33* is especially pertinent to opinions given insurance company financial statements:

> The basic postulates and broad principles of accounting comprehended in the term 'generally accepted accounting principles' which pertain to business enterprises in general apply also to companies whose accounting practices are prescribed by authorities or commissions. (Such companies include public utilities, common carriers, insurance companies, financial institutions, and the like.) Accordingly, the first reporting standard is equally applicable to opinions on companies presented for purposes other than filings with their respective supervisory agencies, and material variances from generally accepted accounting principles, and their effects, should be dealt with in the independent auditor's report in the same manner followed by companies which are not regulated. Ordinarily, this will require either a qualified or adverse opinion on such statements.[15]

The AICPA's audit guide shows acceptable procedures for presenting nonlife insurance company financial statements on a basis that merits an unqualified audit opinion; that is, it sets forth areas where statutory financial statements must be adjusted to bring them into conformity with GAAP.

There are seven major areas of difference between statutory insurance accounting and GAAP for property and liability insurers:

1. Nonadmitted Assets. Solvency oriented statutory valuation rules require that certain items be excluded from the balance sheet by a direct charge to surplus when acquired. Under GAAP, economic resources that have an objectively measurable value and which reasonably can be expected to benefit future periods are shown as assets.
2. Unauthorized Reinsurance. Reinsurance placed with a company

not authorized to transact business in a particular state and hence not subject to that state's regulation, is not recognized under statutory rules unless funds have been deposited with the ceding insurer. General accounting regards reserves for unauthorized reinsurance to be segregated policyholders' surplus rather than a liability if the reinsurer possesses the ability to honor its contractual obligations.

3. Excess Loss Reserves. Minimum loss and loss expense reserves for certain types of coverage are established by statutory formula irrespective of the adequacy of case basis reserves. Under GAAP, the excess of statutory loss reserves, if any, over realistically estimated liabilities for unpaid losses and loss expenses is added to policyholders' surplus.

4. Prepaid Expenses. Statutory accounting treats the costs of acquiring new business as period expenses when these costs are incurred but realizes the corresponding premium revenue into income over the contractual coverage period. This mismatching of revenue and expense creates an equity in the unearned premium reserve. That is, the insurer has used a portion of its policyholders' surplus to pay acquisition expenses prior to realizing premium revenue in the income statement. The insurer is said to have "invested" in the unearned premium reserve an amount equal to these prepaid expenses. The insurer's equity is later recovered as revenues are released from the unearned premium reserve and flow to income. GAAP capitalize acquisition expenses by creating an asset account for deferred charges that are amortized over the same period during which revenues are realized.

5. Capital Gains and Losses. Because equity securities generally reflect their year-end market values, unrealized capital gains and losses are included on the statutory balance sheet. Unrealized changes in capital values are credited or charged directly to surplus while realized capital gains and losses are included in income for the period. The lack of parallel treatment given realized and unrealized gains and losses is bothersome. A unique principle for dealing with this problem only recently has been agreed upon by the accounting profession. This method is similar to the statutory treatment of gains and losses with some specific exceptions, discussed below.

6. Deferred Federal Income Taxes. No adjustment is shown in statutory financial statements for federal income tax charges or credits that arise out of differences between pretax statutory income and taxable income as shown on the company's income

tax return. When financial statements are adjusted to GAAP, deferred income taxes arising from any timing difference are reflected in the statements.

7. Business Combinations and Consolidated Financial Statements. For statutory accounting purposes, investments in subsidiary companies are carried among invested assets at a value equal to the underlying net equity in the subsidiary. Changes in the subsidiary's equity (e.g., arising from retained earnings) are treated as unrealized gains and losses through a direct credit or charge to surplus. The parent insurer realizes investment income from the subsidiary only to the extent that dividends are received. Financial statements prepared in conformity with GAAP deal with subsidiary investments either by fully consolidating all legal entities involved or by using the equity method to reflect results of subsidiary operations in the parent corporation's earnings.

Some of these items have been discussed previously and require no further elaboration. Additional comments on items 4, 5, 6, and 7 are appropriate here.

Prepaid Expenses Under GAAP, costs associated with selling new insurance become expenses during the same period that the related premium revenue is recognized. This is accomplished by capitalizing acquisition costs when they are incurred and later amortizing them proportionately against revenue. Expense deferral removes the statutory paradox of decreasing earnings and surplus in periods of expanding sales. Consider the Hypothetical Insurance Company example used earlier. Under statutory accounting rules the relevant revenue and expense items for 1977 and 1978 were as shown in Table 1-17.

The GAAP procedure would adjust these figures to provide an even matching of expenses and revenues in the manner shown in Table 1-18. As before, the policies yielded an overall underwriting income of $6,300. But under GAAP, there was an even emergence of profit in the two accounting periods whereas a large underwriting loss was followed by a large underwriting profit when statutory rules were employed.

Adjusting for the insurer's equity in the unearned premium reserve due to prepayment of expenses conforms the statutory expense recognition rule to GAAP. Care must be exercised to avoid undue expense deferrals that delay recognition of underwriting losses. Such situations would arise whenever anticipated losses, loss adjustment expenses, and other expenses incurred after policy issue exceeded the difference between premiums written and initial acquisition costs. In such cases, the costs subject to capitalization are limited so that the ratio of anticipated losses and expenses plus acquisition costs cannot exceed

Table 1-17

Abbreviated Statutory Revenue and Expense Allocation

	1977	1978
Premiums written	$210,000	$ 0
Increase in unearned premiums	105,000	(105,000)
Premiums earned	105,000	105,000
Acquisition costs incurred	84,000	0
Revenue net of acquisition costs	21,000	105,000
Losses and expenses subsequently incurred	59,850	59,850
Statutory underwriting profit (loss)	($38,850)	$ 45,150

Table 1-18

Abbreviated GAAP Revenue and Expense Allocation

	1977	1978
Premiums written	$210,000	$ 0
Increase in unearned premiums	105,000	(105,000)
Premiums earned	105,000	105,000
Amortization of deferred acquisition costs	42,000	42,000
Adjusted net revenue	63,000	63,000
Losses and expenses subsequently incurred	59,850	59,850
Adjusted underwriting profit	$ 3,150	$ 3,150

100 percent of premiums earned. Changing a few assumptions in the Hypothetical Insurance Company example illustrates this point, as shown in Table 1-19. Actual expenses incurred act as a limit on the costs subject to capitalization under the original conditions of the example. To defer the entire amount available to meet acquisition costs in this case would amount to deferring profit recognition. Note that the absence of an underwriting profit in the second illustration does not prevent deferral of the full amount of eligible acquisition costs if sufficient revenues are available. A reduction of capitalizable costs does occur when premiums are not adequate to meet all costs associated with the

Table 1-19

Expense Capitalization Limitations

	Original Conditions	Zero Profit	Under-writing Loss
Premiums earned	100%	100%	100%
Anticipated loss ratio	45	46	50
Loss adjustment expense ratio	5	6	8
Other underwriting expense ratio	7	8	10
Subtotal	57	60	68
Available for acquisition expenses	43	40	32
Acquisition expenses incurred	40	40	40
Expenses eligible for capitalization	40	40	32

policies. In such a case, the ineligible costs are expensed when incurred along with the pro rata share of capitalized costs.

Capital Gains and Losses   Realized capital gains and losses are included on the statutory income statement. Unrealized appreciation or depreciation in the value of stocks, carried at market on the balance sheet, is credited or charged directly to surplus. The 1966 AICPA audit guide expressed disapproval for the lopsided treatment accorded realized and unrealized gains and losses. It noted that large realized gains might completely dwarf results of underwriting operations. To avoid this, the guide recommended that adjusted net income be determined exclusive of investment gains or losses. Net investment results then could be shown in a separate statement.

However, the guide noted that "...there is no single approach to the treatment of realized and unrealized capital gains which will simultaneously satisfy all requirements of informative reporting for insurance company operations."[16] The FASB urges adherence to an all-inclusive presentation of income which includes all items of revenue, expense, gain, and loss in the determination of income for the period. Inclusion of both realized and unrealized gains and losses in income substantially limits manipulation of net income through investment activities. Until recently there was authoritative support for more than one approach to reporting capital value changes. This area therefore permitted several alternative procedures, each of which was considered to conform with GAAP. Companies individually adopted an approach they believed best disclosed the results of their underwriting and investment operations. These approaches included:

1. The Statutory Approach. Realized capital gains and losses were included directly in income. Unrealized changes in the value of investment assets did not enter the income calculation but were reflected directly in surplus.
2. The Audit Guide Approach. A separate statement of the results achieved from investment activities was prepared to supplement the income statement. Both realized and unrealized gains and losses were shown on the separate investment statement and were not included in calculating "net income, as adjusted (excluding investment gains and losses)."
3. The All-Inclusive Approach. All capital gains and losses, whether realized or unrealized, were shown on the income statement and entered into the calculation of adjusted net income. This sometimes was referred to as the "flow-through" method because results of investment operations flowed through the income statement to surplus.

A fourth method of dealing with investment gains and losses involved the amortization of both realized and unrealized components through use of a formula approach. This method sought to reflect a long-term yield from appreciation in income without allowing the disruptive fluctuations possible under the all-inclusive approach. Although this proposal received considerable discussion over the years, it was not widely used.

The SEC, by issuing Accounting Series Release No. 183, has mandated a uniform approach for reporting capital gains and losses in financial statements of property and liability insurers filed with the commission. Investments may be shown on the balance sheet at cost or current value provided the basis of valuation for stocks and bonds is disclosed parenthetically. Realized capital gains and losses, less applicable taxes, are included as a component of net income. Unrealized appreciation or depreciation of invested assets are not included in income but are reflected in policyholders' surplus, adjusted for applicable deferred taxes. The change in the value of equity investments occurring during the accounting period is shown parenthetically immediately following the statement of income. An analysis of realized and unrealized capital gains and losses on stocks, notes, and bonds must be given in notes accompanying the financial statements. Changes in the difference between current value and cost for both stocks and bonds must be included even though these assets may be carried on the balance sheet on a basis other than current value.

In 1978, the AICPA's Accounting Standards Division approved for issuance a Statement on Accounting for Property and Liability Insurance Companies. This document states that realized capital gains and losses on investments should be included in the statement of income below operating income and should be net of applicable income taxes. Realized gains and losses on assets not held for investment should be included in the statement of income before applicable income taxes. Unrealized investment gains and losses should be recognized in policyholders' surplus net of applicable income taxes.

Deferred Federal Income Taxes   Preparation of financial statements in conformity with GAAP often gives rise to what are called "timing differences" between earnings on the financial statements and on the federal tax return. A timing difference results from the fact that income recognition rules under GAAP are not identical to those of the federal tax code. GAAP may recognize income earlier than the tax rules and although a tax is not immediately owed the government on the differential income, a deferred credit must be shown currently in the financial statements. In later periods when the amount of income tax actually paid exceeds the tax on GAAP income for that period, the deferred tax liability is discharged.

Three points need to be emphasized here. First, deferred federal income taxes are not amounts currently owed the government and not paid. This account does not reflect benefits of "creative accounting" or the keeping of a "hidden set of books." Indeed, the existence of the deferred income tax account discloses the fact that GAAP income is measured differently than taxable income. The second point to stress is that deferred income taxes are not unique to insurance companies. Many types of business transactions may result in timing differences between income on a corporation's tax return and in its financial statements. Insurance companies as well as other business enterprises may engage in such transactions. A third point follows from these two comments: the fact that insurance company income as reported in stockholder financial statements is adjusted from a statutory income statement is only incidental to income tax deferrals. Timing differences creating deferred income taxes are due to the divergence between GAAP and the federal tax code not between GAAP and statutory insurance accounting principles. This last point notwithstanding, two of the most common areas where GAAP income differs from taxable income happen to be areas where statutory insurance accounting diverges from GAAP. These are the areas of prepaid expenses and unrealized capital gains and losses.

Prepaid Expenses.   Expenses incurred on the statutory income statement generally are deductible for income tax purposes. As noted above, GAAP income capitalizes acquisition costs and amortizes them against income in later periods. This gives rise to higher GAAP income during the current period and hence a deferred federal income tax liability must be recognized. A further extension of the Hypothetical Insurance Company example illustrates the calculation of the deferred tax liability and shows how the account reverses itself in a later period. For the sake of illustration, net investment income is assumed to be $50,000 in both years and an effective tax rate of 50 percent is applied to combined underwriting and investment income.

Net income for the two years totals $53,150 on HIC's tax returns and on its financial statements. Because a 50 percent tax rate is assumed, provision for federal income taxes also totals $53,150 for the two years in each set of statements. Note, however, that GAAP make a uniform provision for taxes in each year. In 1977, HIC pays $5,575 income tax and establishes a $21,000 deferred tax liability. The total provision for federal income taxes is $26,575. A $47,575 income tax payment is made in 1978, but of this only $26,575 is current expense and a $21,000 reduction occurs in the deferred tax account. Thus, the timing difference reverses itself in the second year and the balance in the deferred income tax account goes to zero. In an actual case, as some timing differences reverse, others arise so that a balance in the deferred income tax account should be expected. See Table 1-20.

Unrealized Capital Gains and Losses. Another cause of changes in the deferred income tax liability account is the occurrence of unrealized appreciation or depreciation in the market value of stocks. While a unique treatment of capital value changes is not mandated by GAAP, recognition of potential income tax effects is imposed. An adjustment to surplus is made for unrealized appreciation from prior years' investments the first time GAAP financial statements are prepared. For investments made after 1971, the maximum capital gains tax rate is 30 percent. This rate is applied to net unrealized capital value changes occurring during the current year. In this way, unrealized gains and losses reflected in adjusted surplus are reduced by the related tax that would be paid upon realization.

Assume that the Hypothetical Insurance Company was in its twentieth year of operation in 1977 and that for the first time, it prepared financial statements in conformity with GAAP. Surplus at the beginning of 1977 was $10 million; of this amount $1 million was attributable to unrealized capital gains on investments purchased in 1972 and thereafter. During 1977, the value of marketable securities appreciated $20,000 but no gains were realized that year. At the end of 1977, HIC would show a deferred federal income tax account balance of $306,000 due to unrealized capital appreciation in its investment portfolio. This liability would reduce adjusted surplus by $300,000 for

Table 1-20

Income Effect of Timing Differences

		1977	1978
Taxable Income			
Premiums written		$210,000	$ 0
Change in unearned premiums		105,000	(105,000)
Premiums earned		105,000	105,000
Acquisition expenses incurred		84,000	0
Subtotal		21,000	105,000
Losses and expenses subsequently incurred		59,850	59,850
Net underwriting profit (loss)		(38,850)	45,150
Net investment income		50,000	50,000
Income before federal income taxes		11,150	95,150
Provision for federal income taxes		5,575	47,575
Net income		$ 5,575	$ 47,575
GAAP Income			
Premiums written		$210,000	$ 0
Change in unearned premiums		105,000	(105,000)
Premiums earned		105,000	105,000
Amortized acquisition costs		42,000	42,000
Adjusted net revenue		63,000	63,000
Losses and expenses subsequently incurred		59,850	59,850
Adjusted underwriting profit		3,150	3,150
Net investment income		50,000	50,000
Income before federal income taxes		53,150	53,150
Provision for federal income taxes:			
Taxes currently payable	$ 5,575		$47,575	
Taxes deferred	21,000	26,575	(21,000)	26,575
Net income		$ 26,575	$ 26,575

appreciation experienced in prior years ($1,000,000 × 0.30) and $6,000 ($20,000 × 0.30) for the current year's gain. If HIC sustains a $40,000 unrealized capital loss in 1978, the deferred federal income tax account would be decreased by $12,000 ($40,000 × 0.30) to a new balance of $294,000. Now, suppose all marketable securities were sold in 1979 and the proceeds reinvested. The $980,000 net appreciation from prior years is realized and a capital gains tax becomes payable. No other capital gains or losses occur. Will surplus be affected by the investment transactions? No, it will not. The gain had been reflected in surplus previously on an unrealized basis and had been adjusted for taxes through the deferred federal income tax account. Although income taxes become payable upon realization of the gain, the expense was provided for when the appreciation first was recognized in surplus.

Business Combinations and Consolidated Financial Statements Combination of two or more corporations through intercorporate investments has become common business practice. Within the insurance industry corporate combinations take many forms including mergers, consolidations, and parent-subsidiary relationships. Mergers and consolidations both result in the termination of at least one previously existing entity, usually the acquired company. The difference between the two methods of combination is primarily one of form. When a merger occurs, two or more existing companies combine and only one continues. In a consolidation, a new corporation is established to absorb two or more existing companies which then pass from existence. A parent-subsidiary relationship exists when one corporation owns or controls all or a majority of the voting equity securities of one or more other corporations. When the parent holding company and the subsidiary corporations operate in similar or related activities, the combined entities are called a "congeneric." For example, a property and liability insurance company may be part of a congeneric which includes corporations involved in leasing operations, computer services, real estate development, insurance marketing, consulting and research activities, investment banking, and other related financial services. Affiliated corporations engaged in unrelated operations that provide products and services to distinguishable markets are called collectively a "conglomerate." Such an organization might include, for instance, an insurance company, a steel manufacturer, and a fast-food restaurant chain. Property and liability insurance companies can be found in both congeneric and conglomerate organizational structures either as the parent company or among the subsidiaries.

Methods of accounting for business combinations in conformity with GAAP are set forth in *Opinion No. 16* and *Opinion No. 17* of the Accounting Principles Board and subsequent pronouncements of the FASB. The two APB *Opinions* contain criteria that are used to determine whether a business combination should be treated according to the so-called "pooling of interests method" or the "purchase method." Under the pooling of interests method, the recorded assets and liabilities of the constituent companies that existed prior to the combination are carried forward to the balance sheet of the continuing entity at their precombination values. Stockholders' equities of the constituent companies also are combined on the continuing entity's balance sheet. Income of the constituent companies for the entire accounting period in which the combination occurs is included in the continuing entity's income for the period. Financial statements for prior years are restated to show the status and operating results of the continuing entity as if the constituent companies had always been one. Appropriate adjustments may be necessary to reconcile differences in the accounting methods employed by constituent companies prior to combination.

The purchase method of accounting must be used when the combination does not qualify as a pooling of interests. Under the purchase method, assets and liabilities of the constituent companies are recorded at their fair values on the balance sheet of the continuing entity with any unallocated cost associated with their purchase recorded as goodwill. Income of the constituent companies prior to combination is not considered income of the continuing entity. If the financial accounting methods of the constituent companies differed, accounting methods must be made to conform after the combination is consummated.

Consolidated financial statements are considered to be more meaningful than separate parent and subsidiary statements presented without consolidation. Methods of preparing consolidated statements that conform with GAAP are set forth in APB *Opinion No. 18* and subsequent FASB pronouncements. In general, one of two methods can be used to consolidate the financial statements of related corporations. These are the full consolidation and equity methods. Partial consolidations involve the use of both methods to consolidate the statements of three or more related corporations.

Full consolidation combines the assets, liabilities, revenues, and expenses of related companies and shows these combined amounts on the consolidated financial statements of the parent corporation. This method is appropriate for most situations in which the parent owns 50 percent or more of the subsidiary corporation. If less than 100 percent ownership exists, the minority interest of outside shareholders must be recognized in the consolidation. Intercompany transactions and balances are eliminated in order to avoid double counting and premature income recognition. The resulting financial statements present the financial position and operating results of the congeneric or conglomerate as if it were one entity. While this ignores the legal divisions among constituent corporations, it portrays realistically the economic substance of the affiliated companies.

The equity method is used to account for intercorporate investments in the voting stock of companies that are less than majority-owned. This method usually is appropriate for situations in which one company owns between 20 and 50 percent of the voting equity securities of another corporation. The investing company shows its interest in the owned company on its balance sheet at a value equal to the purchase price of the equity securities, plus its pro rata share of the investee's net income, less dividends received from the owned company since the time of acquisition. The owning company reports its share of the investee's net income for the current period by presenting this amount on a separate line in its own income statement. This treatment has caused the equity method to become known as a "one-line consolidation."

Although use of the equity method is an alternative to full consolidation, both methods may be used by a parent company with multiple subsidiaries. A partial consolidation occurs when there are three or more affiliated entities and the financial statements of at least two companies are fully consolidated while at least one company's statements are presented as a one-line consolidation or are not consolidated.

Property and liability insurers use appropriate GAAP methods to account for business combinations and to prepare consolidated financial statements. Companies such as The Home Insurance Company, Fireman's Fund Insurance Company, Continental Casualty Company, Reliance Insurance Company, and similar property and liability insurers are parts of larger organizations. The format of financial statements issued to stockholders by the parent corporations of such companies differs from that of nonaffiliated insurers. A recent survey of the annual reports of 100 stock and 48 mutual property and liability insurance companies indicated that 91 percent of the stock companies were affiliated with other corporate entities.[17] The most typical relationship witnessed in these business combinations is that of a noninsurance holding company parent which has subsidiary insurance companies. Less typically, a property and liability insurance company may act as parent for other insurance and noninsurance subsidiaries. Financial statements of 78 percent of the stock insurers with intercorporate affiliations were presented on a fully consolidated basis, 10 percent were one-line consolidations, 8 percent were partially consolidated, and 4 percent were not consolidated. Only 27 percent of the stock insurers affiliated with other corporations presented separate financial statements for significant property and liability subsidiaries to supplement their consolidated statements.

Notes to Financial Statements Financial statements based on GAAP are accompanied by a set of notes that disclose information which cannot be presented adequately otherwise. Notes accompanying financial statements are an integral part thereof. While the use of notes in general purpose financial statements is not a difference between statutory insurance accounting principles and GAAP, their utilization changes the form of presentation. The statutory annual statement uses interrogatories to facilitate disclosure of nonquantitative information.

Notes in general purpose statements have a similar purpose but their content is different.

The initial notes explain the significant accounting policies on which the statements are based and disclose any changes in these policies that have occurred since the previous accounting period. These notes state the basis of presentation (GAAP), consolidation policies, and methods of asset and liability valuation. Notes accompanying property and liability insurance company statements discuss the composition of reserves, the nature of the unearned premium reserve, treatment of deferred acquisition costs, restrictions on the distribution of policyholders' surplus, and other important information. The number of notes appearing in financial statements varies among companies and between accounting periods but it rarely is less than six and often exceeds ten.

SUMMARY

This chapter describes the principal types of accounting reports prepared by property and liability insurance companies. The form and content of the statutory annual statement is designed to facilitate regulatory purposes, especially solvency surveillance, the NAIC examination process, and premium tax collection. The annual statement's many exhibits and schedules contain detailed information useful in testing, evaluating, and otherwise amplifying the contents of its summary financial statements. Standards of accounting, referred to as statutory accounting principles, are imposed on property and liability insurers through the requirements for filing an annual statement, the Insurance Expense Exhibit, and other supplementary documents.

Mutual and reciprocal insurance companies prepare reports to their policyholders by extracting and summarizing information from their annual statement. Stock insurance companies also prepare external reports that are filed with the stock exchanges and the SEC. Reports to stockholders usually contain financial statements based on GAAP rather than statutory accounting rules. Material differences in these two sets of accounting standards can have a significant effect on the financial position and operating results reported by an insurer. Notes included in general purpose financial statements explain the basis of accounting used in their preparation and acknowledge the divergence from statutory accounting documents.

Both stock and mutual insurers prepare reports for internal use. Financial accounting data included in management reports is supplemented by other quantitative and nonquantitative information that enables control, planning, and decision making.

Chapter Notes

1. *Best's Aggregates & Averages: Property-Liability,* 36th annual edition (Morristown, NJ: A.M. Best Company, 1975), pp. 64, 12B and 66B.

2. The Committee on Valuation of Securities of the NAIC periodically publishes a booklet on valuation procedures and instructions that must be used in preparation of the annual statement. Stocks and bonds are shown on the balance sheet at "Association Values"; that is, at values determined by application of the NAIC procedures. Bonds in good standing are carried at amortized cost; common and preferred stocks usually are valued at year-end market prices. Specific rules also are given for valuation of equity interests in subsidiary corporations.

3. Some authors use the term "estimated liabilities" for loss and loss adjustment expense reserves because the ultimate costs associated with these items are not known and must be estimated at the time financial statements are prepared. Other obligations of the insurer that can be evaluated more directly are called "liabilities." See, for example, Ruth Salzmann, "Estimated Liabilities for Losses and Loss Adjustment Expenses," in *Property-Liability Insurance Accounting,* Robert W. Strain, editor (Santa Monica, CA: Merrit Company, 1976), pp. 29-79.

4. Factors that encourage claims resistance along with several arguments against the alleged practices are discussed by Jerry S. Rosenbloom, *Automobile Liability Claims: Insurance Company Philosophies and Practices* (Homewood, IL: Richard D. Irwin, 1968), pp. 123-126.

5. State of New York Insurance Department, *Automobile Insurance ... For Whose Benefit?* (1970).

6. Each insured in a reciprocal assumes a proportional share of all loss exposures transferred to the organization, other than his or her own. The term "subscriber" rather than "policyholder" therefore is used to signify the insured's unique relationship with the interinsurance exchange.

7. Joseph C. Noback, *Life Insurance Accounting* (Homewood, IL: Richard D. Irwin, 1969), p. 307. Exhibit 3 on the fire and casualty blank corresponds to Exhibit 12 on the life insurance blank. A statement of changes in financial position was added to the annual statement for 1977.

8. Gerald I. Lenrow and Ralph Milo, "The IRS Issues Its Position on Unpaid Losses," *Best's Review,* Property-Liability Edition, (March 1976), pp. 64-70.

9. Carl B. Drake, Jr., "What An Insurance Executive Expects From Management Reports," *Best's Review,* Property-Liability Edition (May 1973), pp. 78-82.

10. German Alliance Insurance Company v. Lewis, 223 U.S. 389 (1914).

11. Nebbis v. New York, 291 U.S. 502 (1934).

12. See Chapter 2 in *Audits of Fire and Casualty Insurance Companies* (New York: American Institute of Certified Public Accountants, 1966).

13. Gains (losses) are defined as increases (decreases) in net assets other than

those resulting from additions to invested capital or from revenues. Robert T. Sprouse and Maurice Moonitz, *A Tentative Set of Broad Accounting Principles for Business Enterprises* (New York: American Institute of Certified Public Accountants, 1962), p. 9.

14. Eldon S. Hendriksen, *Accounting Theory*, revised edition (Homewood, IL: Richard D. Irwin, 1970), pp. 57-59.
15. Committee on Auditing Procedure of the American Institute of Certified Public Accountants, *Auditing Standards and Procedures, Statement on Auditing Procedure No. 33* (New York: American Institute of Certified Public Accountants, 1963), pp. 70-71.
16. *Audits*, p. 63.
17. *Financial Reporting Trends, Fire and Casualty Insurance* (New York, NY: Ernst & Ernst, 1974), pp. 13-19.

CHAPTER 2

Valuation of
Balance Sheet Accounts—Assets

INTRODUCTION

This chapter is divided into four major sections. The first section presents descriptive information concerning the principal asset accounts of property-liability insurance companies. This nontechnical section introduces the necessary terminology and background material to understand property and liability insurance company balance sheets.

The second section of the chapter focuses on the impact that common stock and bond valuation changes have upon insurance company surplus. Discussion is limited to these two asset types because they represent the greatest portion of insurance company assets and the largest segments of assets over which management can exercise direct control.

The third section of the chapter explains the concepts of insurance exposure and insurance leverage as they pertain to property and liability insurance companies. These concepts are necessary tools to provide a proper understanding of property and liability insurance company investment policy.

The final section of the chapter discusses investment policy for nonlife insurance companies. This section addresses the role of underwriting results, product line mix, and risk/return attributes of common stocks and bonds in the formulation of an investment policy.

77

ASSETS OF PROPERTY-LIABILITY
INSURANCE COMPANIES

The primary thrust of insurance company regulation is insurance company solvency. The insurance policy is a contract obligating the insurance company to make future financial settlements to, or for the benefit of, insureds who incur economic loss. Statutory restrictions and limitations on financial operations are necessary to ensure that insurance companies can meet their financial obligations as they occur.

The states have enacted statutes and promulgated administrative regulations which are intended to provide policyholder safety and maintain investment diversification. For example, when preparing their balance sheets for statutory purposes, insurance companies are prevented from showing as an asset delinquent accounts receivable or loans to company officers and directors whether collateralized or not. Similarly, property-liability insurance companies are restricted in the amount they may invest in any nonaffiliate company.

Assets which an insurance company may show on its statutory balance sheet are termed admitted assets. All other assets owned by the company are nonadmitted assets. Nonadmitted assets, even though substantial in value, are charged to policyholders' surplus of the insurance company during the year in which the nonadmitted assets are acquired.

Nonadmitted Assets

The principal asset categories which are generally considered to have some statement value for other types of companies but which are not admitted to an insurance company's balance sheet are the following:

1. Investments other than those which are legal investments. This would include sums in excess of the maximum amount the company is permitted to invest in a particular security.
2. All premiums due ninety days or more.
3. Notes and accounts receivable which are not secured by collateral which would be a legal investment for an insurance company. This would include notes from agents for premiums ninety days due or more.
4. All prepaid expenses. This would include such expense items as premium taxes and agent's commissions.
5. Office furniture, equipment, and supplies.

Assets which are classified as nonadmitted items generally have one of two attributes: either they are (1) not legal or (2) not liquid. Either attribute may disqualify an asset from being entered upon the insurer's statutory balance sheet. However, as will be shown later in this chapter, illiquidity does not necessarily disqualify an asset from being admitted.

Admitted Assets

There are many types of admitted assets owned by property-liability insurance companies. The different types of assets will be described in the following pages, along with an explanation of how they are recorded in the insurer's financial statements and how they are valued for statutory accounting purposes.

Bonds Bonds are generally the largest single asset type for property-liability insurance companies. Frequently they represent in excess of 50 percent of total admitted assets. Bond investments can be categorized into two basic groups: taxable and nontaxable. This grouping is based on the federal income tax treatment of interest income received by the bondholder.

Bonds are further categorized for statutory purposes into groupings based upon the type of issuer. The statutory bond groupings include:

1. Governments, United States, Canada, other countries
2. State territories, possessions, and political subdivisions thereof
3. Railroads
4. Public utilities
5. Industrial and miscellaneous

Schedule D of the annual statement provides a detailed listing of all bonds owned at year end and all bond transactions for the year.

State regulations limit the amount an insurance company may invest in certain types of bonds. Although the limitations vary by state, their general thrust is to prohibit an insurance company from investing more than a certain percentage of its admitted assets into any one permitted category of bonds. Any investments in excess of these limitations are nonadmitted assets. The excess amount is charged to policyholders' surplus for the year in which the excess first occurs.

There are a number of descriptive terms which must be understood in order to account properly for bonds as property-liability insurance company investments:

1. Par Value—The face value amount which the issuing debtor promises to pay to the bondholder when the bond matures.
2. Premium—The amount paid by the purchaser in excess of the par value of the bond. Typically, a premium is paid when the stated interest rate is greater than current interest rates for bonds of comparable maturity and risk.

3. Discount—The difference in the amount paid by the purchaser and the par value when the purchase price is less than the par value. Generally, bonds can be purchased at a discount when their stated interest rate is lower than current interest rates for bonds of comparable maturity and risk.

4. Amortization of Premium or Discount—For statutory accounting purposes, bond premiums and discounts are prorated over the remaining years to the bond's maturity. The prorated amount is referred to as the amortization.

5. Amortized Cost—The cost at which insurance companies generally report their bond investments for statutory accounting purposes. Amortized cost equals the original purchase price (including any commissions, taxes, and so on) plus or minus the amortization of premium or discount since the date of acquisition.

The following example illustrates the preceding by determining the December 31, 1975 statutory value of a $100,000 par value bond maturing December 31, 1980, purchased at December 31, 1970 for $115,000:

Par value	$100,000
Purchase price December 31, 1970	115,000
Premium	15,000
Annual straight-line amortization ($15,000 divided by 10 years)	1,500
Amortized cost December 31, 1975 (original purchase price minus 5 years of annual amortization of premium)	107,500

For bonds purchased at a premium, a portion of the premium periodically is subtracted from the cost shown in the company's records to reduce the recorded cost to the bonds' face value at or before maturity. Similarly, for bonds purchased at a discount, a portion of the discount is added to the recorded cost so that the cost increases to equal the bonds' face value.

Some bonds have an optional maturity date, referred to as the call date, which allows the bond insurer to retire their bonds at a date earlier than the bond's stated maturity date. All bonds acquired at a premium should be amortized over a period ending with the optional maturity date. Bond discounts can be amortized over a period that ends with either the optional maturity date or the stated maturity date. Amortizing a discount beyond the optional maturity date results in a slower recognition of the discount into income and may be regarded as a more conservative approach than obtained by writing-up the bond value to par prior to the stated maturity date.

Amortized cost should be used as the statutory statement value of all bonds for which the National Association of Insurance Commissions (NAIC) permits such valuation. In its annual publication, *Valuation of*

Securities, the NAIC lists nearly all bonds reported as owned by property and liability insurance companies. The book of valuations indicates for each bond whether amortized cost valuation can be used. Bonds in default with respect to either principal or interest can be admitted on the insurer's balance sheet only at the NAIC determined market value of the bond. The acceptable admitted asset market value is shown also in the valuation book. The difference between amortized cost and admitted asset market value of defaulted bonds is charged to policyholders' surplus for the year in which the difference first occurs. Many companies own a substantial number of state and municipal bonds or subdivisions thereof which for the most part are not listed in the book, and are permitted to be carried at amortized value as long as they are not in default as to principal or interest.

Interest income from bond investments is recorded on an accrual basis. For example, a $100,000 par value bond with a 6 percent stated annual interest rate having interest payable on March 31 and September 30 would provide the bondholder with two semi-annual payments of $3,000. Because the bond interest earned from September 30 to December 31 is not received until March 31, the insurer can report as an admitted asset accrued interest earned. The accrual amount is obtained by dividing the accrual period, in this case one quarter of a year, into the annual interest amount of $6,000, resulting in $1,500.

Common Stocks Other than bonds, common stocks represent the greatest single asset category for property and liability insurance companies. Frequently, common stock investments represent about one-third of a nonlife insurance company's admitted assets. Similar to bonds, common stocks are categorized for statutory purposes into major groupings which reflect the primary business nature of the issuer such as railroads, public utilities, industrials and miscellaneous and so forth. A detailed list of all stocks bought and sold during the year and owned at year end is presented in Schedule D of the annual statement.

Most states have statutory rules and regulations which somewhat restrain investments in common stocks. In general, these limitations restrict a property-liability insurance company from investing in any one stock an amount greater than a prescribed percentage of the insurance company's capital and surplus. They may also limit the amount of stock ownership to a specified percentage of the issuer's outstanding stock. If an insurance company exceeds these limitations, the excess is charged to policyholders' surplus. These regulations have two purposes. First, they are intended to encourage portfolio diversification. Second, they are intended to prevent insurance companies from obtaining proprietary interests in noninsurance related activities.

The admitted asset value of common stocks is the market value shown in the NAIC's *Valuation of Securities.* Unlike bonds, the statutory statement value of common stocks is intended to reflect market variations in common stock prices. As common stock prices fluctuate, changes in market value are applied to policyholders' surplus as either losses or gains. Greater discussion of differences between bond and common stock valuations are presented in the next section.

Mortgage Loans Property and liability insurance companies normally do not make substantial investments in mortgage loans. Generally, mortgage loans are long-term commitments, and until the recent advent of secondary mortgage markets, mortgage loans were more difficult to convert to cash than, for example, bonds. Insurance companies limit their investments to first lien mortgage loans since second mortgages are nonadmissable assets and are charged to policyholders' surplus when acquired.

An insurance company cannot carry, as an admitted asset in its financial statements, a mortgage loan in excess of the appraised value of the secured property. Any violation of these statutory regulations, which differ from state to state, will result in the amount of violation being charged to the policyholders' surplus. Also, the statutory regulations of individual states stipulate limitations on the percentage of admitted assets which an insurance company may have invested in mortgage loans.

The amount recorded as the initial investment in a mortgage loan is the amount of money given for the loan. If a mortgage loan is purchased the remaining amount of principal balance might not equal the consideration given for the loan because the interest rate on the purchased loan might not equal the rate currently charged for similar new mortgage loans. If there is a difference in rates, then the loan is acquired for a premium or discount, (the difference between the consideration paid and the unpaid principal balance). The premium or discount will be amortized to income over the remaining life of the loan subject to certain time limits. The amortization will adjust the interest earned to equate the rate of return on the loan to the interest yield negotiated at time of purchase.

Amortizing premiums or accruing discounts on mortgage loans is prescribed in the *Valuation of Securities* book of the NAIC. Premiums may be amortized and discounts accrued over a five-year period from date of acquisition on FHA or VA mortgages. For mortgages other than FHA or VA mortgages acquired at a premium, the amortization period is three years. Since the period of amortization is usually shorter than the term of the loan, the straight-line method of amortization is generally used. Noninsured real estate mortgages purchased at a discount should be carried at cost.

If a mortgagor defaults on mortgage payments the insurance company may foreclose on the mortgaged property. All expenses incurred such as insurance, taxes, legal fees and other direct expenses that have been incurred to protect the investment or to obtain clear title to the property can be added to the unpaid loan balance provided the loan balance plus capitalized expenses do not exceed the appraised value of the foreclosed property. If the expenses cannot be recovered, they should be expensed when incurred.

Normally payments on mortgage loans are received on a monthly or quarterly basis. The level payments are developed on an amortization schedule so that the amount of the payment applied to the principal each period is exactly sufficient to extinguish the debt at the end of the term for which the loan is granted. The balance of each periodic payment is interest income. The schedule will indicate the amount of each payment received to be credited to the book value of the mortgage loan and the amount to be credited to interest income. During the early years of the loan's term, the greatest portion of each periodic payment is interest income but as the loan is repaid, increasingly larger portions of each payment are used to reduce the principal. The amortization schedule used to divide each level payment between interest and principal results in a constant effective rate of return to the insurer.

In many cases amounts in addition to principal and interest payments are received to pay property taxes and insurance premiums when due so the lender is assured that no lien for unpaid property taxes will be placed on the property and that the value of the property will be recovered should the property be completely or partially destroyed. The amount received for property taxes and insurance is credited to an escrow account and shown as a liability in the annual statement under "amounts withheld or retained by company on account of others."

Mortgage loans that are in default, or which are under foreclosure proceedings, continue to be classified as mortgage loans. Loans for which foreclosure proceedings have been completed, even to the extent of the court granting title to the mortgagee, temporarily retain their status as mortgage loans, since in some states the mortgagor still has the privilege of redeeming the mortgage during a stated redemption period. During this period, the loan remains classified as a mortgage loan until the insurance company obtains clear title; the asset is then transferred to the real estate account.

Interest on mortgage loans is recorded on a cash basis. Therefore, interest earned but not received must be accrued at the end of an accounting period. Interest due and accrued that is over one year past due must be considered a nonadmitted asset.

Real Estate Insurance companies own real estate either as investments or to provide office space for normal business activities. Real estate is reflected in statutory financial statements at original cost, plus additions or improvements, less depreciation and any encumbrances on the real estate. Cost includes the purchase price of the real estate acquired, plus the cost incurred to place the real estate asset in usable condition. Elements of cost also include brokerage, legal fees, demolition, clearing, grading, fees for architects and engineers, and any additional expenditures for service equipment and fixtures that are made a permanent part of the structure. The purchase price must be allocated between land and building since only the cost of the building will be depreciated over future periods. The costs of improvements and additions should be added to the building account. Unless expenditures of this nature have a useful life in excess of one year, they should generally be charged off directly as a current period expense.

Insurance companies are permitted to depreciate buildings on either a straight-line or accelerated depreciation basis. Depreciation allocates the cost of the building to the periods benefiting from its use. Therefore, the estimated useful life and the depreciation method used depend on the circumstances of each individual case. If an insurance company makes any leasehold improvements for the benefit of a lessee; then the costs of the improvements should be amortized over the lease period (ignoring any options to renew).

An insurance company that owns the building housing its own operating office space must charge itself rent expense for statutory financial statement purposes. This rental charge should be a fair and reasonable amount based on what the company normally would have to pay if it did not own its own buildings. Since the company offsets the rental charge to itself by corresponding rental income, there is no effect on the net income. The expense portion is allocated among the three primary operating functions: loss adjustment, underwriting, and investment.

Collateral Loans Collateral loans are not commonly held by property and liability insurance companies. Similar to mortgage loans, collateral loans represent obligations which are secured by collateral. The insurance company retains the collateral to ensure the repayment of the loan in case of default. The loan is considered an admitted asset as long as its unpaid balance does not exceed the market value of the collateral held. Generally, loans to officers or directors, even though they may be collateralized, are considered nonadmitted assets.

Cash Insurance companies may maintain several bank accounts which are designated for specific purposes. These bank accounts may include a general operating account, investment account, payroll account, claim account, loss adjustment expense account, and so forth. In addition to bank accounts, insurance companies may have a portion of their cash in certificates of deposit, cash in transit, and a small amount in petty cash.

It is quite common for insurance companies to use drafts to pay insurance loss settlements rather than checks. When checks are used for payment purposes, the loss account is charged immediately and the bank account reduced.

The insurer can delay reductions in its bank account through the use of drafts. An ordinary check is payable upon demand but a draft is not. The claimant who has been issued a draft on the insurance company's bank account must present the draft to the bank for collection. In turn, the bank must present the draft to the insurer for acceptance. At this point the insurer must have deposited or must then deposit an adequate amount of money to cover the draft. This procedure serves to reduce the amount of idle funds deposited in bank accounts. Drafts can be accounted for either on a draft-issued or draft-paid basis. If a draft-issued basis is used, an accounting entry to debit losses paid and credit outstanding drafts payable is made when the draft is issued. When the draft is presented for payment, and the company authorizes the payment, an accounting entry to debit outstanding drafts payable and credit cash is recorded. If a draft-paid basis is used, no accounting entry is made when the draft is initially issued. When the draft is presented for payment and honored by the company, an entry is made to debit losses paid and credit cash. The draft-issued basis provides more timely accounting but necessitates a monthly reconciliation for the outstanding draft payable account. The incurred losses should not be significantly affected regardless of which method is used, provided the claim reserves applicable to the draft-paid claims are reasonably accurate.

Agents' Balances Agents' balances represent the total amount of premiums which have been recorded, net of commission expense, but not collected. Most agency contracts stipulate the period of time that the agent has to pay the insurance company—generally within thirty to forty-five days after the policy is recorded. Agents will generally either pay based on the insurance company statement, based on their own "account current," or on an individual item basis.

In the first instance, the insurance company compiles a monthly statement that shows all policies which have been recorded but are not paid by the agent. Most insurance companies encourage their agents to pay on this basis since the amount of the agent's check will generally agree to the total of the monthly statement making individual items more easily identifiable.

Each month some insurance agents will submit an account current to the insurance company; this is a list of all policies written during the past month. The account current reflects accounting entries made by the insurance agent and rarely agrees to the monthly statement prepared by the insurance company due to timing differences. The agent frequently prefers to pay on an account current basis since the agent is more familiar with it. Also, the agent may not want to reconcile agency accounting records with those of the insurance company, although this should be done to identify all differences.

Payment on an individual item basis is less frequent than either the company statement basis or the agent account current basis. An agent generally will pay on an individual item basis when there is a dispute with the insurance company.

Agents' balances which are due more than ninety days are declared overdue by statutory provision. Overdue agents' balances are set up as a nonadmitted asset and a corresponding charge is made against surplus. The procedure by which overdue premiums are determined depends largely on the accounting method the insurance company uses—whether ledger balances are posted on either an account current basis or item basis, or a combination of both.

An agent's account current is a summarization of the month's business. Information is listed by premium transaction and may include the policy number or other reference, the premium or return premium, the agent's commission rate and amount, incidental charges such as postage and the current month balance owing either to the insurance company or to the agent. If the summary balance has been due for more than ninety days, it is overdue. In determining overdue amounts, credits can be offset against debit premiums for a specific policy.

When agents' balances are accounted for on an item basis, determination of overdue amounts depends upon the effective date of each transaction. Because December 31 is the annual cutoff date, the following generalizations can be used to classify which premiums in the course of collection should be considered overdue:[1]

1. Premiums on policies effective prior to October 1.
2. Premiums for endorsements on which the effective dates of the endorsement were prior to October 1.
3. Installment premiums due prior to October 1. (If any installment is overdue, all of the unpaid installments are overdue.)
4. Audit and additional premiums determined by audits made prior to October 1, or those charged upon insured payroll statements received prior to October 1. When an audit premium is overdue, all premiums subsequently charged on the same policies should be classified as overdue.

Funds Held by or Deposited with Ceding Reinsurers Reinsurance is an integral part of the insurance industry and involves the transfer of a portion of a loss exposure of the primary insurance company to another insurance company in return for a portion of the insurance premium. When the loss exposure is transferred, the company writing the original policy is referred to as the ceding company, and the company assuming a portion of the loss exposure is referred to as the assuming company. The terms of any reinsurance arrangement are stipulated in a reinsurance contract which documents the agreement reached between the companies. Frequently, the reinsurance contract stipulates that the ceding company will withhold a portion of the premiums to which the assuming company is entitled in an amount equal to the unearned premium reserves and the loss reserves.

The funds held by or deposited with ceding reinsurers represent the amount which is owed by the ceding reinsurer to the assuming company but which is not currently payable. If the balance were currently payable, then it would be reflected in uncollected premiums which is combined with balances due from agents.

Funds held by or deposited with ceding reinsurers are considered to be an admitted asset as long as the account is due from a solvent authorized insurance company. If the insurance company is insolvent, or unauthorized, the balance due from that company must be treated as a nonadmitted asset and charged off to policyholders' surplus.

Bills Receivable Taken for Premium In certain states, insurance premiums can be financed through a bill receivable. Bills receivable usually have an interest rate attached; therefore, accrued interest receivable must be calculated whenever financial statements are prepared. Bills receivable and any related accrued interest are considered admitted assets when the following conditions are met:

1. The note has been signed by the insured.
2. The unpaid balance of the note does not exceed the unearned premium on the policy for which it was accepted.
3. The note is not past due.

Reinsurance Recoverable on Loss Payments As discussed previously, an insurance company transfers a portion of its loss exposure when it enters into a reinsurance contract. The assuming reinsurer receives a portion of the premium and, in return, promises to pay a proportionate share of the losses to which the direct writer is exposed. When a loss claim is settled and a draft is issued to pay damages incurred, the reinsurers should be billed for their portion of the settlement. The receivable from reinsurers for their portion of the loss is recorded in an account called "reinsurance recoverable on loss payments." It is extremely important that an insurance company identify all reinsurers on an exposure and bill them for their portion of a loss at the same time that the loss is being paid.

The method used to notify a reinsurer of its portion of a loss varies by type of reinsurance contract. If the contract is in the form of a quota share treaty, only summary data is provided to the reinsurer. In that situation, a monthly statement is sent to the reinsurer summarizing the premiums and losses which are covered by the treaty. If the reinsurance is a form of facultative cession (reinsurance terms negotiated on a policy-by-policy basis) then the reinsurer receives specific data pertaining to the individual claim for which the reinsurer is liable.

The records for reinsurance recoverable on paid losses are comparable to the records used in agents' balances. There is a need for effective follow-up and collection efforts since disputes frequently arise over the interpretation of reinsurance contracts.

Federal Income Tax Recoverable Property and liability insurance companies file tax returns based on their statutory annual statement. Many of the corporate federal income tax rules apply to insurance companies. If an insurance company incurred a loss and was able to carry that loss back to the preceding three years to generate a federal income tax recovery, the recovery should be set up as an asset. It is considered an admissible asset.

Furniture, Equipment, and Supplies The furniture, equipment, and supplies owned by an insurance company are considered to be a nonadmitted asset. In other words, all desks, filing cabinets, automobiles, office machines, stationery, printed forms, and so forth cannot be reflected on the balance sheet. Even though these assets are nonadmitted for statutory purposes, the company should maintain a formalized control over them. Insurance companies will generally record the purchase of furniture and equipment and depreciate this equipment over a reasonable period. The depreciation expense is reflected in the statement of income, and the accumulated depreciation account further reduces the book value of the furniture and equipment. Similarly, inventory records are maintained for the numerous types of supplies needed by insurance companies. Whenever financial statements are prepared, the change in the net book value of furniture, equipment, and supplies is charged or credited to surplus as being a nonadmitted asset.

One exception to the admissibility of furniture and equipment in many states is major electronic equipment such as computers. This type of equipment generally represents a substantial investment. Recognizing this, many states permit insurance companies to admit the net book value of major electronic equipment if it exceeds a certain dollar amount. These rules generally pertain only to purchased equipment and not to the purchase of software or to the costs associated with developing software internally.

VALUATION OF COMMON STOCKS AND BONDS

As noted in the previous section, common stocks and bonds represent the largest admitted asset accounts of property and liability insurance companies. In combination they may represent in excess of 80 percent of an insurer's admitted assets. It was also noted that for statutory accounting statements, common stocks are shown at market value whereas bonds are shown at amortized cost. In this section alternative valuation methods for common stocks and bonds are discussed. Theoretical valuation models used to determine the intrinsic worth of common stocks and bonds are contrasted to statutory rules that may result in values that differ from those produced by the theoretical models.

Recall that one distinction between admitted and nonadmitted assets is liquidity; that is, admitted assets ideally can be converted into cash without delay and without loss of value whereas nonadmitted assets may be illiquid. The valuation of common stocks at market value assures their liquidity at a relatively well-known market value amount. On the other hand, the valuation of bonds at amortized cost does not assure liquidity of bonds. Bond liquidity occurs only if their amortized cost coincidentally equals their market value. Hence, it would appear that valuing bonds at amortized cost may be inconsistent with statutory objectives of asset liquidity. However, as discussed in Chapter 1, other statutory accounting objectives may have priority over the liquidity objective.

Only basic valuation models for common stocks and bonds are presented here. In the case of common stocks the treatment is brief. It is presented this way because the current common stock valuation method for statutory statements is consistent with statutory desires for asset liquidity. In the case of bonds, the treatment is more detailed. This more thorough treatment is necessary to highlight the consequences that would result if the annual statement rule for showing bonds at amortized cost were changed to show bonds at their market values.

Common Stocks

Owners of common stock are entitled to receive their proportionate share of dividends paid by the firm issuing the common stock. They are also able to sell their stock for whatever price they can obtain for it. Hence, owners of common stock may profit from that ownership through receipt of dividends and increase in value of the common stock. For example, a stock with a $1 quarterly dividend purchased for $50 on

January 1, 1976, and sold December 31, 1976, for $56 would provide the investor with a $10 profit during the year: $4 in dividends and $6 in increased value.

Most models of common stock valuation are predicated on theories of capitalization. In other words, these models discount to present value the stream of future dividends and the future price of the security. For example, consider a common stock which is expected (1) to pay dividends of $4 per share at the end of one year and (2) to sell at $76 per share at the end of the one year. If the rate of discount (or capitalization rate) were 10 percent, then several common stock valuation models would compute the current intrinsic value of the stock, V_s, as follows:[2]

V_s = Present value of dividends + present value of future price

$$= \frac{\$4.00}{1.10} + \frac{\$76.00}{1.10}$$

$$= \$3.64 + \$69.09$$

$$= \$72.73$$

In other words, a common stock paying a $4 dividend and expected to be selling at $76 one year from now is currently worth $72.73, provided the market discount rate is 10 percent.

The above example illustrates that there are at least three parameters that, for any single common stock, can affect the current value of the common stock: dividends; future market price, and the discount rate. Each of these parameters has some degree of uncertainty associated with it.

Common stock dividends are uncertain as to their availability and their amounts in future years. Similarly, the future market price of the stock is an uncertain amount, especially as the time horizon is increased. The discount rate used to determine the current value of a common stock is also uncertain from year to year. The rate may change, reflecting, among other things, alternative investment opportunities. Moreover, due to differing risk characteristics of the securities, the discount rate appropriate for one common stock may not be the same as the discount rate used for another common stock.

The discount rate is an uncertain element in the valuation of all securities. Therefore, for individual common stocks the only pricing parameters that can uniquely affect current value are expected dividends and the expected future market price.

Theoretically, investors make buy-hold-sell decisions by calculating the intrinsic value of a common stock and comparing it to the stock's current market price. According to the model briefly outlined here, an investor capitalizes at an appropriate discount rate the returns expected from a stock during the period in which the investor owns the security. This calculated value then is compared to the stock's market price, and the investment decision is made. As an example, assume a stock is expected to pay a $2.28 dividend at the end of the current year and that annual dividends are expected to grow by 4 percent each year during the foreseeable future. Further assume that the stock's market price is expected to increase from its current level of $24 to $27 at the end of three years. If the investor holds the stock for the three years and then sells it at the expected market price, the stock's current intrinsic value (assuming an 8 percent capitalization rate is appropriate) is determined as follows:

$$V_s = \frac{\$2.28}{(1.08)^1} + \frac{\$2.28\,(1.04)^1}{(1.08)^2} + \frac{\$2.28\,(1.04)^2 + \$27.00}{(1.08)^3}$$

$$= \$2.11 + \$2,03 + \$1.96 + \$\$21.43$$

$$= \$27.53$$

Since the calculated value exceeds the current market price, the investor should purchase the stock. On the other hand, if the investor's capitalization rate for this security is 14 percent and all other assumptions remain the same, the stock's intrinsic value would be below the current market price:

$$V_s = \frac{\$2.28}{(1.14)^1} + \frac{\$2.28\,(1.04)^1}{(1.14)^2} + \frac{\$2.28\,(1.04)^2 + \$27.00}{(1.14)^3}$$

$$= \$2.00 + \$1.82 + \$1.67 + \$18.22$$

$$= \$23.71$$

Based on this evaluation, the stock should not be purchased. In this instance, the stock should not be purchased because its current market price exceeds the value the investor places on the security. A similar decision would be reached by an investor who used the original 8 percent capitalization rate and who shared all the original expectations concerning future dividends but who believed the stock's price at the end of three years would be $20. This set of parameters once again produces an intrinsic value below the current market price:

$$V_s = \frac{\$2.28}{(1.08)^1} + \frac{\$2.28\,(1.04)^1}{(1.08)^2} + \frac{\$2.28\,(1.04)^2 + \$20.00}{(1.08)^3}$$

$$= \$2.11 + \$2.03 + \$1.96 + \$15.88$$

$$= \$21.98$$

These examples explain why the value a particular investor places on a certain common stock may differ from the stock's market price. The investor may have expectations about future dividends and stock prices that are not in agreement with the expectations of others. Similarly, even if all parties shared common expectations, the discount rate used by a particular investor may differ from the discount rate used by others to capitalize future cash flows. Therefore, the value one investor places on a certain common stock may be different from the value of the stock to other individuals. The most objective measure of the stock's current equivalent value in cash is the stock's current market price. However, market prices are not infallible measures of value. Lack of adequate information, political disruptions, temporary economic disturbances, and many other factors may cause the market to under- or over-value common stocks relative to their true worth. Market prices are used to portray values of an insurance company's common stocks on the annual statement because this method is objective and conservative in the sense that it represents realizable values if immediate liquidation is required.

Bonds

Bonds are similar to common stocks in at least three ways. First, they entitle the bondholder to receive periodic payments. Second, they are generally traded in secondary markets which readily enable the bondholder to sell the bond prior to maturity. And third, bond valuation generally is determined by discounting to present value all future periodic payments and the face amount payable at maturity. Due to these similarities, methods of determining a bond's intrinsic value share some of the characteristics of common stock valuation methods.

Definitions There are some basic terms associated with bonds that should be understood in order to comprehend bond pricing. Included are the following:

1. Coupon—The coupon is the stated, fixed, and guaranteed return from the bond. Generally, the coupon is expressed in either dollars or a percentage of the face amount of the bond. For example, a $40 coupon bond or 4 percent coupon rate bond are equivalent; this means a bond with a $1,000 face or par value paying a coupon of 4 percent of the face value is a $40 coupon bond. Coupon yield is often used interchangeably with coupon rate.
2. Current Yield—This amount, expressed as a percentage, is obtained by dividing the coupon amount in dollars by the current selling price of the bond. For example, a 6 percent coupon rate bond having a par value of $1,000 but selling for

only $875 has a current yield of 6.86 percent ($60 divided by $875). The current yield will equal the coupon yield only when the bond sells at par value.

3. Reinvestment Rate—This is the rate(s) of interest at which future coupons are reinvested. For example, a bondholder receiving a $60 coupon may reinvest the coupon in different investments providing different annual interest rates than the bond now held, or the investor may not invest the coupon proceeds at all. The reinvestment rate, when applied to coupons received by the bondholder over the holding period of the bond, produces what is termed interest-on-interest. The impact of the reinvestment rate upon a bond's return can be significant and varied. This will be discussed in this section.

4. Yield-To-Maturity—This figure is simply the interest rate necessary to equate the stream of future coupon payments, plus the return of principal at maturity, to the current price of the bond. That is, the yield-to-maturity is the effective periodic rate of return that can be earned on the bond if (1) it is held to maturity, (2) it is honored for its face amount at maturity, and (3) the coupons are reinvested at the same effective rate of return. By analogy to capital budgeting, the yield-to-maturity may be considered the bond's internal rate of return.

Bond Valuation

Compound Interest. In order to understand and discuss the consequences of various methods of bond valuation, it is necessary to be familiar with elementary mechanics of compound interest. A deposit made in a savings account today paying 5 percent annually is worth $105 at the end of one year and $110.25 at the end of two years. That is:

$$\$105 = \$100 \times 1.05 \text{ and}$$

$$\$110.25 = \$105 \times 1.05 \text{ or alternatively}$$

$$\$110.25 = \$100 \times 1.05 \times 1.05$$

By formula, the future value V_f of an initial sum V_o at the end of n periods compounding at a rate i is as follows:

$$V_f = V_o \times (1 + i)^n$$

As can be seen by the above formula, if either the interest rate or the time horizon is increased, the future value of the initial sum is also increased.

On the other hand, it might be asked: What is the present value, V_o, of the amount V_f to be paid at the end of n periods when the discount

Table 2-1

Percent of Total Return Due to Interest on Interest*

Interest Rate	Time Period in Years				
	2	5	10	20	30
4%	1.9%	7.7%	16.7%	32.8%	46.5%
5	2.4	9.5	20.5	39.5	54.8
6	2.9	11.3	24.1	45.6	62.1
8	3.8	14.8	31.0	56.3	73.5

* Adapted from James E. Bachman and G. C. Lang, "The Impact of Market Valuation of Property/Casualty Bond Holdings," *Best's Review Property/Casualty Edition* (December 1976), p. 12.

rate is i? The answer, which is merely a rearrangement of the above equation is as follows:

$$V_o = \frac{V_f}{(1 + i)^n}$$

If the interest rate were 5 percent and the payoff in 5 years were equal to $1,200, then the present value V_o would be $1,200/(1.05)^5$, or $940.23. If the rate were increased to 10 percent, then the present value would be equal to only $1,200/(1.10)^5$ or $745.11. Increasing either the interest rate or lengthening the time horizon diminishes the present value V_o of the future sum.

The process used to determine the present value of a future sum is referred to as discounting. The rationale for discounting the value of a future amount to a present value figure is simply that an amount to be received in the future has less value than having it now. Discounting reflects the time value of money.

Interest Upon Interest. In the above example, a two-year, 5 percent savings deposit paid $10.25 in interest. A portion ($0.25) of the interest paid was interest on interest. The total amount of interest due at the end of two years can be divided as follows: $10.00 (97.6 percent) interest on the initial deposit and $0.25 (2.4 percent) interest on interest. Table 2-1 shows the percent of total return (excluding the initial deposit) attributable to the interest on interest effect as both the interest rate and time horizon are varied.

The above figures indicate that the portion of return due to the interest on interest effect can be considerable as either the time horizon or the interest rate is increased. For example, in the extreme case of 8 percent interest for thirty years, a $100 deposit would yield $906.27 in

Table 2-2

Realized Annual Rate of Return on a 6 Percent Savings Deposit for Different Time Horizons as the Reinvestment Rate Varies*

Reinvestment Rate	Years			
	5	10	20	30
4	5.8%	5.6%	5.3%	5.0%
6	6.0	6.0	6.0	6.0
8	6.2	6.5	6.8	7.1

* Reprinted with permission from James E. Bachman and G. C. Lang, "The Impact of Market Valuation of Property/Casualty Bond Holdings," *Best's Review Property/Casualty Edition* (December 1976), p. 12.

total interest. Of that sum, $240.00 (26.5 percent) is the total of the annual interest payments on the initial deposit and $666.27 (73.5 percent) is interest on interest.

The significance of the interest on interest effect as it influences total return can be better understood by an example in which the reinvestment rate is different from the rate being paid on the initial deposit. Table 2-2 presents the realized rate of return on a 6 percent savings deposit for different time horizons as the reinvestment rate is varied. If the reinvestment rate equals the rate paid on the initial deposit, then the stated savings rate is the true yield of the account held to maturity. Therefore, the realized annual rate of return is 6 percent, regardless of the time horizon, if the reinvestment rate is 6 percent. However, if the reinvestment does not equal the rate paid on the initial deposit, then the stated saving rate is a misleading guide as to the true yield. The extent to which there is a difference between the stated savings rate and the true yield depends upon two factors: the spread between the reinvestment rate and the rate paid on the initial deposit and the time period for which the account is held. Given the spread between the two rates, it is the interest on interest effect, working through time, that widens the gap between the stated rate and the true yield. Note in Table 2-2 that a reinvestment rate below the stated rate lowers the realized rate, while a reinvestment rate above the stated rate increases the realized rate when compared to the stated rate. This is true regardless of the holding period.

Determining Bond Values. In the most common situation, a bond is an investment security entitling the bondholder to receive a series of fixed periodic payments plus a return of principal at maturity. The periodic payments are referred to as coupons. The principal payoff is the face value of the bond. For example, a $10,000, five year, 8 percent bond purchased at issue entitles the bondholder to receive five annual coupons at $800 each plus a face value amount of $10,000 at the end of the fifth year.[3] Hence, the payment structure of the bond can be divided into two parts: one, the receipt of a stream of future coupon payments; and two, the receipt, in the future, of the face value amount.

The intrinsic value of a bond, V_B, is the sum of present value of the future coupons plus the present value of the face amount. Using the example from above, this formulation is as follows:

$$V_B = \frac{\$800}{(1+i)} + \frac{\$800}{(1+i)^2} + \frac{\$800}{(1+i)^3} + \frac{\$800}{(1+i)^4} + \frac{\$800}{(1+i)^5}$$

$$+ \frac{\$10,000}{(1+i)^5}$$

The first five terms are the present value of receiving an $800 coupon each year for the next five years. Each coupon to be received in the future is discounted to its present value. The final term is the present value of receiving the $10,000 face value amount at the end of the fifth year. The actual price of the bond depends upon the going interest rate for similar bonds with the same risk of default. If the going interest rate, i, is greater than 8 percent (.08) then the would-be bondholder could invest the funds elsewhere and receive a coupon greater than 8 percent; hence, the above bond would be worth less than $10,000. On the other hand, if i is less than 8 percent (.08), the bond would be worth more than $10,000 to the investor because 8 percent coupons would not be attainable elsewhere. Table 2-3 presents the present value of the income stream for the above bond as the interest rate is varied. The bond in the above table pays five annual $800 coupons and a $10,000 face value amount. When discounted at 8 percent, the first coupon has a present value equal to $740.74, the fifth coupon $544.47 and the face value amount $6,805.83. Hence, the bond that pays to the bondholder $14,000 in total has a present value of only $10,000 when discounted at 8 percent. As Table 2-3 indicates, the selection of the interest rate can have a pronounced impact upon the value of the bond. A 25 percent increase in the interest rate (from 8 percent to 10 percent) causes a depreciation of 7.6 percent in the bond's value. This occurs because the present value of each coupon and the face value amount is less when discounted at the 10 percent rate. Decreasing rates 25 percent (from 8 percent to 6 percent) causes an 8.4 percent appreciation in the bond's value. This illustrates the general principle that bond values are inversely related to the prevailing interest rate. Further, note that, as interest rates increase, that portion of the bond's value determined by

Table 2-3

Value of a $10,000, Five-Year, 8 Percent Coupon Bond as the Interest Rate Varies*

Year-End Receipt	Payments	6 percent	8 percent	10 percent
		Present Value When "i" Equals		
1	$ 800 Coupon	$ 754.72	$ 740.74	$ 727.27
2	800 Coupon	712.00	685.87	661.16
3	800 Coupon	671.70	635.07	601.05
4	800 Coupon	633.67	588.02	546.41
5	800 Coupon	597.81	544.47	496.74
5	10,000 Face amount	7,472.58	6,805.83	6,209.21
Total	$14,000	$10,842.48	$10,000.00	$9,241.84

* Adapted with permission from James E. Bachman and G. C. Lang, "The Impact of Market Valuation of Property/Casualty Bond Holdings," *Best's Review Property/Casualty Edition* (December 1976) p. 12.

the return of principal decreases and leaves greater emphasis upon the discounted value of the coupons.

Amortized Cost Valuation. As noted earlier, the general rule for annual statement presentation of bonds that are not in default as to interest or principal is to value them at amortized cost. There are several methods of calculating amortized cost. In general, however, each method results in the difference between the original investment in the security and its maturity value being spread over the years to maturity in a systematic manner. When a bond is purchased for more than its final redemption value, the excess or premium must be charged against periodic coupon payments or a capital loss will be experienced on the redemption date. For example, suppose an investor pays $10,534.60 for a $10,000 par value bond maturing in three years and having an 8 percent coupon rate. It is necessary for a $534.60 premium to be paid because the going market interest rate for this type of bond is 6 percent. The bond valuation model developed above shows this relationship:

$$V_o = \frac{\$800.00}{(1.06)^1} + \frac{\$800.00}{(1.06)^2} + \frac{\$800.00}{(1.06)^3} + \frac{\$10,000.00}{(1.06)^3}$$

$$= \$754.72 + \$712.00 + \$671.69 + \$ 8,396.19$$

$$= \$10,534.60$$

Table 2-4

Straight-Line Amortization Schedule for a Bond Purchased at a Premium

End of Year	Actual Coupon Payment	Amortized Premium	Effective Coupon Payment	Book Value	Effective Rate of Return[†]
0	—	—	—	$10,534.60	—
1	$ 800.00	$178.20	$ 621.80	10,356.40	5.95%
2	800.00	178.20	621.80	10,178.20	6.06
3	800.00	178.20	621.80	10,000.00	6.16
Total	$2,400.00	$534.60	$1,865.40	—	—
Average				$10,267.30	6.06%

[†]On average bond book value during the period.

At the end of the year, the investor will receive an $800 coupon payment. The actual gain is not $800 each year, however, since at the end of three years only $10,000 of the original $10,534.60 investment will be paid. The $534.60 premium must be recovered out of the periodic coupon payments in order to receive the entire amount of principal originally invested in the bond. It is therefore necessary that an amortization process be adopted in order to allocate a certain portion of each coupon payment for recovery of the premium.

The straight-line method of amortization has the advantage of being easy to calculate and understand. Following the straight-line approach, the amount of premium is divided by the number of years remaining until maturity, and the resulting amount is deducted from the periodic coupon payments. Using the example from above, the straight-line amortization procedure is illustrated in Table 2-4. The chief disadvantage of this method is that it results in an increasing return on investment because the book value of the bond decreases as the net coupon payment remains constant.

A somewhat more refined amortization method is called the annuity method because it results in the investor recognizing a constant rate of return on the money invested in the bond. This rate of return is equal to the market rate of interest prevailing at the time the bond was purchased. Although the rate of return is constant, the amortization increases each year. In the earlier illustration, the market value was set so that the bond would yield 6 percent annually on the money invested in it. Therefore, at the end of the first year, the effective coupon should be $10,534.60 × 0.06 = $632.08. But the investor actually receives

Table 2-5

Amortization Schedule Based on the Annuity Method for a Bond Purchased at a Premium

End of Year	Book Value	Effective Coupon Payment at 6 percent	Actual Coupon Payment	Amortized Premium
0	$10,534.60	—	—	—
1	10,366.68	$ 632.08	$ 800.00	$167.92
2	10,188.68	622.00	800.00	177.99
3	10,000.00	611.32	800.00	188.68
Totals	—	$1,865.40	$2,400.00	$534.59[†]

[†]The one-cent error is due to the accumulation of rounding errors.

$800.00; the $167.92 difference is part of the original principal being returned. Consequently, the book value of the bond is reduced to $10,366.68 ($10,534.60 - $167.92). Continuing the procedure throughout the years remaining to the bond's maturity produces the figures shown in Table 2-5.

Regardless of the procedure used, amortization of a bond premium reduces periodic investment income below the actual coupon payment. The straight-line method uses a constant charge against investment income to amortize the premium and thus produce a constantly increasing rate of return on the bond's book value. Some states require that the annuity method be used for annual statement purposes.

These amortization methods are also used to accumulate discounts or deficiencies on bonds purchased below their par value. For instance, suppose the bond in the preceding illustration was purchased at a time when the prevailing market interest rate was 12 percent rather than 6 percent. In this case, the bond valuation model indicates a required purchase price of $9,039.27. This is determined as follows:

$$V_o - \frac{\$800.00}{(1.12)^1} + \frac{\$800.00}{(1.12)^2} + \frac{\$800.00}{(1.12)^3} + \frac{\$10,000.00}{(1.12)^3}$$

$$= \$714.29 + \$637.76 + \$569.42 + \$7,117.80$$

$$= \$9,039.27$$

Since the bond will be redeemed at its par value of $10,000, the discount below par is $960.73. This must be accumulated during the

Table 2-6

Straight-Line Amortization Schedule for a Bond Purchased at a Discount

End of Year	Actual Coupon Payment	Amortized Discount	Effective Coupon Payment	Book Value	Effective Rate of Return[†]
0	—	—	—	$ 9,039.27	—
1	$ 800.00	$320.24	$1,120.24	9,359.51	12.18%
2	800.00	320.24	1,120.24	9,679.75	11.77
3	800.00	320.25	1,120.25	10,000.00	11.38
Totals	$2,400.00	$960.73	$3,360.73	—	—
Averages				$ 9,519.64	11.77%

[†]On average book value during the period.

years in which the bond is held, or a capital gain will be experienced at the maturity date. Table 2-6 illustrates how the discount is accumulated using the straight-line method.

In this case the amortized discount accumulated each period is added to the coupon payment to produce the effective coupon payment. Dividing the effective coupon payment by the average book value of the bond results in a decreasing rate of return during the holding period. Once again, a constant return on investment will be realized if the annuity method of amortization is used. Table 2-7 illustrates the annuity amortization of the discount for this example.

Impact of Maturity Upon Bond Values.   Three factors impact upon the value of a bond. These are the coupon rate, the going interest rate, and the bond's maturity. The first two are beyond the immediate control of the bondholder. The third factor is controllable to the extent that prospective bondholders are able to select among available bond maturities.

As discount rates change, the value of bonds change in the opposite direction. For a given coupon level and a given change in rate, the extent of the bond value fluctuations is determined exclusively by the maturity of the bond. Table 2-8 demonstrates this fact for a $10,000, 6 percent annual coupon bond as the discount rate is increased to 8 percent.

Increasing the maturity of the bond accentuates the impact of a change in the discount rate. A $10,000, five-year, 6 percent annual coupon bond will depreciate 8 percent in value if rates increase to 8 percent whereas a thirty-year bond will depreciate nearly 23 percent.

Table 2-7

Amortization Schedule Based on the Annuity Method for a Bond
Purchased at a Discount

End of Year	Book Value	Effective Coupon Payment at 12 percent	Actual Coupon Payment	Amortized Discount
0	$ 9,039.27	—	—	—
1	9,323.98	$1,084.71	$ 800.00	$284.71
2	9,642.86	1,118.88	800.00	318.88
3	10,000.00	1,157.14	800.00	357.14
Totals		$3,360.73	$2,400.00	$960.73

Table 2-8

Impact of Maturity Upon Value for a $10,000, 6 Percent Bond as the
Discount Rate Is Increased to 8 Percent*

Maturity in Years	Value at 6 percent	Value at 8 percent	Percent Change
5	$10,000	$9,197.32	−8.0%
10	10,000	8,652.13	−13.5
20	10,000	8,030.58	−19.7
00	10,000	7,744.57	−22.6

* Adapted with permission from James E. Bachman and G. C. Lang, "The Impact of Market
Valuation of Property/Casualty Bond Holdings," *Best's Review Property/Casualty
Edition* (December 1976), p. 70.

The reason for the greater depreciation associated with longer termed
bonds is simply that, regardless of the coupon rate, the longer time
period allows the discount factor to compound to a greater value. At the
same time, it should be noted that the impact of maturity increases at a
decreasing rate. Hence, even for bonds with short maturities (less than
ten years), there can be considerable depreciation (up to 13.5 percent for
this example) if the discount rate is increased.

Another way of examining the impact of maturity upon bond
values is to calculate, for a given coupon rate, what required percent
change in the discount rate would be necessary to change the value of
the bond a targeted percent as the maturity is varied. Table 2-9 presents

Table 2-9

Percent Increase in Discount Rate Necessary to Achieve a 15 Percent Reduction in Bond Values for Different Combinations of Coupon and Maturity*

Coupon Rate	Years to Maturity			
	5	10	20	30
0.04	92.8%	51.0%	30.7%	24.3%
0.06	65.3	37.5	24.4	20.6
0.08	51.6	30.9	21.5	19.1

*Adapted with permission from James E. Bachman and G. C. Lang, "The Impact of Market Valuation of Property/Casualty Bond Holdings," *Best's Review Property/Casualty Edition* (December 1976), p. 70.

the percent increase in the discount rate necessary to achieve a 15 percent reduction in bond values as the maturity is varied.

For any coupon level, the shorter the maturity the greater must be the percent increase in the discount rate to achieve the specified depreciation in bond values. For example, a five-year, 6 percent coupon bond would require a 65.3 percent increase in rates (to approximately 9.9 percent) whereas the thirty-year, 6 percent coupon bond would require only a 20.6 percent increase in rates (to approximately 7.2 percent). This occurs because of the interest on interest effect (See Table 2-1). For the five-year bond, the return is dominated by the coupon portion. The interest on interest effect is significant only if the discount rate can be increased significantly. On the other hand, the return of the thirty-year bond is dominated by the interest on interest effect. The coupon portion of the return is less significant. The net result is that a much smaller percentage increase in the discount rate is necessary to cause a similar reduction in bond value, for a given maturity, as the coupon rate is increased.

Impact of Market Interest Rates upon Bond Values. Although market interest rates are not controlled by individual bondholders, it is necessary to understand the impact of interest rates upon bond valuation in order to explain the price behavior of a seasoned bond portfolio in response to interest rate changes. Table 2-10 shows the percent change in value for a "low," "medium," and "high" coupon bond for various changes in the interest rate. Each bond has a twenty-year maturity.

The percent change in value of a "low" coupon bond as the market interest rate increases from 5 to 6.25 percent is 14.7 percent. It is

Table 2-10

Impact of Interest Rate Changes Upon Bond Value for "Low," "Medium," and "High" Coupon Bonds*

Change in Market Interest Rate = 25 percent	20-Year Maturity		
	Low Coupon 4 percent	Medium Coupon 6 percent	High Coupon 8 percent
5% to 6.25%	−14.7%	−13.6%	−12.9%
6 to 7.50	−16.6	−15.3	−14.5
7 to 8.75	−18.2	−16.8	−15.9
8 to 10	−19.6	−18.0	−17.1

* Adapted with permission from James E. Bachman and G. C. Lang, "The Impact of Market Valuation of Property/Casualty Bond Holdings," *Best's Review Property/Casualty Edition* (December 1976), p. 70.

obtained by first pricing a twenty-year, 4 percent coupon bond to yield 5 percent ($875.38), next pricing it to yield 6.25 percent ($747.11), and then computing the percent decrease in price ($875.38 − $747.11 = $128.27; $128.27 ÷ $875.38 = 14.7 percent).

As the figures in Table 2-10 indicate, for any change in the market interest rate, the impact is more severe for "low" coupon bonds than it is for "high" coupon bonds. For all cases shown, "low" coupon bonds are more volatile than "high" coupon bonds. Reading down the table, it can also be seen that as the level of the market interest rate increases, then for a fixed percent increase in the market interest rate the value of the bond becomes more volatile.

Principles of Bond Valuation. There are four principles of bond valuation that warrant summarization. First, bond values are inversely related to changes in market interest rates. That is, as interest rates increase, bond values drop; alternatively, bond values rise as interest rates decline. Second, bond values are more sensitive to interest rate changes as the maturity of the bonds increases. Third, "low" coupon bond values are more sensitive to interest rate changes than "high" coupon bonds, and fourth, as the level of the market interest rate increases, there is a greater change in bond values for a given percentage change in the interest rate.[4] In the following discussion, the impact of maturity upon bond values is emphasized.

Data for Assessing the Effect of Market Valuation In order to assess the impact of market valuation upon the financial structure of property and liability insurance companies, data were collected for a

Table 2-11

Sample Companies*

Major Companies[1]	Nonmajor Companies[2]
Aetna Casualty	Agricultural Insurance
Aetna Insurance	Allied Fidelity
Continental Casualty	Allied Insurance
Continental Insurance	Amco Insurance
Federal	American Benefit
Fireman's Fund	American Druggists
GEICO	American Family Home
Great American	American Integrity
Hartford Accident	American Live Stock
Hartford Fire	
Home	
INA	
Maryland Casualty	
Reliance	
TransAmerica	
Travelers	
U.S.F. & G.	
U.S. Fire	

1. In 1975 the sampled major companies had direct written premiums in excess of $12 billion.
2. Capitalization not to exceed $3 million.

* Reprinted with permission from James E. Bachman and G. C. Lang, "The Impact of Market Valuation of Property/Casualty Bond Holdings," *Best's Review Property/Casualty Edition* (December 1976), p. 71.

representative sample of the companies in the industry. Table 2-11 lists the twenty-seven companies used for data gathering purposes.

The data obtained for each company were balance sheet figures and information contained in Schedule D, Part 1. These data included the coupon rate, payment dates, maturity (month and year), cost, and type of bond (treasury, special revenue, and so forth) for holdings as of December 31, 1975. Of the $11.286 billion in bonds held by these companies, bonds having a value of $3.139 billion were randomly sampled for the analysis; this represented approximately 28 percent of the companies' bond holdings. Table 2-12 summarizes the bond holdings by type of bond, annual coupon rate, and average maturity.

Tax-exempt special revenue bonds comprise the largest segment (nearly 43 percent) of these insurance companies' bond portfolios. They also have the longest dollar-weighted maturity. For summary purposes,

Table 2-12
Coupon Rate and Maturity Characteristics of Bond Portfolios Held by Sample Companies*

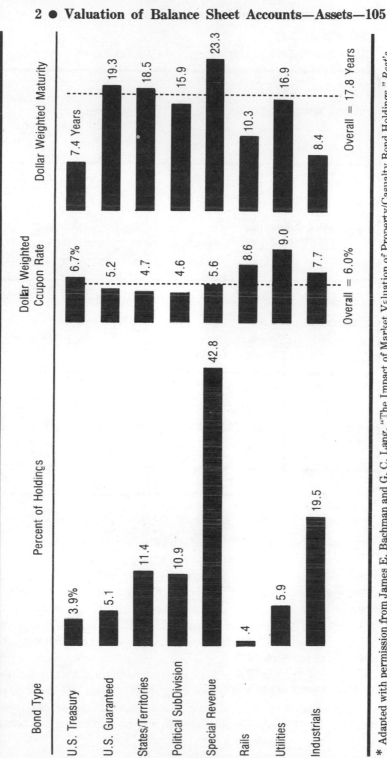

Bond Type	Percent of Holdings	Dollar Weighted Coupon Rate	Dollar Weighted Maturity
U.S. Treasury	3.9%	6.7%	7.4 Years
U.S. Guaranteed	5.1	5.2	19.3
States/Territories	11.4	4.7	18.5
Political SubDivision	10.9	4.6	15.9
Special Revenue	42.8	5.6	23.3
Rails	.4	8.6	10.3
Utilities	5.9	9.0	16.9
Industrials	19.5	7.7	8.4

Overall = 6.0%   Overall = 17.8 Years

* Adapted with permission from James E. Bachman and G. C. Lang, "The Impact of Market Valuation of Property/Casualty Bond Holdings," *Best's Review Property/Casualty Edition* (December 1976), p. 71.

Table 2-13
Bond Classification by Maturity and Coupon Rate*

Coupon Rate	Taxable Bonds					
	Maturity in Years					
	5 or less	6-10	11-20	21-30	More than 30	Total
5% or less	2.95%	1.00%	3.43%	1.69%	0.91%	9.98%
5.01—6	14.52	0.07	2.42	1.56	0.88	19.45
6.01—7	8.26	1.53	1.52	0.86	0.14	12.31
7.01—8	10.80	4.67	0.43	2.02	0.43	18.35
8.01—9	1.90	6.70	1.30	7.20	0.55	17.66
More than 9%	4.59	6.64	5.09	4.43	1.51	22.26
Total	43.02%	20.61%	14.19%	17.76%	4.42%	100.00%

Coupon Rate	Tax-Exempt Bonds					
	Maturity in Years					
	5 or less	6-10	11-20	21-30	More than 30	Total
3% or less	1.61%	1.24%	2.37%	0.39%	—%	5.61%
3.01—4	1.92	2.91	11.63	4.95	1.14	22.55
4.01—5	0.52	1.26	7.56	4.38	1.47	15.19
5.01—6	0.40	0.37	8.69	19.50	7.33	36.29
6.01—7	0.59	0.17	3.30	4.65	2.99	11.70
More than 7%	0.64	0.29	2.07	2.65	3.03	8.68
Total	5.68%	6.24%	35.62%	36.52%	15.96%	100.00%

* Adapted with permission from James E. Bachman and G. C. Lang, "The Impact of Market Valuation of Property/Casualty Bond Holdings," *Best's Review Property/Casualty Edition* (December 1976) p. 71. Percentages are determined on the basis of par valuation. By company, the average discrepancy between par value and cost is less than three-quarters of one percent (¾%).

the bond portfolios can be further categorized as taxable and tax-exempt holdings. In total, approximately 65 percent of the bond holdings are tax-exempt securities. Within each of these categories, bonds are grouped into classes by maturity and coupon rate. Table 2-13 presents these data.

As indicated in Table 2-13, there are several significant differences between the taxable and tax-exempt portfolios. First, over 50 percent of the tax-exempt portfolio have maturities in excess of twenty years, whereas for the taxable portfolio, nearly 65 percent of the bonds are less

Table 2-14

Coupon Rates of Newly Issued Moody A Rated Tax Exempt
Municipal Bonds by Year and Maturity*

End of Year	5	10	20	30
1971	3.59%	4.23%	5.18%	5.52%
1972	3.74	4.26	4.94	5.22
1973	4.34	4.54	5.19	5.53
1974	5.36	5.92	7.25	7.55
1975	5.05	5.91	6.99	7.10
5 Year Average	4.42%	4.97%	5.91%	6.43%

*Reprinted with permission from James E. Bachman and G. C. Lang, "The Impact of Market Valuation of Property/Casualty Bond Holdings," *Best's Review Property/Casualty Edition* (December 1976), p. 72.

than ten years in maturity. Second, in the case of tax-exempt bonds, the higher coupon rates are concentrated in the longer maturity classes. In the case of the taxable portfolio, the higher coupon rates are distributed fairly evenly across all maturities (except beyond thirty years).

The distribution of coupons and maturities among taxable and tax-exempt portfolios points to the likely consequences of market valuation. In general, the taxable portfolio appears to be better insulated than the tax-exempt portfolio against severe depreciation in price. First, the maturity structure of the taxable portfolio is weighted more heavily toward short- and medium-term (less than ten years) bonds. Second, the longer term (greater than ten years) taxable bond portfolio has an apparent concentration (in excess of 20 percent) of funds invested in the high (greater than 8 percent) coupon range. On the other hand, the tax-exempt portfolio has a large concentration (nearly 70 percent) of low to medium (less than 6 percent) coupon bonds with medium to long (greater than ten years) maturities.

The final type of data obtained from the sample is the time series of coupon rates prevailing at year end for each type of bond. Table 2-14 presents a sample of this data for Moody A-rated tax-exempt municipals having maturities of either five, ten, twenty, or thirty years.

The data presented in Table 2-14 demonstrate the normal relationship between coupon rate and maturity. For any year, if the maturity is decreased, then the coupon rate decreases. As can be seen from Table 2-14, shortening the maturity from thirty years to ten years would have reduced the five-year average coupon rate from 6.43 to 4.97 percent or 146 basis points.

Model for Assessing Bond Market Valuation A model is developed here to assess the impact upon the financial condition of insurance companies that would be caused by a change from amortized cost to market valuation for bond investments. The model discounts the stream of receipts for each bond by an appropriate discount rate, computes the total depreciation by type of bond, and subtracts the sum from surplus in order to arrive at a market valued surplus.

The process is as follows: first, for each company, classify the bonds into the type of bond categories shown in Table 2-12. Second, within each type of bond category, further classify the bonds by maturity as to those having maturities of fifty-four months or less, fifty-five to ninety months, and more than ninety months. Third, for the bonds within each type of bond category and maturity class, discount their income streams by the appropriate discount rate. The discount rates used are selected from Moody's rates for three-year, five-year, and ten-year bonds. The rates used, with the exception of bonds of the U.S. Government, are based on Moody A-rated securities. They are classified as the U.S. Treasury, municipals, rails, utilities, and industrials.

A reasonable criticism to this approach is that long-term bonds with maturities in excess of ten years are not discounted by a long-term index. The reason this occurs is that long-term indexes for all types of bonds are not available. However, this does not negate the value of the analysis. The impact of maturity upon price volatility can still be observed for longer term bonds even though the discount rate used is not as large as what twenty- or thirty-year bonds might indicate. Also, to the extent that longer term bonds have higher coupons than the ten-year index assumes, the amount of depreciation resulting from market valuation is understated. Hence, the resulting depreciation in surplus can be correctly viewed as the minimum depreciation that might be expected to occur due to market valuation. It is a consequence that is unavoidable.

Results of the Analysis The results that follow show the impact of valuation for two sets of assumptions. For the first set, it is assumed that the appropriate series of discount rates would be the market interest rates prevailing as of December 31, 1975. The second set assumes the appropriate discount rates would be an average of the corresponding market interest rates during the three-year period ending December 31, 1975. Table 2-15 below shows the percentage decrease in surplus and resulting premiums written-to-policyholders' surplus ratio for the major companies sampled if bonds had been valued at market on December 31, 1975, using the then current market interest rates.

The results displayed in Table 2-15 indicate considerable variation among companies. Overall there is nearly a 36 percent reduction in

Table 2-15

Percent Reduction in Surplus and Resulting Premium to Surplus Ratio—
Market Valuation of Bonds at December 31, 1975 using
Current Discount Rates*

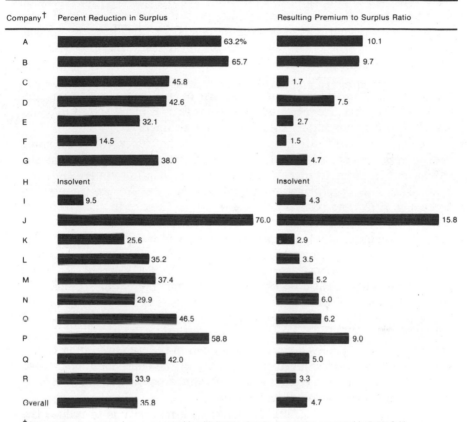

Company[†]	Percent Reduction in Surplus	Resulting Premium to Surplus Ratio
A	63.2%	10.1
B	65.7	9.7
C	45.8	1.7
D	42.6	7.5
E	32.1	2.7
F	14.5	1.5
G	38.0	4.7
H	Insolvent	Insolvent
I	9.5	4.3
J	76.0	15.8
K	25.6	2.9
L	35.2	3.5
M	37.4	5.2
N	29.9	6.0
O	46.5	6.2
P	58.8	9.0
Q	42.0	5.0
R	33.9	3.3
Overall	35.8	4.7

[†]Sequencing of companies does not coincide with listing of major companies presented in Table 2-11.

* Adapted with permission from James E. Bachman and G. C. Lang, "The Impact of Market
Valuation of Property/Casualty Bond Holdings," *Best's Review Property/Casualty Edition*,
(December 1976) p. 73.

surplus and the premiums written-to-policyholders' surplus ratio is increased from 2.9 (not shown) to 4.7. By company, one major company (Company H), is ruined whereas Company I has its surplus reduced only 9.5 percent.[5]

The reasons for the intercompany variation are several. First, the size of each company's bond portfolio relative to its surplus differs among the companies. Second, and perhaps more important, there is wide variation among companies in the yield and maturity structure of their bond portfolios. Several companies possess a preponderance of low-coupon, lengthy maturity, tax-exempt bonds. In fact, it is the special revenue category of bonds which on an aggregate basis presents the companies with the greatest rate of depreciation.

The data presented in Table 2-11 are for the "major" companies only. For the "nonmajor" companies the overall reduction in surplus exceeds 44 percent. The premium to surplus ratio is increased from 3.1 to 5.5. Of the nine "nonmajor" companies, one is ruined.

Using a discount rate based upon the current market interest rates prevailing at the end of the year may be too stringent a test for market valuation.[6] In order to investigate the impact of a less severe test, the analysis was also performed on an average of rates for the three years preceding 1975. The results are presented in Table 2-16. The result of using a three-year average of rates reduces the depressing impact on surplus of valuing bonds at market. The overall reduction in surplus is 20 percent. The premium-to-surplus ratio is 3.6. For "nonmajor" companies (not shown), surplus is reduced 30.4 percent and the premium-to-surplus ratio is changed to 4.4. One "nonmajor" company is ruined when a three-year average of rates is used as the discount factor.

Earlier in this chapter the impact of bond maturity upon market valuation was discussed. One possible method by which insurers can avoid the severe surplus depreciation shown in the two preceding tables would be to shorten the maturity structure of the bond portfolios. Table 2-17 below presents the results across all companies at the end of 1975 if the maturity were shortened as indicated.[7]

The impact of shortening the maximum maturity is to reduce the adverse effect upon surplus of market valuation for bonds. A portfolio with a maximum maturity of ten years causes surplus to fall approximately 24 percent as opposed to the unconstrained drop of nearly 36 percent shown by the companies included in Table 2-11.

Unfortunately, an expected reduction in investment income is associated with the bond portfolio's shorter maturity structure. Based upon the dollar amount of bonds held by the sampled companies ($11.286 billion) each basis point in yield is worth approximately $1.129 million of investment income. The bond investment income of the sample companies during 1975 was approximately $667.460 million. Based on

Table 2-16

Percent Reduction in Surplus and Resulting Premium to Surplus Ratio—
Market Valuation of Bonds at December 31, 1975 using
3 Year Average of Discount Rates*

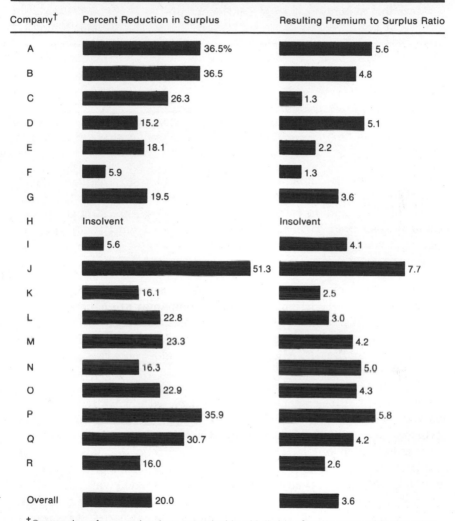

Company†	Percent Reduction in Surplus	Resulting Premium to Surplus Ratio
A	36.5%	5.6
B	36.5	4.8
C	26.3	1.3
D	15.2	5.1
E	18.1	2.2
F	5.9	1.3
G	19.5	3.6
H	Insolvent	Insolvent
I	5.6	4.1
J	51.3	7.7
K	16.1	2.5
L	22.8	3.0
M	23.3	4.2
N	16.3	5.0
O	22.9	4.3
P	35.9	5.8
Q	30.7	4.2
R	16.0	2.6
Overall	20.0	3.6

†Sequencing of companies does not coincide with listing of major companies presented
in Table 2-15.

*Adapted with permission from James E. Bachman and G. C. Lang, "The Impact of Market
Valuation of Property/Casualty Bond Holdings," *Best's Review Property/Casualty Edition*,
(December 1976), p. 73.

Table 2-17

Impact of Market Valuation if Maturity of Bond Portfolio Were Shortened—
December 1975 Market Valuation—Current Rates*

Maximum Maturity in Years	Percent Reduction in Surplus	Premiums Written to Policyholders' Surplus Ratio
20	34.4%	4.4
10	24.4	3.8
5	13.0	3.3

* Adapted with permission from James E. Bachman and G. C. Lang, "The Impact of Market Valuation of Property/Casualty Bond Holdings," *Best's Review Property/Casualty Edition* (December 1976), p. 74.

data presented in Table 2-14, it is reasonable to assume that if maturities were reduced from say twenty years to ten years, then in excess of $105 million (about 94 basis points) of investment income would be sacrificed. Hence, reducing maturities from twenty years to ten years would eliminate approximately 16 percent of the companies' bond investment income.

Summary of Valuation Methods The two principal asset accounts of property-liability insurance companies are common stocks and bonds. This section has discussed methods used to value the securities. For statutory accounting purposes common stocks are reported at market (NAIC) value. This value should very closely represent the liquidating value of the common stock portfolio. On the other hand, bonds are reported in the insurer's financial statement at amortized cost. However, this valuation may not always represent the liquidating value of the bond portfolio because bond values vary inversely to changes in market interest rates. All else being equal, the liquidating value of the insurer's bond portfolio depends upon the maturity structure of the bond portfolio, the distribution of coupon rates of bonds within the portfolio, and the level of bond yields at which interest rates begin to fluctuate. As the results of the analysis presented in this section indicate, amortized cost does not always present insurance company bond holdings at their liquidating value. Whether bonds should continue to be valued at amortized cost rather than at their market values or at some modification of market value is a topic being considered by insurance regulators. The difference between amortized cost and market valuation is an important concept for insurance company managers to understand regardless of the statutory accounting treatment. For companies with cash flows sufficient to cover operating expenditures without liquidating bond investments, amortized cost valuation has the advantage of shielding policyholders' surplus from unnecessary fluctuations due to interim vagaries of the bond market. Companies unable to meet operating expenditures from current cash flow fail to disclose their hazardous financial condition by valuing bonds at amortized cost in excess of market value. Because the subject of valuation is so intimately related to the adequacy of a company's cash flow, the following section presents an analysis of insurance company cash flow and related subjects.

FACTORS AFFECTING INVESTMENT POLICY

A large number of factors directly or indirectly influence the investment policy adopted by a particular property and liability insurance company. This section discusses three important determinants of the investment portfolio's size and composition. Initially, *cash flow* from underwriting operations will be examined and illustrated with a series of examples. Then the concept of *insurance leverage* will be explained. Insurance leverage, other things the same, can have a significant effect on the amount of money an insurance company holds for investment purposes. The concept of *insurance exposure* will also be developed and will be shown to interact with insurance leverage to impact upon investment behavior.

Cash Flow Analysis

The cash flow analysis developed here examines the amount of cash retained by an insurance company and generated from the hypothetical underwriting results of a dwelling fire line of insurance. This amount is termed net cash flow. For purposes of this discussion, cash flow from investment income and portfolio turnover are ignored.

Net cash flow equals premium receipts minus payments for underwriting expenses, loss adjustment expenses, and losses. The computation is made on a calendar-year basis, rather than a policy-year basis, which would prevent calendar-year financial statement analysis. The components of net cash flow require further explanation.

Cash Inflows For purposes of this illustration, assume that the distribution of premium receipts lags premiums written by two months, with 15 percent of the premium received in the month the policy is written, 75 percent in the succeeding month, and 10 percent in the next month. For example, for a $200 written premium in dwelling fire on January 1, the distribution of premium receipts is as follows:

Period	Percentage	Premium Received
January	15%	$30
February	75%	$150
March	10%	$20

Although these percentages are not as precise as those experienced by an actual company, they are sufficiently accurate for the purposes of measuring cash inflows. In addition to the above cash inflow, the insurance company will receive other cash inflows for other policies written immediately before and during the same periods as shown above. To illustrate, assume that on July 1 the company begins to write only one dwelling fire policy each month, and that the policy is written on the first day of each month for a $200 premium. Also, assume that the company discontinues writing dwelling fire policies on the following January 2. The amount of the company's cash inflow for each period is presented in Table 2-18. The amount of premium receipts for any period is affected by the amount of premium written for that period and preceding periods, and by the distribution of receipts.

The total cash inflow available to the insurance company increases through September, after which it plateaus through January. Beyond January it decreases. The growth, equilibrium, and decline in cash inflows is indicative of expansion, equilibrium, and contraction in written premium. The impact of changes in the levels of premium volume upon cash inflow is delayed due to the time lag in receipt of premium.

Cash Outflows for Expenses Payments for underwriting expenses include commissions, premium taxes, acquisition expenses, and all other nonloss-related expenses of the company. In the illustrations that follow, the expense payout distribution is assumed to be as follows: premium taxes plus commissions plus one-half acquisition and other nonloss-related expenses, paid in the first month and the balance spread over the policy term. The distribution employed is 80 percent in the first month, with the remainder evenly distributed over the lesser of either ten months or the policy term. This payout distribution might not be precise for the expense payout patterns of all companies; however, it exemplifies the fact that most nonloss-related expenses occur early in the policy term.

Continuing with the same illustration, assume that these dwelling fire policies are only six-month coverages. Further, 80 percent of the underwriting expense is paid out in the first month, and the remaining 20 percent is paid evenly over the next five months, or 4 percent per

Table 2-18

Monthly Cash Inflows from Dwelling Fire Insurance

Policy Date	Month of Receipt				
	July	August	September	October	November
July	$30	$150	$ 20		
August		30	150	$ 20	
September			30	150	$ 20
October				30	150
November					30
December					
January					
Total Cash Inflow	$30	$180	$200	$200	$200

Policy Date	December	January	February	March
July				
August				
September				
October	$ 20			
November	150	$ 20		
December	30	150	$ 20	
January		30	150	$20
Total Cash Inflow	$200	$200	$170	$20

month. The amount of cash outflow for nonloss expense payments in each period is displayed in Table 2-19 for the case in which the expense ratio is 25 percent.

Total cash outflow for underwriting expense payments increases slowly through December, after which it stabilizes through January and then declines sharply. As with cash inflow, the increase, stabilization, and subsequent decrease in cash outflow for nonloss expense payments are attributable to changes in written premiums, albeit with a longer though lesser impact.

Cash Outflow for Loss and Loss Adjustment Expenses In this section, loss and loss adjustment expense are not distinguished from each other. The amount of cash payment for claims depends upon the amount of losses incurred in the past and present and the distribution over time of their payment. In projecting the loss payment distributions into the future, it is assumed that it is constant from month to month,

Table 2-19

Monthly Cash Outflows from Dwelling Fire Insurance
for Nonloss Expenses

Policy Date	Month of Outflow					
	July	August	September	October	November	December
July	$40	$ 2	$ 2	$ 2	$ 2	$ 2
August		40	2	2	2	2
September			40	2	2	2
October				40	2	2
November					40	2
December						40
January	—	—	—	—	—	—
Total Nonloss Expenses Paid	$40	$42	$44	$46	$48	$50

Policy Date	January	February	March	April	May	June	July
July							
August	$ 2						
September	2	$ 2					
October	2	2	$2				
November	2	2	2	$2			
December	2	2	2	2	$2		
January	40	2	2	2	2	$2	$0
Total Nonloss Expenses Paid	$50	$10	$8	$6	$4	$2	$0

and the proportion of paid to incurred losses is independent of the absolute amount of total incurred losses for any one month.

Assume that the loss payment distribution for dwelling fire policies extends six months from the date the claim is stated as incurred until it is paid in full. Further, assume for the purposes of the illustration that the following distribution accurately represents how claims are paid:

Period	1	2	3	4	5	6
Percentage Paid	0	10	15	25	30	20

For a claim incurred in any month when a dwelling fire policy is in force, 0 percent is paid in that month, 10 percent in the succeeding month, 15 percent in the next succeeding month, and so forth, until at the end of the sixth month, the entire claim has been paid. Assume that each dwelling fire policy from the preceding examples incurs a valid payable loss of $140 one month after it is written. This experience would correspond to a 70 percent loss ratio. The amount of cash outflow for loss payments is presented in Table 2-20.

The amount of cash outflow for loss payments is dependent exclusively upon the dollar amount of the loss and the distribution of payment over time. For a six-month distribution as above, six months

Table 2-20

Monthly Loss and Loss Adjustment Expenses Paid on Dwelling Fires

Policy Date	Month of Outflow					
	July	August	September	October	November	December
July		$0	$14	$21	$35	$ 42
August			0	14	21	35
September				0	14	21
October					0	14
November						0
December						
January	—	—	—	—	—	—
Total Loss Expenses Paid	$0	$0	$14	$35	$70	$112

Policy Date	January	February	March	April	May	June	July
July	$ 28						
August	42	$ 28					
September	35	42	$ 28				
October	21	35	42	$ 28			
November	14	21	35	42	$ 28		
December	0	14	21	35	42	$28	
January		0	14	21	35	42	$28
Total Loss Expenses Paid	$140	$140	$140	$126	$105	$70	$28

are required before the full impact of past results ($140 incurred loss) is transmitted to current results. It is important to recognize that past incurred losses weigh heavily upon current cash outflows.

Net Underwriting Cash Flow   Net cash flow from underwriting is defined as premium receipts minus payments for underwriting expenses, loss expenses, and losses. Applying this definition to the dwelling fire example results in an estimate of the periodic net cash flow to the company. Table 2-21 displays the results.

Net cash flow is the actual amount of cash retained by the company during each period. The cumulative net cash flow to date shown in Table 2-21 represents the sum the company would have available for investment during each period. As indicated in Table 2-21 this sum begins as a deficit amount ($10), peaks at $539 and declines to equal $70. This latter sum is the net cash gain to the insurance company (exclusive of investment earnings) for having underwritten dwelling fire insurance. However, the cumulative net cash flow to date does not equal the cumulative underwriting profit from dwelling fire insurance except at the end of the final period. The statutory underwriting result for any

Table 2-21

Monthly Net Cash Flow from Dwelling Fire Insurance

	Month					
	July	August	September	October	November	December
Premium receipts	$30	$180	$200	$200	$200	$200
Underwriting expense payments	(40)	(42)	(44)	(46)	(48)	(50)
Loss payments	(0)	(0)	(14)	(35)	(70)	(112)
Net cash flow	(10)	138	142	119	82	38
Cumulative net cash flow to date	($10)	$128	$270	$389	$471	$509
	January	February	March	April	May	June	July
Premium receipts	$200	$170	$ 20	$ 0	$ 0	$ 0	$ 0
Underwriting expense payments	(50)	(10)	(8)	(6)	(4)	(2)	(0)
Loss payments	(140)	(140)	(140)	(126)	(105)	(70)	(28)
Net cash flow	10	20	(128)	(132)	(109)	(72)	(28)
Cumulative net cash flow to date	$519	$539	$411	$279	$170	$98	$70

period is defined as earned premium minus loss and loss adjustment expenses incurred minus nonloss underwriting expenses incurred. Changes in the insurance company's reserves for loss and loss adjustment expenses are deducted as incurred losses. Nonloss underwriting expenses are deducted as incurred. Thus, the statutory underwriting profit formula ignores cash flow patterns and emphasizes immediate recognition of losses and expenses.

The earned premium for any one of the six-month dwelling fire policies in the example for any given period is 1/6 times $200. Assuming no losses other than a $140 loss occurring in the first month after each policy is in force, and assuming the same 25 percent expense ratio, the statutory underwriting result for all dwelling fire policies is as displayed in Table 2-22.

Comparing the net cash flow data of Table 2-21 to the statutory profit data of Table 2-22 illustrates several important operating characteristics of property-liability insurance companies. First, as indicated by the net cash flow data, property-liability insurance companies can very quickly accumulate relatively large pools of cash from their underwriting activities. The magnitude of the cash buildup is dependent upon such factors as premium growth, loss ratio, and cash payout patterns. Second, as indicated by the statutory underwriting result data, it would appear that so long as premiums are increasing, property-liability insurance companies are able to accumulate large cash holdings in spite of severe statutory losses. However, it should be noted

Table 2-22

Monthly Statutory Gain from Dwelling Fire Insurance

	Month					
	July	August	September	October	November	December
Written premium	$200	$200	$200	$200	$200	$200
Earned premium	33	67	100	133	167	200
Loss incurred		140	140	140	140	140
Expenses incurred	50	50	50	50	50	50
Statutory underwriting result	(17)	(123)	(90)	(57)	(23)	10
Cumulative to date statutory underwriting result	($17)	($140)	($230)	($287)	($310)	($300)

	January	February	March	April	May	June
Written premium	$200					
Earned premium	200	$167	$133	$100	$67	$33
Loss incurred	140	140				
Expenses incurred	50					
Statutory underwriting result	10	27	133	100	67	33
Cumulative to date statutory underwriting result	($290)	($263)	($130)	($30)	$37	$70

that if premium growth is not achieved (i.e., steady state occurs) then the net periodic addition to cash balances will equal the periodic statutory result. Further, if premium volume declines (i.e., discontinues), then the final resulting accumulated net cash flow will equal the accumulated underwriting profit (or loss) for the entire period.

Cash flow analysis is useful in examining the impact of a line(s) of insurance premium receipt, loss, and nonloss payout patterns upon the accumulation of cash. Provided net cash flow is positive, additional funds are being generated for investment. When net cash flow is negative, investments must be converted to cash in order to meet the insurer's obligations. Depending upon the mix of business among product lines and the length of the time horizon involved, cash flow analysis may produce results dissimilar to strict profit measures. The point to remember about cash flow analysis is that it focuses upon changes in the asset portion of the balance sheet.

Insurance Leverage and Insurance Exposure

In addition to cash flow analysis, other tools that are helpful in examining an insurer's balance sheet include measurements of insurance leverage and insurance exposure. These concepts will be discussed thoroughly in Chapter 5 of this text. They are introduced at this point because of their close association with cash flow analysis as a determinant of investment policy.

Unlike many other types of business, insurance companies normally do not use long-term debt as a source of financing nor do insurers employ relatively large amounts of fixed assets in conducting their activities. This means that the financial structure and asset structure of insurers differ from noninsurance firms. Because of these operating characteristics, traditional measures of financial leverage and operating leverage may not be especially meaningful for insurance companies.

Financial leverage involves the use of funds obtained at a fixed cost to increase returns to net worth. It is measured by the relative portion of assets financed by debt and equity. For the majority of insurance companies that do not directly include debt instruments in their capital structure, the traditional ratio of debt to equity offers little information. Insurers, however, can substitute insurance leverage for financial leverage. This means that an insurer can in effect "borrow" funds from policyholders by increasing the size of its liabilities to policyholders. The two most important policyholder liabilities are the unearned premium reserve and the loss reserves. Thus, the ratio of reserves (debt) to policyholders' surplus (equity) can be used as a measure of insurance leverage.

Operating leverage involves the employment of assets for which the firm pays a fixed cost. The higher the degree of operating leverage, the more sensitive operating profits are to changes in sales. Although not a direct counterpart to operating leverage, the concept of insurance exposure relates the sensitivity of underwriting results to changes in sales. The ratio of premiums written (sales) to policyholders' surplus (equity) is used as a measure of insurance exposure.

Ratios of insurance leverage and insurance exposure focus on the liability-net worth portion of the balance sheet and on sales-net worth relationships. The primary issues to be addressed by investigating insurance leverage and exposure are: (1) the extent to which a given amount of policyholders' surplus can support specific amounts of reserves or premiums; and, (2) the effects on underwriting and investment results that varying levels of insurance leverage and exposure can produce.

Resolving these issues requires recognition of the fact that insurance leverage and exposure are interrelated with each other and also that they mutually influence and are influenced by the investment policy of the insurance company. The remainder of this section deals with insurance leverage and insurance exposure. Direct consideration of investment policy is deferred to the last section of this chapter.

Table 2-23

Basic Insurance Leverage Data*

Product Line[†]	Assumed Average/ Loss Ratio	Reserve Duration in Years
A	70.8%	7
B	62.3%	2

[†]A denotes "liability and bond" lines. B denotes "property" lines.

* Adapted with permission from *Best's Aggregates and Averages* (Oldwick, NJ: A. M. Best Co.), 1957—1974 Stock Companies only.

One significant impact of product line mix is insurance leverage as measured by the ratio of outstanding loss reserves to surplus. It is well known that certain liability lines of insurance can be characterized by the extended period of time during which loss reserves are outstanding. These lines are said to have a "long-tail" with respect to loss payout. On the other hand, most property lines of insurance have reserve amounts from which full and final payments are made rather quickly. These lines are "short-tail" with respect to loss payout.

The data presented in Table 2-23 will be used to illustrate the impact upon insurance leverage that can be achieved by altering the pattern of loss payout. Product line A has a 70.8 percent assumed average loss ratio. Reserves established for this product line are outstanding for up to seven years. Product line A is a "long-tail" line of insurance. Product line B has a 62.3 percent assumed average loss ratio. Reserves established for this line are outstanding no more than two years. Product line B is a "short-tail" line of business.

The loss payout pattern for each line is assumed to follow the rule of 78's.[8] If the reserves are established accurately at the beginning of the first year, each with the respective average loss ratio, then the midyear outstanding reserve for all subsequent years would appear as shown in Table 2-24.

Line A has an assumed average loss ratio of 70.8 percent. The above table indicates that, as of midyear in the first year, 87.5 percent of the initial reserve is still outstanding (that is, $\frac{1}{2}$ of $\frac{7}{28}$ths of the initial losses have been settled). Per hundred dollars of premium, $61.95 (0.875 times $70.80) of initial loss reserve remains outstanding. Similarly, in the fifth year, the midyear percent outstanding is 16.07 percent, equivalent to $11.38 (0.1607 times $70.80) of the initial reserve. If a company were underwriting line A at a constant amount of premium for several years, then according to Table 2-24, at any time after seven years, it would

Table 2-24

Percent and Dollar Amount of Initial Reserves Outstanding at Midyear*

Year	Percent of Initial Reserve Outstanding (midyear)		Dollar Amount of Initial Reserve Outstanding (midyear) Per $100 Premium	
	Line A	Line B	Line A	Line B
1	87.50%	66.67%	$ 61.95	$41.54
2	64.29	16.67	45.52	10.39
3	44.64	—	31.61	—
4	28.57	—	20.23	—
5	16.07	—	11.38	—
6	7.14	—	5.06	—
7	1.79	—	1.27	—
Total			$177.02	$51.93

* Reprinted with permission from James E. Bachman and G. C. Lang, "Investment Portfolio Composition, Product Line Mix, and Their Impact Upon Operating Leverage and Solvency," *Best's Review Property/Casualty Edition* (April 1976), p. 20.

have $177.02 of outstanding reserves per hundred dollars of premium. In the case of line B there would be $51.93 of outstanding loss reserves per hundred dollars of premium. Thus, for any line of insurance, given an assumed average loss ratio and a particular loss payout pattern, it is possible to compute for that line a reserve to premiums written ratio.

The ratio of reserves to premiums written is important for two reasons: first, given a level of insurance exposure (the premiums written-to-policyholders' surplus ratio) it is now possible to measure the resulting insurance leverage (reserves-to-surplus ratio) and second, having the ratio of reserves to premiums written by line of insurance, it is possible to measure the impact of product line mix not only upon underwriting results but also upon investment results for any given investment portfolio mix.

Insurance leverage is defined as the ratio of reserves to policyholders' surplus. Insurance exposure is defined as the ratio of premiums written to policyholders' surplus. The relation between these two concepts is as follows:

Table 2-25

Insurance Leverage (Reserves to Policyholders' Surplus) for Various Product Line Mix Combinations and Differing Levels of Insurance Exposure*

Premium to Surplus	25 Percent Liability	40 Percent Liability	50 Percent Liability	60 Percent Liability	75 Percent Liability
1	0.83	1.02	1.14	1.27	1.46
2	1.66	2.04	2.29	2.54	2.91
3	2.50	3.06	3.43	3.81	4.37
4	3.33	4.08	4.58	5.08	5.83
5	4.16	5.10	5.72	6.35	7.29

* Adapted from James E. Bachman and G. C. Lang, "Investment Portfolio Composition, Product Line Mix, and Their Impact Upon Operating Leverage and Solvency," *Best's Review Property/Casualty Edition* (April 1976), p. 20.

Insurance Leverage = Insurance Exposure × Reserves/Premiums Written

$$\frac{\text{Reserves}}{\text{Policyholders' Surplus}} = \frac{\text{Premiums Written}}{\text{Policyholders' Surplus}} \times \frac{\text{Reserves}}{\text{Premiums Written}}$$

For example, if a company issued only liability contracts having the same loss characteristics as line A in the above tables, and if the premiums written-to-policyholders' surplus ratio were, say 3 to 1, then the resulting reserves-to-policyholders' surplus ratio would be 5.31 to 1.

$$\frac{\text{Reserves}}{\text{Policyholders' Surplus}} = \frac{\text{Premiums Written}}{\text{Policyholders' Surplus}} \times \frac{\text{Reserves}}{\text{Premiums Written}}$$

$$= \frac{3}{1} \times \frac{177.02}{100.00}$$

$$= 5.31$$

This is a measure of the insurance leverage being employed by this insurer. On the other hand, if the company issued only property contracts having the same loss charcteristics as line B and if the premiums written-to-policyholders' surplus ratio were again 3 to 1, then the resulting measure of insurance leverage would be only 1.56 to 1. Table 2-25 presents the measure of insurance leverage that occurs as the mix between liability (line A) and property (line B) is altered for various assumed premiums written-to-policyholders' surplus ratios.

As Table 2-25 indicates, a company issuing a 50-50 mix between property and liability contracts at a premiums written-to-policyholders' surplus ratio of 3 to 1 can achieve greater insurance leverage (3.43 to 1) than if the mix were 75-25 property-liability and the premiums written-to-policyholders' surplus ratio were 4 to 1 (3.33 to 1). For whatever value of the premiums written-to-policyholders' surplus ratio, a company that tends to emphasize liability lines of insurance can achieve greater insurance leverage than a company emphasizing property lines. This greater insurance leverage provides more funds for investment operations and may increase the company's earnings if underwriting and investment activities are profitable.

Cash flow analysis highlights property-liability insurance companies' potential for accumulating cash for investment. Using the concepts of insurance exposure and leverage, it can be shown that product line mix has a significant impact upon the amount of funds available for potential investment. Instead of concentrating upon the asset side of the balance sheet as in the case of cash flow analysis, the concepts of insurance exposure and insurance leverage concentrate on the buildup of liability accounts relative to surplus. Cash flow analysis points to the use of funds generated from insurance operations, whereas leverage and exposure concepts point to the sources of these funds.

PROPERTY-LIABILITY
INSURANCE COMPANY INVESTMENT POLICY

In this section it is assumed that property and liability investment policy is concerned only with the composition of the investment portfolio as between common stocks and municipal bonds, and the maturity structure of the bond portfolio. By making this assumption, several aspects of investment policy are ignored. First, there is no discussion as to whether or not property and liability insurance companies should "buy and hold" or "actively trade" the securities in their investment portfolios. Second, there is no discussion as to how individual securities are selected, evaluated, purchased, or traded in a property and liability insurance company investment portfolio. Third, there is no discussion as to the mechanics of organizing, developing, and maintaining an investment department within a property and liability insurance company. And finally, there is no discussion as to the merit or difficulties of making the investment portfolio responsive to short-term deviations in long-run insurance underwriting profit expectations. While these omitted topics are important, emphasis here is placed on the interaction of investment objectives, asset valuation, insurance leverage, and insurance exposure.

This section begins by presenting possible corporate objectives for insurance companies to pursue. Next, a model is developed that can be used to specify a long-term investment policy that is consistent with these corporate objectives. The impact of bond valuation changes is investigated by use of this model which incorporates the concepts of insurance exposure and insurance leverage.

Insurance Company Objectives

Property and liability insurance companies must be responsive to the needs of at least two of their constituents: their policyholders and their stockholders. Because mutual organizations have no stockholders, the demands of policyholders are relevant.

Focusing upon what might be considered the foremost concern of each constituent group, it should be possible to specify insurance company objectives. Existing policyholders have as their primary concern the solvency of the insurance company. Having paid premiums to the insurer, the policyholders are concerned about the company's ability to meet its legal obligations to them. On the other hand, firms organized for profit must be able to satisfy stockholder demands that profits be obtained. Additionally, stockholders may require that profits or at least a portion thereof be distributed. Hence there exists a potential conflict of interest between policyholders and stockholders. At the extreme, management or regulatory practices overly responsive to the security interests of policyholders may deny stockholders an adequate return. Conversely, management practices which focus only upon stockholder return considerations may prevent policyholders from ever receiving their contractual rights.

One way of specifying the needs of each constituency into a single objective for insurance company management to pursue would be to maximize profit subject to an acceptable level of risk. This objective addresses the needs of both policyholders and stockholders. The needs of policyholders are represented in the level of risk assumed. Once this has been determined, the interests of stockholders are represented through the maximization of profit.

Investment Portfolio Composition

To determine investment portfolio composition it is necessary to measure the return and risk parameters developed by the operating objective of the insurance company. It will be seen that rational choices can be made among competing investment policies on the basis of their return and risk characteristics.

Return Measure The total return available to the insurance company is the sum of underwriting returns and investment returns. The underwriting returns depend upon the mix of business across lines of insurance as well as the profit margins for each line of insurance. The investment returns depend upon investment portfolio composition and the return opportunities available from each type of investment.

The total "rate" of return on equity depends not only upon the underwriting profit margin and investment return but also upon insurance exposure and insurance leverage. The latter determinant is the result of product line mix. For example, consider the following data:

Liability underwriting profit margin	1.00% (99.0 combined ratio)
Property underwriting profit margin	2.50% (97.5 combined ratio)
Liability reserves to premium	1.77 to 1
Property reserves to premium	0.52 to 1
Stock rate of return	6%
Bond rate of return	3%

If the mix between property and liability insurance were 50-50 and the premiums written-to-policyholders' surplus ratio were 3 to 1, then the rate of return on equity from underwriting would be:

Underwriting return from property	+	Underwriting return from liability	=	Total underwriting return
$(3 \times 0.5 \times 2.5\%)$	+	$(3 \times 0.5 \times 1.0\%)$	=	5.25%

Further, if the investment portfolio composition were 50-50 as between stocks and bonds, then the rate of return would be 4.5 percent ($0.5 \times 6\% + 0.5 \times 3\%$), and the rate of return on equity from investment would be:

Investment return from property	+	Investment return from liability	=	Total investment return
$3 \times 0.5 \times 0.52 \times 4.5\%$	+	$3 \times 0.5 \times 1.77 \times 4.5\%$	=	15.46%

The total rate of return from policyholder supplied funds is the sum of underwriting (5.25 percent) and investment (15.46 percent) returns or 20.71 percent. Adding to this latter figure the investment return on the surplus funds (4.5 percent) results in a total rate of return on equity from all sources of 25.21 percent.

As the example indicates, it is possible to increase total return several ways, provided the underlying sources of return are positive: first, increase insurance exposure, and second, increase investment in common stocks. Note, however, that increasing insurance leverage may not offer a clear-cut opportunity to increase return. In the above data,

Table 2-26

Total Rate of Return for Various Combinations of Insurance Product
Line Mix and Investment Portfolio Composition*

Premiums Written to Policyholders' Surplus	25% Bonds/75% Stocks		75% Bonds/25% Stocks	
	60-40 Property/ Liability	40-60 Property/ Liability	60-40 Property/ Liability	40-60 Property/ Liability
2:1	14.51%	16.54%	11.45%	12.73%
3:1	21.77	24.80	17.18	19.09
4:1	29.02	33.07	22.90	24.45

* Reprinted with permission from James E. Bachman and G. C. Lang, "Investment Portfolio Composition, Product Line Mix, and Their Impact Upon Operating Leverage and Solvency," *Best's Review Property/Casualty Edition* (April 1976), p. 20.

the increase in insurance leverage accomplished by shifting from property to liability lines of insurance would be associated with a reduction in underwriting returns. The advantages gained by a shift from low-leveraged property insurance to high-leveraged liability insurance would depend upon the underwriting profit margin of each line and the investment portfolio composition. Table 2-26 illustrates this point.

The data in Table 2-26 indicate that a shift from property to liability lines would have a favorable impact upon total rate of return— at least on the basis of the earlier contrived data. It would seem that the opportunity for increased leverage and the subsequent increased investment returns offsets the reduction in underwriting profit resulting from the shift. Hence, at first blush, it is tempting to view the optimum policy from management's viewpoint to be an emphasis of liability insurance and increased investment in common stocks.

Risk Unfortunately, the returns presented in Table 2-26 have associated with them various levels of risk. The riskiness of a particular product mix/portfolio composition pattern is defined as the variability of its possible returns. There is uncertainty that, for example, the future underwriting profit margin of liability insurance will actually be 1 percent. For now, the specific causes of the uncertainty are not important. It is sufficient to recognize that any single period's result will not necessarily equal the anticipated value. Similar statements can be made with respect to the underwriting profit margin of property insurance and the rates of return for stocks and bonds. In order to rationally select among various product line mixes and investment

Figure 2-1

Areas Under a Normal Curve

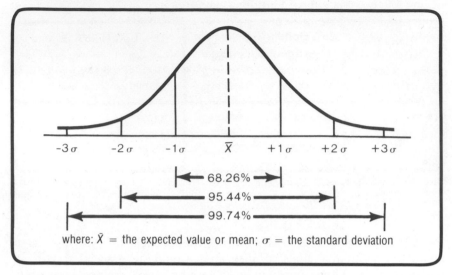

where: $\bar{X}$ = the expected value or mean; σ = the standard deviation

portfolio combinations, it is necessary to quantify the amount of risk associated with each income producing source: liability insurance, property insurance, and stock and bond investments.

Standard Deviation. The risk measure employed is the standard deviation of possible returns which measures the extent to which, on average, any actual observed return deviates from its expected value. As the standard deviation increases, the uncertainty as to what the future actual return will be also increases. This is equivalent to an increase in risk.

If it is assumed that returns from each income source behave according to a particular law of probability, called the normal probability law, it is possible to make predictions about the probability of the returns to be realized from various investments. For the symmetric, "bell-shaped" curve of the normal distribution, approximately 68 percent of the distribution falls within one standard deviation on either side of the expected return; about 95 percent falls within two standard deviations; and about 99.7 percent falls within three standard deviations. This relationship is shown in Figure 2-1.

To illustrate how the standard deviation can be used as a measuring rod to set a confidence range for obtaining a particular return, consider the following example. Suppose the expected rate of return from a particular common stock is 6 percent and the standard deviation of the possible returns is 4 percent. According to the normal curve, there is a 95.44 percent chance that future rates of return will be between –2.0

percent and 14.0 percent ($0.06 \pm 2 \times 0.04\%$). On the other hand, if the expected rate of return remains at 6 percent but the standard deviation of possible returns is 8 percent, then the 95.44 confidence range would be from –10.0 percent to 22.0 percent ($0.06 \pm 2 \times 0.08\%$).[9] Thus the width, or dispersion, of the distribution of returns indicates the level of risk involved in the investment. A distribution with a small standard deviation relative to the expected rate of return exposes the investor to little risk; a high degree of confidence can be placed in the outcome. As the standard deviation becomes larger relative to the expected rate of return, the investor's risk increases and the degree of confidence wanes. In the discussion that follows, it is assumed that probability distributions of rates of return can be described in terms of their expected return and the standard deviation of possible returns.

Risk can unfavorably impact upon the earnings of an insurer when net worth has been leveraged. For example, assume that for each $100 of equity there is available for investment an additional $200 of policyholder supplied funds. The insurance leverage ratio is 2 to 1. If the total amount of funds ($300) is invested in an income-producing source having a 6 percent expected return and an 8 percent standard deviation, there is approximately an 8.5 percent chance that the return on investment will be –5 percent or less. However, the –5 percent or less return on investment implies a –15 percent or less return on equity. If there were no leverage there is only a 0.4 percent chance that the return on equity would be –15 percent or less.[10] If either the standard deviation or leverage is increased, then the chances of suffering more severe losses are increased. While it is true that high leverage and large standard deviations allow for the possibility of very large gains, it is also true that they pose the hazard of unacceptably large losses.

Covariance.   There is an additional element of risk among income-producing sources termed *covariance*. Covariance measures the extent to which various observed rates of return for each income source tend to move either toward or away from their respective expected values simultaneously. Covariance reduces risk when the movement of the observed returns is offsetting (i.e., one moves towards its expected value at the same time the other moves away from its expected value). Covariance increases risk when the movement of the observed return is in phase (i.e., each moves either towards or away from its respective expected value at the same time).

In order to estimate the expected returns and risk for each of the four income-producing sources introduced earlier, data were collected covering the period 1956-1974.[11] From the raw data the expected return parameters were estimated. The expected return and risk measures are presented in Table 2-27. They are shown on an aftertax basis.[12]

Table 2-27

Summary Data for Underwriting Profit Margins and Rates of Return on Common Stocks and Long-Term Municipal Bonds*

	Property	Liability	Stocks	Bonds
Aftertax expected return	0.83%	−0.36%	5.56%	4.31%
Standard deviation (risk)	2.21%	1.15%	11.52%	1.18%
Covariance (risk) matrix				
Property	4.87	−0.07	2.05	0.74
Liability	−0.07	1.33	5.51	−0.70
Stocks	2.05	5.51	132.74	−5.40
Bonds	0.74	−0.70	−5.40	1.40

* Reprinted with permission from James E. Bachman and G. C. Lang, "Investment Portfolio Composition, Product Line Mix, and Their Impact Upon Operating Leverage and Solvency," *Best's Review Property/Casualty Edition* (April 1976), p. 20.

During the nineteen-year period, property insurance provided an average aftertax underwriting profit margin of 0.83 percent ($0.83 per $100 of premium), whereas liability types lines incurred an average aftertax underwriting loss of −0.36 percent. During the same time period, stocks earned an average aftertax total return of 5.56 percent, and bonds had an average aftertax current yield of 4.31 percent. The risk, as measured by the standard deviation for property insurance, liability insurance, and stocks and bonds, is 2.21 percent, 1.15 percent, 11.52 percent and 1.18 percent, respectively. These values are obtained by taking the square root of 4.87, 1.33, 132.74, and 1.40, which are the variances of return for property insurance, liability insurance, and stocks and bonds respectively. (Note that the diagonal elements of the covariance matrix list each income source's variance.)

Using the standard deviation alone, stocks have by far the greatest level of risk; the 95 percent confidence range of return is from −17.02 percent to 28.14 percent. On the other hand, bonds provide the most likely favorable outcome; the 95 percent confidence range return is from 1.70 percent to 6.92 percent. Property insurance has a 95 percent confidence range of return from −3.50 percent to 5.16 percent. The 95 percent confidence range of return for liability insurance is −2.61 percent to 1.89 percent, which makes it more predictable than property insurance although more likely to produce underwriting losses.

The off-diagonal elements of the covariance matrix indicate (by their negative signs) that the fluctuations in returns from property and liability insurance have a slight tendency to be offsetting. The same is also true for stocks and bonds, and bonds and liability insurance.

Table 2-28

Summary Data for Underwriting Profit Margins and Rates of Return on Common Stocks and Short-Term Municipal Bonds at Market*

	Property	Liability	Stocks	Bonds
Aftertax expected return	0.83%	−0.36%	5.56%	3.57%
Standard deviation (risk)	2.21%	1.15%	11.52%	1.57%
Covariance (risk) matrix				
Property	4.87	−0.07	2.05	1.38
Liability	−0.07	1.33	5.51	0.58
Stocks	2.05	5.51	132.73	4.27
Bonds	1.38	0.58	4.27	2.47

* Reprinted with permission from James E. Bachman and G. C. Lang, "Investment Portfolio Composition, Product Line Mix, and Their Impact Upon Operating Leverage and Solvency," *Best's Review Property/Casualty Edition* (April 1976), p. 20.

To further illustrate the effect of valuing bonds at market, an index for short-term bonds is also presented.[13] For this short-term index there are tax consequences resulting from the buy-sell activity of the bonds. Capital gains and losses are adjusted to an aftertax basis to reflect price appreciation and depreciation. Table 2-28 is identical to Table 2-27 except for the replacement of the long-term bond yield data with short-term bond data reflecting price movements.

The impact of valuing bonds at market is twofold. First, the expected return is reduced. This occurs because of the continued price depreciation that occurred during the observation period. Second, the risk associated with bonds is increased from 1.18 percent in Table 2-27 to 1.57 percent in Table 2-28. This occurs because of the price volatility of bonds which is now factored into their return. The 95 percent confidence range of return for bonds when they are valued at market is from 0.49 percent to 6.65 percent. Bonds still retain their first place rank with respect to the ability to minimize the likelihood of unfavorable results.

An Investment Model

In order to combine the elements of risk and return into a structure that can be used to determine investment portfolio composition, a model must be developed. The model is an application of the theory of the so-called "random walk" hypothesis to the gambler's ruin problem. The essence of the problem can be stated as follows. For an individual entering games of chance having particular probabilities of success or

Figure 2-2

Analogy of the Gambler's Ruin Problem*

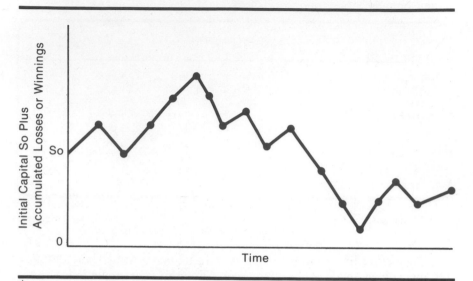

* Adapted from James E. Bachman and G. C. Lang, "Investment Portfolio Composition, Product Line Mix, and Their Impact Upon Operating Leverage and Solvency," *Best's Review Property/Casualty Edition*, (April 1976), p. 20.

failure, what amount of capital is necessary to assure the individual, with any given amount of certainty, that his initial capital plus any accumulated winning will not be eventually lost? For clarity, consider the diagram in Figure 2-2.

The gambler begins with an initial amount of capital (S_o). Changes to this amount are the result of winning or losing each gamble. If the probability of success or failure of each game is known, then what is the probability that the gambler is at some point ruined, given that he started with a certain amount (S_o)? The probability of ruin measures the probability that a gambler beginning with a fixed amount of capital will be eventually ruined.

An analogy of the gambler's ruin problem to an insurace company is possible. The company commences operation with an initial amount of net worth (S_o). It earns, in each period (say every calendar year) a rate of return, positive or negative, reflecting its underwriting and investment success or failure. The sign of the return, positive or negative, depends upon the level of returns from each line of insurance and each type of investment security. It also depends upon product line mix and investment portfolio composition. The magnitude of the "rate" of the return depends upon insurance exposure and, in combination with insurance exposure, the amount of insurance leverage resulting from reserve levels associated with the product line mix. The likelihood of the company being ruined is diminished when, for a given level of return, the risk is reduced, thus providing a lesser frequency of potentially unfavorable outcomes. Stated another way, for a given level of risk, the likelihood of ruin is decreased if the rate of return is increased, thus providing a greater cushion to protect against adverse results.

Application of the Model The objective of the insurance company is presumed to be maximization of profit subject to an acceptable level of risk. The probability of ruin has been taken as the appropriate measure of risk faced by the insurer. It measures the likelihood that with a particular method of operation (investment portfolio composition and product line mix) the insurer will be unable to meet its obligations to policyholders. In the figures that follow, the ruin probability was arbitrarily established at one in one million.[14] Figure 2-3 presents the maximum expected aftertax return available to the insurer when bonds are valued on an amortized cost basis as product line and investment portfolio compositon vary.

Figure 2-3 illustrates the impact of investment portfolio composition upon the total expected aftertax return. Regardless of the product line mix, investment portfolios that emphasize bonds appear to enable the insurer to obtain high returns. Further, because the ruin probability is fixed, policyholder security is not jeopardized. When the investment portfolio is all bonds (that is, 0 percent stocks), it is possible to simultaneously increase total return and the amount of liability insurance exposure. In the figure, total return and the exposure in liability lines of insurance both increase as the company's operating position moves from point A toward point A′. As the percent of the investment portfolio committed to common stocks increases (the company's position moves from line AA′ to line BB′) and as the company increases its exposure in liability lines (its position moves from point B toward point B′), the total return first rises, then plateaus, and thereafter declines. When the portfolio is invested equally in bonds and stocks (the company is operating on line CC′) any increased exposure in liability lines of insurance (the company's position moves from point C toward point C′) only serves to reduce total return. The reason that expected total return falls as the company increases its stock investments and expands its exposure in liability insurance is that both of these changes introduce greater variability of returns. However, the company's probability of ruin must remain fixed at the predetermined level of one in one million. In order to accommodate a larger relative commitment to stock investments and liability lines of insurance, while at the same time keeping the probability of ruin constant, the company must reduce its premiums written-to-policyholders' surplus ratio. It is

Figure 2-3

Total Expected Net After-tax Rate of Return When Probability of Ruin is One in One Million for Various Combinations of Product Line Mix and Investment Portfolio Composition (Bonds Valued at Amortized Cost)*

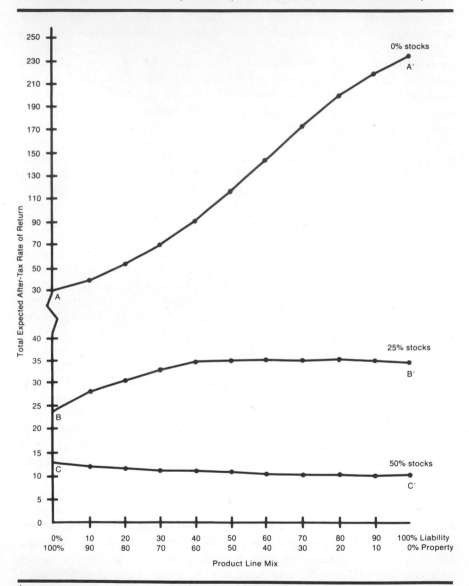

* Reprinted with permission from James E. Bachman and G. C. Lang, "Investment Portfolio Composition, Product Line Mix, and Their Impact Upon Operating Leverage and Solvency," *Best's Review Property/Casualty Edition*, (April 1976), p. 20.

this reduction in insurance exposure, together with the concomitant reduction in insurance leverage and the combination with the investment portfolio composition and product line mix, that causes a reduction in expected total return.

The model illustrated in Figure 2-3 indicates that for a particular combination of desired total return, product line mix, and solvency objective (ruin probability) there is only one investment portfolio composition possible. If the insurer increases the proportion of its portfolio invested in common stocks beyond this amount, then insurer solvency will be jeopardized. Alternatively, an increased investment in bonds, other things being the same, will add an extra margin of solvency. Another implication of this analysis is that for a given level of policyholder security (fixed ruin probability), an increased investment in stocks, accompanied by increased liability insurance exposure, necessitates a reduction in the premiums written-to-policyholders' surplus ratio leading to a reduction in overall return.

From the stockholders' vantage point, an optimum investment portfolio composition and insurance exposure combination is one for which high insurance exposure is maintained and for which the investment portfolio is all bonds (for a fixed ruin probability, policyholders should be indifferent). Also, increased exposure in liability lines is desirable, but there are constraints other than policyholder security and stockholder returns which would prevent the industry (although perhaps not individual companies) from operating with the optimum proportion of liability insurance.

The results displayed in the figure are very sensitive to the basis by which bonds are valued for the insurers' financial statements. Regardless of management's intent with respect to buy-hold decisions for bonds, bond values do fluctuate, and at the very time the company may need their "statement value" to pay claims and losses, it will realize market values. Figure 2-4 presents the total expected aftertax return possible if the probability of ruin is specified at one in one million for various combinations of product line mix and investment portfolio composition when bonds are valued at market.

As Figure 2-4 indicates, under the assumptions of the model used here, regardless of the product line mix, an all-bond investment portfolio offers the insurance company the greatest total expected aftertax rate of return. As the percent of the investment portfolio committed to common stocks increases (the company's position moves from AA′ to BB′ to CC′) and as exposure in liability lines is increased (the company's position moves from A toward A′, B toward B′, or C toward C ′), the total expected aftertax rate of return decreases. Although the expected rates of return shown in Figure 2-4 are lower than those shown in Figure 2-3, the general patterns of returns

Figure 2-4

Total Expected Net After-Tax Rate of Return When Probability of Ruin Is One in One Million for Various Combinations of Product Line Mix and Investment Portfolio Composition: Bonds Valued at Market*

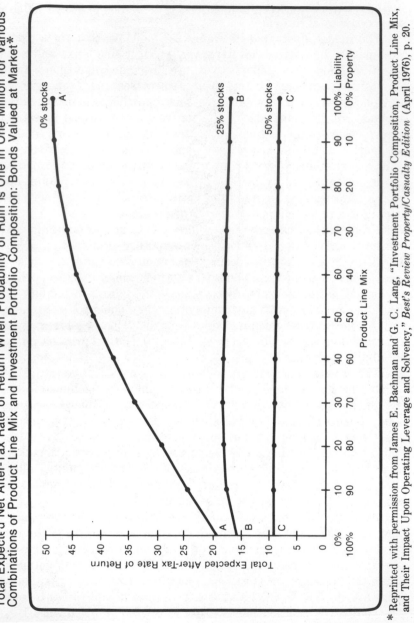

* Reprinted with permission from James E. Bachman and G. C. Lang, "Investment Portfolio Composition, Product Line Mix, and Their Impact Upon Operating Leverage and Solvency," *Best's Review Property/Casualty Edition* (April 1976), p. 20.

resulting from alternative investment/product mix strategies are similar. Again, an optimum operating position can be determined and balanced against constraints imposed by numerous practical influences.

SUMMARY

The annual statement's balance sheet provides twenty-one categories for the classification of a property and liability insurance company's admitted assets. Seven of the categories are designated for cash and portfolio investments. The remaining categories list various receivables and other assets that qualify for presentation on the statutory balance sheet. This chapter has described the various asset categories and emphasized the valuation of stock and bond investments which comprise the majority of a typical nonlife insurer's admitted assets. For annual statement purposes stocks are shown at values prescribed by the NAIC; these values generally are the year-end market values of the stocks. Bonds generally are valued at amortized cost, and their statement value may differ significantly from their year-end market value.

In order to relate valuation to the formulation of investment policy, concepts of underwriting cash flow, insurance exposure, and insurance leverage were explained. Typical underwriting cash flow patterns result in an accumulation of funds for investment by the insurance company. Funds accumulate more rapidly as the degree of insurance exposure, which is measured by the premiums written to policyholders' surplus, increases. The length of time required to settle losses also influences the amount of funds available for investment. Liability lines of insurance which require the buildup of loss reserves increase the amount of insurance leverage, as measured by the reserves-to-policyholders' surplus ratio, employed by an insurer and influence the returns to net worth and the riskiness of the insurer's operations.

The interaction of underwriting cash flows, insurance exposure, insurance leverage, expected returns, and risk were analyzed in the context of an investment policy model. Results obtained from the analysis highlight several facets of insurance company investment policy. It is possible to develop an investment policy that encompasses the needs of policyholders and stockholders. This can be done in a way that does not jeopardize policyholder security for the sake of stockholder returns or vice versa. Formulation of such an investment policy crucially depends upon the method used to value portfolio securities—especially bonds. The method of bond valuation is one of the most significant determinants of portfolio composition and expected total return. When bonds are valued on an amortized cost basis, it is possible to achieve greater insurance exposure and insurance leverage. As pointed out in

Chapter 1, valuing bonds at amortized cost fails to meet the liquidity objective usually desired for admitted assets. Nevertheless, because this valuation basis does permit effective utilization of policyholders' surplus, it is preferable over market valuation if forced liquidation of bonds is unlikely. Insurance company management, however, must be familiar with bond market values as well as their amortized cost because of the valuation method's influence on investment decision making.

Product line mix also influences investment portfolio composition by affecting the company's expected total rate of return. This means that investment decisions cannot be made independent of selecting a desired product line mix or decisions regarding the degree of insurance exposure.

Chapter Notes

1. Gerald W. Huff, "Assets," in *Property-Liability Insurance Accounting,* Robert W. Strain, editor (Santa Monica, CA: Merritt Co., 1976), pp. 22-23.
2. Recall that the present value of $1 to be received n years from now is equal to $1 \div (1.00 + i)^n$; where the exponent n is the number of years before payment is received and i is the annual interest discount rate. Thus, $1 payable at the end of the current year and discounted by 10 percent has a present value of:

$$\frac{\$1}{(1.10)^1} = \$0.9090$$

   Compound interest functions are reviewed at more length in the bond valuation discussion that follows.
3. It is common practice for bond interest to be paid semiannually rather than once a year. Therefore, a $1,000 par value bond that has semiannual coupons of $40 each is said to have coupon rate of 8 percent because it pays $80 per year. In order to avoid the unnecessary refinement of using semiannual interest rates, all the illustrations in this chapter are based on annual coupon payments.
4. See Sydney Homer and Martin L. Leibowitz, *Inside the Yield Book* (Englewood Cliffs, NJ: Prentice-Hall, 1972).
5. The figures above do *not* reflect consolidated results of company groups. To the extent that depeciation in the bond portfolio of a subsidiary company diminishes the parent company's carrying value of that subsidiary, there would be an additional reduction in surplus of the parent. No such accounting has occurred in this analysis. Hence, the extent of surplus reduction may be understated.
6. On the other hand, if bond portfolios of property-liability insurers are valued at market, it is precisely such stringent tests, however infrequently they occur, that must be passed.
7. The procedure used to obtain the results in Table 2-17 is twofold: (1) limit the remaining years to maturity of any bond in the sample of the companies' bond holdings to the maximum maturity; and (2) for any bonds so limited, fix the coupon rate as the lesser of either the bond's stated coupon rate or the coupon rate of the index used to obtain the bond's current market value.
8. The rule of 78's is similar to the sum-of-the-year's-digits formulation for calculating depreciation charges. For example, an asset with a five-year depreciable life would have a sum-of-the-years' digits equal to 15 (5 + 4 + 3 + 2 + 1). The depreciation charged in the first year would be 5/15, in the second, 4/15, etc.
9. In the two examples, the precise 95 percent confidence range would be between –1.8 percent and 13.8 percent in the first case and between –9.7 percent and 21.7 percent in the second case. Another way to use the normal

curve is to ask what is the probability that the actual return is greater than some minimum level, say 0.0 percent. If the expected return is 6 percent and the standard deviation is 4 percent, the probability of achieving a positive return is slightly more than 93 percent; but if the expected return is 6 percent and the standard deviation is 8 percent, then the probability of a positive return being earned is slightly less than 73 percent.

10. A return of –5 percent or less lies at least 1.375 standard deviations below the expected return of 6 percent ($0.11 \div 0.08 = 1.375$). Since more than 91.5 percent of all possible rates of return in this distribution are above the point 1.375 standard deviations below the expected return, less than an 8.5 percent chance exists for a return of –5 percent or less. Similarly, in the no-leverage case, a return of –15 percent or less lies 2.625 standard deviations below the expected return ($0.21 \div 0.8 = 2.625$). About 99.6 percent of all possible rates of return in the distribution lie above this point.

11. Liability and property data were obtained from *Best's Aggregates and Averages* for a large subsection of all stock property-liability companies. Stock data were computed from the Standard and Poor's 500 Stock Price and Dividend Index. Bond data were computed from the Standard and Poor's 15 Domestic Longterm Municipal Bond Index.

12. For underwriting, the assumed tax rate is 48 percent. For common stocks, the assumed tax rates are 48 percent of 15 percent in the case of dividends and 30 percent in the case of capital gains. For municipal bonds, there are no applicable taxes.

13. Short-term bonds are preferred to long-term bonds when market valuation is considered because the impact of interest rate fluctuation is less severe upon the prices of short-term bonds than upon the prices of long-term bonds.

14. A ruin probability of one in one million is a very small number. It relates to the probability of (1) a royal flush (fifteen in ten million); (2) a straight flush (fourteen in one million); and (3) four of a kind (twenty-four in one hundred thousand) when using five-card poker hands.

CHAPTER 3

Liabilities and Policyholders' Surplus

INTRODUCTION

The right side of a property and liability insurance company balance sheet contains the familiar categories, liabilities and owners' equity. Although the general categories are the same, liabilities and owners' equity are quite different in a property and liability insurance organization. Even a casual observer would note that liabilities of a nonlife insurer are composed predominantly of two accounts: loss reserves and the unearned premium reserve. These two liabilities derive from the unique nature of the business transacted by these insurers. Insurance premiums are collected in the present in order to pay insured losses in the future. Exchanging present dollars for a future promise creates certain obligations or liabilities for an insurer.

Loss reserves as of a certain date are, in theory, those amounts that would pay for all incurred and unsettled claims against the insurer. If losses were reported and paid for immediately, no loss reserves would exist. Since delays occur between the time the loss is incurred and when it is finally settled, loss reserves are necessary to properly recognize the insurer's current obligations. Reserves are established for losses that have been recorded in the statistical records of the insurance company but have not yet been paid and for losses that are estimated to have been incurred during the accounting period but have not been reported to the insurer. The liability for this second category of losses generally is referred to as the "incurred but not reported" (IBNR) reserve. Loss reserves are not established for losses that are expected to occur in the future; that is the function of the unearned premium reserve.

The unearned premium reserve results from the fact that the premium is collected at the beginning of the coverage period, but the

141

insurer is obligated to fulfill its performance throughout the entire term of the policy. While the premium has been received in full, it is not considered to be fully earned until the end of the coverage period. The total of all the unearned portions of premiums written by an insurer is represented by the unearned premium reserve. In theory, the unearned premium reserve represents the aggregate amount that an insurer would require in order to return to each insured the unearned portion of the premium in the event that the insurer decided to cancel all its contracts and retire from business.

A number of variables affect both loss reserves and unearned premium reserves. The type of insurance written (product mix) significantly affects loss reserves. The length of the policy term influences the size of the unearned premium reserve. Both loss reserves and unearned premium reserves can be calculated by a number of different methods. Due to the variations brought on by estimation problems, methodology, and unplanned events, both reserves may not necessarily be an appropriate or correct representation of an insurer's liabilities. A substantial portion of this chapter will be devoted to a discussion of the variables that affect these two key liabilities.

The owner's equity account of a property and liability insurance company is referred to as *policyholders' surplus*. This term may seem to be a misnomer, since the account in many cases (stock insurance companies) is a combination of capital stock and surplus. An explanation of the derivation of the term should clear up any misunderstanding.

The policyholders' surplus account is meant to act as a safety cushion for policyholders in the event that an insurer suffers adverse results in the various aspects of its insurance business. If an insurer were to become insolvent, policyholders could lose their unearned premiums, and, more seriously, they could find themselves without insurance protection for an outstanding property or liability claim. Thus, whether the owners' equity account is composed of capital and surplus, as in a stock company, or just surplus, as in a mutual insurer, in both cases the account acts to protect policyholders.

Four principal variables affect policyholders' surplus: (1) underwriting results, (2) investment performance, (3) loss reserve developments, and (4) growth through increases in the unearned premium reserve. The first two variables are discussed in other chapters. The latter two variables will be discussed in this chapter. Chapter 6 examines some of the legal requirements that influence the policyholders' surplus account.

This chapter will be divided into three main subject areas. The first covers loss reserves. The second discusses the unearned premium reserve. The final section is devoted to a discussion of the policyholders' surplus account.

LOSS RESERVES

General Concepts

Aggregate loss reserves are generally the largest and certainly the most important liability item on a property and liability insurer's balance sheet. Loss reserves of an insurer are, in theory, those amounts that would liquidate all unsettled claims against the insurer. These include not only those claims of which the insurer has knowledge but also unknown claims which will subsequently be reported.

Loss reserves are more important for some lines of insurance than others. In general, the so-called third-party lines produce larger loss reserves. These lines include auto bodily injury liability, workers' compensation, medical malpractice, and other bodily injury liability (e.g., products, premises, and umbrella). These lines of insurance typically cover liability situations that tend to result in longer periods of time between the occurrence of a claim and its final disposition. These longer time periods result from the fact that the injuries are to persons. While property damages can be determined in reasonably short periods of time, estimating various bodily injuries like permanent disabilities, long-term hospital confinements, and pain and suffering require relatively longer periods. Because of the extended time required before losses are ultimately settled, bodily injury liability lines of insurance commonly are referred to as "long tail" lines. Other insurance coverages that are relatively quick to settle are called "short tail" lines.

Even though losses are settled relatively quickly, loss reserves are set up for first-party lines (e.g., fire, allied lines, auto collision and comprehensive, burglary and theft, and marine) and property damage liability claims. With few exceptions, property losses are direct obligations of the insurer, with the claimant and insured being the same party. Typically, property losses are reported quickly and settlement is rapid. Even property damage liability claims are usually handled rapidly, as damages can be determined quickly and without complicating factors such as pain and suffering.

The financial strength of a property and liability insurer is dependent upon the status of its loss reserves. Serious under-reserving that results in inadequate loss reserves overstates the financial strength of an insurer and may lead to insolvency. Due to the importance of proper reserving, loss reserves are required by insurance regulatory law. State insurance departments (commissions) spend considerable effort in evaluating loss reserves in their periodic examinations of property and liability insurance companies.

Emphasis by state regulatory officials is on maintaining adequate loss reserves. Insurance commissioners would generally rather have the insurance company err on the side of over-reserving than under-reserving. Yet, this emphasis has limits, as excessive over-reserving may lead to unwarranted rate increases. In addition, tax authorities may become concerned and eventually assess penalties for over-reserving since artificially high loss reserve levels have the effect of deferring income recognition and related taxes.

It should be remembered that loss reserves are not cash or liquid asset funds. The aggregate loss reserve is a liability account—an accounting entry on the balance sheet—indicating a financial obligation of the insurance company. This liability is only as strong as those assets that offset the accounting entry. Thus, the proper valuation and stability of the insurer's assets are of critical importance, as was discussed in the previous chapter.

Methods of establishing loss reserves are discussed later in this chapter. Estimation of loss reserves is not strictly a process whereby actuaries, adjusters, and accountants plug numbers into some pre-determined formula. True, various quantitative methods are employed, yet subjective elements are often present. Sometimes a difficult reserving situation will have to be handled by an "educated guess." Top managerial input is usually included before a final figure for loss reserves is determined. The point to be made is that the estimation of loss reserves is a difficult process where quantitative techniques frequently have to be supplemented by subjective considerations and managerial judgment.

Whether or not loss reserves are properly estimated can be determined only over time. This can be accomplished by comparing loss reserves for a certain set of claims with the actual dollars that ultimately are paid for those claims in the future. It is impossible to say with certainty that the current loss reserves of an insurer represent the dollar amounts needed to settle the corresponding claims. The best indication of a company's current reserving proficiency is generally its record of past reserving. Various techniques, including schedules in the annual statement, can be used to measure past loss reserving performance. Some of the techniques will be discussed in later parts of this chapter.

Improper estimation of loss reserves, whether deliberate or by an error in methodology, will eventually affect the future financial condition of an insurer. When loss reserves are underestimated in a particular year, underwriting profits for that year will be overstated. As claims associated with these loss reserves are eventually settled, more monies will be required than were set aside in loss reserves. Consequently, underwriting profits in the future will be decreased due to under-reserving in the current year. Over-reserving produces precisely the opposite effect. When loss reserves are overestimated, current underwriting profits will be understated. As claims are settled, less monies than estimated will be required, and hence future underwriting profits will be increased. Underwriting profits and losses are channeled (via accounting entries) into the policyholders' surplus account. Thus, the process of incorrect estimation of loss reserves directly affects policyholders' surplus and consequently the financial strength of the insurance organization.

Because of the leeway a company has in settling loss reserves, a company experiencing poor financial results may tend to under-reserve. While this may improve their current reported financial position, additional losses will result in the future due to the under-reserving. Alternatively, a company experiencing favorable financial results may tend to over-reserve. While an insurer's estimation of loss reserves should in theory be totally independent of its financial performance, it would be naive to assume that the relationship is totally ignored by the management of an insurance organization.

In the estimation process, loss reserves are established to cover two areas: (1) claims that have been reported and are still in the process of adjustment, and (2) claims that have been incurred but not reported. The first area involves estimating the amount of dollars that may have to be paid. The second area requires estimating the number of claims as well as the dollar amount which may have to be paid for these claims. The various methods for estimating each of these types of loss reserves will be discussed in the following two sections.

Methods of Estimating Reported Loss Reserves

Before discussing the different methods of estimating reported loss reserves, definitions of various reporting periods need to be made. Three different cost accounting periods—calendar year, policy year, and accident year—are used by property and liability insurance companies. The calendar-year method of accounting is comparable to conventional accounting procedures used in most businesses. Each transaction is related to a particular calendar year in which it took place.

The policy-year method is unique to the insurance business. In this method, each transaction is related to the policy of insurance to which it applies. The aggregate transactions of all policies that become effective in a particular year determine the performance of these policies on a policy-year basis. The policy-year method is the only way an ultimate claims experience record can be obtained for a particular group of policies.

The accident-year method is also unique to the insurance business. In this method, each transaction is related to the year in which the accident (loss) occurred. Accident-year accounting is used to trace the ultimate cost of a group of accidents (losses) that occurred in a particular year. This method is used extensively in evaluating the historical development of loss reserves.

To illustrate how the three cost accounting methods are used, consider the following example. Suppose an insurer issued 200,000 one-year dwelling fire insurance policies that were effective July 1, 1975. During the coverage period, 6 percent of the insureds experienced an insured loss. Although losses occurred evenly throughout the year, there was a one-month delay between the occurrence of a fire and the time the loss was recorded by the insurance company in its statistical records. No other policies were issued in this line until the following July 1 when 220,000 new fire policies were issued and became effective. The new contracts experienced the same loss and reporting pattern as the initial block of policies. Once again, no new policies were sold until the following July 1, when 242,000 contracts were issued and became effective; the loss and reporting experience was identical to that of prior years. No new policies were issued in the dwelling fire line after July 1, 1977. It is further assumed that the insurer consistently understated the number of IBNR claims by 10 percent. Data for this example are shown in Table 3-1. These hypothetical numbers are claims counts only but could be converted to dollar figures by multiplying by an assumed average claim value.

Calendar-year reported claims can be determined by summing the columns in Table 3-1. In 1975, 5,000 claims were reported from policies issued during that year. The 12,500 claims reported for 1976 were from 1975 policies that continued into 1976 and from new 1976 policies. Similarly, 13,750 claims were reported in 1977, and 8,470 claims reports were made in 1978. In addition to calendar-year reported claims, the company would have to estimate the number of incurred but not reported claims in each calendar year. The fact that the estimate may be incorrect (as is true in this case) does not affect the method of allocating claims to cost accounting periods. Total claims incurred in a particular year equal reported claims, plus the number of IBNR claims at year-end, minus IBNR claims at the beginning of the year. Calendar-year total claims are shown in the last row of Table 3-1.

Table 3-1

Hypothetical Claims Count Data

Policy Effective Date	Year Claim Is Reported				Policy Year Total
	1975	1976	1977	1978	
1975	5,000	7,000	—	—	12,000
1976	—	5,500	7,700	—	13,200
1977	—	—	6,050	8,470	14,520
Calendar-year reported claims	5,000	12,500	13,750	8,470	39,720
Plus: ending IBNR estimate	900	990	1,089	0	2,979
Minus: beginning IBNR estimate	0	900	990	1,089	2,979
Calendar-year total claims	5,900	12,590	13,849	7,381	39,720

Policy-year claims can be determined from the table by summing across each row. All claims attributable to policies that took effect in July 1975 have been reported by the end of 1976. Therefore, the claims count for the 1975 policy year is 12,000; for 1976, the policy-year claims count is 13,200; and for 1977, the policy-year claims count is 14,520. Under this approach, claims developing in years subsequent to the effective date are assigned to the year in which the policy took effect. In this way, the total claims cost ultimately developed by a particular block of policies can be compared to the actual premium charged for these policies.

Accident-year claims are assigned to the year in which the accidents occur. Therefore, hindsight allows the 1,000 claims that occurred in 1975 but were not recorded until 1976 to be reassigned to the earlier period. The claims count for accident year 1975 is 6,000; in the 1976 accident year, 12,600 claims were incurred (6,000 from 1975 policies and 6,600 from 1976 policies); in the 1977 accident year, 13,860 claims were incurred (6,600 from 1976 policies and 7,260 from 1977 policies); and in 1978, 7,260 claims were incurred from policies effective July 1, 1977. Note that the inaccurate IBNR estimate that affected calendar-year loss data does not affect the ultimate accident-year claims count. Statistical data compiled on an accident year basis are important because they aid in tracing trends in loss data such as changes in claims frequency, inflationary influences on settlement costs, and so forth.

Accident-year claims data are often compared to earned premiums calculated on a calendar-year basis. For example, in the illustration used above, the 12,600 claims that had an accident date of January 1, 1976, through December 31, 1976, would be related to premiums earned in calendar-year 1976. This produces a calendar-accident-year data base for analyzing price adequacy.

With these definitions in mind, the discussion will turn to the various methods used to estimate reported loss reserves. In studying this section, the reader should keep in mind the general observations on loss reserves made in the previous section.

There are four principal methods used to set the value of reserves for known claims: (1) individual estimate method (claim-file reserves), (2) average value method, (3) loss ratio method (formula reserves), and (4) tabular value method. Numerous other methods exist, but these four approaches to reserve estimation, and combinations thereof, are the most generally applied procedures. As explained later, insurance companies sometimes are restricted in the choice of reserving method used for certain lines of business; in other lines they are free to select from among the general methods discussed here and any others that produce accurate results. Reserving procedures need not be mathematically complex, but they should facilitate statistical treatment so that reasonable confidence can be achieved. The insurance company's true liability for unpaid losses is the same regardless of the method chosen; the company's statisticians must select reserve valuation procedures that consistently result in close approximations of the true liability.

Individual Estimate Method As a part of the claim settlement process, insurance companies typically establish claim files in which all records relating to claims are maintained. When a loss is reported to the insurer, a reserve is calculated by field or home office claims personnel and entered in the claim file as the amount estimated to be adequate for settlement of the claim. These individual estimates are aggregated in the statistical records of the company and continuously revised for changes in the estimated amount needed to pay the claim. Individual estimates are based upon the judgment of adjusters and claims department officials who are responsible for settling the loss. This method can be used for any line of insurance, but it is most effective in situations where the claim is definite, the number of claims for a particular line is too small for reliable averages, or the variation in the amount of claims is too great to permit the use of averages. Thus, the individual estimate or claim file method of estimating loss reserve values may be most appropriate for property insurance and suretyship.

Average Value Method Aggregate reserves for a line of insurance can be based on the average value for claims of various types that have been, or may be, received by the insurer. This value usually is determined from the insurer's past experience on closed claims of different ages and categories and modified as necessary by actuarial projections of future payments. For each category this average is multiplied by the number of unsettled claims of the particular type on hand and the number estimated to have occurred but not yet reported. This method is used in varying degrees by insurance companies; some use it for smaller claims only, while others use it for a certain line, such as automobile physical damage claims. Still other companies may average reserve all claims for a given period of time, such as ninety days, and then individually estimate all claims remaining open after that time. The average value method is especially appropriate for estimating claim reserves for lines of business in which losses are settled quickly, claims are not subject to reopening, the number of outstanding claims is large, and the relative variation among loss amounts is small. If the frequency and severity of losses in a particular line are relatively stable or growing at a constant rate over time, the claims count and average costs can be stored and updated on computer files and aggregate reserve calculations generated automatically by data processing personnel.

Loss Ratio Method Ultimate losses for a particular line of insurance can be estimated by applying an assumed loss ratio to premiums earned during a selected period. Losses and loss adjustment expenses paid to date are then deducted from the ultimate loss figure to derive the current loss reserve. This method is known as the loss ratio or formula method and is the required approach for establishing minimum statutory loss reserves in certain lines of business. Specific steps taken to calculate loss ratio reserves are described later in this chapter.

The loss ratio method has the advantage of being simple to understand and economical to apply. However, this method is not widely applied because the formula approach results in inaccurate and somewhat arbitrary estimates of the true liability for losses. The assumed loss ratio often differs from the ratio of incurred losses to premiums earned actually experienced by the insurer.

Tabular Value Method This method is employed for certain types of claims in which the amount payable will depend upon the duration of life, the remarriage of the beneficiary, or some other contingency. Tabular reserves are established for claims involving total permanent disability, partial permanent but nondismembering disability, survivorship benefits, and the like. These types of reserves are called "tabular reserves" because probabilities of the contingencies upon which the length of benefit period depends are taken from mortality, morbidity, and remarriage tables.

Although this is the least used reserving method, its application is essential for setting reserves in those lines of insurance in which benefits are subject to tabular valuation. A specific table may be mandated in some states for use in determining certain reserves—for instance, the table of remarriage rates used to evaluate income benefits payable under workers' compensation insurance to a surviving spouse until remarriage.

Methods of Estimating
Incurred But Not Reported Loss Reserves

Insurance companies must provide a liability for claims that have already happened but have not been reported. As pointed out earlier, these unknown claims are called "incurred but not reported" (IBNR). The estimation process for IBNR reserves is much more complicated than the reserving process for reported losses because both the number and amount of the unreported claims must be estimated. Since the loss is unreported, there is obviously no indication of the basic nature or facts of the claim. Hence any estimation process involving individual case estimates is not possible.

IBNR reserves are usually estimated on the basis of past experience and then modified for current conditions, such as increased exposure, changed claim processing cutoff dates, rising claim costs, severity and frequency of recent claims, and so on. In sizable companies, the total number of IBNR claims may be great enough to permit a statistical approach based on a formula modified for the aforementioned factors. The formula basis is ordinarily used for normal losses only. Catastrophe and other large losses are excluded from experience statistics and separate estimates made.

The IBNR estimate should take into account company claim reporting practices and the anticipated effect of present conditions on the company's activities. It is not practical for companies to review, evaluate, and record reserves for every claim reported through December 31. A consistent processing cutoff date between years makes IBNR reserve developments more meaningful and reliable. Many companies end processing for the year on December 15 (assuming a December 31 year-end) and use the IBNR reserve to provide for two types of losses: (1) those reported but not recorded before year-end due to processing time limitations; and (2) those incurred but not reported at December 31.

Normal reporting delays for each type of loss and transfer delays between branches and the home office affect the IBNR reserve development. Exposure by line of insurance is an important consideration. Third-party bodily injury claims tend to produce the most difficult reserve estimation challenges.

Problems in estimating IBNR loss reserves recently have arisen in the area of medical malpractice insurance. As losses mounted in the medical malpractice area, insurers became more concerned with their IBNR loss reserve levels. Traditionally, medical malpractice insurance has been written on an occurrence basis. This means that the insurance company whose policy was in force when the mistreatment took place (not when it was discovered and a claim was made) is responsible for that claim. The classic example is the sponge which is left in the patient's body (mistreatment) and does not cause any discernible problems until years later when a claim is made. As medical malpractice losses soared, insurers reacted by substantially increasing their IBNR loss reserves. The amount of the increase was largely determined by managerial judgment rather than by statistical formula.

Since large IBNR cases occur sporadically, composition of the previous year's "reserve development" must be evaluated before it is used to predict the current reserve. Reserve development refers to changes in the estimated amount needed to settle incurred losses adjusted for loss payments. The term is quantified by adding reserves for losses incurred prior to the current year and still outstanding to payments made in the current year for losses incurred prior to the current year and then subtracting the previous year's loss reserve estimate. To evaluate reserves set in prior years, it may be necessary, for example, to separate the catastrophe and noncatastrophe losses in order to get a true picture of the previous year's actual development.

Present conditions play a significant part in establishing the IBNR loss reserves. The previous year's development should be modified to reflect:

- change in amount of premiums in force or units of exposure by line
- change in composition of premiums in force
- claim severity during the last quarter
- accident frequency for the quarter
- results of development over several previous years

Table 3-2

IBNR Reserves as a Percent of Paid Losses*

Coverage	Minimum	Maximum	Average
Fire	5%	19%	12%
Boiler and Machinery	0	255	48
Fidelity	35	109	76
General Liability (BI and PD)	44	148	85
Automobile Liability (BI and PD)	12	41	25
Workers' Compensation	19	48	30

* Reprinted with permission from Warren, McVeigh, Griffin, "Risk Management Notes: IBNR Reserves by Line," *Business Insurance*, 17 April 1978, p. 30.

Past experience, once modified, may then be used to compute percentages over some base that can be applied to the current year. The IBNR reserve can then be computed as a percentage of:

- premiums written during the period
- premiums in force at the end of the period
- earned premiums during the period
- incurred losses
- unpaid reported losses

It can also be related to the number of claims reported in a recent period. The important considerations are that the base chosen has proven to be reliable and that it is used consistently.

There is little uniformity in IBNR reserve estimates among insurance companies. A study of the IBNR reserves established by ten different insurers found substantial variations among the ratios of their unreported claims to paid losses. Results of the study are shown in Table 3-2. Three of the six coverage groups show average reserves for unknown claims equal to almost 50 percent or more of paid losses. Clearly, IBNR reserves can have a significant impact on an insurance company's financial position and operating results.

Evaluation of Loss Reserves

Since loss reserves are estimated, it is necessary to periodically evaluate the accuracy of the estimates. Certain exogenous variables, like inflation, can affect loss reserve development. In addition, the insurer may be deliberately manipulating loss reserve levels to adjust its reported financial status.

Numerous parties may be interested in the evaluation process. State insurance regulators, through periodic examinations, are able to closely analyze the adequacy of loss reserve levels. Their primary objective is to maintain solvency, so they are most concerned with companies whose reserves are inadequate. Although of less importance, regulators are also concerned with excessive loss reserving which may lead to unwarranted rate increases.

Reinsurers, particularly when they are deciding whether to assume an existing block of business, are most concerned with loss reserve adequacy. Company management is also interested in the development of their own loss reserves. Even though management can influence loss reserve levels, it is interested in the effects of exogenous variables as well as the ability of its technical people to accurately estimate reserves.

Accountants preparing independent audits of a property and liability firm test loss reserves. Tax authorities, concerned with deferred tax payments resulting from excessive over-reserving, may also examine loss reserves. Investors interested in the purchase of an insurer's common stock or control of the company might seek information on loss reserve practices. Finally, buyers of insurance, particularly sophisticated corporate buyers, may want data on loss reserve performance.

Evaluating the judgment of those who originally established loss reserves can be difficult. In the case of first-party claims, however, the evaluation is usually fairly simple. All policies for fire or similar type losses provide that when the policyholder presents proper proof of loss, the company will pay, within a reasonable time, up to the amount that the policy provides. Courts have decided that sixty to ninety days is usually a reasonable period of time, but generally these cases are settled within a few days or weeks. Since first-party claims usually involve physical damage to property, it is not too difficult to estimate the cost of settlement in advance by comparing available repair estimates to the claim amount. As a result, the evaluation of these claim reserves usually does not pose a difficult problem.

A third-party liability claim is an entirely different proposition. The insurance contract states that the insurance company will indemnify the claimants for damages for which the insured is legally liable under the terms of the policy. Two questions therefore arise: (1) Is the insured liable? and (2) What is the amount of liability?

Unlike property damage, where the extent of damage can be measured by a qualified adjuster, a precise estimate of the value of a bodily injury is not easily determined. This uncertainty as to whether or not liability attaches, together with the extent of damages is part of the nature of liability claims. Furthermore, in injury cases, a period of time may elapse before an individual realizes the extent of an injury. For instance, the claimant may submit a claim for a broken rib and then find that more serious internal injuries have developed. Ultimately, the adequacy or inadequacy of claim reserves is determined by developing and analyzing the reserves.

Workpapers that are used by outside auditors or insurance company management to develop and analyze loss reserves are designed to indicate any emerging trends. Analysis and interpretation of loss reserve developments require a great deal of informed judgment. Understanding the company's overall operating philosophy with respect to claim reserving and payment practices is essential.

In evaluating loss reserve developments, some key indicators as to the adequacy or inadequacy of loss reserves are:

- consistent shortages or savings on prior years' developments
- accident year loss ratios that are higher or lower than the company's previous experience
- average reported costs for an accident year that are higher or lower than the developed cost of prior accident-year reported claims

These indicators cannot be properly evaluated without first considering current trends and conditions such as:

- changes in company policy or practices
- expected inflationary trends
- anticipated leniency in court settlements, or legislated limits on the amount of the claim
- trends in average cost of settlement
- trends in average settlement period
- change in geographical exposure
- change in reinsurance treaties

In small companies, statistical analysis of claim reserves is usually not reliable because of the small volume of cases; and in new companies, historical data are simply not available. For these companies, the following actions are especially critical to the evaluation of reserve adequacy:

- Review of the method by which claim reserves are established.
- Study of the accident-year loss ratios to form an opinion on the expected loss ratio. Any major variance in loss ratio should be examined to determine the cause.
- Appraisal of the personnel involved in the overall management of the company. The claim department adjusters should also be appraised for their ability to establish loss reserves.
- Comparison of the company's experience with industry experience.

Whenever primary carriers experience reserve problems, it has been found that reinsurers assuming business from them encounter the same problem, only at a later date, because of the lag in receiving claim information. Therefore, assumed reinsurance contracts should be reviewed for trends in the reserve and reserving levels. If a company is assuming large amounts from another company, an attempt should be made to obtain the same type of statistical data as used for preparing loss reserve developments on direct business.

In the next two sections, techniques for evaluating loss reserves will be discussed. The first involves the use of various workpapers that develop information on the degree of past under- or over-reserving. The second section describes various development schedules present in the annual statement. Familiarity with these schedules will allow the reader to use them for testing loss reserve levels.

Workpapers The following set of workpapers normally will aid company management or outside parties to appraise the adequacy of the loss reserves carried at the annual statement date. There are many other excellent methods of appraising claim reserves; but in the absence of actuarial assistance, these workpapers will generally produce the desired results.

The statistical data necessary to develop these workpapers should be classified by coverage between direct and assumed business, net of applicable ceded reinsurance. Any change in the reinsurance program must be considered if the results are to be comparable from year to year.

Some general guidelines for completing the workpapers are:

- Losses paid should be segregated by reported year within the accident year.
- Salvage, subrogation, and reinsurance recoveries should be segregated for claims paid in prior years, indicating the date the claim was reported, the accident year, and the year the claim was paid. Recoveries on claims paid in the current year should be segregated the same as losses paid (by reported year within the accident year).

- Reported loss reserves at the end of the period must be processed the same as losses paid.
- Reported and IBNR claim reserves at the beginning of the period should be shown by accident year.
- Claim counts are required for loss reserves and for new claims reported during the year; they should be segregated by accident year.

Development of Reported Loss Reserves. The worksheet in Table 3-3 is for automobile bodily injury, general bodily injury, and workers' compensation claims. These lines are grouped together because they generally take a long time to settle and require very careful analysis to ensure the adequacy of their loss reserves. However, this worksheet could be used for all lines of business.

This table is prepared for reported claims only to study the overall averages established at the end of each accident year and to follow the claims to their ultimate cost. The current provision for unpaid claims is evaluated by comparing the average developed cost to date for each accident year. The trends are then used to predict the ultimate cost for each accident year.

The six categories of data presented in Table 3-3 provide the following information:

Item 1a. The number of claims in reserve at the end of the accident year is the number of claims still pending from among the claims reported during an accident year.

Item 1b, c, d. The number of claims still pending one year after the end of the accident year, and so forth.

Item 2. The cumulative loss payments are the sum of the amounts paid during the years following the accident year.

Item 3. The claim reserves, Items 3a, 3b, 3c, 3d, and 3e, represent the reserves in dollars outstanding at the end of each of the years indicated, beginning with the end of the accident year on claims outstanding as of that date. These amounts represent the aggregate of the reserves pertaining to the number of claims shown in Items 1a, 1b, 1c, 1d, and 1e.

Item 4. Cost represents the total cost to date of all reported claims pending at the end of the accident year. This is arrived at by combining the respective lines of Items 2 and 3.

Item 5. The savings or loss on development of loss reserves is the difference between Item 3a, the claim reserve at the end of the accident year, and the developed cost, Item 4, at the end of the respective year of development. Savings

Table 3-3

Development of Reported Loss Reserves by Accident Year

	Coverage: Auto Bodily Injury and Related Lines				
		Accident Year			
Item	1970	1971	1972	1973	1974
1. Number of claims in reserve at:					
a. End of accident year	151	154	160	180	211
b. One year later	113	108	101	114	
c. Two years later	69	59	76		
d. Three years later	51	43			
e. Four years later etc.	39				
2. Cumulative loss payments after:					
a. One year's development	$115,867	125,999	129,058	137,969	—
b. Two years' development	189,116	227,845	234,742		
c. Three years' development	256,324	271,883			
d. Four years' development etc.	299,978				
3. Claim reserves:					
a. At end of accident year	241,298	249,172	261,836	309,674	346,251
b. One year later	146,420	151,355	132,778	299,871	
c. Two years later	136,893	133,439	114,829		
d. Three years later	97,167	89,555			
e. Four years later	56,777				
4. Cost:					
a. At end of accident year (3a)	$241,298	249,172	261,836	309,674	346,251
b. One year later (2a + 3b)	262,287	277,354	261,836	437,840	
c. Two years later (2b + 3c)	326,009	361,284	349,571		
d. Three years later (2c + 3d)	353,491	361,438			
e. Four years later (2d + 3e)	356,755				
5. Savings (loss):					
a. At end of one year (3a − 4b)	$ (20,989)	(28,182)	—	(128,166)	—
b. At end of two years (3a − 4c)	(84,711)	(112,112)	(87,735)		
c. At end of three years (3a − 4d)	(112,193)	(112,266)			
d. At end of four years (3a − 4e)	(115,457)				
6. Average cost:					
a. At end of accident year (4a ÷ 1a)	$ 1,598	1,618	1,636	1,638	1,641
b. At end of one year (4b ÷ 1a)	1,737	1,801	1,636	2,317	
c. At end of two years (4c ÷ 1a)	2,159	2,346	2,185		
d. At end of three years (4d ÷ 1a)	2,341	2,347			
e. At end of four years (4e ÷ 1a)	2,363				

indicate that prior loss reserves were excessive. A loss indicates prior loss reserves were inadequate.

Item 6. Average cost represents the developed average cost of claims for the year-end outstanding claims and is obtained by dividing the totals on the respective lines in Item 4 by Item 1a.

Development of IBNR Reserves. The workpaper in Table 3-4, in addition to providing the amount of savings or loss in the provision for incurred but not reported claims, also provides information as to the length of time required to receive notice of all claims. Some companies

Table 3-4

Development of Incurred But Not Reported Loss Reserves by Accident Year

Coverage: Auto Bodily Injury and Related Lines

Item	Accident Year				
	1970	1971	1972	1973	1974
1. Total cumulative number of claims reported:					
a. One year later	29	31	28	33	
b. Two years later	37	37	35		
c. Three years later etc.	41	42			
2. Cumulative loss payments:					
a. At end of one year	$ 19,750	27,300	28,600	29,100	
b. At end of two years	43,100	51,900	47,800		
c. At end of three years	74,600	77,700			
d. At end of four years	89,000				
3. Loss reserves:					
a. At end of accident year (Initial IBNR)	$49,000	56,000	82,500	87,500	91,000
b. One year later	45,000	43,000	51,900	54,000	
c. Two years later	42,000	47,000	43,000		
d. Three years later	25,400	28,000			
e. Four years later	17,500				
4. Cost (2 + 3):					
a. At end of accident year (Initial IBNR)	$ 49,000	56,000	82,500	87,500	91,000
b. One year later (2a + 3b)	64,750	70,300	80,500	83,100	
c. Two years later (2b + 3c)	85,100	98,900	90,800		
d. Three years later (2c + 3d)	100,000	105,700			
e. Four years later	106,500				
5. Savings (loss):					
a. At end of one year (3a − 4b)	$(15,750)	(14,300)	2,000	4,400	
b. At end of two years (3a − 4c)	(36,100)	(42,900)	(8,300)		
c. At end of three years (3a − 4d)	(51,000)	(49,700)			
d. At end of four years (3a − 4e)	(57,500)				

treat reopened claims as IBNR claims; therefore, the evaluator should be aware of how the company treats such claims before interpreting the results derived from their analysis.

The developed cost data forms a basis for determining the IBNR claim provision. Data presented in Table 3-4 differ slightly from the information provided in Table 3-3. The following items are included in the analysis of IBNR reserve development:

Item 1. Total cumulative number of claims reported is the total count of all claims resulting from accidents during such accident year and reported subsequent to the end of the year.

Item 2. Cumulative loss payments is the amount of payments on claims reported in Item 1.

Item 3. The loss reserves, Items 3a, 3b, 3c, 3d, and 3e, represent the reserves outstanding at the end of the years indicated, beginning with the end of the accident year. In many cases, especially in the liability lines, losses are reported more than one year after the accident year. Therefore, the loss reserve in years subsequent to the accident year might include a provision for additional IBNR in addition to the claims already reported.

Item 4. Cost represents the total of the respective lines of Items 2 and 3.

Item 5. The savings or losses on loss reserves is the difference between Item 3a, the loss reserve at the end of the accident year, and the cost to date, Item 4, at the end of the respective year of development. Again this is the key item indicating the degree of over-reserving or under-reserving.

Analyzing reserve development along the lines illustrated in these working papers provides a retrospective test of an insurer's reserving practices. Because loss reserves typically are the largest liability on a property and liability insurance company's balance sheet, being able to judge the accuracy with which these reserves are estimated is essential to proper evaluation of the company. The annual statement contains schedules that, although not identical, are similar to the working papers illustrated in Tables 3-3 and 3-4.

Annual Statement Development Schedules The annual statement contains four schedules relating to loss reserve adequacy. Schedule G covers the reserves and development of fidelity and surety losses; Schedule K covers reserves for credit losses; Schedule O shows the development of loss reserves other than those covered in Schedule P; Schedule P shows the reserves, experience, and development of bodily injury, workers' compensation losses, package policies, ocean marine, aircraft, and boiler and machinery.

The annual statement development schedules are one of the primary tools used by state insurance department (commission) officials in examining an insurer's loss reserve adequacy. Many of the schedules are quite detailed and require a laborious effort for proper analysis. This section offers the reader guidelines as to the more relevant portions of the schedules. Only Schedule O and Schedule P will be discussed, since they are the two key loss reserve development schedules.

Schedule O. This schedule basically covers first-party property lines of insurance. As mentioned previously, these lines of insurance tend to be settled more quickly. Schedule O requires information on payments during the year, plus liabilities at the current year-end for claims unpaid at the close of the last two previous calendar years. Calculation of the development requires sorting losses paid, salvage, reinsurance, and unpaid claims as follows:

- Incurred in the current year
- Incurred in the previous year
- Incurred in the second prior year

A review of Schedule O in a 1976 annual statement would give a one-year development of the reserves carried at December 31, 1975, and a two-year development of reserves carried at December 31, 1974. Because most claims treated in Schedule O are settled within twenty-four months, the two-year development is adequate for an accurate evaluation of reserves for these lines of insurance.

The deficiency in Schedule O is that it is a "catch-all." It tests the overall accuracy of the combined loss reserve provided by the adjusters for individual reported cases and the reserve for incurred but not reported losses. It does not test each one of them separately.

A copy of Schedule O from the 1976 annual statement is included in the appendix of this text. The column headings are reasonably self-explanatory. The reader might find it useful to examine the development of losses and loss reserves. For purposes of analysis, the reader should be directed to the final two columns, 18 and 19. Column 18 shows the difference between columns 14 and 16, i.e., the difference between the loss reserve established at the end of the previous year and the actual development of the claims associated with that loss reserve. A positive number in column 18 indicates that actual loss development exceeded the loss reserve of the previous year; i.e., the loss reserve was inadequate. A negative number in column 18 indicates that actual loss development was less than the loss reserve of the previous year; i.e., the loss reserve was excessive.

Column 19 is similar, except that it compares the loss reserve of two years ago with actual development of claims associated with that loss reserve. Again, a positive number indicates that the company was under-reserved for this particular set of claims. A negative number indicates that the company was over-reserved for this set of claims.

A brief examination of columns 18 and 19 in Schedule O indicates the extent of over- or under-reserving for the last two years by line of insurance. Since the first-party lines of insurance in Schedule O are settled without much delay, this schedule gives an accurate picture of loss reserve development for these lines. Unfortunately, a company's main loss reserving problems are concentrated in the third-party lines, namely, bodily injury liability insurance. An entire schedule, Schedule P, has been constructed specifically for these lines.

Schedule P. Schedule P is considered to be the most important loss reserve development schedule in the annual statement. It is the development schedule used for those lines omitted from Schedule O: auto liability, other liability, workers' compensation, package policies, ocean marine, aircraft, and boiler and machinery. These lines are developed separately because it normally takes longer to settle these claims than it does for those lines included in Schedule O. A minimum reserve is required for claims occurring in the most recent three years, since it is assumed to take at least three years to estimate adequate reserves. The computation of the minimum reserve is explained later in this chapter.

Schedule P consists of three parts, the first of which is the cumulative loss experience by accident year and is the basis used to determine the minimum statutory reserve. The second part shows the historical development of the incurred losses, and the third part compares the claims settling experience of the last seven accident years.

PART 1.   This schedule consists of:

> Part 1A—Auto Liability including Property Damage
> Part 1B—Other Liability including Property Damage
> Part 1C—Medical Malpractice
> Part 1D—Workers' Compensation
> Part 1E—Farmowners Multiple Peril, Homeowners Multiple Peril, Commercial Multiple Peril, Ocean Marine, Aircraft, and Boiler and Machinery
> Part 1F —Incurred But Not Reported Losses

Prior to 1969 Schedule P was prepared on a policy-year basis. In 1969 a change was initiated using accident-year data for losses and loss expenses while premiums were to be reported on a calendar-year basis. The effect of the change to the accident-year basis was to incorporate data into Schedule P beginning in 1969 on the accident-year basis and to continue to use the policy-year basis for prior years. Therefore, in the 1970 annual statement, accident-year data were used only for the 1969 and 1970 years. Since Schedule P Part 1 includes data for eight individual years, there is no policy-year data after 1975. Each part, except 1F, contains common information for each line of insurance.

Column 1 shows the years in which premiums were earned and losses were incurred. Column 2 shows the amounts of earned premiums. The premiums earned for the current year are entered from the corresponding lines of business in column 4, Part 2.

A mutual or a participating company may load its premiums for the specific purpose of paying predetermined dividends. Such a company files with the state insurance department a statement specifying the amount of the loading. It may deduct this loading from the earned premiums for the calendar years involved.

Column 3 is obtained by adding to the prior year's column 3 the net losses paid as shown in the applicable lines in column 6, Part 3 of the

Underwriting and Investment Exhibit of the annual statement. Loss payments should comprise all payments for indemnities, including first aid and medical attention.

Columns 4, 4a, 5, and 5a account for the liability loss expense payments. Column 4 shows the payments for allocated loss expenses. Allocated loss expenses are expenses incurred in connection with specific claims. In other words, they are identified on the records as direct expenses in connection with the settlement, negotiation, or adjustment of a specific claim. As with loss payments, allocated loss expense payments during any calendar year may pertain to a number of accident years. Each such payment must be allocated to the proper accident year. Companies keep records for allocating the loss adjustment expenses by accident years similar to those records kept for allocating liability loss payments to accident years.

Column 4a shows the percentage of allocated expenses to losses paid, by accident year. These percentages help in deciding whether the reserve is large enough to cover adjusting expenses. Allocated adjusting expenses are generally paid after the claims are settled. Normally, attorneys' fees, adjusting fees, and so forth, are not billed and so are not paid until after the claims are settled.

Column 5 shows a breakdown by accident year of the unallocated loss adjustment expenses. These are expenses incurred in connection with investigation and adjustment of claims that cannot be directly allocated to any specific claims. These expenses include the general overhead of maintaining a claims department in companies that do not adjust their own claims but contract the adjustment to bureaus or independent adjusters. They also include all costs of claims adjustment in companies that adjust claims through their own claims adjustment offices where salaried employees handle the adjustment of claims. In these latter companies, the bulk of loss adjustment expense will be unallocated. In the companies that use independent adjusters or adjustment bureaus, the reverse will be true.

The unallocated portion of adjustment expense must be allocated by accident year. Companies may have their own methods of allocation for management statistical reports. The method of allocation by accident year for the annual statement is prescribed in Schedule P Part 1 of the annual statement.

The breakdown for unallocated loss expense between lines of coverage varies with each company. The uniform accounting instructions that are discussed in Chapter 4 of this text deal with the various methods of allocating expenses by line of insurance.

Column 5a gives the percentage of the unallocated loss expenses paid to losses paid. This is inserted for the same purpose as the percentage of allocated expenses to losses paid in column 4a. However, the validity of this analysis is not as apparent as that of the allocated expenses because of the arbitrary uniform method of allocation for this type of expense.

Column 6 shows the totals of the figures for each accident year in columns 3, 4, and 5 (the total loss and loss expense payments). Column 7 gives the percentage of the total payments as indicated in column 6 to premiums earned as shown in column 2. This indicates the percentage of earned premiums used to pay loss costs to date. This is the final loss ratio for those years in which all claims have been liquidated.

Column 8 shows the number of claims outstanding. Column 9 shows the total estimated reserve for liability losses. This includes a reserve for losses incurred but not reported allocated by accident year. The total of column 9 must equal the respective lines of column 5 of Part 3A of the Underwriting and Investment Exhibit of the annual statement. The same estimates will eventually be included in the total loss reserve entry as the main liability item in the insurer's balance sheet.

Column 10 shows the total estimated reserve for loss expenses relating to the estimated reserve for liability losses shown in column 9. This includes a reserve for loss adjusting expenses on claims incurred but not reported. The total of column 10 must equal the respective lines in column 6 of Part 3A of the Underwriting and Investment Exhibit of the annual statement.

Column 11 shows the total of losses and loss expenses incurred by accident year. This is the total of columns 6, 9, and 10 (the total of all payments plus the estimated liability on claims still outstanding).

Column 12 shows the loss ratios by accident year. These are the ratios of the losses in column 11 to the premiums earned in column 2.

Parts 1A, 1B, 1C, and 1D involve a computation of excess of statutory reserves over statement reserves. Any reserve resulting from these computations is recorded on line 16, excess of statutory reserves over statement reserves, on the balance sheet. The charge or credit is recorded as a surplus adjustment and is not reflected in the income statement.

The computation is made separately for each part, as follows: the percentage used should be 60 percent if fewer than three of the five years immediately prior to the most recent three years have at least $1 million of earned premiums reported in column 2. In other cases the percentage used should be the lowest ratio reported in column 12 for any of the five years immediately prior to the most recent three years which have at least $1 million reported in column 2, but not less than 60 percent nor more than 75 percent (not less than 65 percent for workers' compensation).

The computation is made for the most recent three calendar years.

Table 3-5

Schedule P—Loss Ratio Development

Accident Year	Premiums Earned Column 2	Ratio Column 12
1969	$ 302,000	54.7%
1970	546,000	77.4
1971	1,337,000	69.5
1972	1,095,000	88.0
1973	1,370,000	69.7
1974	1,237,000	72.7
1975	1,653,000	62.3
1976	1,945,000	60.4

Table 3-6

Schedule P—Excess Statutory Loss Reserves

	Premiums Earned	Ratio	Amount	Total Losses and Expenses Incurred Column 11	Excess Reserve
1974	$1,237,000	69.5%	$ 859,715	$ 899,306	—
1975	1,653,000	69.5	1,148,835	1,029,418	$119,417
1976	1,945,000	69.5	1,351,775	1,175,699	176,076
					$295,493

This is based on the assumption that the company's reserves are not reliable until they have matured at least three years. An example of information found in Schedule P and used in the calculation is shown in Table 3-5.

Premium volume is over $1 million for three of the five years immediately prior to the most recent three years. The lowest ratio with premiums earned in excess of $1 million was 69.5 percent in 1971. Calculation of excess reserves is shown in Table 3-6.

PART 1F. This section shows the provision for incurred but not reported losses at the end of the most recent year allocated by accident year for Parts A through E. It also shows a one-year development of the IBNR losses included in losses paid, column 3, and losses unpaid, column 9, of Parts A through E. The amounts are subtracted from the last year's provision to determine the degree to which the previous year's IBNR reserve was under- or over-reserved.

PART 2. This part shows the separate development of incurred losses from Parts 1A through 1E. The left-hand column of this schedule gives the accident years for which reports are required. The rest of the schedule consists of six columns headed "Incurred Losses and Loss Expense Reported at End of Year" and six columns headed "Incurred Loss and Loss Expense Ratio Reported." Each column head is one of the six calendar years involved. Each of these columns shows the cost to date of the losses and loss expenses incurred to the end of each of these years (from column 11 of Part 1).

An example should be most helpful here. The appendix of this text contains Part 2 of Schedule P. Suppose estimated auto liability losses and loss expenses for accident year 1971 reported at the end of calendar year 1971 were $17,473,000. This incurred figure is composed of paid losses and expenses and a loss reserve for unpaid losses and expenses. Since the claims are quite recent, a considerable portion of this incurred figure will be composed of the loss reserve. As claims of accident year 1971 are paid in calendar year 1972, the paid figure will increase and the loss reserve will decrease. If the increase in the paid figure precisely equals the decrease in the loss reserve, the losses and expenses incurred figure at the end of calendar year 1972 will be the same as the corresponding figure at the end of 1971. This means loss reserves associated with claims paid in 1972 were perfectly accurate. Of course this rarely happens.

The more common situation will produce a loss and expense incurred figure at the end of 1972 which is smaller or larger than the incurred figure estimated at the end of 1971. A larger incurred amount means that paid losses in that year exceeded the corresponding decrease in loss reserves; i.e., loss reserves were inadequate. A smaller incurred amount means that paid losses in that year were less than the corresponding loss reserve decrease; i.e., loss reserves were excessive.

As one moves to the right for a particular accident year, more claims are settled and the incurred figure is comprised more of paid losses and expenses and less of loss reserves. Thus, the incurred figure becomes more precise, with a lesser degree of estimation. The incurred loss and expense figure for accident year 1971 at the end of the most recent calendar year is $18,600,000. This indicates that the loss reserves for accident year 1971 established at the end of calendar year 1971 were under-reserved by an amount equal to $1,127,000 ($18,600,000 − $17,473,000). Using this schedule, the loss reserves for any particular accident year can be evaluated as of the most current calendar year.

This process can be accomplished by line of insurance for those lines included within Schedule P.

PART 3.   This schedule is divided into six parts: a Part 3 Summary; Auto Liability, 3A; Other Liability, 3B; Medical Malpractice, 3C; Workers' Compensation, 3D; and package policies and certain other lines, 3E. This schedule shows for each of the five lines the calendar-year premiums earned and the accident-year loss and loss expenses incurred, and the ratio of the loss and loss expenses incurred to premiums earned. It also breaks down the loss and loss expenses incurred between paid and unpaid losses and expenses and shows the ratio of each to earned premiums.

The schedule is designed to relate the losses and loss expenses incurred on policies to the year in which the premiums were earned. The incurred figures are those that were developed in Part 2 of Schedule P. The result shows the percent of each dollar of earned premium required to pay claims and claim expenses and the relationship of unpaid losses and loss expenses to total incurred losses and loss expenses for five years. Since, as more time elapses, more of the claim and claim expense reserves have been closed by payment, a more precise estimate of incurred claim and claim expenses is provided. As a result, one is able to use this schedule as an analytical tool to compare the ratios of the most recent years with those of earlier years for which the reserves should be more reliable.

As a tool to help evaluate the loss reserves currently provided, Schedule P has its defects. It is weakened because it combines coverages (such as bodily injury with property damage) and because it combines loss and loss expense experience for both reported claims and claims incurred but not reported. Nevertheless, both Schedules O and P are important and widely used tools in appraising loss reserves. The user, however, must be aware of their limitations. The schedules do not provide information to study trends in average cost or average reserves pending, and they do not provide a breakdown between the cost of reported claims and claims incurred but not reported.

Loss Adjustment Expense Reserves

Loss adjustment expense reserves are established to cover all future expenses required to investigate and settle claims already incurred but not paid, whether reported or not. There are two types of loss adjustment expenses, allocated and unallocated. Allocated loss expenses are those which can be allocated to a specific claim, such as legal fees and outside claims adjusters' fees. Unallocated loss expenses are those which cannot be allocated to a specific claim, such as salaries and rent.

Different methods are used to set the reserves for allocated and unallocated loss adjustment expenses.

The relation of allocated to unallocated adjustment expense varies with the company and methods of adjusting. Some companies will have a minimum of allocated expenses and a maximum of unallocated expenses. Some will not allow anyone but their own salaried employees to adjust their claims unless absolutely unavoidable; for example, company adjusters cannot be used when an accident or loss is reported in some distant territory where it is cheaper to hire a local adjuster on a contract basis. Others will not hire any staff for adjusting purposes but will handle every claim through adjustment bureaus or independent adjusters.

Some companies still include allocated loss adjustment expenses in the estimates on the open claims. For instance, when they set up a reserve for a claim, they may estimate the claim will cost $1,000 plus $100 for the independent adjusting. Therefore, the reserve is set at $1,100.

The better practice, which today is followed by most companies, is to keep claim reserves and adjustment expense reserves separately. The reserves for allocated and unallocated loss adjustment expenses are usually determined separately. Allocated expense reserves might be determined on a case basis or by a study of the relationship of allocated loss expenses paid to losses paid. Unallocated loss expense reserves are usually based on time studies or on a relationship of unallocated loss expenses paid to losses paid.

Since allocated loss expense payments are chargeable to specific claims, individual payments can be recorded in the same detail as the claims themselves. The coverage, class of risk, accident date, reported date, state territory, and so forth can all be pinpointed. It follows that any method used to establish or test loss reserves can also be used to establish or test allocated loss expense reserves.

In the next two sections, methods for establishing and evaluating reserves for allocated loss adjustment expenses and unallocated loss adjustment expenses will be discussed. Although these are important topics, the reader should be aware that reserves for losses are more significant than reserves for loss adjustment expenses. In terms of absolute amounts, reserves for loss adjustment expenses are a small percentage of total loss reserves (5 to 20 percent depending on the business mix). In addition, estimating amounts needed for loss adjustment expenses is generally easier than estimating amounts needed for losses.

Allocated Loss Adjustment Expense Reserves Two ways are used to determine allocated loss adjustment expense reserves: the case basis and the formula basis. When using the case basis, the claims adjuster reviews the claims file and determines what the reserve for allocated loss expenses should be. Most companies, however, determine the reserves on a formula basis.

Over the years formula reserves have been calculated by a calendar-year "paid-to-paid" method. This approach involves calculating the ratio of allocated loss expenses paid to losses paid by line. Frequently, this ratio is averaged over a period of three years in order to reduce the impact of yearly fluctuations in the ratio. The ratio is then multiplied by the reserve for losses to obtain the reserve for allocated loss expenses. Frequently, the ratio is multiplied by the entire IBNR loss reserve and 50 percent of the reported loss reserves, using the theory that, on the average, one-half of the allocated loss expenses have already been paid on reported claims.

In the past few years the problem of computing adequate loss adjustment expense reserves has received much attention. A review of state examiners' reports indicates a significant increase in the number of adjustments for deficiencies in such reserves. The calendar-year "paid-to-paid" method of calculating reserves generally results in an understatement, because the method is based on the assumption that each paid loss carries with it the same ratio of allocated adjustment expense regardless of how long it has remained unsettled. Actually, this does not always occur, particularly on the Schedule P lines of business. These lines can incur expensive litigation costs over many years before all claims are settled.

Generally, a large number of claims are paid within one or two years of the accident, with little or no related attorneys' fees or costs. On the other hand, the insurance company may resist an unreasonable claim in court over a period of several years. If the company wins the case, it will pay no loss, but it will have paid substantial attorneys' fees and court costs. It is this type of settlement that causes the difficulty in estimating the loss adjustment expense reserves. The pending loss reserve tends to consist of proportionately more claims that will involve costly loss adjustment expenses than the whole population of claims settled in a calendar year.

The calendar-year paid-to-paid method of calculating allocated loss adjustment expense reserves is likely to result in an inadequate provision for this liability. It is therefore quite important that the development of prior years' reserves be closely reviewed as a check on the adequacy of the reserves. The need to review reserve developments of prior years' reserves is more significant for companies writing liability lines than for those writing primarily property lines on which claims tend to be settled more quickly. If a company establishes allocated loss expense reserves on a calendar-year paid-to-paid basis and a development of prior years' reserves shows this produces inadequate reserves, a change in method is both appropriate and prudent.

Unallocated Loss Adjustment Expense Reserves Unallocated loss adjustment expenses (ULAE) are generally defined as those expenses connected with the adjustment and recording of policy claims that cannot be related to specific claims. Although a company's employees may do work that could theoretically be related to specific claims, the statutory rules require that salaries paid to employees be treated as an unallocated loss adjustment expense. A reserve for unallocated loss adjustment expenses is required by statutory accounting practices and is currently provided for under generally accepted accounting principles as well.

A common method used to calculate the reserve for ULAE is to relate the paid ULAE to paid losses for a prior period or periods (often a three- or five-year average) and to apply the developed ratios to unpaid losses at the statement date. This method is based on two assumptions which are generally recognized in the industry:

1. The ratio of unallocated loss adjustment expenses paid to paid losses applies to any loss, regardless of how long it has been in the loss reserve. In other words, all claims carry with them a percentage of the unallocated adjustment expense, and this percentage is applicable to all claims. Thus, the calendar-year paid-to-paid ratio is applicable to all claims as far as unallocated loss expenses are concerned.
2. A substantial amount of the unallocated expenses for a particular claim is expended when the claim is first reported, and the remainder is expended when the claim is closed. Accordingly, the ratio developed is reduced by the estimated portion of ULAE expended when a loss is set up; this is usually 50 percent when applied to unpaid reported losses, and the full ratio is applied to IBNR reserves.

While 50 percent is the most common estimate of the portion of ULAE incurred when a claim is set up, the actual percentage will vary by company and by line of business. For example, the unpaid ULAE for a workers' compensation claim will probably be less than 50 percent since a large reserve is often established for related monthly payments which incur very little expense.

The current ratio of paid ULAE to paid losses is usually sufficient for providing the ULAE reserve for reported losses for Schedule O lines which are usually settled in a relatively short period. The trend of the ratio, however, should be reviewed for the IBNR calculation and Schedule P lines, since the ratio in future periods will be applied to all outstanding claims regardless of the incurred date or reported date of the claim. If the ratio of the paid ULAE to paid losses is increasing, the ULAE reserve based on the current ratio would not be adequate. This would have particular significance to IBNR claims since the full ratio of future periods will be applied to such claims when reported.

While the ratio method discussed above is probably the most common method, other more sophisticated methods are also used. One such method is the payment projection method, which is based on studies to determine (1) what percent of ULAE paid in a calendar year is applicable to a particular accident year, and (2) what percent of the total ULAE to be paid for a particular accident year has been paid to date.

By definition, developments cannot be used to test the adequacy of unallocated loss adjustment expense reserves. The adequacy of the reserve for unallocated loss adjustment expenses depends primarily on the use of sound cost accounting and expense allocation methods, as well as the proper method of calculating the reserve.

Insurance companies classify their expenses in accordance with uniform procedures set forth in Regulation 30 of the New York Department of Insurance and adopted by other states. All expenses are classified into twenty-one major expense categories, such as advertising, salaries, employee health and welfare, travel, taxes, director fees, etc. The expenses are further broken down into five functional areas: (1) investment expenses; (2) loss adjustment expenses; (3) acquisition field supervision and collection expenses; (4) taxes; and (5) general expenses.

Because the way the company allocates its expenses will have an impact on the calculation of the unallocated loss adjustment expense reserve, company management and outside auditors periodically review the basis of allocation. Questions such as the following assist the review of the expense allocation:

1. Who was responsible for developing the allocation methods?

2. When were these methods developed?

3. Has the company's mode of operation changed since the methods were developed?

4. Has the increase or decrease in volume been considered since the methods were developed?

5. Were interdepartmental services considered in arriving at total departmental cost?

6. How was company overhead allocated to department?

7. Was officers' compensation distributed logically?

8. Were the bases used to distribute costs truly indicative of the operation?

In addition to being satisfied as to the reasonableness of the costs assigned to the loss adjustment expense classification, we must also be satisfied with the accuracy of the distribution of unallocated loss adjustment expenses by coverage. The best way to distribute unallocated loss adjustment expenses to coverages is to determine the unit cost involved each time a claim file is reviewed. Ideally, this would involve conducting time studies to determine the time spent in handling claims, although in practice such time studies are rare.

While, as indicated above, the adequacy of the ULAE reserve cannot be tested retrospectively, it is included in the Schedule P development. Schedule P requires 50 percent of the ULAE paid during the year to be allocated to losses paid during the year and 50 percent to losses reported during the year. The 50 percent allocated to paid losses is distributed to accident years in direct proportion to the amount of losses paid. Of the 50 percent allocated to losses reported during the year, 45 percent is allocated to the current accident year, and 5 percent is allocated to the next most recent year on the theory that 10 percent of all claims reported in a year were incurred in the previous year (IBNR). In accordance with this calculation, it is estimated that 5 percent of the ULAE to be paid in the next year will be attributable to IBNR claims. Some companies will attempt to calculate the ULAE reserve to meet the Schedule P test. To accomplish this, the reserve established will be the sum of 50 percent of the paid ULAE to paid loss ratio times the total estimated liability for unpaid losses plus 5 percent of the unexpected ULAE to be paid in the following year.

The purpose of the ULAE reserve is to set aside a large enough amount to cover the costs of all services (other than those classified as allocated loss expenses) that are necessary for liquidating the company's entire liability associated with unsettled claims as of the statement date. While many methods can be used, it is essential that the established ULAE reserve be adequate.

UNEARNED PREMIUM RESERVE

The unearned premium typically approximates one-third of the total liabilities in a property and liability insurance company's balance sheet. This liability represents, at least in theory, the aggregate amount a carrier would need to return the unearned portion of the premium of each policy in force to each policyholder should the carrier go out of business and cancel all outstanding policies as of a given date. Assuming policies are in force, the unearned premium may be thought of as that amount required to provide for losses and expenses during the unexpired term of the policy.

The insurance contract permits either the company or the policyholder to terminate the insurance coverage at any time. Once a policy is canceled, the company must return the unexpired portion of the premium. If the company cancels the policy, the return premium must equal the pro rata portion of the unexpired premium. If the policyholder cancels, the company uses a formula to calculate a return premium which is somewhat less than the pro rata portion of the premium in order to recover initial expenses. This is sometimes called the "short rate" method of cancellation.

Since it would be too expensive to compute the unearned premium of each policy as of the financial statement date, companies employ approximation methods that produce reasonably accurate aggregate reserves. The first step in calculating this liability is to develop the "premiums in force" figure which serves as the source for the computation. Premiums in force is a total of all policies in force as of a certain date, since each new policy is automatically placed in premiums in force and remains there until it expires or is canceled.

Every policy is segregated in the in-force record according to its term and expiration date. At any financial statement date, the in-force record is tabulated by policy term (six months, twelve months, eighteen months, two years, and so forth) and by month and year of expiration. This facilitates the application of fractions or percentages to the various group totals to determine the unearned portion. The sum of the group calculation represents the total liability for unearned premiums. The Underwriting and Investment Exhibit (Part 2) in the annual statement displays the summarized information and the final calculations for the total unearned premium reserve.

Methods of Calculating the Unearned Premium Reserve

A number of different methods are used in calculating the unearned premium reserve. Special methods exist for handling installment and retrospective premiums. The methods will be described in the following sections.

Monthly Pro Rata Method Because so many transactions are involved, determining the exact amount of unearned premium on each policy in force would be costly and impractical. For this reason a simplified method, the monthly pro rata method, is commonly used. This method assumes that the statistical average of a large number of policies that provide identical coverage yields an unearned premium not materially different from the combined results of individual computations. Many states now insist on the monthly pro rata method since it is generally more accurate than the annual pro rata method, which assumes that all policies are written evenly throughout the year.

The monthly pro rata method of calculating unearned premiums assumes that, on the average, the same amount of business is written each day of the month. Consequently, it is assumed that the effective date for the premiums written during the month will be the fifteenth day. Thus, the year is divided into twenty-four half months. At the end of the month, one twenty-fourth (1/24) of the month's writing will have been earned on policies written for a one-year term and twenty-three twenty-fourths (23/24) will be unearned. If the policy was written for a three-year term, one seventy-second (1/72) would be earned and the unearned premium would be seventy-one seventy-seconds (71/72) of the month's in-force premiums. If the policy was written for a six-month term, one-twelfth (1/12) would be earned and the unearned premium would be eleven-twelfths (11/12) of the month's in-force premium. An important point to note is that the longer the policy term, the greater the size of the unearned premium reserve at the end of the period in which the premiums were written.

Daily Method The daily method of calculating unearned premiums is based on the exact number of days the policy is in force. This method has not been widely used, as the day of expiration is generally not included in the premiums in force statistical data and because additional computer capacity is required. The formula is the unexpired number of days remaining divided by the days in the period, multiplied by the premiums in force.

For a company writing personal lines, the difference in unearned premiums resulting from changing to a daily pro rata method from the monthly pro rata probably would not be significant since these policies are usually written evenly throughout the month. For a company writing commercial lines, however, the change could substantially reduce the unearned premiums since these policies are often effective the first of the month.

Retrospective Premiums A retrospectively rated insurance policy is one for which the premium is adjusted at the end of the coverage period to reflect the insured's loss experience during the policy term. The current year's experience determines the year's premium within predetermined maximum and minimum limits. An initial premium is due at the beginning of the year, and the final cost is fixed after the policy term has expired. Retrospective rating is used for workers' compensation, general liability, automobile liability, automobile physical damage, burglary, and glass insurance.

Retrospectively rated policies generally are written for an annual term; the premium deposit is fully earned by the end of the year. It is not a final premium so the insurance company may make either an additional charge or a refund, depending on whether the actual cost proves to be more or less than the originally estimated cost. This additional charge or credit may take the form of either (1) an increase or reduction in the subsequent premium, or (2) an actual invoice to the policyholder or a refund by the insurance company. Whichever form it takes, the refunds must be recognized by being included in the reserve for unearned premiums.

Statutory insurance accounting principles require that an amount be established in the unearned premium liability for any rate credits or return premiums due the policyholder. Either of two methods may be used to compute this liability. The first method develops a ratio of retrospective return premiums to earned standard premiums by analyzing each line of insurance over past policy years. The standard premium is the premium based on the insured's experience rate, with allowance for the appropriate premium discount. This ratio of return-to-earned standard premiums is applied to the earned standard premiums currently in force for which the current year's retrospective calculation has not been made. This results in the required unearned premium for liability return premiums in the particular line of insurance.

The second method used to determine unearned premium credits considers each retrospectively rated exposure separately. The basic premium, losses, loss conversion factor, and premium tax multiplier for each exposure are used to arrive at an estimate of the return premium due the insured. Although highly accurate estimates can be obtained by use of this method, it is impractical if more than a small number of policies are involved.

Not all retrospectively rated exposures receive rate credits at the end of the policy term; upward adjustments are made subject to predetermined maximum limits if the insured's loss experience during the term has been adverse. Insurance companies may not currently recognize any anticipated additional charge on in-force policies that are subject to retrospective rating. Any additional "retrospective charge," when made, will be a premium invoice on a policy that already has expired. This charge is not considered to be an admitted asset.

Installment Premiums Installment premiums on policies with terms of more than one year are generally treated as successive one-year policies. Thus a three-year policy in equal annual installments is entered as if it were three one-year policies.

Audit Premiums Audit premiums are obtained through an examination of the insured's books or other records to determine the premium due the insurance company for protection furnished. Since the protection has been furnished, such premiums are considered earned when recorded by the company. Policies written on workers' compensation and certain general liability lines of business commonly have audits made because the exposure base on many of these policies is not known at the time the policy is written. These policies usually include a deposit premium and provide for monthly, quarterly, or semi-annual audit premiums in addition to a final audit premium after the policy expires. Audit premiums are based on reports prepared by the insured and subject to audit by the insurance company.

Various methods are used to recognize how and when the deposit premium is earned. Care must be taken to select a method that does not result in overstating the earned premium. This can happen, especially in the case of workers' compensation, when the deposit is not proportional to the period covered (i.e., a six-month audit period might require a deposit of 75 percent of the estimated annual premium). Some methods in use are:

1. The deposit is earned over the period covered by the deposit. When the audit premium is received, the deposit premium is reversed and reinstated for the following period.

2. The full estimated annual premium is entered, and modified accordingly, when the audit premiums are received.

3. The deposit is earned pro rata over the life of the policy. The pro rata unearned deposit premium is then increased by some amount (often one-twelfth of the deposit premium) to prevent overstating the earned premium when the audit premium is received.

Advance Premiums Advance premiums are premiums on policies that have been issued but do not become effective until after the date of the statement. This happens most often in companies that write renewals thirty to sixty days before expirations. These companies include as premiums written the premiums on advance business. However, the more common practice is to record the premiums as they become effective.

Important Considerations of the Unearned Premium Reserve

The unearned premium reserve results from the fact that insurance premiums are collected in advance for a service to be performed in the future. The calculation for this reserve assumes that premiums, losses, and expenses are spread evenly over the period of the policy. Of course in the insurance business this is not the case. A disproportionate amount of expenses is incurred at the beginning of the policy period. These expenses include commissions, underwriting costs, policy writing costs, and other acquisition expenses. Since premiums must be recognized as being earned evenly over the period although these initial expenses must be recorded immediately, a statutory accounting underwriting loss will occur early in the period. This loss will result in a drain on policyholders' surplus.

It is important to note that the underwriting loss is an "accounting" loss and not a cash loss. The accounting loss results from accruing revenues (premiums earned) evenly over the period while expenses must be recognized immediately. The accounting losses and subsequent accounting drains on surplus can be particularly severe in the case of a newly organized insurer that is growing rapidly. Coupled with large immediate outlays for organizational and operating expenses, a new insurer can expect to experience a considerable decrease in policyholders' surplus.

The statutory accounting method of calculating the unearned premium reserve portrays a company as being worse off than it actually is. The difference between the reported and the actual position can be found in an excessive unearned premium reserve. The reserve is "excessive" in that it should be able to pay for both losses and expenses as if they were incurred evenly throughout the term of coverage, but the disproportionately large initial expenses have already been recognized. Thus as the unearned premium reserve is decreased over time to cover losses and expenses, not all of the unearned premium reserve will be required. Because initial expenses have previously been recognized, the unearned premium reserve is shown to have been overstated by approximately the amount of these initial expenses. This redundant amount is referred to as the "equity" in the unearned premium reserve. The amount of this equity varies but may be in the range of 20 to 40 percent of the unearned premium reserve. Investors interested in purchasing property-liability company stock commonly make an adjustment in annual statement data by adding a certain percent of the unearned premium reserve to the policyholders' surplus of the company. However, limits should be placed on the amount of this adjustment. See

Table 1-19 for an illustration of how this adjustment is limited in general purpose financial statements prepared on the basis of GAAP.

If an insurer were to stop writing all new business, the equity in the unearned premium reserve would eventually flow to the surplus account. Since such an action is unrealistic, an insurer suffering substantial surplus drains will often reinsure a portion of its business. The effect on the accounting statements is an immediate recognition of a surplus increase due to the release of the equity in the unearned premium reserve of reinsured business. This occurs, under the most typical arrangement, because the reinsurer assumes the obligation for the unearned premium reserve and pays the ceding insurer a commission to reimburse it for expenses associated with originating the business.

One might logically question why the system is not changed since it does not accurately reflect the company's true financial position. This system is required by state insurance regulatory law which has as its primary objective the maintenance of insurance company solvency. The realization rule imposed by regulation is basically conservative in that it anticipates expenses prior to realizing the related revenues. Insurance regulators know that a safety cushion equal to the equity in the unearned premium reserve is available to bolster policyholders' surplus. The objective of maintaining solvency apparently outweighs the propriety of having statutory accounting statements reflect the financial condition of insurers on a going concern basis.

The length of the policy period affects the magnitude of the unearned premium reserve. In general, the longer the policy period the greater will be the unearned premium reserve. Companies that write predominantly longer term business like fire, homeowners, and fidelity bonds will have a relatively higher unearned premium reserve. The problem of surplus drain mentioned above will be particularly severe for a new fast-growing company writing a substantial portion of longer term business. The trend of insurers toward shorter term policies mitigates the effects of statutory accounting unearned premium reserving rules.

Finally, an important distinction should be made between a company's loss reserves and its unearned premium reserve. A considerable estimation or judgment component is present in the calculation of loss reserves. The unearned premium reserve is basically a straightforward arithmetical computation. Assuming the company is honest, the unearned premium reserve may be accepted as being adequate. No need exists, as in loss reserves, to test for adequacy by using historical development schedules. Of course, the unearned premium reserve is excessive due to the equity component, but given the proper information this amount can be determined.

POLICYHOLDERS' SURPLUS

The total capital and surplus of an insurance company, according to statutory accounting terminology, is called "surplus as regards policyholders" or policyholders' surplus. It is the difference between an insurer's admitted assets and liabilities; that is, it is the company's net worth on the statutory balance sheet. On the annual statement the policyholders' surplus section is subdivided into special surplus funds, capital paid-up, gross paid-in and contributed surplus, unassigned funds, and treasury stock. Several of these classifications require explanation; some are significant only to stock insurance companies.

Special surplus funds that have been authorized by the board of directors for a specific purpose are merely segregations of otherwise unassigned surplus. As an example, an insurance company writing lines of business that have widely fluctuating loss ratios may decide to establish a specially earmarked subdivision of policyholders' surplus and call it "reserve for extraordinary losses." Note that the use of the term "reserve" to classify a portion of surplus does not change this net worth account into a liability. The variety of titles used to designate special surplus accounts makes a complete listing here inappropriate; the most frequently used captions relate to underwriting loss and investment value fluctuations. With the creation of post-insolvency insurance company guaranty funds (discussed in Chapter 6), a segregation of surplus to provide for assessments by state guaranty funds has become common. Regardless of their intended purpose, these earmarked surplus accounts restrict the amount of funds available for stockholder or policyholder dividends.

Capital paid-up is the aggregate par or stated value of the company's capital stock outstanding. Stock may be preferred or common; however, in most states only one kind of stock is permitted— common stock. The classes of stock authorized and issued by an insurance company, along with other details concerning the corporation's equity shares, are described in item seven of the general interrogatories found on page thirteen of the annual statement. A stock insurer cannot obtain a license to operate unless all of its outstanding stock is issued for at least its par or stated value. This encourages those organizing a new stock insurance company to set the per share par value of the company's stock relatively low to facilitate rapid sale and encourage wide distribution of the equity shares.

Gross paid-in and contributed surplus is created by the sale of stock for an amount in excess of the stock's par or stated value per share and by any subsequent contributions of funds from stockholders. Thus, if a $5.00 par value common share is issued for $7.50, $2.50 is credited to the gross paid-in and contributed surplus account. After the corporation's initial capitalization is completed, the need may arise for additional equity. This need commonly arises as sales volume increases and new lines of insurance are written. If the corporation has issued all of its authorized capital stock, it will be necessary for it to seek state approval of a change in its charter before additional stock can be sold. This can be time consuming and costly. An alternative source of new equity is to procure contributions from existing stockholders. These contributions— which may be in the form of cash, donated assets other than cash, or forgiveness of indebtedness—also are credited to the gross paid-in and contributed surplus account.

Unassigned funds represent the net retained earnings since the inception of the company and reflect all adjustments to surplus, such as the charge for unauthorized reinsurance, additional liability for Schedule P loss reserves, and unrealized capital gains or losses on investments. The amount of unassigned surplus sets a limit on the amount that can be distributed as nonliquidating dividends to policyholders or stockholders. A liquidating dividend is a return *of* the owner's investment in the company while a nonliquidating dividend is the return *on* the owner's investment. Because nonliquidating dividends can come only from unassigned surplus, this account is sometimes referred to as "free surplus."

Treasury stock is a corporation's own stock, once issued and later reacquired either for holding as treasury stock or for cancellation. The cost of treasury stock is deducted from otherwise available capital and surplus in order to arrive at the corporation's total net worth (surplus as regards policyholders).

State insurance codes specify the minimum amounts of capital paid-up and paid-in and the contributed surplus required to obtain a certificate of authority as well as the minimum amount of surplus as regards policyholders required to continue writing business. These state insurance regulatory capitalization requirements are described in greater detail in Chapter 6.

Four variables principally affect policyholders' surplus of a property and liability company: (1) its underwriting results, (2) its investment performance, (3) developments in its loss reserves, and (4) its growth rate. Favorable results in any of these four areas will provide an increase in the policyholders' surplus account. Hence, for a going concern, these four variables may be thought of as the primary sources of policyholders' surplus. Alternatively, unfavorable results in any of these four areas will cause a decrease in policyholders' surplus. The purposes of policyholders' surplus, then, may be thought of as providing a safety cushion to absorb such adverse results. Policyholders' surplus protects the policyholder as well as the company by maintaining the company's solvency during periods of unfavorable operating results.

A property and liability company is primarily in the business of writing insurance. When underwriting gains result, policyholders' surplus is increased by these gains minus any applicable taxes. While any business is subject to unprofitable years, the insurance business is particularly vulnerable when rapid economic or societal changes are occurring. Since losses and expenses must be estimated, failure to anticipate and respond to adverse future developments may produce underwriting losses. An insurer's position is also complicated by delays in obtaining desired premium increases due to political pressures. When underwriting losses do occur, policyholders' surplus must be sufficient to cover these losses.

Due to the nature of the insurance operation, an insurer is also heavily involved in making investments. Policyholders' funds, rather than sitting idly until they are needed, are channeled into a wide variety of investments. Investment income (dividends, interest, and rents) constitutes a positive flow to surplus in virtually all situations. Property and liability companies typically hold a substantial portion of their investments in common stocks. The sale of the stocks may produce realized gains or losses. Since common stocks must be carried on the balance sheet at market value, unrealized (paper) gains and losses also result. In recent years, unrealized gains and losses have produced considerable shifts in companies' policyholders' surplus accounts.

The effects of loss reserve developments on policyholders' surplus have been described in early portions of this chapter. Loss reserve developments are reflected in underwriting results and can cause considerable increases and decreases in policyholders' surplus.

The growth variable is an anomaly in the insurance business. Generally, growth of a business is a positive factor and can be assumed to increase the firm's net worth. In property and liability insurance, however, due to the surplus drain resulting from an increasing unearned premium reserve, rapid growth may appear detrimental to the company's financial position. Assuming that profitable business is being sold, accounting funds will eventually flow to the surplus account as growth levels off or moderates. From a long-run standpoint, growth through writing profitable business can be expected to bolster policyholders' surplus. Yet during periods of rapid growth, one of the principal purposes of policyholders' surplus becomes apparent, namely, to absorb drains on the account due to an increasing unearned premium reserve. Adjusting statutory financial statements for general purpose use in conformity with GAAP removes the irregular impact that sales growth has on surplus.

SUMMARY

The principal liabilities of a property and liability insurance company are the loss and loss adjustment expense reserves and the unearned premium reserve. The aggregate loss and loss adjustment expense reserves that appear on an insurer's annual statement are supposed to disclose the amount needed to fully pay all unsettled claims that have occurred up to that date. Because estimates must be made in advance of ultimate settlement, the ability to judge the accuracy of an insurer at setting loss reserve levels is important. Loss development schedules in the annual statement give insight into the over- or under-reserving tendencies of particular insurers.

Loss reserves do not represent liabilities for losses that have not yet occurred on policies that have been written. This is the function of the unearned premium reserve. The reserve for unearned premiums represents the proportionate premium revenue received or in the course of collection on policies that currently are in force. As the protection service afforded by the policies is provided, revenues are released from the unearned premium reserve and realized as a contribution to income. While realization of revenue is deferred through the unearned premium reserve, expenses associated with issuing the corresponding insurance are realized as incurred. This results in an "investment" of the company's surplus in the unearned premium reserve because expenses are charged off immediately while premium revenue is deferred.

Capital and surplus of a property and liability insurance company serves several functions. First, it provides the initial funds to establish the company and begin operations; second, it is a continuing source of funds for financing increased sales and expansion; third, it provides a safety cushion to absorb adverse underwriting and investment experience without loss to policyholders. Capitalization requirements imposed by state insurance regulations set minimum net worth requirements that must be complied with by insurers that remain in operation. Company management must be cognizant of the factors that impact on policyholders' surplus and must guard against losses that threaten the financial strength and continued existence of the insurer.

CHAPTER 4

Revenue and Expenses

INTRODUCTION

When insurance is placed in force, an entry to record the sale is made in the insurance company's accounts. Usually, the entry debits accounts receivable and credits premiums written. As the premiums are collected, cash is debited and the accounts receivable account is credited. Out of these funds and other operating funds, the insurance company pays the agent's commission and any other operating expenses. The remaining money is available for the payment of claims, in some cases for policyholder dividends, and for profit.

Losses may be reported to the insurer during the period of coverage or at some later date. In certain lines of insurance, such as glass insurance, claims are settled almost immediately after they occur; in other lines, for example medical malpractice written on an occurrence basis, claims may be paid long after the policy has expired; and, in still other lines, loss settlement payments are made over a number of years, as in the case of survivorship benefits under workers' compensation. While awaiting payment of claims, the insurer will establish a liability based on what management believes will be the ultimate cost of the settlements.

Net funds received after payment of commissions and underwriting expenses are invested as soon as possible, consistent with other objectives and constraints. The funds are invested in various types of investments, but mostly in bonds and stocks. The amount invested in each category depends on the investment strategy of the company, subject to state regulatory restrictions. Theoretically, funds are invested until they are needed to pay the claims; in actual practice, however, current revenue from premiums is used to pay claims so that existing investments do not have to be liquidated.

Previous chapters of this text deal with the balance sheet accounts that are affected by the premium collection and the expense and loss payment cycle. Chapter 2 discusses asset accounts, asset structure, and investment strategy. Chapter 3 examines the principal liabilities arising out of the premiums written and the loss settlement processes. Those earlier chapters deal with accounting variables that are considered to be *stock variables*. Stock variables are balance sheet accounts that have a value at one point in time but do not have a value through time. In this sense, stock variables are static. This chapter deals with revenues and expenses; these accounting variables are *flow variables*. Flow variables appear on the income statement, have a value through time, and thus are considered to be flows. For example, the annual statement account entitled "cash on hand or on deposit" is a stock variable because it has a specific value as of the balance sheet date; on the other hand, the "premiums earned" account is a flow variable because its value exists over a time period between consecutive income statement dates. While the distinction between stock and flow variables may seem obvious, failure to recognize the distinction can be the source of confusion. As the presentation in the text turns from a consideration of balance sheet stock variables to flow variables found on the income statement, the transition is explicitly noted.

The two principal revenue sources for an insurer are premium collections and investment receipts. The annual statement reflects premium revenue by line of business, such as automobile liability, workers' compensation, fire, and accident and health. It shows the losses paid and incurred in the same way. Investment receipts are also shown in detail on the annual statement. The schedule of interest, dividend, and real estate income analyzes the investment income by type of investment. State insurance regulators desire the ability to analyze the profitability of each line of business sold. Consequently, the Insurance Expense Exhibit was developed to provide an analysis of the operations of the insurer by line of business. Premiums, losses, loss adjustment expenses, commissions, taxes, and other expenses are all allocated by line. Investment income is also allocated to individual lines of business in order to study each line's total contribution for rate-making purposes.

This chapter examines the accounting treatment of revenues, losses, and expenses of an insurance company and their relation to the financial statements. The effects of reinsurance, investment income, and capital gains and losses also will be explained. Various methods and records (like the annual statement) for monitoring revenues and expenses will be analyzed.

PREMIUMS WRITTEN CYCLE

A premium is the consideration received from an insured in exchange for the insurance company's contractual obligation to insure the exposure against financial loss. The premium accounting cycle includes all phases of premium recognition by the insurance company—from policy inception to expiration. The functions involved in the premium cycle include:

- Sales and policy issue
- Underwriting
- Premium recording
- Premium collecting

Figure 4-1 depicts a rather simplified picture of the premium cycle. In certain situations the sequence of these procedures may be in a different order than shown in the figure; for instance, in cases where coverage is bound by agents and the policy is issued from the agency, the diagram should be modified.

Several of the steps in the premium accounting cycle that precede premium collection and recording are discussed below. This is not meant to be an exhaustive discussion of the functions but should contribute to better understanding of the revenue cycle.

Sales and Policy Issue

As in any other business, the premium or revenue cycle begins with a sales effort. Depending on the company, sales are generated through general agents, local and regional agents, brokers, and on a direct marketing basis. Insurance sales represent a substantial effort on the part of the insurance marketing personnel and provide an important service to the interests insured.

The insurance policy is a contract between the insurer and the insured and contains all the terms and conditions of their agreement. Policy issue can take place at:

- the producer's office,
- the company's branch office, or
- the company's home office.

Policy issue can be done before or after underwriting, depending on who writes the policy and the legal authority of the producer.

If a producer writes a policy, the home or branch office performs the underwriting function after the policy is written on the basis of a daily

Figure 4-1

The Premium Accounting Cycle

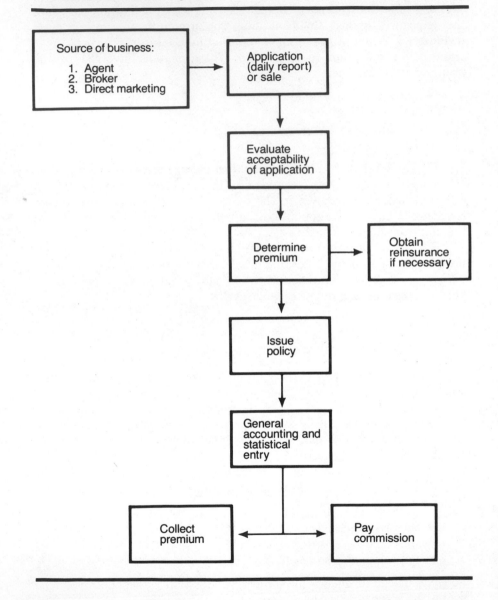

report (a copy of the policy's declaration page submitted to the company from the producer). When the branch or home office writes a policy, the company underwrites from an application submitted by a producer. The application contains applicant underwriting information upon which the company bases its decision to accept (continue coverage) or reject (flat cancellation) the opportunity to provide coverage.

The distribution of copies of the policy generally includes the policyholder (for evidence of coverage), the producer (for confirmation of coverage and use in servicing policyholders), the branch office (for use in servicing producers or policyholders through decentralized loss and policy issue control), and the home office (for use by the accounting, statistical, audit, and inspection departments).

Underwriting

The underwriting function includes an evaluation of the acceptability of the loss exposure, a determination of the premium, a review of contract conditions and terms, and an evaluation of the company's capacity to assume the entire exposure (that is, whether or not to reinsure). The first underwriting function—evaluation of the acceptability of the loss exposure—involves a recognition of hazards and potential losses based on a review of dailies and contract endorsements. In addition, an investigation of loss exposures is conducted according to company procedures and, in some cases, in compliance with state statutes. For example, applicants for automobile insurance may be checked against driving records issued by state departments of motor vehicles. Applications for other coverages may require an engineering survey, a fire hazard survey, or other information.

The underwriting function determines the premiums on policies written by the company, and checks the premiums on policies written by agents against bureau or company rate manuals. Of course, underwriting expertise also will play a role in determining or reviewing premiums. Interrelated with selection and pricing of acceptable business is determination of appropriate policy terms and conditions. An unacceptable or improperly priced submission can be converted into an acceptable insurance arrangement through modification of contract provisions.

Reinsurance requirements are determined in accordance with company underwriting policy and expertise. A number of purposes are served by reinsurance; these include the ability to:

- increase the insurer's capacity to accept business,
- stabilize underwriting results,

- finance a portion of the business being written, and
- protect surplus from catastrophic losses.

Often, an agent can bind insurance coverage before the underwriting is completed and the application is accepted by the company. In such cases, a review of the coverage is made in the field office, and the daily is recorded. The company can record the policy before the ultimate underwriting decision is made, and if subsequently rejected, the exposure in the policy can then be canceled.

Premium Recording

Premium recording includes the coding and processing of transactions evidenced by originating documents such as dailies and endorsements. This process produces the written premium and statistical premium data needed to calculate premiums in force and premiums earned. The exact nature of a particular company's premium recording process depends on whether the insured is billed by the agent or by the company. The flow chart shown in Figure 4-2 illustrates the processing of a premium transaction in a situation in which the agency issues the policy and bills the insured. The premium is collected by the agency from the insured and remitted to the insurer according to the agency or company account current records and the agency agreement. Although somewhat simplistic, the flow chart illustrates the basic steps in the policy issue and premium recording process.

A policy is written in the agent's office on policy forms supplied by the insurance company. A copy of the information contained in the policy declarations is made; and this daily report, along with any supporting documents, is submitted to the insurer. The agent may also collect a full or partial premium payment at this point or arrange for premium financing. Upon receipt of the daily and any accompanying documents, the company records the policy identification number in order to maintain control of policy forms. The underwriting process then begins. If the loss exposure is unacceptable, a cancellation notice is issued by the company; otherwise, the company begins the process of recording the policy data in its accounting and statistical records. Note: if the process involves the agent's submission of an application for coverage and the company's selection of its insureds prior to policy issue, the policy would be prepared at this point. A copy of the policy would be sent to the interests insured and a daily report sent to the agency.

Dailies and endorsements can be coded either during or after the underwriting process. Coding involves assigning an alphanumeric label to each transaction so that it can be stored according to an indexing

Figure 4-2
Simplified Premium Transaction Processing

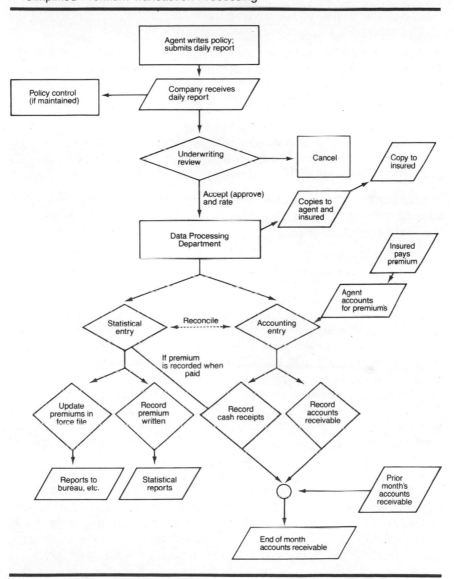

system and retrieved expeditiously. A major reason to code information is to facilitate compilation of data for the annual statement. For example, state codes are necessary to produce Schedule T (premium written by state), and insurance line codes are necessary to produce the Underwriting and Investment Exhibit.

Once policy data are recorded in the company's information system, various statistical reports can be prepared, such as premium tax schedules, rating bureau reports, experience rating reports, and activity reports to management, and so forth. The data simultaneously are used as the source of accounting entries. For example, if premiums are recognized at policy issue, the initial accounting entry might be as follows:

Accounts Receivable (debit)	$160
Commission Expense (debit)	$ 40
Premiums Written (credit)	$200

Within forty-five to sixty days, the agency will remit its payment on its account current. At that time, the cash receipt would be recorded and the agent's commission paid:

Cash (debit)	$160
Accounts Receivable (credit)	$160

These entries are posted to the company's ledger accounts monthly, or more frequently, and periodic receivables and receipt records are updated. Some companies may defer recognition of premiums written until cash receipts actually are recorded rather than at the time of policy issue. In many cases, both methods of premium recognition are used by the same company for different lines of insurance.

Premium processing creates a series of premium records or files. These files appear in a number of different forms and fulfill several purposes. An *accounting file* is used to maintain a record of agents' balances (accounts receivable) and to determine overdue agents' balances, which are nonadmitted assets for statutory purposes. A *statistical file* is used to record, test, and verify data and to produce premiums in force and unearned, premium written registers, board and bureau reports, and producer performance reports. In addition, the statistical file may be used to control policy expirations, installment premium billings, timing of policy audits, and reinsurance ceded records. The statistical file is necessary to determine the two basic premium amounts:

- Premiums written—the amount of premiums billed less premiums returned to the insured. This figure is recorded to the general ledger as premium revenue.

Figure 4-3

Original and Written Premiums

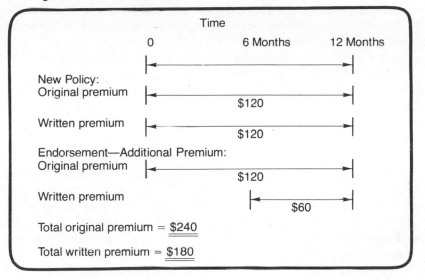

- Original premiums—the amount of premiums for the full term of a policy for the current coverage at the latest premium rate shown in the policy or endorsement to the policy. This figure is used in compilation of in-force premiums; it is the basis for calculating unearned premiums.

Figure 4-3 shows an example of how the original premium differs from the written premium. Assume a company issues a policy with an annual term for a premium of $120. Six months later the insured doubles the coverage. The company issues an endorsement for an additional premium for the six months (50 percent pro rata portion of $120).

The original premium concept is the basis for determining the premiums in force, which is the aggregate of the original premiums from all policies that have been recorded but that have not expired or been canceled. Premiums in force are determined by updating the previous cumulative premiums in force by the periodic contribution to the premiums in force.

The statistical file input also produces the premiums written register. New policy and endorsement transactions are used to produce monthly premium registers simultaneously with or before the updating of the statistical file.

Statistical file premiums written input (gross premiums before agent's commissions) is then reconciled with accounting file input. After reconciliation, the accounting file can be maintained on a net of agents' commissions basis.

Premiums written is derived and recorded from the processing of the monthly transactions, but then must be converted to premiums earned. From an accounting viewpoint, premiums earned equals premiums written for the period, plus the unearned premium reserve at the beginning of the period, less the unearned premium reserve at the end of the period. This accounting entry by line of insurance is included in Part 2 of the Underwriting and Investment Exhibit in the annual statement. Barring premium rate changes, if an insurance company writes the same mix and the same amount of business each year, premiums written and premiums earned will be equal, as the unearned premium reserve will remain constant. A company that is growing will experience an increasing unearned premium reserve, causing the earned premiums figure to be less than written premiums. The opposite will occur in a company suffering from negative growth. A detailed discussion of the effects of changes in the unearned premium reserve is included in the preceding chapter.

Premiums written may be thought of as a cash measure of premium income. Premiums earned, on the other hand, may be thought of as an accrual measure. In a sense, premiums earned is the more important measure because it is used as the measure of revenue in the statement of income in the annual statement. Premiums earned is also the figure commonly used in the denominator of the loss ratio.

The unearned premium reserve is a nonledger liability representing two concepts. First, it represents the statutory concept in which unearned premium represents a liability to pay potential losses, loss expenses, and return premiums for the unexpired policy period. It also represents the generally accepted accounting principle (GAAP) concept in which unearned premium represents deferred revenue that is recognized on a pro rata basis as the policy period passes.

Statistical file data may be used for other premium-related controls, including:

- *Premium transactions.* These are coded by reinsurance agreement and summarized by reinsurer for payment.
- *Policy expiration notices.* Notices are prepared by comparing the expiration date of each policy with a control date. This procedure helps agents to renew policies on time and controls removal of expired premiums from the in-force file.
- *Installment premium billings.* By use of special coding, these billings can also be controlled by a file designed to generate billings on the next due date.

- *Policies subject to periodic audit for the determination of premium.* These policies require quarterly or other periodic premium billing based on payroll or gross receipts. The timing of premium audits is most important for consistent premium recording. The audited premium is determined after the exposure period and is earned when billed and recorded.
- *Participating policies, loss experience, policy profitability and earned premium.* Participating policies provide for a partial return of premium (or dividend) to the policyholder, based on policy profitability. However, dividends are a company obligation only when they are declared. Statutes prohibit promising dividends, contractually or otherwise.
- *Accounting for reinsurance assumed and ceded.* This may be integrated with premium processing. Both premiums written and unearned premiums include reinsurance premiums, whether assumed or ceded.
- *Nonadmitted agents' balances.* This is determined by a simple comparison of dates in the accounting files of agents' balances after ninety days.

Premium Collecting

The premium collecting function includes billing premiums, receiving cash, applying cash to agents' balances, and satisfying agents' commisions. Three basic methods are used for billing premiums: (1) agents are billed by the company, (2) accounts are rendered to the company by agents, and (3) policyholders are billed directly by the company. These three methods will be discussed in the following sections.

Agents Billed by the Company First, the company prepares monthly statements using recorded transactions. The statements usually include policy number, name of the insured, effective date of the policy, gross premium, commission rate, and amount of commission for each policy. In connection with this procedure, monthly premium transactions are added to, and remittances are removed from, the unpaid premium accounting file.

Accounts Rendered to the Company by Agents Under this method, agents send a monthly statement to the company listing individually all transactions for which the agent's records show a premium is due. For the most part, the company will have previously recorded these transactions as premium revenue and agents' balances from dailies received or issued.

The company compares the account submitted by the agent to the transactions it recorded earlier. Any differences are accumulated and classified as:

- items included in agents' account currently but not yet recorded by the company,
- items recorded but not currently included in the account, or
- discrepancy in amounts when an item is both reported by an agent and recorded by the company.

The company usually controls differences by treating the account rendered by the agent as a unit and establishing ledger control over differences.

Policyholders Billed Directly by the Company Companies can have a direct bill operation whether or not they have agents. Those companies without agents generally use company-paid sales persons to sell their insurance coverages. In a direct bill operation, the premiums are billed directly to the policyholders by the insurance company.

The recording of direct bill premiums written is done in either of two ways. One method is to record premiums written when the policyholder is billed, usually thirty to sixty days in advance of the effective date of the policy. The other method is to record premiums written as the premiums are collected. Since the premiums are billed in advance, they should be collected prior to the effective date of the policy. If the premium is not collected by the effective date, the policy is canceled.

For companies paying commissions to the persons producing the business, a summary of the collections is prepared monthly, by producer, and the commission is paid on that basis. This is different from an agency type operation in which the agent collects from the policyholder and remits net of commission to the company.

Four basic methods are used for premium settlement or payments (receiving cash) billed directly by the company: lump sum prepayment, audit or reporting premium, installment payment, or deposit premiums. Each is described briefly below.

> *Lump sum prepayment* is the most common method of premium payment. The entire policy premium due is received at the beginning of the period. This method is used extensively in personal lines and for small commercial lines accounts.

> *Audit or reporting premium* is an earned premium determined from data developed from periodic audits of the policyholder's records or from periodic reports submitted by the policyholder.

The amount of the premium depends on the exposure base, which can be determined only after the passage of time. An initial deposit premium is determined (and collected) based on an estimate of the anticipated exposure and later adjusted to reflect the actual exposure. Payroll and gross receipts are typical exposure bases.

Installment premiums are means by which insureds finance their insurance expense. Two methods are used to record installment premiums: premiums are recorded as each installment becomes due, or when the policy is written. In the latter case, separate control of the installments due is established for subsequent billing.

Deposit premiums are used in situations in which the exposure base is not known at the time the policy is written. Consequently, a deposit premium is charged at the inception of the policy. Workers' compensation and general liability lines of insurance (where the premium will be determined based on payroll or gross receipts) will charge an initial deposit premium either quarterly or annually. The premium is then earned on a pro rata basis according to the payment pattern. At the end of the period an audit may be made of the policyholders' report of premiums based on the measure of exposure. The additional or return premium is considered earned at that time. Premiums in force or unearned premiums are not affected by this premium adjustment.

At the end of any accounting period, companies writing this type of business will generally have premiums earned but unbilled which have not been recorded as an asset or as revenue. Some companies estimate this asset and record it as a receivable with a credit to premiums earned. The majority of companies, however, do not reflect this item in their financial statements.

LOSS CYCLE

The loss cycle includes a number of functions: loss processing, loss adjustment and loss reserve estimates, loss recording, loss settlement, and loss reserve evaluation. These various functions are illustrated in Figure 4-4. The purpose of this section is to describe these functions and to show how they are interrelated.

Figure 4-4
Simplified Claim Processing Cycle

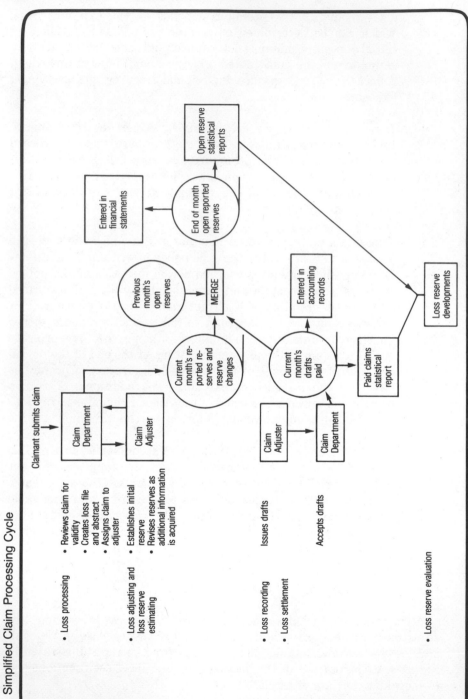

Loss Processing

After a loss, the claimant sends a notice of the loss either directly to the company or to the policyholder's agent or broker. The claimant and the policyholder are the same person for first-party losses and different individuals for third-party claims. A claim notice is generally required from the claimant and includes (1) a brief summary of the loss or injury, (2) the time and date of the loss or injury, (3) how the loss or injury happened, and (4) the policyholder's name and policy number.

There is always a delay between the date of the loss or injury and the claim report date, although the length of the delay varies depending on the type of loss. When a loss report is received, the validity of the claim is first determined by comparing the loss notice to the proof of insurance coverage in force. Next, a loss file is created and assigned an identifying number for use throughout processing. All documents on reporting, adjusting, recording, and settling the claim are kept in that file.

A loss abstract (often called a claim label or face sheet) prepared from information in the loss report, adjuster's report, and the daily, is used to record the new loss in subsidiary records. It is sometimes used as a summary of transactions for that loss file. The loss abstract contains coded information as outlined in Table 4-1.

Loss Adjustment and Loss Reserve Estimates

When insurance coverage has been verified, an adjuster is assigned. Which adjuster is selected will depend on where the loss occurred, the type and amount of the loss, and the experience of the adjuster. The adjuster may be an independent adjuster, the company's own employee, or the company's agent.

An adjuster investigates the loss to determine that it actually occurred, that coverage is in effect, and that the claim is otherwise valid. Photographs, surveillance reports, medical reports, and any other reports are assembled to substantiate the loss. If the policy contains any special limiting provisions, a determination must be made as to the policyholder's adherence to these provisions.

The adjuster estimates the amount of the loss and loss adjustment expenses. For property losses, the approximate amount of salvage value is also reported to the company. The adjuster also finds out, if possible, if any subrogation rights are available.

The claims adjuster bases the original estimate of the value of the loss on information available at the time of the original report. As

Table 4-1

Outline of Information in a Loss Abstract

I. Dates

    A. Accident occurrence date
    B. Accident report date

II. Loss Identification Data

    A. File number
    B. Cause and location of loss
    C. Type of loss or injury
    D. Claimant identification
    E. Catastrophe code

III. Policy Identification Data

    A. Policy number, term, and effective date
    B. Agent or producer
    C. Lines and amounts of coverage
    D. Amount of deductibles to be absorbed by the insured
    E. Reinsurance arrangements, if any

IV. Monetary Information

    A. Original estimate of the loss incurred value
    B. Loss expense and loss adjustment expense payments
    C. Reserve changes and amount of current reserve
       outstanding, and subrogation, salvage, and reinsurance
       receipts

additional information is acquired, the estimate is revised until the case is closed. The estimate made by the adjuster is reviewed by a company claims examiner or a supervisor to make sure the estimate is sound and consistent with company guidelines.

Loss Recording

The loss recording function accumulates data on loss costs and loss adjustment expenses incurred by claim. The loss cost incurred on a claim has two parts, the unpaid or loss reserve portion and the paid portion.

Details on losses incurred are kept on a gross and net basis. The gross basis provides for the loss cost before reinsurance, subrogation, or salvage recoveries. The net basis provides for the amount of loss incurred by the company after reinsurance, subrogation, and salvage.

Financial statements show losses on a net basis. In the Underwriting and Investments Exhibit of the annual statement, Parts 3 and 3A, a record of the composition of net losses incurred is shown.

Insurance companies do not reflect estimated amounts of subrogation and salvage recoverable in their statutory financial statements either as a reduction of outstanding loss reserves or as an estimated receivable. The amount of any subrogation or salvage receivable is not recorded until the cash is received.

Gross and net loss detail may be required for a claim, depending on the volume of transactions affected and the type of reinsurance treaties in force. These records may be kept manually, or they may be a part of the electronic data processing (EDP) master loss files.

Throughout the life of the claim, the cumulative paid portion and reserve portion are maintained separately for each claim. A record of loss adjustment expenses incurred, which are directly attributable to a specific claim (these are called allocated loss adjustment expenses), is somtimes maintained. Many companies do not keep allocated loss adjustment reserves on an individual case basis, but compute these reserves on an overall formula basis. All companies, however, should separately maintain a record of cumulative allocated loss expenses paid for each claim.

Table 4-2 summarizes some of the transactions that may be included in the loss records during the life of the claim. Subsidiary records support both ledger and nonledger accounts. Loss reserve totals may be reconciled from month to month by summarizing transactions for these categories.

The loss reserve, any related reinsurance recoverable, and loss adjustment expense reserve are added to the outstanding loss file tape or other subsidiary record. No entry is made in the general ledger because these are all nonledger assets and liabilities. The adjuster or a claims supervisor makes reserve changes from a reevaluation of facts or evaluation of new facts. Changes are added to the subsidiary record from coded change notices.

Once the loss settlement is recorded, loss and loss adjustment payments are put on record. A payment affects both the general ledger (because paid losses must be charged and cash credited) and the subsidiary record of losses (because the loss reserve is decreased and the amount of loss paid increased). Payment of loss in excess of the company's retention results in a receivable and a bill to the reinsurer.

Subrogation or salvage recovered is coded and entered in the general ledger and subsidiary loss records. Once losses paid and salvage received have been recorded separately, they are combined in the records. They are listed separately because, as was noted above, a record of the composition of net losses incurred is required in the Underwriting and Investment Exhibit of the annual statement. Total loss paid and

Table 4-2

Accounting Effects of Selected Loss Transactions

	Effect on Loss Reserve (Nonledger)	Effect on Loss Paid (Ledger)	Effect on Incurred Loss
To record new claim	Increase	None	Increase
To increase the estimate of total cost of the loss	Increase	None	Increase
To decrease the estimate of total cost of the loss	Decrease	None	Decrease
To make partial payment in settlement	Decrease	Increase	None
To make final settlement payment at amount less than the loss reserve	Decrease to zero	Increase	Decrease (called a savings on reserve)
To make final settlement payment at amount greater than the loss reserve	Decrease to zero	Increase	Increase (called deficiency on reserve)
To receive subrogation or salvage	None	Decrease	Decrease

salvage received are combined to determine the net total amount of loss incurred. Subrogation or salvage received reduces the total loss incurred.

Property and liability insurance companies compile and maintain detailed loss data in order to complete the annual statement and produce other reports for management. Detailed loss data appears in Parts 3 and 3A of the Underwriting and Investment Exhibit and in Schedules O and P of the annual statement. Examples of management reports containing extensive loss data include reports showing losses by producer; losses by line, location, or department; losses on reinsured business; loss experience for large loss exposures; loss experience on retrospectively rated policies; and analyses of unallocated loss adjustment expenses.

Loss Settlement

Loss settlement includes not only partial and final payment to the claimant for the loss liability but also payment of allocated loss adjustment expenses. Loss adjustment expenses are divided into two categories: *allocated* loss expense payments and *unallocated* loss expense payments. Allocated loss adjustment expenses are those identified by claim file in company records; on the other hand, unallocated loss adjustment expenses are not identified with a particular claim file but are all remaining expenses associated with the loss adjustment operation.[1] Unallocated expenses may be thought of as expenses in need of allocation; allocated expenses have already been assigned to a claim.

Final settlement requires a release from the claimant as evidence that the claim has been settled satisfactorily. When the loss payment is made by check the claimant must sign a release, which is a separate document. Draft loss payments have a release printed on the draft. The release is effective when the draft is endorsed.

After final payment is made to all claimants, the loss file is reviewed to make sure all necessary procedures have been followed. Final payment should have been approved and coded to remove the reserve from the outstanding loss records. All loss adjustment expense payments are verified, and any open loss adjustment expense reserve is removed from the company records. Paid loss records are checked to see that they contain the correct amount of loss and loss adjustment expense payments. Reinsurers should have been notified of their portion of loss and loss adjustment expenses, and the related receivable should be recorded. Any salvage and subrogation possibilities should be recorded and collection efforts followed. Policy records should be updated so that future underwriting will have loss information available. Coverage on property that no longer exists should be canceled. If all procedures have been followed properly, the loss file or loss pocket should be stamped "closed" or "paid."

Loss Payments

Loss payments are made by draft or check. Checks are controlled and treated as outstanding when issued. Drafts are controlled, either on an issued or honored basis. Draft payments have advantages over checks because they are subject to company review before being honored. Draft-signing authority is sometimes delegated to a lower responsibility level than check-signing authority. In addition, use of drafts rather than checks allows more flexible management of insurance company cash balances.

When drafts are controlled as issued, they are recorded immmediately as paid losses and credited to a liability account called outstanding loss drafts. The draft copy is input to reduce the loss reserve, to increase losses paid in the subsidiary loss records, and to record the paid loss in the general ledger. Drafts presented for payment by the bank and approved by the company are credited to cash and charged to the liability account—outstanding loss drafts. Insurance companies issuing large volumes of drafts usually record the drafts as issued.

When drafts are controlled as paid, they are recorded when honored. This method typically is employed by insurers that do not have large volumes of loss payments and therefore are able to maintain control over unprocessed drafts.[2] Drafts issued and not yet presented for payment have no effect on the financial statements since the amount of the unpaid loss remains in the loss reserve. This is a very significant distinction between the two methods of accounting for loss payments made by drafts. If drafts are recorded as issued, any over- or underestimation of the loss reserve is recognized immediately. On the other hand, if the draft is not recorded until it is paid, any inaccuracy in loss reserves remains until payment of the draft.

The draft copy is used to record the loss payment after it is matched with the cleared draft. A system is needed to control both the original draft and the copy because either one can be received first by the company when drafts are issued by independent or field adjusters. Suspense accounts are normally used for this control. The account is debited when the draft is purchased from the bank and credited when the draft copy is received.

EXPENSES

A substantial portion of each premium dollar is used to pay expenses associated with the insurance transaction. Expenses incurred by a property and liability insurer arise out of the company's marketing, underwriting, policy servicing, claims administration, and investment operations. The degree to which the company can effectively perform these activities while limiting their costs determines the internal operating efficiency of the insurer. Other things the same, an insurance company that operates efficiently can offer lower premium rates and generate higher profits. Proper monitoring and control of expenses, therefore, is an essential determinant of successful performance.

Part 4 of the Underwriting and Investment Exhibit of the annual statement is a schedule of expenses paid and incurred. Expenses are classified into three functional expense groups: (1) loss adjustment expenses, (2) other underwriting expenses and (3) investment expenses. They are also classified by object or purpose. Both the functional expense groups and the object expense classifications are those prescribed by the uniform accounting instructions (Regulation 30 of the State of New York). These instructions define the items going into each expense classification and the methods of allocating expenses by functional expense groups, as well as by major and minor lines of business. The allocation of expenses to lines of business is necessary to prepare the Insurance Expense Exhibit that companies must file annually. This exhibit contains an analysis of premiums, losses, expenses, and net income by line of business before federal income taxes.

There are twenty-one expense classifications shown in the Insurance Expense Exhibit. The classifications are identical to those used in Part 4 of the Underwriting and Investment Exhibit of the annual statement. The total expenses in the twenty-one classifications equals the total amount of expenses incurred during the year. The total loss adjustment expenses and other underwriting expenses shown in the Exhibit are carried to lines 3 and 4 of the statement of income, and the total investment expenses incurred are carried to line 11, Part 1 of the Underwriting and Investment Exhibit.

Uniform Accounting Instructions

The New York Insurance Department historically has been a leader in regulating insurance company expenses. Separate insurance expense exhibits for casualty insurance and fire and marine insurance were adopted in New York in the 1920s and 1930s. These exhibits showed expense allocations to functional areas by line of business. A need for greater uniformity in expense reporting prompted the New York Department to work with the NAIC to develop its "Uniform Classification of Expenses of Fire and Marine and Casualty and Surety Insurers," Regulation Number 30, which became effective January 1, 1949. The National Association of Insurance Commissioners adopted uniform accounting instructions identical to those in New York's Regulation 30. The commissioners of insurance of all the other states required their fire and marine and casualty and surety companies to adjust their records as of January 1, 1950, to comply with these instructions which have been part of the annual statement since that time. The development of uniform expense allocation rules has established cost accounting within the insurance industry and has enabled valuable comparisons to be made among companies for expense analysis and control purposes.

The objective of uniform accounting instructions is to allocate insurance company expenses uniformly within prescribed principal groupings. Expenses are allocated

1. by companies, wherever more than one company is operated jointly;
2. by nature of expense (major expense classification);
3. by functions (such as investment, loss adjusting, other underwriting); and
4. by lines of business (such as automobile liability, automobile physical damage, workers' compensation, and so forth).

The uniform accounting instructions provide specific rules for the allocation of expenses to these various categories. Where a specific rule is not feasible, the instructions prescribe procedures and methods of determining the proper allocation.

The allocation of expenses as set forth by the uniform accounting instructions is based on four principles:

1. All direct expenses, or those expenses obviously incurred for specific companies or purposes whether by function, line of insurance, coverage or nature of expense, are to be allocated as incurred.
2. Other expenses not directly allocable but related to some direct expenses are allocated in the same porportion as the direct expenses to which they are related.
3. General expenses not related to any direct expenses are allocated on the basis of time studies (or other special studies that can help classify the expenses into categories consistent with their nature).
4. Those general expenses (such as general advertising) not subject to allocation based on time and special studies are to be allocated on the basis of premium volume.

All bases of allocation are to be compiled or calculated from the transactions or procedures for the period applicable to the expenses to be allocated unless the use of any other period is justified by investigation made during the applicable period. In most insurance companies, employee salaries constitute the major item of expense that cannot always be directly allocated. Once salaries are properly allocated, the bulk of the job is done. In fact, so many other general expenses bear such a close relationship to salaries that once salaries have been allocated they can serve as the basis for allocating the other general expenses.

Basic Expense Classifications   Under the uniform accounting instructions, all expenses are segregated and correspond precisely to those contained in Part 4 of the Underwriting and Investment Exhibit. Table 4-3 shows this exhibit from the 1977 annual statement filed by the Insurance Company of North America and its affiliated fire and casualty insurers. Columns 1, 2, and 3 indicate the functional expense groupings, and rows 1 through 21 classify expenses according to the purpose for which they were incurred. For example, during 1977, INA and its affiliates incurred legal and auditing expenses (line 17) that totaled $6,764,260. The loss adjustment function was responsible for $634,896; underwriting functions other than loss adjustment incurred $4,536,657; and investment operations accounted for $1,592,707 of the total audit and legal expense.

The twenty-one expense classifications are, in effect, general ledger expense accounts and should include all expenses of the particular type incurred by the company during the year. It does not matter which department of the company or line of insurance may have been involved.

Uniform accounting instructions indicate what kinds of disbursements should be included in each of the expense classifications. As an example, the following are rules for including expenses in classification number 6, "surveys and underwriting reports."

- Include the cost of the following:
  - Survey, credit, moral hazard, character, and commercial reports obtained for underwriting purposes
  - Commercial reporting services
  - Appraisals for underwriting purposes
  - Fire records
  - Inspection engineering, and accident and loss prevention billed specifically
  - Literature, booklets, placards, signs, etc., issued solely for accident and loss prevention
  - Maps and corrections
  - Services of medical examiners for underwriting purposes
- Exclude:
  - Compensation to employees (see salaries)
  - Expenses of salaried employees (see travel and travel items)
  - Items includable in boards, bureaus, and associations; claim adjustment services; and allowances to managers and agents
  - Cost of character or credit reports on employees or applicants for employment (see employee relations and welfare)

Table 4-3

Underwriting and Investment Exhibit of the Insurance Company of North America and Its Affiliated Fire and Casualty Insurers—Annual Statement for the Year Ended December 31, 1977

Part IV—Expenses

	1 Loss Adjustment Expenses	2 Other Underwriting Expenses	3 Investment Expenses	4 Total
1 Claim adjustment services				
(a) Direct	$113,097,894			$113,097,894
(b) Reinsurance assumed	12,302,406			12,302,406
(c) Reinsurance ceded	16,936,108			16,936,108
(d) Net claim adjustment services (a+b−c)	$108,464,192			$108,464,192
2 Commission and brokerage				
(a) Direct		$294,321,095		294,321,095
(b) Reinsurance assumed		190,045,331		190,045,331
(c) Reinsurance ceded		172,199,370		172,199,370
(d) Contingent—net		29,676,565		29,676,565
(e) Policy and membership fees				
(f) Net commission and brokerage (a+b−c+d+e)		$341,843,621		$341,843,621
3 Allowances to managers and agents	132,163	353,349		485,512
4 Advertising	305	2,525,484		2,525,789
5 Boards, bureaus, and associations	19,351	11,061,529		11,080,880
6 Surveys and underwriting reports	2,752	2,961,982		2,964,734
7 Audit of assureds' records		130,239		130,239
8 Salaries	38,738,485	114,066,149	$ 490,999	153,295,633

9	Employee relations and welfare	4,328,864	14,086,462	48,539	18,463,865
10	Insurance	71,560	690,759	77,216	839,535
11	Directors' fees		78,597		78,597
12	Travel and travel items	3,367,244	10,821,299	39,669	14,228,212
13	Rent and rent items	5,106,492	17,511,225	112,751	22,730,468
14	Equipment	2,655,083	10,958,012	37,363	13,650,458
15	Printing and stationery	1,430,645	5,898,253	39,303	7,368,201
16	Postage, telephone and telegraph, exchange and express	3,902,305	9,702,336	45,811	13,650,452
17	Legal and auditing	834,896	4,536,657	1,592,707	6,764,260
17a	Totals (Items 3 to 17)	$ 60,390,145	$205,382,332	$2,484,358	$268,256,835
18	Taxes, licenses, and fees				
	(a) State and local insurance taxes		45,014,771	9,481	45,024,252
	(b) Insurance department licenses and fees		738,347	15,123	753,470
	(c) Payroll taxes	4,762	11,310,515	4,483	11,319,760
	(d) All other (excluding federal and foreign income and real estate)		2,143,268	436	2,143,704
	(e) Total taxes, licenses, and fees	4,762	$ 59,206,901	$ 29,523	$ 59,241,186
19	Real estate expenses		291	1,267,678	1,267,969
20	Real estate taxes			509,206	509,206
21	Miscellaneous (itemize)				
	(a) Outside services	4,781,934	11,880,260	561,001	17,223,195
	(b) Income and charges from special services	-2,103,342	-7,613,827	1,148,154	-8,569,015
	(c) Contributions	331	6,226		6,557
	(d) Other	58,751	755,134	12,608	826,493
22	Total expenses incurred	$171,596,773	$611,460,938	$6,012,528	$789,070,239
23	Less unpaid expenses—current year	277,333,260	55,151,632	171,525	332,656,417
24	Add unpaid expenses—previous year	237,214,198	42,330,935	109,869	279,654,702
25	TOTAL EXPENSES PAID	$131,477,711	$598,640,241	$5,950,572	$736,068,524

— Fee for physical examination of employees or applicants for employment (see employee relations and welfare)
— Income from inspections, which shall be classified according to the instructions for "income from special services"

Whenever personnel or facilities are used in common by two or more companies, or whenever the personnel or facilities of one company are used in the activities of two or more companies, the expenses involved follow the rules for joint expenses. Each company allocates these apportioned expenses to the same operating expense classifications as if it had borne all the expense alone. This does not apply to the allocation of the following expenses which are covered by separate instructions:

- Reinsurance commission and allowances
- Commission and brokerage paid to managers and agents
- Allowances to managers and agents
- Expenses allocable according to the instruction "income from special services"

Functional Expense Groups. There are five functional expense groups established by uniform accounting instructions: (1) investment expenses; (2) loss adjustment expenses; (3) acquisition, field supervision, and collection expenses; (4) taxes, licenses, and fees; and (5) general expenses. These functional expense groups are shown on the Insurance Expense Exhibit but not in the annual statement. General expenses; acquisition, field supervision, and collection expenses; and taxes, licenses, and fees are classed as other underwriting expenses for annual statement purposes. Uniform accounting instructions for each expense group set forth general principles for allocating all expenses to one of these five functional groups. Each functional expense group consists of several expense classifications. The general principles governing the composition of the expense groups are described in this section.

Investment expenses comprise all expenses incurred, even those expenses only partly incurred in connection with investing funds and obtaining investment income. These include related expenses incurred in (1) initiating or handling orders and recommendations; (2) doing research; (3) pricing; (4) appraising and valuing; (5) paying and receiving; (6) entering and keeping general and detailed records; (7) safekeeping; (8) collecting, recording, calculating, and accruing investment income; (9) conducting general clerical, secretarial, office maintenance, supervisory, and executive duties; (10) handling personnel, supplies, mail; and (11) all other activities reasonably related to the investing of funds and the obtaining of investment income.

Loss adjustment expenses comprise all expenses connected, in whole or in part, with the adjustment and recording of policy claims, including the totals of the operating expense classification and claim adjustment services. This also includes the types of employee-related claim adjustment expenses incurred in (1) estimating amounts of claims; (2) paying and receiving; (3) entering and keeping general and detailed records; (4) general clerical, secretarial, office maintenance, supervisory, and executive duties; (5) handling personnel, supplies, and mail; and (6) all other activities reasonably related to the adjustment and recording of policy claims.

Acquisition, field supervision and collection expenses comprise all expenses incurred wholly or partially in the following activities:

1. Soliciting and procuring business and developing the sales force.
2. Writing policy contracts, and checking and directly supervising the work of policy writers.
3. Receiving and paying premiums and commissions; entering into or setting up records of premiums and commissions receivable and payable for collection purposes; balancing and maintaining such records; corresponding with and visiting insureds and producers for the purpose of collecting premiums or adjusting differences; checking current accounts from producers; auditing records of delinquent agents; and monitoring services of collection agencies.
4. Compiling and distributing expiration lists, notices of premiums due, lists of premiums or premium balances receivable and payable, contingent and other commission statements, production statements for acquisition and field supervision purposes, and similar data.
5. Maintaining goodwill of policyholders and producers, activities of field agents, contact work related to acquisition, field supervision and collection, making contracts and agreements with producers, and activities in connection with agency appointments and replacements.
6. Rendering service to agents and other producers, such as obtaining agents' licenses and providing office space, personnel, and telephone.
7. Advertising and publicity of every nature related to acquisition, field supervision, and collection.
8. Miscellaneous activities of agents, brokers and producers other than employees; inspections, quoting premiums, signing policies; examining and mailing policies, applications and daily reports; compiling figures for current accounts; and correspondence and other bookkeeping and clerical work.

9. Other activities reasonably attributable to acquisitions and field operations such as: keeping general and detailed records; paying and receiving; general clerical, secretarial, office maintenance, supervisory and executive work; and handling personnel, supplies, and mail.

Taxes, licenses, and fees include state and local insurance taxes, insurance department licenses and fees, payroll taxes, and other similar expenses. Federal and foreign income taxes and real estate taxes are not included in this expense category.

General expenses comprise all expenses not assignable to other expense groups. An effort is made to allocate as many expenses as possible to one of the first four expense categories in prefence to using the general expense classification.

Table 4-4 shows to which functional group each type of expense should be allocated or the basis to be used to allocate such expense. For those operating expense classifications that allow overhead on salaries to be used as the basis for allocation, companies may adopt any other basis that yields more accurate results.

Allocation of Expenses to Lines of Business. Expenses are allocated to various lines of business in Part II of the Insurance Expense Exhibit rather than in the annual statement. The Insurance Expense Exhibit is described later in this chapter but the basis for line of business expense allocations is presented in this section. Expenses are allocated to lines of business on a basis best suited to each expense item. Allocations are made by functional expense groups. Each expense classification, within each functional expense group, is allocated separately to the various lines of business.

All bases used in such allocations are required to be appropriate to the expense group of which the expense is a part. For example, expenses allocated to lines of business as an overhead on salaries should be computed only in relation to the salaries included in the same expense group.

Uniform accounting instructions stress that a direct allocation must be made wherever possible. For instance, the salary and expenses of an adjuster who handles nothing but automobile bodily injury cases should be allocated to that line of business. If the adjuster handles both bodily injury and property damage claims, a special study must be made of the proportion of his or her time involved in handling each type of claim, and the adjuster's salary must be distributed between automobile bodily injury and property damage. On the other hand, the salary of the supervisor of an entire claim department must be allocated to all lines of insurance and to all coverages. The best basis for that allocation would be the proportion of the department employees' salaries directly

Table 4-4

Expense Allocations

Type of Expense Incurred	Expense Function or Basis of Expense Allocation
(1) Claim adjustment services	
Direct	Loss adjustment expenses
Reinsurance assumed	Loss adjustment expenses
Reinsurance ceded	Loss adjustment expenses
(2) Commission and brokerage	
Direct	See commission and allowances
Reinsurance assumed	Acquisition, field supervision, and collection expenses
Reinsurance ceded	Acquisition, field supervision, and collection expenses
Contingent—net	Acquisition, field supervision, and collection expenses
Policy and membership fees	Acquisition, field supervision, and collection expenses
(3) Allowances to managers and agents	See commission and allowances
(4) Advertising	Acquisition, field supervision, and collection expenses
(5) Boards, bureaus, and associations	General expenses
(6) Surveys and underwriting reports	General expenses
(7) Audits of assureds' records	General expenses
(8) Salaries	See special instructions relating to the allocation of salaries and other expenses
(9) Employee relations and welfare	Overhead on salaries
(10) Insurance	Special studies
(11) Directors' fees	Overhead on salaries
(12) Travel and travel items	Special studies
(13) Rent and rent items	Overhead on salaries
(14) Equipment	Overhead on salaries
(15) Printing and stationery	Overhead on salaries
(16) Postage, telephone and telegraph, exchange and express	Overhead on salaries
(17) Legal and auditing	Special studies
(18) Taxes, licenses, and fees	Taxes
(19) Real estate expenses	Investment expenses
(20) Real estate taxes	Investment expenses
(21) Miscellaneous	Special studies

allocated to each line and coverage. For those expenses not susceptible to direct and accurate allocation, other bases permitted are (1) premiums, (2) overhead on salary, and (3) special studies. For those expense classifications permitting the bases "overhead on salaries" or "premiums," any other basis of allocation may be used if it yields more accurate results.

General Procedures in Allocating Salaries Whenever possible, salaries of employees who work solely with a specific company, expense group, or primary line of business shall be directly allocated to the specific company, group, or line of business. When a direct allocation is not possible, salaries should be allocated on one of the following bases, or a combination of bases: (1) number of items or units, (2) time studies, (3) overhead on other allocations, (4) premiums, (5) dollar volume of losses, and (6) other special studies. These bases will all be described in greater detail below.

All bases of allocation and their application should be subject to the restrictions, modifications, and exceptions contained in the general instructions regarding allocation bases. Weightings may be applied in using any basis of allocation provided that the justification for these weightings is explained. Weightings are not to be used to give effect to a basis that the instructions prohibit.

Number of Items or Units. Item and unit counts may include the number of premium entries, number of policies, number of loss entries, number of accidents, number of employees, or any other unit or item counts that aid in the allocation of expenses. To the greatest practical extent, unit or item counts should be applied only to expenses incurred in activities directly related to the bases.

To determine whether the number of premium entries is an appropriate basis of allocation, a company should consider the number of premiums on original policies, plus additional premiums, return premiums, reinsurance premiums, and return premiums on reinsurance. It may also be important to consider whether more than one data processing card is keypunched or more than one entry is made covering a single amount. A final consideration when evaluating the basis for allocation may be how procedural differences for different types of entries affect cost.

In determining whether the number of policies is a good basis for allocation, one should consider policies underlying another policy, policies covering more than one line of business, and policies for various terms. Again, procedural differences for different types of policies may affect cost, and if so, they should be a consideration.

To see if the number of loss entries is an appropriate basis of allocation, one should consider the number of gross entries, plus salvage entries and reinsurance entries for paid losses, or for outstanding losses, or for both. In addition, the manner in which procedural differences for different types of loss entries affect cost should be included.

In determining whether the number of accidents makes an appropriate basis of allocation, an examination should be made of accidents on which specific estimates are set up, accidents on which no specific estimate is made, and accidents for which no claim is made. The cost effect of procedural differences for various types of accidents may be a further factor.

The number of employees should be used as a basis of allocation only when the cost logically follows the number of employees. It may be of use, when properly weighted, in allocating such company entities as the cafeteria, personnel department, and payroll department.

Time Studies.   Time studies are actual measurements of the time required to complete a routine or regularly occurring procedure. Before deciding to use a time study as a basis of allocation, a company would want to consider how many motions must be studied to obtain a valid average and whether there might be any conditions during the study that might distort the average.

Overhead on Other Allocations.   Salaries of supervisors and executives may be distributed as an overhead on the salaries of employees whom they supervise. Salaries of departments, such as a mail department or word processing group, may be distributed as an overhead on the salaries of people whose work is handled. However, salaries should not be distributed as an overhead if any other basis of allocation is more appropriate.

Premiums.   Premiums are not to be used as a basis of allocation except in three instances: one, when specifically noted as a permissible basis; two, when the expense is incurred as a percentage of premiums (subject to instructions under commissions and allowances); or three, when the expenses are logically allocable on the basis of premiums. Premiums should never be used as a basis of allocation in connection with clerical, technical, secretarial, office maintenance, supervisory, or executive activities unless such basis is clearly appropriate or unless all other reasonable bases of allocation have been considered and found to be inappropriate.

In determining whether premiums are an appropriate basis of allocation, a review should be made of direct and reinsurance premiums, and written, earned, and unearned premiums, as well as their subdivisions.

Dollar Volume of Losses.   Dollar volume of losses is to be used as a basis of allocation only when dollar amounts of losses influence the activities resulting in expense. If all other reasonable bases of allocation have been considered and found less appropriate, then dollar volume of losses may be considered. In determining whether dollar volume of losses makes a good basis of allocation, a company should consider its direct and reinsurance losses and its paid, incurred, and outstanding losses, as well as their subdivisions.

Other Allocation Bases. It is usually possible to allocate indirect salaries fully by use of one or a combination of the five bases just described. Other allocation bases are permitted but only if their usage can be shown to produce more accurate results. This can be shown from special cost studies conducted by the insurer. Usually, companies prefer to use the established bases.

NET INVESTMENT INCOME

Investment income is a very important part of an insurance company's operation. Since a large portion of collected premiums is invested shortly after the policy is written, substantial investment earnings result. In 1976, for instance, the investment income of property and liability insurance companies amounted to $3,628,913,621, while underwriting operations produced a loss of $1,405,967,932 according to *Best's Aggregates and Averages* 1977 edition.

A large investment base is possible because insurance premiums are usually collected in advance of expense and loss payments. After acquisition costs are paid, the balance of the payment is invested until needed to settle a loss. Because of the importance of investment income, the industry is continually studying ways to accelerate cash flow so additional investments can be made.

Investment strategies vary from company to company. Some companies will stress equity securities, thereby giving up some investment income for potential capital appreciation. Others will invest their funds in debt issues to gain investment income.

Some state insurance departments, recognizing the importance of investment income in the operations of a company, require investment income to be used in developing premium rate structures for personal lines business. The Insurance Expense Exhibit requires that investment income be allocated by lines of business.

Federal income tax status of the insurance company also will influence the use of investment funds. In a period of underwriting profit, investible funds are placed in tax-exempt bonds, while in a period of underwriting loss, high yielding corporate and government bonds will receive the investment funds.

Net investment income is the amount of investment income earned less the investment expenses. Interest and other income accruals are inventories put into the statement as nonledger assets. To determine the actual amount of interest earned, the interest collections for the year are added to or subtracted from the difference between the accruals at the beginning and at the end of the year. This gives the same result as if the interest accruals were recorded on the books throughout the year. An insurance company usually does not record these items on the books; it makes the computation for financial statement purposes only.

In many instances the purchase price of a bond is above or below the par value of the bond. Thus, if bonds are amortized, interest income includes the amortization and represents the effective rate of interest earned on the assets. The bond premium, or discount, is just an adjustment of the nominal interest rate. Some companies record these adjustments on the books monthly. Others compute them less frequently.

Dividends earned for the year are obtained by adding the dividend collected during the year to the dividends receivable at the end of the year less the dividends receivable at the beginning of the year.

Mortgage loan investment income earned is the gross amount collected during the year adjusted for any interest paid in advance and for the accrued interest at the beginning and end of the year. If the mortgage loan was purchased for an amount different than the unpaid balance, the difference is amortized in accordance with statutory rules. This amortization is an adjustment to mortgage interest earned.

Real estate income usually consists of the amount charged for occupancy of an insurance company's own buildings plus any rents received from tenants. The amount charged for occupancy of its own buildings is investment income and, at the same time, rental expense to the various functional areas of operations. If the property is mortgaged, the interest payments are deducted from rental income.

Investment expenses are handled in the same manner as "other underwriting expenses." Certain items are charged directly to investment expense accounts; allocations are made from other expense accounts in accordance with uniform accounting instructions. In addition to investment expenses, other expenses such as depreciation of real estate and interest on borrowed funds are taken as deductions to arrive at net investment income.

Part 1 of the Underwriting and Investment Exhibit in the annual statement is a report on investment income collected and a calculation of investment income earned during the year. It is in itself a summary of figures that appear in Schedules A, B, C, D, N, and BA of the annual statement. All of these schedules are listings of assets owned as follows: Schedule A, real estate; Schedule B, mortgages; Schedule C, collateral loans; Schedule D, bonds and stocks; Schedule N, bank accounts; and

Schedule BA, other invested assets. Totals of the interest, dividends, and other income collected; the interest, dividends and rentals paid in advance; and the accruals of interest and dividends at the end of the year, as shown in the various schedules, are carried over into Part 1 of the Underwriting and Expense Exhibit. The items paid in advance and the accruals at the end of the previous year are carried over from Part 1 of the previous year's annual statement.

After all of these figures are included, the amount earned can be calculated.

ADD: Amounts collected, current year
                          Amounts paid in advance, end of previous year
                          Amounts accrued, end of current year
SUBTRACT: Amounts paid in advance, end of current year
                          Amounts accrued, end of previous year
EQUALS: Investment income, current year

The total of these earned items represents total interest, dividends, and real estate income earned. From this total of earned investment income is deducted the total investment expenses incurred (from Part 4 of the Underwriting and Investment Exhibit which shows the expenses incurred and the allocation of expenses between functional groups) and the depreciation of real estate, for those companies that depreciate real estate annually on a formula basis. The difference between the total interest, dividends, real estate income, and total deductions is known as the *net investment income*. The net investment income is carried over to line 8 of the Underwriting and Investment, Statement of Income.

This schedule of net investment income earned is typical of the method for determining the income and the costs of operations of an insurance company for annual statement purposes. Income earned is determined by taking the cash collections, adding the accruals as inventoried at the end of the current year, and substracting the accruals as inventoried at the end of the previous year.

Part 1A of the Underwriting and Investment Exhibit reports the profits and losses on investments disposed of during the year and the gains and losses from changes in the admitted value of investments. The first column shows the profits on sales or maturity by types of investments: bonds, stocks, mortgage loans, real estate, collateral loans, cash and bank deposits, and other invested assets and options. The second column shows the losses on sales or maturity. Columns 3 and 4 show the increases or decreases, by adjustment in book value, for the amortization of premiums or accrual of discount on securities and for the depreciation on real estate. These adjustments are made here only in those cases where amortization of premiums or accrual of discounts are not included in interest income and depreciation on real estate is not shown as a reduction of real estate income in the preceding schedule.

The increases or decreases by adjustment in the book value of investments shown in columns 3 and 4 are supported by details in Schedules A and D. The annual statement blank allows companies to choose between reflecting accruals of discounts and amortization of premiums as adjustments to interest earned or as unrealized gains or losses. If they are reflected in interest earned, they are not included in Part 1A. Companies occasionally make adjustments in book values of real estate to reflect appraisals or write-downs of values authorized by the company's board of directors and appropriate committees of the board. Such adjustments are reflected in Part 1A.

Column 5 shows the changes resulting from market fluctuation or change in admitted value of securities. Again, these are inventory figures; that is, the figures are not contained in the company's ledger but are determined during preparation of the annual statement. They represent the change in the difference between the admitted value of each group of securities and their book value at the beginning and end of the year. The securities at the beginning and at the end may be entirely different since a 100 percent turnover during the year is possible. In each case, the profits and losses on the liquidation or other disposition of securities will be shown in columns 1 and 2. Any adjustments in book value will be shown in columns 3 and 4. Column 5 shows the residual difference (in the value of each group of securities) resulting from revaluation (at the end of the year as compared to the beginning of the year) of the inventory of securities on hand.

After all these figures are calculated, the net difference, or the net gain or loss from all sources, is calculated. This total—the "total capital gain or loss for the year"—is then broken down on lines 11 and 12 to show two separate amounts (which together must equal the grand total on line 10), representing (1) the net realized capital gains and losses and (2) the net unrealized capital gains and losses. The realized gains or losses are normally the net of columns 1 and 2. The unrealized gains or losses are generally the net of columns 3, 4, and 5. This distribution is necessary because the net realized capital gains and losses are carried to the income statement. The unrealized capital gains and losses are carried over to the capital and surplus account.

OTHER INCOME

Items of income or expense that are not related to the underwriting or investment function are recorded in the Other Income section of the Statement of Income.

Agents' balances recovered or charged off consist of agents' balances written off during the period less the amounts recovered on balances previously charged off. As described in Chapter 1, agents' balances that are more than ninety days old are considered a nonadmitted asset and charged to surplus. Under generally accepted accounting principles, the company will make a provision for bad debts and charge the accounts written off against such provision.

Finance and service charges not included in premiums are used when a company charges policyholders a fee for paying their premiums on an installment plan. Other types of accounts included in this section are items such as outstanding checks charged off, sale of furniture and equipment, and interest expenses.

GAINS AND LOSSES IN SURPLUS

The year-to-year change in a property and liability insurance company's net worth is not fully explained by the current year's net income. Gains and losses that, according to existing accounting rules, do not flow through the income statement but are direct adjustments in surplus can be analyzed by studying the capital and surplus account. This account is appended to the statutory Statement of Income and, together with the income statement, reconciles balance sheet surplus between the year's beginning and end. As an illustration, the capital and surplus account from INA's 1977 annual statement is shown in Table 4-5.

Net unrealized capital gains or losses result from reporting investments on the balance sheet at an admitted value which is different from book value. The most common entry in this category is stocks. Stocks are generally shown at market value which can vary from cost or book value. When that happens, surplus is affected, so an entry must be made in the reconciliation of surplus to explain the difference in value. Column 5 of Part 1A of the Underwriting and Investment Exhibit summarizes net gains and losses arising from differences between book and admitted values of assets. For instance, in INA's 1977 annual statement, as illustrated in Table 4-6, bonds ($5,597,412) and preferred stocks ($7,166,273) were written-up in value while common stocks of unaffiliated companies ($47,334,143) and of affiliates ($41,569,350) were written-down in value. The net unrealized capital loss of $76,139,808 calculated in Part 1A of the Underwriting and Investment Exhibit is carried forward to line 23 of the capital and surplus account.

In accepted insurance accounting practices, this "unrealized" gain or loss is reflected in the company's surplus. However, no provision is made for federal income taxes which would become payable if such

Table 4-5

Annual Statement for the Year 1977 of the Insurance Company of North America

Capital and Surplus Account	Current Year	Previous Year
21. Surplus as regards policyholders, December 31 previous year	$454,248,899	$389,449,063
Gains (+) and Losses (−) in Surplus		
22. Net income (from Item 20)	+115,555,360	+20,156,476
23. Net unrealized capital gains or losses (Part 1A)	−76,139,808	+99,036,694
24. Change in non-admitted assets (Exhibit 2, Item 33, Col. 3)	+8,818,324	−4,105,286
25. Change in liability for unauthorized reinsurance	−7,094,328	+9,990,555
26. Change in foreign exchange adjustment	−893,753	+401,592
27. Change in excess of statutory reserves over statement reserves		+2,241,023
28. Capital changes:		
(a) Paid in		
(b) Transferred from surplus (stock divd.)		
(c) Transferred to surplus		
29. Surplus adjustments:		
(a) Paid in		
(b) Transferred to capital (stock divc.)		
(c) Transferred from capital		
30. Net remittances from or to Home Office	−50,583,756	−51,058,674
31. Dividends to stockholders (cash)		
32. Change in treasury stock	+164	+225
33. Tower Insurance Pool		−13,341,660
34. Federal income tax—prior year		
35. Loss expense reserve adjustment—prior year		+1,478,891
36. Foreign exchange on foreign income taxes—prior year	+1,698,081	
37.		
38.		
39. Change in surplus as regards policyholders for the year	−8,639,716	+64,799,836
40. Surplus as regards policyholders, December 31 current year	$445,609,183	$454,248,899

Table 4-6

Annual Statement for the Year 1977 of the Insurance Company of North America

Part 1A—Capital Gains and Losses on Investments

	1 Profit on Sales or Maturity	2 Loss on Sales or Maturity	3 Increases by Adjustment in Book Value	4 Decreases by Adjustment in Book Value	5 Net Gain (+) or Loss (−) from Change in Difference Between Book and Admitted Values	6 Total (Net of Cols. 1 to 5 incl.)
1. U. S. government bonds	$ 1,167,766	$ 867,447				$ 300,319
1.1 Bonds exempt from U.S. tax	1,125,662	2,399,430				−1,273,768
1.2 Other bonds (unaffiliated)	3,299,770	3,640,842			$ +5,597,412	5,256,340
1.3 Bonds of affiliates						
2.1 Preferred stocks (unaffiliated)	293,116	6,777,795			+7,166,273	681,594
2.11 Preferred stocks of affiliates						
2.2 Common stocks (unaffiliated)	11,982,060	14,935,713			−47,334,143	−50,287,796
2.21 Common stocks of affiliates	101,744,342	50,066,062			−41,569,350	10,108,930
3. Mortgage loans						
4. Real estate				2		
5. Collateral loans						
6. Cash on hand and on deposit						
7. Other invested assets		3,716,813				−3,716,813
8. Equipment	458,375	407,795				50,580
9.						
10. TOTALS	$120,071,091	$82,811,897			$−76,139,808	$−38,880,614

(Distribution of Item 10, Col. 6)

11. Net realized capital gains or losses[1]	Column 1, plus 3, minus columns 2 and 4	$ 37,259,194
12. Net unrealized capital gains or losses[1]	Column 5	−76,139,808

1. Attach statement or memorandum explaining basis of division.
2. Excluding $152,309 depreciation on real estate included in Part 1, Item 12.

income is realized; nor is any provision made for tax refunds for unrealized capital losses. The failure to consider these adjustments does not seem to agree with FASB Statement No. 12, *Accounting for Certain Marketable Securities.* Therefore, this practice does not fully conform with GAAP, and an adjustment must be made when statutory financial statements are converted for general purpose use.[3]

It should be pointed out that unrealized capital gains and losses have caused considerable fluctuations in the capital and surplus (policyholders' surplus) accounts of property-liability insurance companies. Property-liability companies typically have carried a significant percentage of their assets in common stocks. As explained above, since common stocks are carried at market value, any increase or decrease in the market value of the portfolio must be directly offset by a corresponding increase or decrease in the policyholders' surplus account.

As an example, a 40 percent drop in the Dow Jones Industrial Average occurred between December 31, 1972, and December 31, 1974. The related overall stock market decrease greatly eroded the policyholders' surplus accounts of most property-liability insurers. Coupled with the disastrous underwriting losses of 1974, a number of companies teetered on the brink of insolvency. The significance of unrealized capital gains and losses became even more apparent in 1975. That year marked the worst period of underwriting losses ever experienced by the insurance industry. Had the stock market not recovered to offset these underwriting losses in 1975, the policyholders' surplus accounts of an unacceptably large number of companies would have dropped to the point of technical insolvency.

Change in nonadmitted assets is the difference between the nonadmitted assets carried at the beginning of the accounting period and those carried at its end. This entry is necessary to reflect the gain or loss in surplus for the nonadmitted assets. Nonadmitted assets include such items as agents' balances over three months due, past due bills receivable (taken for premiums), equipment, furniture, and supplies. Exhibit 2 in the annual statement is an inventory of the assets considered nonadmitted at the beginning and end of the year.

Change in the liability for unauthorized reinsurance records the change in the liability a company must set up when reinsurance is placed with a company not licensed in the state where the annual statement is being filed. Schedule F—Part 2 of the annual statement is an inventory of the unauthorized companies at balance sheet date. The appropriate columns of Part 2 are transferred to lines 14, 15, and 16 of the liabilities page in the balance sheet. The difference between years of line 15 is the amount charged or credited to surplus.

The change in foreign exchange adjustment is used when a company has assets and liabilities in a foreign country. These assets and liabilities must be converted to United States currency for financial statement purposes. The change in the foreign exchange adjustment, located on line 17 of the liabilities, between financial statement dates is charged or credited directly to surplus.

Change in excess of statutory reserves over statement reserves (Schedule P) consists of the change between periods of the excess of the statutory reserve over the case basis reserve and the loss expense reserve for certain lines of business which is reflected on line 16 of the balance sheet. Note that changes in excess reserves affect surplus but not income.

Capital changes are segregated by source of increase or decrease. The captions "paid in" and "transfers to and from surplus" are used to record changes in capital stock during the year. Paid in is used whenever capital stock is issued for cash. Transfers from surplus are used to record the stock issued when a stock dividend has been declared. Transfers to surplus are used when the par value of the stock has been lowered but the number of shares outstanding has stayed the same.

Surplus adjustments consist of adjustments to surplus related to the capitalization of the company and are also segregated by source of the increase or decrease. The captions "paid in" and "transfers to and from capital" are used to record changes in gross paid in and contributed surplus. Paid in is used to reflect cash received in excess of par value when additional capital stock is issued for cash or for surplus contributions by existing stockholders. Transfers to and from capital are used to reflect stock dividends and reduction of par value of outstanding stock, as described in the preceding paragraph.

Net remittances to or from home office are used to record transfers of cash between a United States branch of a foreign company and the foreign company's home office. Change in treasury stock reflects the change in ownership of treasury stock at cost.

In addition to the captioned items in the capital and surplus statement, some companies make a direct charge to surplus for such items as adjustments to prior years' income taxes, effects of changes in accounting method, and errors noted in prior years' financial statements. Also, some companies provide a reserve for taxes on unrealized capital gains and show the change in the reserve as a write-in item in the statement.

INSURANCE EXPENSE EXHIBIT

The Insurance Expense Exhibit is a supplement to the annual statement. This Exhibit contains an analysis of profitability by line of business, showing net income before federal income taxes. The Exhibit also contains a detailed analysis of expenses by classification and function.

The Exhibit has three main purposes. First, it presents the company's expenses on a uniform basis for each account by function, and for each function by line of business. Second, it reports the operating gain or loss by line of business after consideration of the statutory underwriting result, the investment income assigned, and policyholders' dividends. Third, it furnishes aggregate expense data by line of insurance which can be used as source data for expense loadings in rate making.

The Exhibit is made up of four separate parts. A brief description of the information contained in each part is given below. Each part is illustrated with an excerpt from the 1977 Insurance Expense Exhibit of INA and its affiliated fire and casualty insurers.

Part I—Allocation to Expense Groups

Part I is an expansion of Part 4 of the Underwriting and Investment Exhibit in the annual statement. Expenses are itemized in this section for the five functional expense groups discussed earlier in this chapter:

- Loss adjustment expenses
- Acquisition, field supervision, and collection expenses
- General expenses
- Taxes, licenses, and fees
- Investment expenses

Note that the total incurred expense figures shown in Table 4-7 correspond with those shown previously in Part 4 of the Underwriting and Investment Exhibit shown in Table 4-3.

Part II—Allocation of Lines of Business

Part II is divided into two sections:

- Section A—Premiums, Losses, Expenses and Net Income, and Ratios to Earned Premiums
- Section B—Adjusted Direct Premiums and Expenses, and Ratios to Adjusted Direct Premiums.

Underwriting expenses shown by function in Part I of this Exhibit are allocated to the principal lines of business in Part II. Profitability for individual lines of business is determined by disaggregating data shown

224—Insurance Accounting and Finance

Table 4-7
Insurance Expense Exhibit of the Insurance Company of North America and Its Affiliated Fire and Casualty Insurers for the Year Ended December 31, 1977

Part I—Allocation to Expense Groups

Operating Expense Classifications	1 Loss Adjustment Expenses	2 Acquisition, Field Supervision and Collection Expenses	Other Underwriting Expenses — 3 General Expenses	4 Taxes, Licenses and Fees	5 Investment Expenses	6 Total Expenses
1. Claim adjustment services:						
a. Direct	$113,097,894					$113,097,894
b. Reinsurance assumed	12,302,406					12,302,406
c. Reinsurance ceded	16,936,108					16,936,108
d. Net claim adjustment services	$108,464,192					$108,464,192
2. Commission and brokerage:						
a. Direct		$294,321,095				294,321,095
b. Reinsurance assumed		190,045,331				190,045,331
c. Reinsurance ceded		172,199,370				172,199,370
d. Contingent—net		29,676,565				29,676,565
e. Policy and membership fees						
f. Net commission and brokerage		$341,843,621				$341,843,621
3. Allowances to managers and agents	132,163	353,349				485,512
4. Advertising	305	2,462,896	$ 62,588			2,525,789
5. Boards, bureaus and associations	19,351	17,099	11,044,430			11,080,880
6. Surveys and underwriting reports	2,752	112,001	2,849,981			2,964,734
7. Audit of assureds' records			130,239			130,239

8. Salaries	38,738,465	32,910,864	81,155,285		$ 490,999	$ 153,295,633
9. Employee relations and welfare	4,328,864	3,463,984	10,522,478		48,539	18,463,865
10. Insurance	71,560	45,818	844,941		77,216	839,535
11. Directors' fees			78,597			78,597
12. Travel and travel items	3,367,244	2,683,158	8,138,141		39,669	14,228,212
13. Rent and rent items	5,106,432	5,065,999	12,445,226		112,751	22,730,468
14. Equipment	2,655,083	819,454	10,138,558		37,363	13,650,458
15. Printing and stationery	1,430,845	964,194	4,934,059		39,303	7,368,201
16. Postage, telephone and telegraph, exchange and express	3,902,305	2,637,575	7,064,761		45,811	13,650,452
17. Legal and auditing	634,896	660,172	3,876,485		1,592,707	6,764,260
17a. Totals (items 3-17)	$60,390,145	$52,196,563	$153,185,769		$2,484,358	$268,256,835
18. Taxes, licenses, and fees:						
a. State and local insurance taxes and fees				45,014,771	9,481	45,024,252
b. Insurance department licenses and fees				738,347	15,123	753,470
c. Payroll taxes	4,762		19,286	11,291,229	4,483	11,319,760
d. All other (excl. fed. and foreign income and real estate)				2,143,268	436	2,143,704
e. Total licenses, and fees	$4,762		$19,286	$59,187,615	$29,523	$59,241,186
19. Real estate expenses				291	1,267,678	1,267,969
20. Real estate taxes					509,206	509,206
21. Miscellaneous (itemize):						
a. Outside services	4,781,934	3,626,960	8,026,728	226,572	561,001	17,223,195
b. Income and charges from special services	-2,103,342	-1,357,024	-6,256,803		1,148,154	-8,569,015
c. Contributions	331		6,226			6,557
d. Other	58,751	327,997	427,137		12,608	826,493
22. TOTAL EXPENSES INCURRED	$171,596,773	$396,638,117	$155,408,343	$59,414,478	$6,012,528	$789,070,239

in the annual statement. The following revenue and expense categories are included:

- Revenue
  - Net premiums written
  - Net premiums earned
  - Net investment gain or loss and other income

- Expense
  - Net losses incurred
  - Loss adjustment expenses paid
  - Loss adjustment expenses incurred
  - Commission and brokerage incurred
  - Other acquisition, field supervision, and collection expenses incurred
  - Boards, bureaus, and association expenses incurred
  - Other general expenses incurred
  - General expenses incurred (total of above two items)
  - Taxes, licenses, and fees incurred
  - Dividends to policyholders

Table 4-8 illustrates a portion of Part II from the consolidated Insurance Expense Exhibit of INA and its affiliates.

Net investment income is generally a significant part of an insurance company's net income. A great portion of the investment income is derived from investing unearned premium funds and funds that ultimately will be used to pay outstanding claims and adjustment expenses. In recent years, some states have explicitly incorporated investment income on policyholder-supplied funds in their rate-making calculations. As a result, the expense exhibit was changed in 1971 to include investment income and dividends to policyholders. Since investment income is also derived from the funds made available by the company's net worth, a separate category called capital and surplus accounts was included in the Exhibit to credit that account with its share of investment income. Including investment income ensures that the net income before federal income taxes as shown in the Expense Exhibit agrees with the same item in the statement of income in the annual statement.

Section A of Part II includes the effect of reinsurance assumed and ceded by the company. The presence of substantial reinsurance activities can distort many of the income and expense classifications if an adjustment is not made. To eliminate this distortion, Section B was developed to more clearly indicate the costs associated with writing direct business.

Section B is a better source for analyzing or determining expense loadings for rate-making purposes. Section B relates the expense classifications to direct premiums written whereas Section A shows the expense classifications to net premiums earned. It is generally agreed that expenses such as commissions, taxes, and other underwriting expenses bear a closer relationship to premiums written than to premiums earned.

Part III—Summary of Workers' Compensation Expenses and Ratios to Earned Premiums

Part III of the Insurance Expense Exhibit produces a national workers' compensation expense ratio on a standard premium basis. An example of this part of the Exhibit is shown in Table 4-9. The standard premium is computed using the rates in effect before the premium is adjusted under premium discount or retrospective rating. This is accomplished by eliminating, on line 2, the adjustments for premium discounts and retrospective rating from earned premiums. The net result is entered on line 3.

Line 4 contains the premiums, if any, applicable to war projects of national defense projects. The total of lines 3 and 4 equals the standard premiums on regular business plus war projects. Lines 6 through 10 are all the underwriting expenses except losses incurred. These amounts are taken from Part II and are related to total net earned premiums to obtain itemized expense ratios.

Line 12 shows the effect of expense graduation. Expense graduation is the amount by which the full expenses included in the standard premium exceed the expenses provided for in the net discounted premium.

Part IV—Exhibit of Workers' Compensation Earned Premiums and Incurred Losses by States

Part IV of the Insurance Expense Exhibit shows the earned premiums, losses incurred, and loss ratio, on a direct premiums written basis, for workers' compensation insurance by state. This part of the exhibit allows state insurance regulators to closely monitor experience in this politically sensitive social insurance line of business. The reinsurance assumed and ceded experience is shown at the bottom of the page on a national basis in order that this part should agree with the workers' compensation amounts included in Part II of this Exhibit and in the annual statement. An abbreviated version of Part IV is contained in Table 4-10.

Table 4-8

Insurance Expense Exhibit of the Insurance Company of North America and Its Affiliated Fire and Casualty Insurers for the Year Ended December 31, 1977

Part II—Allocation to Lines of Business

A. PREMIUMS, LOSSES, EXPENSES AND NET INCOME, AND RATIOS TO EARNED PREMIUMS.	31 Total All Lines (Cols. 1 to 30.1 incl.) Amount	%	1 Fire Amount	%	2 Allied Lines Amount	%	3 Farmowners Multiple Peril Amount	%	4 Homeowners Multiple Peril Amount	%	5 Commercial Multiple Peril Amount	%
1. Net Premiums Written (Annual Statement Pg. 8, Part 2C, Col. 4)	$2,140,493,419	—	$73,849,670	—	$34,639,904	—	$8,995,232	—	$161,456,576	—	$391,305,190	—
2. Net Premiums Earned (Annual Statement Pg. 7, Part 2 Col. 4)	2,069,967,397	100.0	82,763,596	100.0	37,431,598	100.0	8,494,428	100.0	146,997,173	100.0	364,992,902	100.0
3. Net Losses Incurred (Annual Statement Page 9, Part 3, Col. 7)	1,341,014,576	64.8	50,996,936	61.6	12,008,547	32.1	5,151,623	60.6	77,981,660	53.0	179,977,079	49.3
4. Loss Adjustment Expenses Paid (Annual Statement Pg. 11, Col. 1, Line 25)	131,477,712	—	3,070,063	—	1,102,994	—	370,985	—	7,803,753	—	17,915,923	—
5. Loss Adjustment Expenses Incurred (Part I, Col. 1, Line 22)	171,596,773	8.3	2,854,066	3.4	1,059,671	2.8	864,050	10.2	8,620,673	5.9	28,189,568	7.7
6. Commission and Brokerage Incurred (Part I, Col. 2, Line 2 (f))	341,843,681	16.5	6,922,853	8.4	7,349,280	19.6	1,885,038	22.2	34,346,950	23.4	72,600,563	19.9
7. Other Acquisition, Field Supervision and Collection Expenses Incurred (Part I, Col. 2, Line 22 minus Line 2 (f))	54,794,496	2.6	4,754,147	5.7	682,162	1.8	12,473	0.1	3,067,891	2.1	10,174,769	2.8
8. Boards, Bureaus and Associations Expenses Incurred (Part I, Col. 3, Line 5)	11,044,430	0.5	1,174,935	1.4	934,596	2.5	10,013	0.1	379,205	0.3	1,670,935	0.5
9. Other General Expenses Incurred (Line 10 minus Line 8)	144,363,913	7.0	8,377,876	10.1	3,503,351	9.5	1,071,608	12.6	11,138,507	7.5	26,421,851	7.2

Item												
10. General Expenses Incurred (Part I, Col. 3, Line 22)	135,408,343	7.5	9,552,811	11.5	4,437,947	12.0	1,081,621	12.7	11,512,712	7.8	28,092,786	7.7
11. Taxes, Licenses and Fees Incurred (Part I, Col. 4, Line 22)	59,414,478	2.9	5,565,890	4.6	1,173,222	3.2	255,770	3.1	4,787,872	3.2	10,914,757	2.9
12. Total Expenses Incurred (Lines 5, 6, 7, 10 and 11)	783,057,711	37.8	27,769,767	33.6	14,702,282	39.2	4,096,952	46.3	62,341,098	42.4	149,972,433	41.0
13. Net Investment Gain or Loss and Other Income (Sum of Items 9A and 17, Page 4, of Annual Statement)	−45,116,785 / 228,303,139	—	3,456,506	4.2	652,667	1.7	273,680	3.2	3,999,694	2.7	19,021,512	5.2
14. Dividends to Policyholders (Item 18A, Page 4, of Annual Statement)	10,159,679	0.5	13,112	—	225,338	0.6		—	127,119	0.1	5,670,326	1.6
15. Net Income before federal and foreign income taxes (Line 2 plus 13 minus 3, 12 and 14, to agree with Item 18B, Page 4 of Annual Statement)	80,851,216 / 164,038,630	—	7,443,287	9.0	11,148,298	29.8	$480,487	−5.7	10,546,990	7.2	48,394,576	13.3

B. ADJUSTED DIRECT PREMIUMS AND EXPENSES (SEE NOTE C) AND RATIOS TO ADJUSTED DIRECT PREMIUMS.

Item												
16. Direct Premiums Written (Annual Statement Page 8, Part 2C, Col. 1)	2,204,908,515	—	135,071,193	—	55,819,914	—	9,993,302	—	168,874,657	—	416,582,644	—
17. Adjusted Direct Premiums Written (See Note C)	2,203,245,416	100.0	137,653,265	100.0	56,995,313	100.0	10,666,774	100.0	179,541,698	100.0	416,575,506	100.0
18. Direct Commission and Brokerage Incurred (Part I, Line 2 (a) plus direct contingent commission and policy and membership fees)	320,507,367	—	25,808,664	—	11,006,668	—	2,122,621	—	36,210,587	—	75,897,258	—
19. Adjusted Direct Commission and Brokerage Incurred (See Note C)	323,864,168	14.7	26,017,895	18.9	11,100,545	19.5	2,360,772	22.1	39,470,759	22.0	75,897,238	18.2
20. Other Acquisition Expenses Incurred (Line 7)	48,369,949	2.2	4,754,147	3.5	682,162	1.2	12,473	0.1	3,067,891	1.7	10,174,769	2.4
21. General Expenses Incurred (Line 10)	153,213,644	6.9	9,352,811	6.9	4,437,947	7.3	1,081,621	10.1	11,512,712	6.4	28,092,786	6.7
22. Taxes, Licenses and Fees Incurred (Line 11)	59,005,221	2.7	3,685,890	2.7	1,173,222	2.1	255,770	2.4	4,787,872	2.7	10,914,757	2.6
23. Adjusted Direct Premiums Earned (Line 10)	2,102,488,604	100.0	143,131,872	100.0	59,603,928	100.0	9,901,447	100.0	162,593,760	100.0	388,857,768	100.0
24. General Expenses (Line 10) ratio to Line 23	—	7.4	—	6.7	—	7.4	—	10.9	—	7.1	—	7.2

Table 4-9

Insurance Expense Exhibit of the Insurance Company of North America and Its Affiliated Fire and Casualty Insurers for the Year Ended December 31, 1977

Part III—Citing Adjustment for Effect of Premium Discounts and Retrospective Rating

Summary of Workmen's Compensation Expenses and Ratios to Earned Premium

Category	Item	Amount	Percentage of Total Premium
Regular Business (Excluding War Projects)	1. Net Earned Premiums (Line 2, Col. 16 Part II in part)	$329,524,148	XXX
	2. Adjustment for Premium Discounts and Retrospective Rating	18,908,502	XXX
	3. Net Earned Premiums—Standard Basis (1) + (2)	348,432,650	XXX
War Projects	4. Net Earned Premiums (Line 2, Col. 16 Part II in part)	$ 0	XXX
Total Business	5. Total—Net Earned Premiums—Standard Basis on Regular Business plus War Projects (3) + (4)	$348,432,650	100.0%
Expenses Incurred	6. Loss adjustment expenses (Line 5, Col. 16 Part II)	$ 35,223,199	10.1
	7. Commission and brokerage (Line 6, Col. 16 Part II)	17,889,035	5.1
	8. Other Acquisition, Field Supervision and Collection Expenses (Line 7, Col. 16 Part II)	6,018,535	1.7
	9. General Expenses (Line 10, Col. 16 Part II)	26,480,671	7.6
	10. Taxes, Licenses and Fees (Line 11, Col. 16 Part II)	14,097,420	4.1
	11. Total Expenses excluding federal and foreign income taxes (Line 12, Col. 16 Part II)	99,708,860	28.6
	12. Effect of Expense Graduation	24,436,789	7.0
	13. Total of Item 11 plus Item 12.	$124,145,649	35.6

Table 4-10

Insurance Expense Exhibit of the Insurance Company of North America and Its Affiliated Fire and Casualty Insurers for the Year Ended December 31, 1977

Part IV—Exhibit of Workmen's Compensation Earned Premiums and Incurred Losses by States (Direct Business)

1 State		Code	2 Earned Premiums (Direct Business)	3 Incurred Losses (a) (Direct Business)	4 Loss Ratio 3÷2
Alabama		01	$ 2,418,890	$ 1,846,909	76.4%
Alaska		54	63,101,858	51,889,489	82.2
Arizona		02	4,588,085	5,023,928	109.5
Arkansas		03	1,705,638	1,011,988	59.3
California		04	79,724,140	54,395,331	68.2
Colorado		05	676,267	988,325	146.1
Virginia		45	3,333,046	2,908,926	87.3
Wisconsin		48	3,278,135	3,672,829	112.0
All Other		80	15,137,638	121,753,619	804.3
(1) Total—Direct Business		81	$399,466,536	$459,813,740	115.1
(2) Reinsurance Assumed		82	158,590,386	79,741,654	50.3
(3) Reinsurance Ceded		83	228,532,774	275,516,844	120.6
(4) Total—Net Basis, (1) + (2) − (3)		84	$329,524,148	$264,038,550	80.1
(5) Other Reconciliation Items		85	0	2,325,217	—
(6) Grand Total		86	(b) $329,524,148	(c) $266,363,767	80.8

ACCOUNTING FOR REINSURANCE TRANSACTIONS

A detailed discussion of reinsurance can be found in Chapter 7 of CPCU 5. No attempt is made in this text to thoroughly describe the nature and purpose of reinsurance or the institutional characteristics associated with this area of company operations. This section reviews some of the principal accounting aspects of reinsurance, especially from the viewpoint of a ceding insurance company.

Reinsurance Procedures

Reinsurance has been defined as a contractual arrangement under which one insurer, known as the ceding company, buys insurance from another insurer, called the reinsurer, to cover some or all of the losses incurred by the ceding company under insurance contracts it has issued or will issue in the future. Reinsurance can be viewed as one insurance company purchasing insurance from another insurer. The original insured is not a party to the reinsurance contract, and the reinsurance company is usually not directly obligated to the insured. In all reinsurance contracts, both parties must be insurance companies, a risk must be transferred; and although a contractual relationship exists between the ceding company and the reinsurer, no contract exists between the insured and the reinsurer.

Reinsurance may be categorized in several ways. The first major categorization is by the method used to effectuate reinsurance coverage. In general, there are two basic methods—*facultative* and *treaty* reinsurance. Facultative reinsurance requires the ceding company to negotiate a separate reinsurance agreement for each policy it wishes to reinsure. Treaty reinsurance is more automatic. The ceding company agrees in advance to cede certain classes of business to the reinsurer in accordance with the terms and conditions of the treaty, and the reinsurer agrees to accept the business ceded. Several variations of these two reinsurance methods exist.

The second way of categorizing reinsurance is according to the method of spreading the loss between the ceding company and the reinsurer. Under a *pro rata* contract, both contracting parties share the loss from the first dollar in the same ratio as they shared the premium. Under an *excess of loss* contract, the primary insurer retains all the loss up to a stated amount, after which the reinsurer pays all loss (or 80 to 90 percent of the balance of the loss) up to the limit set in the contract. The reinsurer's limits and its percentage of participation are always stipulated.

A pro rata contract usually runs for the term of the underlying policies and, upon cancellation, normally requires a return of portfolio (unearned premiums). An excess of loss contract usually runs for a stated period of time.

One of the purposes served by reinsurance is to increase the premium capacity of the ceding insurer; that is, it permits the primary company to increase the aggregate premium volume it can write. Reinsurance to allow this increased premium capacity can be arranged prior to premium volume expansion or after the primary company's existing capacity becomes strained. In the latter circumstance, a type of cession known as *portfolio reinsurance* can be arranged. Portfolio reinsurance is not attached as business is written. Instead, a block of business already in force is ceded. This procedure may be followed when a company wishes to withdraw from a line, territory, or agency. Frequently the portfolio is reinsured 100 percent by the assuming company.

Reinsurance Premiums and Commissions

Cessions under a pro rata contract are made on the basis of the premium stated in the policy and usually involve a 30 to 45 percent commission to the ceding insurer. In most contracts this is a provisional rate and may be adjusted up or down by about five or six points, depending on the loss ratio. For example, the reinsurance treaty might provide for a provisional commission of 35 percent, to be adjusted after the end of the year according to the commission rates and loss ratios shown in Table 4-11.

Excess of loss premiums usually are computed by using an agreed-upon percentage of the total premiums written or earned for the line. An exception is auto liability. Here it is common practice to pay the reinsurer the excess limits portion of the premium charged the insured. Recently this has proven inadequate, and an additional amount is usually added to the rate, very often a percentage of the basic premium or of the entire premium. Contracts of this type rarely provide for a commission. The rate quoted is usually provisional, however, and is subject to adjustment based upon the loss ratio.

It is important to know whether the premiums are being ceded on a written or earned basis. In other words, are the premiums due the reinsurer at the inception of the policy or as they are earned? Obviously, this provision in the contract governs the amount of the liability for reinsurance premiums payable. It also determines whether the ceding company can take credit in the unearned premium reserve for the

Table 4-11

Retrospective Ceding Commission Scale—Pro Rata Reinsurance

Actual Loss Ratio	Commission Rate
50% or more	35%
49% but less than 50%	35.5
48% but less than 49%	36
47% but less than 48%	36.5
46% but less than 47%	37
45% but less than 46%	37.5
44% but less than 45%	38
43% but less than 44%	38.5
42% but less than 43%	39
41% but less than 42%	39.5
40% but less than 41%	40
less than 40%	41

premiums ceded. Since one of the principal reasons for using reinsurance is surplus aid, or more properly stated, the recovery of acquisition costs before the premium is earned (early release of equity in the unearned premium reserve), most contracts are on a written premium basis, with a provisional commission equal to the ceding company's acquisition costs on the portion of the premium ceded.

For example, consider the reduction in policyholders' surplus occasioned by writing business at an acquisition expense ratio of 30 percent:[4]

Insurance premium	$100
Acquisition expenses	30
Company receives	70
Unearned premium reserve	100
Beginning surplus of $1,000 reduces to	970

Policyholders' surplus declines by the amount of acquisition expenses paid by the insurer.

The policy is reinsured to the extent of 60 percent under an existing pro rata reinsurance treaty. This creates the following:

Reinsurance premium	$60
Commission paid to ceding insurer	18
Ceding company pays reinsurer	42
Credit to unearned premium reserve	60
Increase in surplus	18

The amount of premium transferred to the reinsurer equals the unearned premium reserve obligation the reinsurer assumes. The commission paid the ceding insurer reimburses it for prepaid acquisition expenses on that portion of the business reinsured. Policyholders' surplus increases by the amount of the reinsurance commission. After completion of the reinsurance transaction, the net impact on the primary insurer of writing and reinsuring this policy is as follows:

Net premium to primary company	$ 40
Net acquisition expense	12
Company receives	28
Net unearned premium reserve	40
Surplus	988

Note that the ratio of direct premiums written-to-policyholders' surplus is .103-to-1 but improves after reinsurance is completed to .040-to-1 ($40/$988).

Reinsurance contracts written on an earned premium basis usually are identified with excess of loss and catastrophe reinsurance. There may or may not be a commission allowance. Since the premiums are earned when ceded, there is no surplus help in this type of contract.

Reinsurance Losses

Loss recoveries are governed by the contract. In the case of pro rata coverages, losses are shared in the same proportion as the premiums. For other types of reinsurance, the proportion is stipulated in each contract.

Losses recoverable appear under two categories: recoverable on paid losses and recoverable on pending losses. The first is usually shown as an admitted asset; the second is deducted from the loss reserve. In either case, however, if the amount recoverable is due from a nonadmitted company, the amounts shown must be offset by inclusion in the reserve for unauthorized reinsurance.

Reinsurance Recoverable

Upon receiving notice of a loss, the loss department determines whether there is any right of recovery under a reinsurance agreement. In the case of a pro rata reinsurance (other than quota share) the daily report, showing appropriate reinsurance information, is inspected. Recoveries under quota-share reinsurance agreements are usually based on the appropriate total loss figures for the period. In the case of excess of loss reinsurance, the loss examiner bases his decision on the terms of the applicable reinsurance contract.

Recoveries under catastrophe reinsurance are usually determined on the basis of data compiled by the statistical department. Each catastrophe is assigned a code number and a recovery is set when the total incurred losses for any one catastrophe exceed the company retention.

When it has been determined that there will be reinsurance recoverable on a loss, the estimated amount is usually entered in the claim file and in the data processing records on a separate reinsurance recoverable loss reserve card. In most cases, notices of losses are sent to reinsurers in accordance with the terms of reinsurance contracts only for losses reinsured on a facultative basis and for the larger losses.

The annual statement provides for reporting gross unpaid losses, related reinsurance recoverable, and net unpaid losses. Listings prepared from the data processing records at statement dates give the required information. The estimated amounts of unpaid losses recoverable from reinsurers are not recorded, except in very rare cases, on the general records. When losses and loss expenses are paid, however, most companies record the actual amount of reinsurance recoverable both in the general ledger and in subsidiary records. Some companies maintain a record of reinsurance recoverable on paid losses on a memorandum basis until collection is made.

Reinsurance recoverable must be divided into amounts recoverable from authorized companies and amounts recoverable from unauthorized companies. Insurance companies are required to provide a reserve for reinsurance recoverable from unauthorized companies in the amount that such receivables exceed the funds held or retained for account of unauthorized companies.

Reinsurance Accounting Records

In the case of facultative reinsurance, a monthly listing (or bordereau) detailing the particulars of each risk reinsured is the ceding company's standard method of reporting to the reinsurer. Quota share reinsurance is frequently handled in monthly or quarterly totals only.

The accounting entries involving reinsurance ceded are relatively simple. Recall that the ceding company is in the position of a purchaser of insurance coverage from the reinsurer. A charge is made to premiums on reinsurance ceded, offset by credits to commissions on reinsurance ceded and on ceded reinsurance balances payable. Conversely, since the reinsurer takes the position of the seller, it records the transaction by charging uncollected premiums and commissions on reinsurance assumed and crediting premiums on reinsurance assumed. One of the objectives of accounting rules for reinsurance transactions is that the accounting records of the ceding insurer complement those of the reinsurer. Both sets of records should show the same asset and liability transfer.

When pooling arrangements are in effect, no reinsurance records are prepared until the direct writing records have been summarized and monthly or quarterly totals are complete. In other words, under a pooling arrangement, the only reinsurance entries required are prepared from totals of business written.

SUMMARY

This chapter traces revenue and expense flows through a property and liability insurance company. The premiums written cycle begins with the sale of insurance and includes premium recording and premium collecting. Companies utilizing direct billing methods may differ in their premium accounting procedures from companies using agent billing. Many insurers make use of both billing methods for various lines of business. Direct billing is advantageous to the insurance company if premium volume in a particular line is large enough to justify employment of personnel and mechanical billing equipment to perform the collection function. Direct billing may also increase the velocity of premium payments by eliminating the 30, 45, or 60-day credit period associated with the payment of agents' accounts current. Effective cash management requires close monitoring and control of premium collections.

Investment operations are also a source of revenue to a property and liability insurance company. Investment income is comprised of interest, dividends, and real estate income. A periodic determination of investment income is made on an accrual accounting basis and reported in the annual statement. Sales and maturities of invested assets contribute additional cash flow to the insurer. Net realized gains and losses on investments are included in investment income during the year in which the asset matures or is sold. Net investment income for the year is arrived at by charging investment expenses incurred, real estate depreciation, and interest on borrowed funds against investment income plus net realized capital gains or losses.

The losses paid cycle encompasses one of the most important operations of an insurance company. Careful monitoring and control of claims processing is necessary to assure equitable treatment of policyholders and third-party claimants and to synchronize the insurance company's cash flow. Loss records must be sufficiently detailed to permit in-depth management reports, to provide statistical data for rate-making purposes, and to facilitate preparation of financial accounting reports. In the annual statement, information on salvage and reinsurance recoveries is merged with loss payments on direct business and reinsurance assumed to determine net losses paid during the accounting period. Net payments plus changes in accrued losses equal the period's losses incurred.

Expenses of an insurance company represent a substantial portion of the premium dollar, and controlling these expenses is vital if a company is to be successful. Uniform expense classification and allocation rules have been developed for statutory reporting purposes. Uniformity allows comparisons to be made among companies for expense analysis purposes and also facilitates use of inter-company data in rate making. Statutory expense reporting usually is not adequate for management information needs. More frequent and detailed expense reports are prepared for internal analysis and control.

Some items of income or expense are not properly classified as either underwriting income or investment income on the annual statement. These items are recorded under the caption "Other Income" and affect both net income and policyholders' surplus.

Certain changes in balance sheet asset and liability values are not reflected in the statutory measurement of periodic income. Instead, direct charges or credits are made to policyholders' surplus. Statutory accounting fails to recognize the potential federal income tax effects related to unrealized capital gains and losses credited or charged to surplus in this manner.

Reinsurance may reduce a ceding insurance company's unearned premium, loss and loss adjustment expense reserve requirements, and lower the ceding company's net loss payments. Whether or not these benefits are reflected in surplus is determined by the reinsurance company's authority to act as a reinsurer within a particular regulatory jurisdiction. The accounting treatment given reinsurance transactions is determined by the reinsurer's legal status.

Chapter Notes

1. Ruth Salzmann, "Estimated Liabilities for Losses and Loss Adjustment Expenses," in *Property-Liability Insurance Accounting*, ed. Robert W. Strain (Santa Monica, CA: The Merritt Co., 1976), p. 43.
2. Ernie Burch, "Loss and Loss Expense Processing and Accounting," *Property-Liability Insurance Accounting*, p. 195.
3. The Accounting Standards Division of the American Institute of Certified Public Accountants presents its position on the preferable accounting treatment of taxes on realized and unrealized capital gains, and other aspects of nonlife insurance accounting, in its *Proposed Statement of Position on Accounting for Property and Liability Insurance Companies* (New York: AICPA, 1977), p. 13.
4. This example is adapted from Robert J. Murphy, "Reinsurance Accounting," *Property-Liability Insurance Accounting*, pp. 267-268.

CHAPTER 5

Financial Analysis

INTRODUCTION

Insurance is purchased to guarantee financial recovery in case an insured loss occurs. Given this fundamental purpose for the insurance purchase, it would be illogical to buy insurance from a company of questionable financial strength in order to obtain a lower initial premium, more lenient underwriting conditions, broader coverage, or for any other reason. However, determining the financial strength of competing insurers is not a trivial exercise; the price of insurance and the breadth of coverage do not automatically indicate an insurer's ability to honor its contractual promises. A company with lower premiums than its competitors may be just as strong as other insurers or it may be financially weaker. Similarly, a small, regional insurer may be as safe or safer than a widely-known national company.

In addition to those parties whose interests are insured, insurance agents, brokers, risk managers, and ceding insurance companies are concerned with financial analysis of insurers. Agents and brokers have a professional obligation to place insurance with solvent and financially sound insurers. They also may have a fiduciary obligation to fund loss payments or return unearned premiums on insurance placed with an insurer that becomes insolvent. The embarrassment as well as the time and expense involved in dealing with a client whose insurance company has failed can be avoided by producers who select companies wisely. Often risk managers request the assistance of insurance producers in evaluating insurance companies. Ultimately however, the risk manager is responsible for recommending the company(ies) selected. The risk manager or insurance producer may be willing to deal with a particular primary insurer only because of that company's reinsurance arrange-

241

ments. In such cases, it may be prudent to include an endorsement in the insurance contract that allows the insured to proceed directly against the reinsurer if the primary insurer is in financial distress at the time of a loss. Whether such a "cut-through endorsement" is necessary requires an ability to judge the primary insurer's financial strength. On the other hand, a ceding insurance company desiring stabilization of underwriting results and protection from catastrophic losses needs to be able to evaluate the financial strength of the reinsurers it deals with.

Appraising the solvency and stability of insurance companies is an important task that requires an understanding of insurance accounting and finance. Most insurance consumers lack the motivation and technical knowledge necessary to evaluate the financial condition of insurance companies. Agents, brokers, risk managers, and insurance company personnel must be able to perform an individualized financial analysis of insurers or must be familiar with financial reporting services that evaluate and recommend insurance companies.

GOALS AND OBJECTIVES OF INSURANCE COMPANIES

The social goal of the insurance industry is to make available adequate insurance protection on an affordable basis for all economic entities that desire such coverage and simultaneously earn an adequate profit. In attempting to achieve this goal, the insurance industry justifies its presence in society. This broad statement of purpose for the industry also provides a valid goal for management of an individual insurance company.

While this statement of purpose is correct and laudable, it is not easily translated into operational decision making. One might expect that insurance company top management has a well-defined corporate objective. However, researchers have found that insurance company management often is unable to precisely state what it really wants the company to achieve. Discussions with the top managers of several prominent insurers revealed multiple corporate objectives, including a desire to (1) maintain market share, (2) raise profits, (3) avoid insolvency, and (4) adhere to some notion of socially responsible conduct.[1] Financial analysis assumes that the fundamental strategic objective of an insurance company's management is to maximize the rate of return on company equity for a given level of assumed risk, consistent with statutory solvency requirements. There is reason to believe that this is an important objective of most insurers and it provides a direct criterion for operational decision making. Furthermore, this criterion is consistent and supportive of the industry's social goal. Insurance companies, like other business enterprises, can best serve society by providing service in an efficient and profitable manner. Whether or not this is in fact being accomplished ought to be reflected in the financial reports of insurance companies. These reports contain a wealth of information which can be extremely illuminating if properly analyzed and understood. This chapter develops tools of financial analysis that can be used to evaluate the progress of property and liability insurers toward meeting their fundamental financial objective.

UNIQUE CHARACTERISTICS OF INSURANCE OPERATIONS

In many respects, financial analysis of insurance companies follows the same basic principles applied to the study of any corporation's financial stature. Concepts of liquidity, leverage, profitability, and growth are as appropriate in the insurance industry as elsewhere. The unique characteristics of insurance operations, however, cause some modification of how these concepts are applied. It may be well to review a few of these characteristics as background for the discussion which follows.

Other business enterprises usually are able to estimate their costs accurately before pricing their products. Insurance companies operate in a significantly different manner. They must establish prices in advance of knowing the costs associated with the services they provide. Current prices must be established from forecasts of the ultimate costs expected to arise from exposures underwritten during the period in which the rates are used. This unique pricing environment impacts on the financial statements primarily through the loss reserves. Judging the accuracy with which these reserves are established and maintained is fundamental to evaluation of a property and liability insurer.

The fact that insurance companies are financial intermediaries also affects analysis of their financial statements. Essentially, an insurer manages two risky portfolios that can be described in terms of expected returns and variances. An insurer raises funds by binding itself to selected insurance contracts. This creates what might be called its underwriting portfolio. The results achieved from insurance operations are unknown in advance and contingent upon ultimate loss settlement and expense experience. The other risky portfolio is the investment portfolio which consists of securities that are expected to yield a return but which may result in a loss depending upon the outcome of investment activities. As a financial intermediary, the insurer must simultaneously manage both portfolios in a manner that achieves corporate goals and complies with insurance regulatory requirements.

Insurers also exhibit an unusual capital structure. Capital structure refers to the relative importance of various forms of permanent financing as represented by long-term debt, preferred stock, and common equity. Traditionally, insurance companies have not included long-term debt or preferred stock in their permanent capital. Instead, capital has been raised from owner supplied equity and retention of earnings. The virtual absence of long-term debt from the capital structure causes many of the leverage ratios common to financial analysis to be inappropriate to insurers unless these ratios are modified.

Regulatory insurance accounting practices greatly influence how insurance company financial statements can be analyzed. Chapter 1 listed a number of ways in which statutory insurance accounting differs from accounting practices used outside the insurance industry. These differences make conventional methods of financial analysis somewhat difficult to apply to insurance companies.

Over the years a set of basic measurement statistics has been developed and used within the property and liability insurance industry. The statistics initially were based only on statutory financial data but gradually have been adjusted to make the relationships they measure more comparable to those of noninsurance enterprises. Recently, the National Association of Insurance Commissioners (NAIC) developed a set of financial ratios, or tests, designed to be of help in identifying companies in need of particularly close solvency surveillance. In the discussion that follows, financial ratios traditionally used within the property and liability insurance industry are described. Ratios developed from both statutory and adjusted financial data are included in the discussion. The tests that currently constitute the NAIC Early Warning System are presented in Chapter 6.

Basic Operating Statistics

The determination of underwriting gain or loss is illustrated in Table 5-1. The calculation begins with *premiums earned*. This differs from the normal sales revenue figure found in most businesses' income statements. As pointed out in Chapter 1, not all premiums received during the year are recognized currently in the income calculation. *Premiums written* give a more accurate indication of sales activity during the accounting period but, because revenue recognition is deferred, premiums written are not shown on the income statement. Instead, premiums earned during the year must be developed from written premiums and changes in the unearned premium reserve. This is done at the bottom of Table 5-1 and in Part 2 of the Underwriting and Expense Exhibit on the NAIC annual statement. Three categories of

Table 5-1

Net Underwriting Gain or Loss—Statutory Basis

Premiums earned (see below)		$120,836,210
Deductions		
Losses incurred (see below)	$69,645,325	
Loss adjustment expenses incurred	7,247,083	
Other underwriting expenses incurred	40,667,942	
Total underwriting deductions		117,560,400
Net Underwriting Gain or Loss		$ 3,265,810
Development of Premiums Earned:		
Net premiums written		$122,438,476
Plus: Unearned premiums previous year		59,190,359
Minus: Unearned premiums current Year		60,792,625
Premiums earned during current year		$120,836,210
Development of Losses Incurred:		
Loss payments (net of reinsurance and salvage)		$ 61,400,377
Plus: Net losses unpaid current year		69,885,690
Minus: Net losses unpaid previous year		61,640,742
Losses incurred current year		$ 69,645,325

deductions are shown: (1) losses incurred, (2) loss expenses incurred, and (3) other underwriting expenses incurred. Participating insurers might also deduct policyholder dividends at this point to arrive at a modified net underwriting figure.

Several important ratios can be constructed from the data shown in Table 5-1. The *loss ratio* measures the fundamental cost of underwriting operations. It expresses the relationship between losses and premiums in percentage terms. While there are several bases for expressing the loss ratio, the most useful basis for financial analysis purposes is to divide losses incurred during the year by premiums earned in the same period:

$$\text{Loss Ratio} = \frac{\text{Losses Incurred}}{\text{Premiums Earned}}$$

The numerator of this ratio, losses incurred, includes changes in loss reserves for known claims and for claims not yet reported. Because these reserves must be estimated they have the potential to distort operating results if the reserves are inaccurately set. The vulnerability of this form of the loss ratio to improper reserve estimates is greatest in liability lines where it is difficult to properly place a value on currently incurred losses that will not be settled until several years in the future. Settlement of property claims does not usually involve as great a time period so the ratio may be more meaningful in these lines. Nevertheless, the companywide ratio is readily determinable from the statutory income statement and is widely used as a benchmark of financial results. Using premiums earned in the ratio's denominator instead of premiums written results in a better matching of losses with the more nearly related revenues in all instances when premium volume fluctuates between accounting periods.

The loss ratio may be calculated with or without including loss adjustment expenses in the numerator. Most analysts and independent reporting services, such as Best's, include loss adjustment expenses so that all costs associated with losses are contained in one statistic. Using the data in Table 5-1, the loss ratio can be constructed in the following manner:

$$\text{Total Loss Ratio} = \frac{\$69,645,325 + \$7,247,083}{\$120,836,210} = 63.6\%$$

It should be noted that the premiums and losses shown in the statutory income statement and illustrated in Table 5-1 are net of all reinsurance transactions. Losses under reinsurance assumed are included in losses incurred by the company, but loss recoveries from reinsurers reduce the numerator of the loss ratio. Similarly, premiums are increased by premiums earned on reinsurance assumed and reduced by premiums paid on insurance ceded to reinsurers. These adjustments for reinsurance transactions result in a *net loss ratio*. Unless otherwise defined, reference to the loss ratio means that losses incurred have been added to loss adjustment expenses and the sum has been divided by premiums earned with all figures net of reinsurance transactions.

A second important ratio developed from the statutory income statement expresses the relationship between underwriting expenses and premiums. Like the loss ratio, this ratio can be constructed in several alternative ways. For financial analysis purposes the *expense ratio* is formed by dividing expenses incurred by premiums earned. The numerator includes all the expenses shown in the Underwriting and Expense Exhibit, Part 4 under the caption Other Underwriting Expenses. Included are acquisition and premium collection and field supervision costs plus general expenses, taxes, licenses, and fees. Investment expenses are not included in calculation of underwriting gain or loss and therefore are not involved in computation of the expense ratio. The expense ratio for the data shown in Table 5-1 is:

$$\text{Expense Ratio} = \frac{\$40,667,942}{\$120,836,210} = 33.7\%$$

The *combined ratio* is formed directly by adding the loss ratio to the expense ratio, assuming both losses and expenses are related to premiums earned:

Combined Ratio = Loss + Expense Ratio

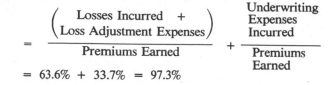

$$= \frac{\left(\begin{array}{c}\text{Losses Incurred } + \\ \text{Loss Adjustment Expenses}\end{array}\right)}{\text{Premiums Earned}} + \frac{\begin{array}{c}\text{Underwriting}\\\text{Expenses}\\\text{Incurred}\end{array}}{\begin{array}{c}\text{Premiums}\\\text{Earned}\end{array}}$$

$$= 63.6\% + 33.7\% = 97.3\%$$

Underwriting gain or loss is equal to 100 percent minus the combined ratio:

$$\text{Underwriting Gain} = 100\% - 97.3\% = 2.7\%$$

The combined ratio summarizes in one statistic the overall underwriting performance of the insurer during an accounting period. It is useful for comparing results among various lines of insurance, among companies, and for comparing the result of a single insurer over several accounting periods. Its component parts are also significant. A company's loss ratio—overall and by the line of insurance—gives a general indication of the quality of business it writes and may give information on the adequacy of the company's premium rates. Operating efficiency and effectiveness are measured by the expense ratio. Comparisons of expense ratios among successive time periods offer an initial indication of overall expense trends and may flag the need for increased attention to cost control.

Capacity Statistics

The operating statistics developed from statutory income statement data may not seem to be related to solvency measurement. Although the relationship is not immediately apparent, they can be used to give an indication of how adequate an insurer's capitalization is relative to the volume of business being done. Before developing this relationship, however, some basic concepts relating capacity and capitalization need to be discussed.

Capitalization refers to the net assets, net worth, or equity of a company. For a stock insurance company, capitalization includes capital stock and retained earnings or surplus. Mutual and reciprocal insurers have no capital stock, only surplus. A general term, *policyholders' surplus* or surplus with regard to policyholders commonly is used within the insurance industry to refer to an insurer's equity. In essence, it is assets minus liabilities, regardless of what it is called.

Financial analysis of a corporation's capitalization usually centers on the relationship between debt and equity. The prospects of higher returns to stockholders through the use of debt encourages a high debt/equity ratio. On the other hand, the increased risk of being unable to meet debt obligations and the related prospect of being forced into liquidation by unsatisfied creditors recommends a smaller amount of debt relative to equity. Achieving the debt/equity balance appropriate for the rate of growth desired by the company is a continuous concern of financial management.

In an insurance company, long-term debt is almost never used as part of the firm's capital structure. The company's principal liabilities are obligations to policyholders arising from underwriting operations, especially the unearned premium reserve and reserves for losses. Due to the absence of long-term debt and the significance of insurance related liabilities, insurance companies are said to substitute "insurance leverage" for financial leverage. Insurance leverage arises from the use of equity capital to support the issuing of new insurance and the concomitant increase in insurance liabilities. Two sources of income are associated with insurance leverage: underwriting profit and investment profit. The leverage effect can be positive so long as the combined sources of revenue produce net income. From this it would appear that an insurer should expand sales continuously if the increased use of insurance leverage results in net income from underwriting and investment operations. However, two factors constrain a company's ability to increase premium volume. First, the statutory accounting treatment of acquisition expenses causes a reduction in policyholders' surplus as new sales occur. This places an absolute limit on a company's capacity to write new business because a required minimum policyholders' surplus must be maintained in order to avoid becoming technically insolvent.

The second capacity constraint is imposed by company management. Variability in underwriting and investment experience causes unexpected fluctuations in policyholders' surplus. These fluctuations could render the company technically insolvent unless an adequate surplus buffer has been maintained above the minimum statutory level. The question that arises is what level of policyholders' surplus can be considered adequate for a desired rate of growth in premium volume. This commonly is called the *capacity problem* although it actually involves the twin problems of capacity and capitalization.[2]

Several approaches may be used to estimate capital adequacy. One approach uses actuarial techniques to develop the theoretical aggregate loss distribution of an insurance company. Knowing the statistical properties of the loss distribution would facilitate management decisions as to the desired level of surplus.[3] These techniques as yet have not been developed to a point of providing clearcut answers to the capacity problem. One needs only to consider the nature of this approach to appreciate the difficulties involved. Estimating the overall loss distribution requires that the form and parameters of the underlying frequency (often assumed to be Poisson or normal) and severity (log normal or Pareto) distributions be modeled. In addition, the interrelationships between the loss distribution and the distribution of returns from investment operations also must be estimated. For a multiple-line insurance company operating in a dynamic economy these relationships are not easily approximated.[4]

A simplistic approach to the capacity problem is to apply conventional rules-of-thumb. The most popular of these benchmarks are the so-called Kenney Rules which are widely perceived as indicating industry standards. There are two major rules found in Roger Kenney's book, *Fundamentals of Fire and Casualty Insurance Strength*. One rule applies to insurers writing primarily property insurance. It states that the ratio of policyholders' surplus to the unearned premium reserve should be 1-to-1; that is, the insurance company should have one dollar worth of policyholders' surplus for each dollar of unearned premium. Strict application of this rule would require curtailment of new insurance sales as the unearned premiums reserve approached the size of policyholders' surplus. Thus, it acts to limit an insurer's capacity to accept more business. The rationale behind this rule is that the principal liability for a property insurer is the unearned premium reserve; therefore, a 1-to-1 ratio means that the company has two dollars in assets for each dollar obligated to policyholders. Although Kenney offers little justification for this rule, it may have been derived from a belief that essentially all assets held by an insurance company are current assets and the unearned premium reserve is a current liability. The Kenney "Fire Ratio" of 1-to-1 would equate to a current ratio of 2-to-1 following this line of reasoning if it is assumed that the unearned premium reserve is the only current liability. If a 2-to-1 current ratio is desirable for noninsurance corporations then, by analogy, a ratio of one dollar in the unearned premium reserve for each dollar of policyholders' surplus is appropriate for property insurers.

A second Kenney Rule is applied to companies that write primarily casualty insurance. It states that the ratio of premiums written to policyholders' surplus should not exceed 2-to-1. Here, premiums written are viewed as a source of future obligations to policyholders either in the form of premium refunds or loss payments. Premiums written-to-policyholders' surplus therefore is used as a substitute ratio of debt-to-equity.[5]

A slightly different rule-of-thumb approach for judging financial strength was developed in Great Britain and used by surplus lines associations in this country. Once again, ratios are established that relate premiums written to various balance sheet accounts. Several *cover ratios* are developed following this approach.

One rule recommends that loss reserves plus policyholders' surplus should "cover" net premiums written by 2.5 times or more:

$$\frac{\text{Loss Reserves + Policyholders' Surplus}}{\text{Premiums Written}} \geq 250\%$$

Another rule is used for workers' compensation insurance. It is felt that the company should at all times maintain loss reserves at least equal to the premium volume written during the year in this line of insurance:

$$\frac{\text{Loss Reserves for Workers' Compensation}}{\text{Premiums Written in Workers' Compensation}} \geq 100\%$$

The most general cover ratio prescribes the proper relationship between admitted assets and net premiums written during the year in all lines of business. This ratio has a distinct advantage over the Kenney Rules in that it is independent of errors in the loss reserve estimates. Both ratios in the Kenney system incorporate policyholders' surplus which will be overstated or understated if loss reserves are either inadequate or excessive. Relating admitted assets to premium volume avoids the necessity of judging loss reserve adequacy. An assets-to-premiums ratio of at least 1.25-to-1 is considered desirable while smaller ratios are interpreted as indicators of financial weakness:

$$\frac{\text{Admitted Assets}}{\text{Premiums Written}} \geq 125\%$$

Although the Kenney Rules are almost completely devoid of logical, theoretical, or empirical justification, they furnish a quick solution to the complicated problem of determining an insurance company's capital adequacy and capacity to underwrite new business. Over the years, state insurance regulators often have referred to these popular benchmarks in judging whether an insurance company is overextending its capital through rapid premium growth. The following example shows how these rules can be combined with the operating statistics discussed earlier.

Assume an insurer's combined ratio is 90 percent and that its premiums written-to-policyholders' surplus ratio is 2-to-1. In the absence of investment losses, insurance leverage clearly is favorable in this instance since underwriting gain equal to 10 percent of premiums earned is being achieved. If the combined ratio is assumed to indicate the underwriting gain that will be experienced on business currently being written, the percentage gain can be multiplied by the premium/surplus ratio to find the rate at which surplus will grow. In this case, the rate of surplus growth will be 10 percent × 2, or 20 percent per year. But if the insurer had been operating at a 5-to-1 premium/surplus ratio, surplus growth would have been 50 percent per year. The prospect of doubling net worth within two years certainly might entice increased use of insurance leverage. Balancing the lure of potentially rapid surplus growth is the impact of underwriting losses on the surplus of a highly levered insurer.

If an insurance company has a combined ratio of 110 percent, it will suffer a decline in surplus of 10 percent × 2, or 20 percent per year when the premiums written-to-policyholders' surplus ratio is 2-to-1. Again, this assumes that underwriting experience on business currently being written will be identical to results on currently earned premiums. High degrees of leverage in this case would be disastrous for the insurer. With a 5-to-1 premium/surplus ratio, a 10 percent × 5 or 50 percent loss of surplus would occur each year. While these simple illustrations completely ignore investment operations, they serve to demonstrate the increased fluctuations in surplus that can be caused by high degrees of leverage.

Calculating ratios of debt to equity gives an indication of the potential drain on policyholders' surplus associated with leverage. Whether or not an insurer will be able to meet its obligations to policyholders also depends on the payment schedule associated with claims in the process of settlement and on the revenues being generated by underwriting and investment operations. In the short run the insurer's ability to remain solvent when faced by adversities rests upon the liquidity of its assets and the ability of cash flow to meet expenses and pay claims. Survival and growth over the long term is a function of profitability. How rapidly a company grows depends on the interaction of insurance leverage and profitability. Financial analysis therefore looks beyond ratios of debt-to-equity and evaluates the liquidity and profitability of the insurer as well.

Liquidity

Conventional financial analysis addresses the concept of liquidity in two ways: (1) by comparing short-term financial resources to short-term financial obligations; and (2) by examining the turnover of receivables and inventory. The current ratio compares current assets to current liabilities. An "acid test" or quick ratio deletes the least current of the current assets, inventory, and relates the remaining current assets to short-term obligations. Activity or turnover ratios are used to discern the rates at which receivables and inventories are being converted to cash.

Almost all admitted assets of an insurer are readily marketable. The only inventories consist of operating supplies which are extremely illiquid and classified as nonadmitted assets. Agents' balances or uncollected premiums less than ninety days due the insurer are analogous to net accounts receivable in a noninsurance company. These premium balances customarily are less than one-tenth of the company's assets. Due to the absence of significant investments in accounts receivable and inventories, traditional turnover ratios are not especially important for insurance company financial analysis. The vast majority of admitted assets are held in cash and marketable securities. Judging the liquidity of these items and relating these to short-term obligations gives a measure of balance sheet liquidity.

Liquidity refers to the firm's ability to meet obligations as they come due. This ability depends upon cash flow, the relationship between assets and liabilities, and the nature of assets available to discharge debt. In judging the liquidity characteristics of particular assets, the time required to convert the asset to cash and the proportion of value expected upon conversion must be considered. Currency and demand deposits therefore are the most liquid assets. Securities that experience little price fluctuation and for which an active market exists are highly liquid. Liquidity declines as the time required to convert the asset to cash increases and/or the certainty of the amount realizable upon conversion decreases.

An insurer's liquidity can be judged by comparing its cash and high-grade marketable securities to the total of the unearned premium and the loss reserves. If highly liquid assets equal or exceed liabilities to policyholders, the insurer's position is satisfactory. But if assets with relatively low liquidity characteristics would have to be called upon to satisfy underwriting obligations, the insurer lacks sufficient liquidity. Poor liquidity exposes the insurer to investment losses in the event that liabilities have to be settled from the forced sale of assets below their carrying values. For example, at the end of 1974 the Government Employees Insurance Company had a bond portfolio of approximately $412 million valued at amortized cost and policyholders' surplus equal to $103 million, as shown in Table 5-2. The company had experienced disastrous underwriting results during the year with a statutory underwriting loss of almost $10 million. Moreover, it incurred investment losses of $3.88 million. Because of the high interest rates prevailing at the time, the market value of GEICO's bond portfolio undoubtedly was below the value shown on the statutory balance sheet.

Table 5-2

Government Employees Insurance Company—1974 Balance Sheet
(in millions)

	Statutory Values	Bonds at 75% Statutory Values
Assets		
Bonds	$412	$309
Other admitted assets	319	319
Total admitted assets	$731	$628
Liabilities and policyholders' surplus		
Liabilities	$628	$628
Policyholders' surplus	103	—
Total liabilities and policyholders' surplus	$731	$628

If the total bond portfolio had been liquidated at 75 percent of its statement value, policyholders' surplus would have evaporated.

A measure of an insurer's balance sheet liquidity can be formed by relating cash and the current value of invested assets to the company's policyholder obligations:

$$\text{Liquidity Ratio} = \frac{\text{Cash} + \text{Invested Assets (Market Value)}}{\text{Unearned Premium Reserve} + \text{Loss and Loss Adjustment Expense Reserves}}$$

If the calculated value of this ratio is 1.00 or less, an undesirable situation is indicated. Ratio values greater than unity show that the insurer could cover the balance sheet values of its obligations to policyholders by converting invested assets to cash at current prices. Market values for most securities are listed in Schedule D of the annual statement and may be included in notes to general purpose financial statements. (Tax-exempt bonds generally are shown at amortized cost rather than market in Schedule D.)

Another aspect of liquidity is disclosed by analyzing cash flows to and from the insurance company. Underwriting and investment operations provide cash through premium writings, interest, dividends, and rents, proceeds from the sale and maturity of investments, and the recapture of previously paid federal income taxes. Funds are applied to loss and expense payments, investment purchases, and dividends to policyholders and stockholders. Any remaining funds are used to increase the company's cash position or are invested in short-term securities. A cash flow statement is not contained in the NAIC annual statement, but a statement of changes in financial position was added in 1977. Companies that prepare audited financial reports based on generally accepted accounting principles (GAAP) issue a statement of changes in financial position that summarizes cash flows during the accounting period. The liquidity demands of underwriting operations can be discerned by comparing the sources and uses of funds as portrayed in this statement. For a growing insurance company, underwriting operations should make a substantial net contribution to the company's cash reservoir.

Profitability

Several measures of profitability are used for property-liability insurers. The most commonly quoted figure is underwriting gain or loss. Other profit measurements are constructed by (1) making adjustments to statutory underwriting profit or loss; (2) combining underwriting and investment results; (3) relating profits to sales, assets, and net worth; and (4) expressing earnings on a per share of stock basis.

Underwriting Profit The concept of underwriting gain or loss as being equal to 100 percent minus the combined ratio was discussed earlier. In that presentation the combined ratio was formed by relating both losses and expenses incurred to premiums earned. A different form of the expense ratio may be used to form an alternative measure of underwriting results. The so-called trade-basis expense ratio relates expenses incurred-to-premiums written. It is believed that combining a loss ratio based on premiums earned and an expense ratio based on premiums written produces a more meaningful measure of underwriting profit when premium volume is increasing or decreasing. The rationale of this approach lies in the fact that acquisition costs are a function of premiums written and, in compliance with statutory accounting rules, must be expensed as incurred. A trade basis combined ratio is published by financial reporting services such as Best's for individual insurance companies and company groups.

Consider the following financial information for a particular year:

Premiums Written	$200,000
Premiums Earned	100,000
Acquisition Expenses Incurred	80,000
Other Underwriting Expenses Incurred	5,000
Losses and Loss Adjustment Expenses Incurred	50,000

The combined ratio on the financial basis (which uses premiums earned as the denominator) relates losses and all expenses incurred to premiums earned:

$$\text{Combined Ratio (Financial Basis)} = \frac{\$50,000 + \$80,000 + \$5,000}{\$100,000} = 135\%$$

While the financial basis produces a combined ratio which, when subtracted from 100 percent, accurately reflecting the statutory percentage margin on premiums earned, it fails to indicate that significant acquisition expenses have been prepaid. Results of underwriting operations are unduly depressed following this approach.

On the trade basis, losses incurred once again are divided by premiums earned, but all expenses other than for loss adjustment are related to premiums written:

$$\text{Combined Ratio (Trade Basis)} = \frac{\$50,000}{\$100,000} + \frac{\$80,000 + \$5,000}{\$200,000} = 92.5\%$$

This results in a combined ratio of less than 100 percent by relating acquisition expenses to the corresponding premiums. Note that Other Underwriting Expenses Incurred which are not a direct function of premiums written also are included in the numerator of the expense ratio. Because these other expense items are small in comparison to acquisition costs, the distortion caused by lumping all expenses together is not great. Nonetheless, an underwriting gain of 7.5 percent (100 percent – 92.5 percent) slightly overstates the true profit margin for this example.

Another approach can be used to adjust for premium volume increases or decreases. This procedure restates the financial basis combined ratio in such a way as to recognize expense prepayments. In the example, acquisition expenses were 40 percent of premiums written. If the unearned premium reserve grew by $100,000 as premiums written increased, an adjustment to reflect the company's equity in the unearned premium reserve is made by multiplying $100,000 by 40 percent. The $40,000 figure represents an increase in the insurer's equity in the unearned premium reserve which arises from prepayment of acquisition expenses. Subtracting this equity increase from the financial basis combined ratio's numerator gives an accurate measure of underwriting results:

Adjusted Combined Ratio =

$$\frac{\$50,000 + \$80,000 + \$5,000 - \$40,000}{\$100,000} = 95\%$$

The true pretax underwriting profit margin is 100 percent minus 95 percent, or 5 percent of premiums earned. This approach implies that it is possible to segregate costs that are functionally related to premiums written from costs which properly are considered period expenses. An insurer's own expenses would have to be analyzed over several operating periods in order to develop a proper segregation. The expense ratio used to adjust for changes in the insurer's equity in the unearned premium reserve cannot exceed 100 percent minus the current loss ratio. This is illustrated in Table 1-19 in Chapter 1. In fact, the adjustment ratio should probably be smaller than this amount in recognition that some expenses are not associated with current sales.

Investment Profit Property and liability insurance companies tend to have a positive cash flow due to prepayment of insurance premiums. Net operating cash flow plus funds provided by policyholder surplus are invested to yield a profit over and above any gain realized from underwriting operations. Investment income is an integral part of an insurance company's overall profitability. The importance of investment income can be seen in Figure 5-1. Investment income as a percentage of average admitted assets is compared in the diagram to underwriting profit (loss) as a percentage of earned premiums for a large number of stock property and liability insurers. In thirty-three of the fifty years from 1927 through 1976 the investment earnings rate of return exceeded the underwriting profit margin on premiums earned. In dollar amounts, investment income exceeded underwriting profit in forty-four of the fifty years. Income from investments exceeded underwriting profit on a percentage basis in each year since 1955 and on a dollar basis every year after 1955.

Two components of investment gain or loss are shown in the statutory income statement. Net investment income earned is the excess of interest, dividend, and real estate revenues over related investment department expenses. Net *realized* capital gains or losses arise from the sale or maturity of securities for amounts in excess of their carrying values. *Unrealized* gains and losses in the investment portfolio are not included in investment income; rather these changes are reflected directly in policyholder surplus without passing through the statutory income statement. Financial reports prepared to conform with GAAP generally follow the statutory approach of defining investment income

Figure 5-1

Investment Income and Underwriting Results—Stock Companies

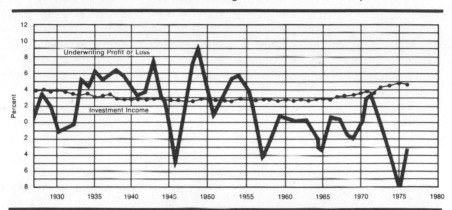

exclusive of unrealized gains or losses. A separate disclosure of unrealized appreciation or depreciation in the value of securities is presented along with an adjustment to reflect deferred federal income taxes on unrealized changes in market values.

Investment income traditionally has been considered separate from underwriting income within the property and liability insurance industry. Returns from investment operations are considered to belong to the company and its owners rather than the policyholders in their role as consumers. It has been asserted that investment returns reimburse the insurance company for an advance credit given to the insured in the form of a premium discount. Stock insurance companies have used investment earnings as the source of dividend payments to stockholders and as a source of surplus growth. Two justifications for this viewpoint are offered. First, stockholders must be rewarded for using their capital to establish and maintain the company. A return on their investment commensurate with the opportunity cost of not employing these funds in an alternative enterprise of similar risk is deemed to be appropriate. Second, returns to equity are necessary to accumulate and attract new capital for expanded growth of the insurance industry. As Figure 5-1 shows, returns have not been forthcoming from underwriting activities and therefore must come from investments. A similar line of reasoning is applied to mutual insurers. Investment income in a mutual serves either to reduce the cost of insurance for policyholder owners or it is added to surplus to increase the company's stability and capacity.

In recent years, political and regulatory pressure has mounted against the traditional proprietary view of investment income. Explicit inclusion of net investment income and realized capital gains in the ratemaking process has been advocated widely and adopted in some jurisdictions. The industry's response has been to reemphasize the need for growth in underwriting capacity through capital formation. The fact that capital at times has been drained from property and liability insurers by holding companies desiring to employ funds at higher rates of return is offered as evidence that returns are inadequate within the industry. In addition, the dual impact inflicted on surplus by underwriting losses and depressed securities markets in 1974 and 1975 is said to illustrate the need for increased earnings accumulations to provide stability within the industry. Company officials cite the need to expand underwriting capacity rapidly in order to keep pace with coverage needs heightened by economic growth and inflation.[6] These factors demand a more rapid accumulation of earnings than has been experienced recently in order to strengthen the industry and provide for increased insurance capacity. Divergence of investment income away from corporate control appears to be inconsistent with the need for capital.

Analysis of an insurer's investment operations should include attention to several points. The composition of the investment portfolio may say something about management's risk-taking attitude since investments in equity securities are considered more risky than investment in bonds. Of course it must be recognized that state regulators place limitations on how the company can invest its assets. Generally speaking, an insurer must invest an amount equal to its minimum required capital and surplus in obligations of the United States government, the company's own state of domicile, or similar assets. The amount of funds equal to liabilities to policyholders may be invested in government obligations, bonds, preferred stock, certain mortgages, and real estate. Only after minimum capitalization and policyholder-supplied funds have been invested can the insurer acquire common stocks and other assets considered to be more risky.

Stock property and liability insurance companies typically invest an amount equal to policyholders' surplus in various types of equity securities, principally common stocks. Mutual insurance companies tend to invest smaller portions of their assets in equities. One explanation of this difference is that stock companies use realized capital gains on common stock as the source of dividends to their stockholders. According to this line of reasoning, equity investments offer higher returns than alternative portfolio assets and therefore will support a larger dividend while still allowing the company to grow. Mutual insurance companies, on the other hand, use investment earnings on funds provided by policyholders' surplus to lower insurance costs and build surplus. Management in a mutual company is said to be less interested in seeking the higher rates of return associated with riskier investments and therefore may be content with lower but more stable returns. Generalizations are not always appropriate for individual companies because many factors influence portfolio decisions. It is highly unlikely that management attitudes toward the risk/return characteristics of the company's investment portfolio are strongly influenced by the insurer's legal organizational form. Factors other than the need to pay dividends to stockholders have a greater effect on the portfolio's composition. The tax treatment afforded investment returns is far from insignificant. Tax-exempt municipal bonds, for example, may be attractive to an insurer taxed as a "small" mutual but not to a stock insurer with a tax-loss carryover. The favorable tax treatment (85 percent exemption) afforded intercorporate dividend payments may encourage investment in common and preferred stock. Significant differences between a particular company's asset composition and industry averages or a sudden shift in the company's portfolio mix signals the need for further inquiry.

Two important relationships should be considered jointly when analyzing investment operations: (1) the degree of insurance leverage, and (2) the proportion of assets invested in common stock. If both are high, there is a potential for disastrous results. The premiums written-to-policyholders' surplus ratio therefore should be inversely related to the proportionality of stock in the investment portfolio. Judgments in this area should incorporate knowledge of underwriting profitability. Heavy use of insurance leverage in a company which historically earns an underwriting profit may be consistent with substantial investments in common stock. On the other hand, a history of underwriting losses would not recommend combination of an equity oriented investment portfolio and a high premiums written-to-policyholders' surplus ratio.

The interrelationship among insurance exposures, the underwriting profit margin, the amount invested in common stock, and fluctuations in policyholders' surplus can be illustrated by an example. Consider the data in Table 5-3.

All three companies begin the year with assets of $2.2 million. Cash flow during the year increases average invested assets by 60 percent of premiums written. Each company invests one quarter of its assets in common stock and each realizes net investment earnings equal to 9 percent of average invested assets. By year-end, all three insurers have suffered unrealized capital losses equal to 22 percent of their investments in common stock. A price decline of this magnitude is equivalent to the Dow Jones Industrial (DJI) average falling from 900 to 700 during a one-year period; an insurer's common stock portfolio usually would be more diversified than the thirty blue chip stocks that make up the DJI average. Companies A and B exhibit a 3-to-1 premiums to surplus ratio while Company C operates with a 1.5-to-1 ratio. Only Company A has an underwriting gain (5 percent); Companies B and C incur underwriting losses (-5 percent). The effects that these various

Table 5-3

Assumed Financial Data For Three Property and Liability Insurance Companies

	Company A	Company B	Company C
Beginning assets	$2,200,000	$2,200,000	$2,200,000
Average invested assets	4,000,000	4,000,000	3,100,000
Common stock investments	1,000,000	1,000,000	775,000
Premiums written	3,000,000	3,000,000	1,500,000
Beginning policyholders' surplus	1,000,000	1,000,000	1,000,000
Combined ratio	95%	105%	105%
Net investment income	$ 360,000	$ 360,000	$ 279,000
Unrealized capital losses	222,222	222,222	172,222

Table 5-4

Operating Results of Three Property and Liability Insurance Companies

	Company A	Company B	Company C
Beginning policyholders' surplus	$1,000,000	$1,000,000	$1,000,000
Underwriting gain or loss	+150,000	−150,000	−75,000
Net investment gain	+360,000	+360,000	+279,000
Unrealized capital loss	−222,222	−222,222	−172,222
Ending policyholders' surplus	$1,287,778	$ 987,778	$1,031,778
Change in policyholders' surplus	$ 287,778	($ 12,222)	$ 31,778

combinations of insurance leverage, equity investments, and underwriting margins have on policyholders' surplus at year-end are shown in Table 5-4.

The risk inherent in combining high degrees of insurance leverage with substantial equity investments has been recognized for some time. In 1964, the NAIC established a Subcommittee to Draft Legislation to Relate Holdings of Equity Investments to the Surplus of the Insurance Company. The Subcommittee recommended that the question of equity investments be combined with the question of the proper relationship between premiums written and policyholders' surplus. A proposal was made that the ratio of premiums written plus equity investments-to-policyholders' surplus be used as a legal limit on underwriting capacity.

A ratio of 3-to-1 would signal a problem company and a ratio above 4-to-1 would not be permitted. This proposal later was withdrawn and the Subcommittee was discharged. One reason for resistance to arbitrary legal limits like the one outlined is illustrated by the three company example:

$$\frac{\text{Premiums Written} + \text{Equity Investments}}{\text{Policyholders' Surplus}} = \begin{array}{ccc} A & B & C \\ \dfrac{4}{1} & \dfrac{4}{1} & \dfrac{2.275}{1} \end{array}$$

Both Companies A and B are at the proposed legal limit of 4-to-1 while Company C has not yet reached the 3-to-1 red flag benchmark. Yet Company A is highly profitable, Company C is barely profitable, and Company B sustains a substantial loss. Failure of the ratio to account for differences in underwriting profitability appears to be a critical omission. Nonetheless, it is important that surplus be judged in regard to both premium volume and portfolio composition.

Company A's underwriting and investment gains are more than sufficient to absorb the unrealized capital loss. Insurance leverage served to magnify both underwriting and investment results because the business written was profitable in itself and generated investable funds which earned an attractive return. The underwriting loss experienced by Company B was magnified by the volume of business written. Although this company also earned the same return on investments as Company A, the combination of an underwriting loss and falling securities prices resulted in a depletion of policyholders' surplus. The adverse effect of combining substantial equity investments with insurance leverage is illustrated further by contrasting Company C's results with those of Company B. Though writing only one-half as much business, Company C was able to operate with an equally bad combined underwriting ratio and still earn investment income in excess of its underwriting and unrealized capital losses.

Profit Ratios Four types of ratios are useful in analyzing property and liability insurance company profitability: (1) those showing profits in relation to revenues (premiums earned), (2) those showing profits in relation to investment, (3) those showing profits in relation to net worth, and (4) those showing profits in relation to the number of shares of common stock outstanding. The three sources of insurer profit—underwriting income, investment income, and capital gains—individually or in combination can be related to revenues (premiums earned), invested assets, or net worth. Because there is a multiplicity of profit measurements and ratios it is easy to become confused when evaluating an individual insurance company's or the industry's operating results. For the financial analyst to get an accurate idea of performance, a clear understanding of what each profit ratio measures is essential.

Underwriting Profit. The first profit ratio already has been introduced. It is the underwriting profit ratio adjusted for prepaid expenses. The ratio can be calculated directly or found by subtracting the adjusted combined ratio from unity:

$$\text{Underwriting Profit Ratio} = \frac{\text{Adjusted Underwriting Gain (Loss)}}{\text{Premiums Earned}}$$

$$= 1.00 - \text{Adjusted Combined Ratio}$$

This ratio is analogous to the net profit margin for noninsurance business:

$$\frac{\text{Adjusted Underwriting Gain (Loss)}}{\text{Premiums Earned}} = \text{Net Profit Margin} = \frac{\text{Net Profit}}{\text{Sales}}$$

It differs from the net profit margin in that only a portion of the insurer's current operating income is included. No recognition is given to investment income or portfolio gains. The emphasis here is on the efficiency of underwriting and not on overall profitability. Observation of trends in the underwriting profit ratio and comparisons of a particular company's ratio with industry averages may be helpful in evaluating performance. Some analysts may adjust the numerator of this ratio to reflect current and deferred income taxes.

Return on Investable Funds. A second type of profit ratio is widely used in financial analysis but has received only limited use in the property and liability insurance industry. It relates total return to total investable funds. This type of ratio was stressed in studies made by the Arthur D. Little organization of prices and profits in the property and liability insurance industry. Total investable funds for an insurer are defined to equal capital, surplus, the unearned premium reserve, and loss reserves. Essentially, this simply enumerates the sources of funds shown on the balance sheet's right-hand side. It would be more concise to say that total investable funds equal total assets minus current liabilities, but listing each important fund source emphasizes that the return is made possible by contributions from numerous interests. Total return includes adjusted underwriting gains, net investment gain, and realized and unrealized capital gains. Ideally, an adjustment should be made to approximate current income taxes and the deferred tax liability associated with prepaid acquisition expenses, excess statutory loss reserves, and potential capital gains not yet realized. The ratio is formed as follows:

$$\frac{\text{Net Profit}}{\text{Investable Funds}} = \frac{A + B + C + D}{X + Y + Z + W}$$

where A = after tax underwriting gain (loss) adjusted for prepaid acquisition expenses and deferred federal income taxes; B = net investment gain (loss) from interest, dividends, and real estate less expenses and taxes; C = net realized capital gain (loss) less taxes thereon; D = net unrealized capital gain (loss) less allowance for deferred federal income taxes; X = unearned premium reserve minus the insurer's equity for prepaid expenses; Y = loss reserves established on case-based estimates minus any equity due to overreserving practices; Z = capital stock, if any; and W = surplus, adjusted for prepaid expenses, statutory loss reserves in excess of case-based reserves, unrealized capital gains (losses), and related tax effects. Adjusted surplus also includes unauthorized reinsurance and nonadmitted assets which have economic value. Policyholder dividends are included in the ratio's numerator although the deductibility of this item has been recognized in determining income taxes.

This type of ratio is meant to compare total income from ongoing operations to all funds permanently invested in the company. Investable funds are treated in the same way regardless of their source. The ratio is especially appropriate for public utilities which issue long-term debt in order to finance their substantial investment in fixed assets. Utility company rates are regulated in such a way as to guarantee a permissible return to stockholders after all expenses have been absorbed. Included are the costs associated with borrowing funds. The utility is granted a monopoly position in exchange for the services it can provide through efficient employment of its resources. A ratio measuring the return on all resources permanently committed to the utility is intended as a meaningful measure of how effectively assets are being utilized.

The appropriateness of using investable funds as a basis for evaluating insurance company profits has been questioned. Insurers are not monopolies, they do not invest heavily in tangible fixed assets, and they do not issue long-term debt on which explicit interest expenses are incurred. Moreover, insurance rates are not developed from a cost-plus formula that uses a company's cost of capital as a component of the rate base. These fundamental differences suggest that the rate of return on investable funds may not be especially meaningful for insurance companies. The ratio does indicate how efficiently company management utilizes its resources and it may be useful as a basis for comparing insurance company profits to those being earned in other industries.[7]

Several variations on the investable funds ratio are used by insurance reporting services to monitor the investment performance of property and liability insurers. One ratio shows the relationship between net investment income and average admitted assets:

$$\text{Investment Earnings Ratio} = \frac{\text{Net Investment Income}}{\text{Average Admitted Assets}}$$

Investment income includes interest, dividends, and real estate income, less investment expenses, but before federal income taxes.

This ratio gives a narrowly defined measure of investment assets. A broader rate of return figure for investment operations also is reported. It compares total *realized* investment profit or loss to average admitted assets:

$$\text{Investment Profit Ratio} = \frac{\text{Total Investment Profit (Loss)}}{\text{Average Admitted Assets}}$$

The numerator of this ratio adds realized capital gains (losses) to investment income and produces an overall index of investment performance. Best's publishes both investment return ratios annually in a series dating back to 1913. Care should be taken in comparing investment return ratios with the underwriting profit ratio since the latter ratio relates underwriting results to premiums earned rather than assets. In other words, the two ratios are not meaningful when added together.

Return on Net Worth. The third type of profitability ratio relates profits to the book value of the company's net worth (policyholders' surplus):

$$\text{Return On Net Worth} = \frac{\text{Net Profit}}{\text{Policyholders' Surplus}}$$

Either statutory accounting or GAAP data can be used. If statutory results are being measured, net profit includes underwriting gain (loss), investment income, and realized capital gains. Policyholders' surplus at the end of the current year normally is used as the base of this profitability ratio. When constructed in this fashion, the ratio is logically inconsistent. Unrealized investment gains and losses are included in policyholders' surplus but not in profit. A better measurement is given by adjusting the statutory data to conform with GAAP. An adjusted profits-to-adjusted net worth relationship is formed:

$$\text{Adjusted Return On Net Worth} = \frac{\text{Adjusted Net Profit}}{\text{Adjusted Policyholders' Surplus}}$$

Adjusted net profit includes the four elements of the numerator in the investable funds ratio: A, B, C, and D as defined earlier. This ratio's denominator does not include all investable funds. Only capital (Z) and adjusted surplus (W) are used here.

The rate of return on net worth is especially appropriate for comparisons among insurance companies. It avoids problems caused by differences in premium volume, underwriting and investment gains by summarizing overall operating success relative to the firm's net resources. Stockholders view this ratio with interest because it indicates the company's earning power and ability to grow.

Earnings per Share. One of the most widely used profitability ratios applicable to the financial analysis of stock insurance companies is the earnings per share (EPS) figure. EPS is a measure of net income available to common stockholders expressed on a per share of stock basis:

$$EPS = \frac{\text{Net Income Available to Common Stockholders}}{\text{Weighted Average Number of Common Shares}}$$
Outstanding During the Accounting Period

Stock insurers may publish EPS figures based on statutory net income as well as an EPS figure based on GAAP income. Reporting both earnings ratios serves to highlight the fact that regulatory accounting principles result in profit measurements that are significantly different from those based on GAAP.

The Financial Accounting Standards Board requires that the guidelines set forth in *APB Opinion No. 15* and subsequent interpretations by the American Institute of Certified Public Accountants be followed in calculating and reporting EPS. These guidelines apply to both insurance and noninsurance companies. Essentially it is necessary to deduct the claims on net income of senior securities (for instance, preferred stock) from the ratio's numerator and for corporations with a complex capital structure, to report primary and *fully diluted* EPS. A corporation which has a simple capital structure consisting of common stock and nonconvertible senior securities needs only to report primary EPS. In such a case, primary EPS would be calculated according to the ratio presented earlier in this section. A corporation's capital structure is complex if it includes convertible securities, stock options, warrants, or other agreements that have a potential to dilute net income per share available to common stockholders. For such firms, disclosure must be made of the impact on EPS resulting from the exercise of conversion or stock purchase privileges. This is accomplished by reporting two EPS figures: (1) primary EPS which is net income divided by the number of outstanding common shares and securities that are equivalent to common shares; and (2) fully diluted EPS which reflects the maximum reduction of current EPS that would have resulted if all conversion and purchase privileges had been exercised at the beginning of the accounting period.[8] Complex capital structures often are found to exist in companies that have intercorporate affiliations. Consolidated earnings of conglomerate or congeneric groups that include property and liability insurers typically are reported in both a primary and fully diluted form.

Several other per share statistics may be reported by stock insurers or calculated by the financial analyst and compared to EPS. The dividend paid per share of stock is of interest to investors who wish to estimate the future dividend yield available from ownership of the insurer's stock. A comparison of EPS to dividends per share may indicate the likelihood that the current dividend will be continued or increased in the future. Another figure that is helpful in this regard can be determined by dividing the insurance company's unassigned surplus by the number of common shares outstanding. Statutory unassigned surplus represents the maximum amount of accumulated earnings potentially available for distribution. Although most companies intend to retain unassigned surplus to support current obligations and to finance future growth, the ratio of statutory unassigned surplus per share indicates the insurer's ability to continue stockholder dividend payments even during a year when EPS falls below the company's historical dividend per share payment.

Summary of Financial Ratios

Financial ratios that may be used to analyze property and liability insurance companies are summarized in Table 5-5. Ratio values calculated for a particular insurer should be interpreted with circumspection. Such values have little inherent meaning; normally, they become meaningful only when compared to industry norms and to values determined for the same company in prior years or forecasted for the future. Where appropriate, the benchmarks that traditionally have been used to define acceptable relationships are included in the table. These standards are not always inviolate rules. For instance, aggregrate industry data for 1976 revealed a premiums written-to-policyholders' surplus ratio of approximately 2.45-to-1, a value greater than the normally acceptable bound. Numerous individual insurers were operating at much larger writings-to-surplus ratios without threatening policyholder security. On the other hand, an insurer whose liquidity ratio dropped below 1-to-1 clearly would be in an undesirable situation. Additional care should be exercised in comparing profitability ratios. While comparisons of profit indexes among insurers may be meaningful, comparisons of insurance company rates of return with those of other

Table 5-5
Summary of Financial Ratios

Ratio	Formulation	Acceptable Value
I. CAPACITY		
Kenney's "fire" ratio	$\dfrac{\text{Policyholders' Surplus}}{\text{Unearned Premium Reserve}}$	$\geq 1{:}1$
Kenney's "casualty" ratio	$\dfrac{\text{Premiums Written}}{\text{Policyholders' Surplus}}$	$\leq 2{:}1$
Cover ratio "1"	$\dfrac{\text{Loss Reserves + Policyholders' Surplus}}{\text{Premiums Written}}$	$\geq 2.5{:}1$
Cover ratio "2"	$\dfrac{\text{Loss Reserves for Workers' Compensation}}{\text{Premiums Written in Workers' Compensation}}$	$\geq 1{:}1$
Cover ratio "3"	$\dfrac{\text{Admitted Assets}}{\text{Premiums Written}}$	$\geq 1.25{:}1$
II. LIQUIDITY		
Liquidity ratio	$\dfrac{\text{Cash + Invested Assets (Market Value)}}{\text{Unearned Premium + Loss Reserves}}$	$> 1{:}1$
III. PROFITABILITY		
Return on investable funds	$= \dfrac{\left(\begin{array}{l}\text{Underwriting Gain + Net Investment Gain}\\ \text{+ Realized and Unrealized Capital Gains}\\ \text{- Federal Income Taxes}\end{array}\right)}{\left(\begin{array}{l}\text{Policyholders' Surplus + Unearned}\\ \text{Premium Reserve + Loss Reserves}\end{array}\right)}$	
Investment earnings ratio	$= \dfrac{\text{Net Investment Income Before Federal Income Taxes}}{\text{Average Admitted Assets}}$	
Investment profits ratio	$= \dfrac{\text{Net Investment Income Before Taxes + Realized Capital Gains}}{\text{Average Admitted Assets}}$	
Return on net worth	$= \dfrac{\begin{array}{l}\text{Net Underwriting Gain + Net Investment Gain}\\ \text{+ Realized Capital Gains - Federal Income Taxes}\end{array}}{\text{Policyholders' Surplus}}$	
Adjusted return on net worth	$= \dfrac{\begin{array}{l}\text{Adjusted Underwriting Gain + Net Investment Gain}\\ \text{+ Realized and Unrealized Capital Gains}\\ \text{- Federal Income Taxes}\end{array}}{\text{Adjusted Policyholders' Surplus}}$	
III. PROFITABILITY		
Underwriting profit (Financial basis)	$= 1.00 - \text{Combined Ratio (Financial Basis)}$ $= 1.00 - \dfrac{\left(\begin{array}{l}\text{Losses and Loss Adjustment Expenses Incurred}\\ \text{+ Acquisition Expenses Incurred}\\ \text{+ Other Underwriting Expenses Incurred}\end{array}\right)}{\text{Premiums Earned}}$	
Underwriting profit (Trade basis)	$= 1.00 \quad \text{Combined Ratio (Trade Basis)}$ $= 1.00 - \left[\dfrac{\left(\begin{array}{l}\text{Losses and Loss}\\ \text{Adjustment}\\ \text{Expenses Incurred}\end{array}\right)}{\text{Premiums Earned}} + \dfrac{\left(\begin{array}{l}\text{Acquisition Expenses}\\ \text{Incurred}\\ \text{+ Other Underwriting}\\ \text{Expenses Incurred}\end{array}\right)}{\text{Premiums Written}}\right]$	

III. PROFITABILITY (contd.)

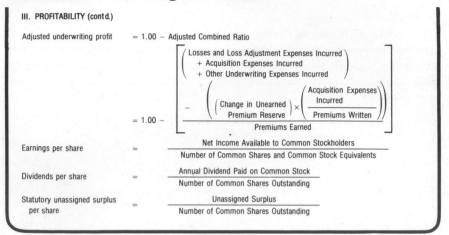

Adjusted underwriting profit $= 1.00 -$ Adjusted Combined Ratio

$$= 1.00 - \left[\left(\begin{array}{c} \text{Losses and Loss Adjustment Expenses Incurred} \\ + \text{ Acquisition Expenses Incurred} \\ + \text{ Other Underwriting Expenses Incurred} \end{array} \right) - \frac{\left(\begin{array}{c} \text{Change in Unearned} \\ \text{Premium Reserve} \end{array} \right) \times \left(\frac{\text{Acquisition Expenses Incurred}}{\text{Premiums Written}} \right)}{\text{Premiums Earned}} \right]$$

Earnings per share $= \dfrac{\text{Net Income Available to Common Stockholders}}{\text{Number of Common Shares and Common Stock Equivalents}}$

Dividends per share $= \dfrac{\text{Annual Dividend Paid on Common Stock}}{\text{Number of Common Shares Outstanding}}$

Statutory unassigned surplus per share $= \dfrac{\text{Unassigned Surplus}}{\text{Number of Common Shares Outstanding}}$

types of businesses should not be made without an adjustment to reflect financial and operating risks in both sectors.

FINANCIAL RATINGS OF INSURANCE COMPANIES

Financial analysis of individual insurance companies can be a laborious, time-consuming and costly procedure. For these and other reasons, persons seeking to appraise the financial condition of a particular insurance company may refer to the specialized financial evaluation provided by an insurance reporting service and expressed as a grade or rating. The predominate insurance company rating service in the United States is A.M. Best Company which annually publishes ratings for life insurance and property and liability insurance companies. The rating system applied to nonlife insurers by Best is described here, based on *Best's Insurance Reports Property-Casualty*, published annually.

Companies Subject to Rating

The 1977 edition of *Best's Insurance Reports* presented financial information on more than 1,500 stock, mutual, reciprocal, and American Lloyds insurance organizations. Nearly 1,000 of these insurers were assigned a policyholders' rating and were classified by financial size. A rating for the remaining insurers was omitted for one or more reasons. In some cases the rating was omitted because the company either refused to supply information to the reporting service or information was furnished too late to enable completion of a full-fledged analysis of the company. Ratings were omitted for insurers that disputed Best's application of its rating system to their companies' information or that disagreed with Best's interpretation of certain items appearing in their annual statement. Some companies that were analyzed did not qualify for a rating within the classification system used by Best's and consequently did not receive a rating. Insurers with fewer than five consecutive years of operating data are not considered to have developed adequate experience and were not rated. Best's requirement that at least five years' data be available effectively precludes new insurers from receiving the visibility associated with a rating published in a nationally recognized reporting service. Nevertheless, Best's supplies financial information on a large number of insurance companies and expresses its evaluation of most companies in the form of a policyholders' rating.

Best's Policyholders' Ratings

Best's rates companies on a continuous scale ranging from excellent to fair. Letter notation is used to designate a company's position within this range. A percentage distribution of the policyholders' ratings assigned by Best's in 1977 is shown in Table 5-6.

The ratings express Best's opinion on a particular company's relative position within the industry based on comparisons with broad industry standards. The highest rating category is subdivided into four classifications (A+, Contingent A+, A, and Contingent A), but all companies rated "excellent" are considered to be outstanding on a comparative basis. The "very good" (B+ and Contingent B+) and the "good" (B and Contingent B) categories are similarly subdivided. Only one grade or rating is used to denote companies classified as "fairly good" (C+) or "fair" (C). Best's indicates that only small variances from industry standards exist among companies classified as excellent. For lower classifications variances from industry standards are greater.

The fact that 657 companies, more than two-thirds of all companies that received ratings in 1977, were classified as excellent indicates that Best's rating system is not meant to disclose slight differences among insurers. Rather, the ratings rank individual insurers in broadly defined groups by comparing each insurer's performance in five areas to industry averages which serve as standards for appraisal. The five factors used to measure a company's stability and strength are (1) underwriting performance, (2) management economy, (3) reserve adequacy, (4) adequacy of net resources, and (5) soundness of investments. In certain situations, for example to meet requirements of lending institutions or governmental agencies, an excellent rating by Best's may be set as a minimum for defining acceptable insurers.

Table 5-6

Best's Policyholder Ratings for Property and Liability Insurance Companies, 1977*

Rating	Interpretation	Approximate Number of Companies with Rating	Approximate Percentage of Companies with Rating
A+	} Excellent	384	40%
Contingent A+		54	6%
A		163	17%
Contingent A		56	6%
B+	} Very Good	106	11%
Contingent B+		18	2%
B	} Good	67	7%
Contingent B		11	1%
C+	Fairly Good	24	3%
C	Fair	20	2%
Rating deferred or omitted		70	5%

* Reprinted with permission from *Best's Review Property/Casualty Edition*, August 1977, p. 6.

Underwriting Performance Underwriting profit margins are developed using the trade basis combined ratio as previously defined:

$$\text{Underwriting Profit} = 1 - \left(\frac{\text{Losses and Loss Adjustment Expense Incurred}}{\text{Premiums Earned}} + \frac{\text{Expenses Incurred}}{\text{Premiums Written}} \right)$$

This type of underwriting profit ratio is used because it makes allowance for changes in the insurer's equity in the unearned premium reserve.

The amount of underwriting profit or loss, as calculated, is compared to earned premiums; this serves as a measure of the company's ability to successfully conduct insurance operations. A comparison of underwriting profit to the insurance company's net resources (adjusted surplus) also is made so that the importance of the year's underwriting profit or loss can be judged relative to the company's net safety factor. The same underwriting profit or loss may be insignificant to an insurer with large net resources but critical to an insurer with small net resources.

Management Economy The ratio of expenses incurred, other than loss adjustment expenses, to premiums written is used as a measure of management's ability to control operating expenses. Best's rating system recognizes that the percentage expense ratios of two multiple-line insurance companies may be identical but one company may be managed much more economically than the other. The distribution of each company's business among various lines of business, some of which have high and others low expense ratios, is considered in evaluating a company's overall expense ratio. Also considered are the amount of reinsurance commissions and the relationship between gross and net premiums written.

Reserve Adequacy Except in unusual instances, Best's regards the insurer's reserves for unearned premiums to accurately reflect the true value of this liability. Loss and loss adjustment expense reserves are not automatically accepted at their statement values. Reserve development schedules included in the insurers' annual statements are studied to detect any reserve deficiencies or excesses. If aggregate statement reserves are found to be inaccurate estimates of an insurer's true liability for unsettled claims, the discrepancy is considered in evaluating the adequacy of the insurer's policyholders' surplus.

Adequacy of Net Resources After allowance has been made for the insurance company's equity in the unearned premium reserve and any necessary adjustments have been made in loss reserves, the adequacy of policyholders' surplus, as adjusted, is evaluated. Adjusted surplus represents the net resources available to absorb adverse loss, expense, and investment experience. The evaluation includes, but is not limited to, a comparison of premiums written to adjusted surplus. Also considered are the profitability of underwriting operations, the insurer's product mix, the character of its assets, and the diversification of underwriting commitments.

Soundness of Investments Investments are evaluated on the basis of their quality, diversification, and liquidity. If assets are judged to be of such a character that they cannot be converted to cash quickly without significant loss of value, the insurer's net resources may be insufficient to guarantee policyholder security. As in the case of the other factors upon which company ratings are based, this factor is judged relative to conditions prevailing in the industry during the period under study. Therefore, the quality of a particular company's investment portfolio may decline in one year but the company's relative position to the industry may remain unchanged or actually may improve.

Best's Financial Classification

In addition to the policyholders' rating, each rated insurer is classified into a financial category determined by Best's estimate of the size of the company's adjusted surplus. Adjusted surplus includes policyholders' surplus from the annual statement, modified for conditional or required reserves in excess of estimated reserve requirements, plus the company's equity in the unearned premium reserve, less any estimated reserve deficiencies. Financial categories of alien insurers are based upon financial statements of the alien companies which include assets and liabilities of their United States branches.

Best's traditionally has used distinctive notation to differentiate the financial category and the policyholders' rating. Prior to 1976, the financial category was indicated by two or more letters ranging from AAAAA (for companies with adjusted surplus equal to $25 million or more) down to CC (for companies with $250,000 or less in adjusted surplus). Beginning in 1976, Best's changed its notation and increased the amount of adjusted surplus represented by its top six categories. To prevent confusion with policyholders' ratings, roman numerals now are used to denote financial categories. The financial classification system in use by Best's in 1977 is shown in Table 5-7.

Effect of Company Size

It should be noted that an insurer's size is reflected only in the financial category to which it is assigned and does not influence the policyholders' rating assigned the company. Small insurers can be equally as safe as larger insurers. Best's explicitly acknowledges the desirability of insurance coverage from a small, prudently managed, and adequately financed insurer in preference to a larger insurance company that is operated less successfully.

Changes in Ratings

The large underwriting losses experienced by property and liability insurers in 1974, 1975, and 1976 caused Best's to reduce its policyholders' ratings for a large number of companies. As shown in Table 5-6 the

Table 5-7

Best's Financial Categories For Property and
Liability Insurance Companies, 1977*

Class	Size of Adjusted Surplus	
I	250,000	or less
II	250,000 to	500,000
III	500,000 to	750,000
IV	750,000 to	1,000,000
V	1,000,000 to	1,500,000
VI	1,500,000 to	2,500,000
VII	2,500,000 to	3,750,000
VIII	3,750,000 to	5,000,000
IX	5,000,000 to	7,500,000
X	7,500,000 to	12,500,000
XI	12,500,000 to	25,000,000
XII	25,000,000 to	50,000,000
XIII	50,000,000 to	75,000,000
XIV	75,000,000 to	100,000,000
XV	100,000,000	or more

*Reprinted with permission from *Best's Review Property/
Casualty Edition,* August 1977, p. 6.

majority of rated companies still are classified as excellent but more than a fourth of these companies were assigned contingent or lower ratings during this time period. Best's assigns new ratings during the spring of each year and publishes them in August. Occasionally, extraordinary developments discovered after ratings are published cause a change in the assigned rating. In such cases, subscribers to Best's reporting services receive notification of rating changes through its weekly or monthly publications.

Changes in an insurance company's policyholders' rating should be interpreted as an indication of the direction in which the company is heading. A downward trend over the course of several years is a cause for concern. It has been suggested that insurer selection should be limited to companies that have been assigned an A+ policyholders' rating for six or more consecutive years in order to be reasonably sure of avoiding delinquent companies.[9] While application of such a rule might unreasonably restrict available sources of insurance, it very likely would assure the financial strength of the company.

SUMMARY

Several groups have an interest in evaluating the financial condition of insurance companies. Insureds, investors, insurance producers, insurance regulators, and others may be concerned with the solvency, liquidity, and profitability of one or more insurance companies. Most persons however have little knowledge of insurance accounting and are unable to evaluate insurance company finance. Individuals who have chosen insurance as their professional interest can rightfully be expected to be familiar with a subject others may consider to be complex, obscure, and arcane. Some basic tools for financial analysis of property and liability insurers have been presented in this chapter.

The rather long list of ratios discussed here does not constitute an exhaustive treatment of the subject. It is necessary to go beyond calculation of financial ratios; statistics developed for a particular insurer should be compared to standard averages within the industry and trends should be studied over several accounting periods. Rates of growth in a company's premiums, profits, and surplus should be balanced against the risk faced by the insurer. Financial reporting services are a valuable source of financial information on individual insurers and as a source of data for comparisons. Care must be taken to direct the analysis toward the future rather than allowing it to be only a compilation of past performance.

Chapter Notes

1. John L. Markle and A.E. Hofflander, "A Quadratic Programming Model of the Non-Life Insurer," *The Journal of Risk and Insurance*, Vol. 43, No. 1 (March 1976), pp. 99-120.
2. In actuarial literature a more technical name is associated with the capacity/capitalization problem. It is called the "ruin problem" because it deals with how large liabilities can grow for a given amount of equity without the probability of the company being ruined (becoming insolvent) increasing beyond a selected small value. For example, if the ratio of liabilities to policyholders' surplus increases to 6 to 1 during a given time interval, say, three years, will the probability of ruin be greater than 0.001?
3. Theoretical and empirical papers have proposed the use of quadratic or chance-constrained programming models as aids to insurance company operational decision making. Leading articles in this area include: Yehuda Kahane and David Nye, "A Portfolio Approach to the Property-Liability Insurance Industry," *The Journal of Risk and Insurance*, Vol. 42, No. 4 (December 1975), pp. 579-598; Clement G. Krouse, "Portfolio Balancing Corporate Assets and Liabilities with Special Application to Insurance Management," *Journal of Financial and Quantitative Analysis*, Vol. 6 (September 14, 1971), pp. 77-104; John L. Markle, and A. E. Hofflander, "A Quadratic Programming Model of the Non-Life Insurer," *The Journal of Risk and Insurance*, Vol. 43, No. 1 (March 1976), pp. 99-120; Tapan S. Roy and Robert Charles Witt, "Leverage, Exposure Ratios and the Optimal Rate of Return on Capital for the Insurer," *The Journal of Risk and Insurance*, Vol. 43, No. 1 (March 1976), pp. 53-72; and Howard E. Thompson, John P. Matthews, and Bob C. L. Li, "Insurance Exposure and Investment Risks: An Analysis Using Chance-Constrained Programming," *Operations Research*, Vol. 22 (September-October 1974), pp. 991-1007.
4. The Poisson or normal distribution commonly is employed to measure the frequency with which independent losses occur. It is much more difficult to fit an appropriate theoretical distribution to loss severity data. Several distributions, including the exponential, gamma, normal, or Pareto may be candidates for the distribution of severity data. Conditions that govern the use of a particular distribution are discussed in R. E. Beard, T. Pentikainer, and E. Pesonen, *Risk Theory* (London: Methuen, 1969).
5. In Chapter 2 of this text, the concepts of *insurance exposure* and *insurance leverage* were defined. Insurance exposure is measured by the ratio of premiums written-to-policyholders' surplus. Insurance leverage is measured by the ratio of reserves-to-policyholders' surplus. Obviously the two concepts are closely related; increases in net premiums written result in increased reserves relative to surplus. When the ratio of premiums-to-surplus is used as a surrogate debt-equity ratio, the two concepts are combined and the terminology insurance leverage seems most appropriate.

6. "Industry Need to Double Capital," *The National Underwriter*, Property and Casualty Insurance Edition, July 1, 1977, p. 1.
7. Regardless of which rate of return ratio is being employed, interindustry profit comparisons should recognize differences in the riskiness of the industries being compared. Variation within a rate of return distribution often is used as the proper measure of risk, although this is not a universally agreed upon concept. In general, a company or an industry that experiences greater variation in its rates of return is considered more risky than one that does not, and it should earn a higher average rate of return to compensate for this uncertainty. Risk adjustment techniques are discussed in Paul H. Cootner and Daniel M. Holland, "Rate of Return and Business Risk," *The Bell Journal of Economics and Management Science*, Vol. 1, No. 2 (Autumn 1970), pp. 211-226; Stephen W. Forbes, "Rates of Return in the Nonlife Insurance Industry," *The Journal of Risk and Insurance*, Vol. 38, No. 3 (September 1971), pp. 409-442; Irving H. Plotikin, "Rates of Return in the Property and Liability Insurance Industry: A Comparative Analysis," *The Journal of Risk and Insurance*, Vol. 36, No. 2 (June 1969), pp. 173-200; Richard W. McEnally, and Lee A. Tavis, "'Spatial Risk' and Return Relationships: A Reconsideration," *The Journal of Risk and Insurance*, Vol. 39, No. 3 (September 1972), pp. 351-368; and James S. Trieschmann, "Property-Liability Profits: A Comparative Study," *The Journal of Risk and Insurance*, Vol. 43, No. 1 (March 1976), pp. 53-72.
8. The determination of EPS in accordance with FASB requirements can be complicated for a firm with a complex capital structure. Readers interested in pursuing this topic further are referred to the discussion and illustrations contained in Leopold A. Bernstein, *Financial Statement Analysis: Theory, Application, and Interpretation*, rev. ed. (Homewood, IL: Richard D. Irwin, 1978) pp. 330-353.
9. Herbert S. Denenberg, "Is 'A-Plus' Really A Passing Grade?" *The Journal of Risk and Insurance*, Vol. 34, No. 3 (September 1967), pp. 371-384.

CHAPTER 6

Establishing and Maintaining Insurance Company Solvency

INTRODUCTION

The insurance mechanism can reduce the uncertainty of economic loss only to the extent that the mechanism itself is secure. Unfortunate consequences occasioned by the collapse of an insurance company can be devastating to innocent members of the public unable to collect first- and third-party claims, and prepaid but unearned premiums. Likewise, the adverse financial and public relations effects of an insurer insolvency reverberate throughout the entire industry and are deleterious to all associated with it. Previous chapters of this text have described how statutory accounting, policyholder reserve requirements, asset valuation, and investment controls help to ensure company solvency. Other techniques used to establish and maintain the financial integrity of the insurance mechanism are discussed in this chapter. In addition, arrangements are described that have been set up to protect the public from loss once a default occurs. Alleged deficiencies of the current backup system, which is based on state insurance guarantee funds, are noted and some alternative ways of providing protection against insurer insolvencies are reviewed.

ESTABLISHING SOLVENCY

The Meaning of Solvency

Solvency can be defined in several different contexts. Using the analogy of the gambler's ruin problem introduced in Chapter 2 and

277

discussed in Chapter 5, a probabilistic definition of solvency can be given: An insurer is solvent if the probability is at least 1-e (for instance, 99.9% for $e = 0.1\%$) that it will be able to discharge present and future losses and expenses by using its current capital and surplus together with future premiums assuming it ceases business at the end of some specified time period (say, one year). Given the current level of capital and surplus and employing certain assumptions in regard to the probability distribution of losses, expenses, and investment returns, a mathematical formulation can be used to determine whether a particular insurance company's ruin probability is sufficiently small. If the company's probability of ruin (the calculated value of e) is greater than what is considered to be socially acceptable (say, 0.1%) the insurer is insolvent and must be removed from the marketplace. Although this definition is theoretically sound, its application in practice is prevented by the inability to include the actual probability distributions and appropriate parametric values that will apply to future operations. Moreover, nonsystematic risks, such as management dishonesty, are not comprehended in such a mathematical model. This approach to solvency therefore may be more useful for management decision making than to external parties.

In a regulatory context, an insurance company is solvent if its admitted assets exceed liabilities by a margin at least equal to the minimum capital and/or minimum surplus required by law. This meaning is said to define "technical" solvency. In theory, an insurer is technically solvent so long as the value of its admitted assets less properly valued liabilities is at least equal to the required minimum capitalization. It becomes insolvent the moment capital or surplus drops below the minimum level. Realistically, such a situation probably would not be discovered until some time after capital had been impaired.

Solvency also may be defined to mean that an insurance company maintains the ability to meet its obligations as they are due, even though some claims arising from current operations will be settled a number of years in the future. This emphasizes the need for continued liquidity, adequate loss reserves, and appropriate premium rates. However, this definition cannot fully explain solvency because it fails to acknowledge the legal requirement that an insurance company must maintain at least a prescribed level of net worth.

For insurance company management purposes, a practicable definition of solvency is obtained by combining the previous approaches. A solvent insurer (1) collects premiums that realistically can be expected to satisfy anticipated loss settlements and meet all operating expenses; and (2) maintains admitted assets sufficient to cover its existing liabilities, with a remaining safety margin that is at least equal to statutory net worth requirements. This defines a *minimum* solvency standard for management. In most, if not all, cases insurance companies choose to operate with a larger net worth than prescribed by statutory minimums. Indeed, the capitalization requirements prescribed by law in many states are grossly inadequate solvency safeguards.

Minimum Net Worth Requirements

The minimum amount of initial net worth required in order for a company to obtain a license to transact a certain type of insurance business is governed by the respective state insurance laws. In addition to statutory minimums for initial capital and surplus, many states require that minimum levels of net worth be maintained so long as the company is a going concern. These continuing minimums are commonly lower than the initial standards.

Initial Minimums One of several initial minimums will apply to a particular insurance company depending on (1) the state in which the license is obtained, (2) the lines of insurance in which the company wishes to engage, and (3) the company's legal form. There is little similarity among net worth requirements set by the various states. For example, a stock fire insurance company needs $1.4 million of capital and surplus to meet the initial requirements in Illinois but only $150,000 if it is organized in Pennsylvania. If the company intends to transact marine insurance and reinsurance business as well as fire insurance, Pennsylvania mandates that initial capital and surplus be increased to $300,000. On the other hand, if the insurer restricts its activities to fire insurance but is organized as a mutual in Pennsylvania, it must have an initial surplus of only $100,000. The property and liability insurance industry is predominantly made up of stock and mutual companies writing multiple lines of insurance but other organizational forms (reciprocals and Lloyds associations) and other operating methods (monoline) do exist. It is questionable whether the diverse initial net worth requirements witnessed among state laws can be justified by the pluralism within the insurance marketplace.

A stock insurance company acquires its initial capitalization from the sale of the corporation's common stock to investors who are interested in becoming stockholders of the new company. Organizers of the corporation, most of whom will later be active in its management, usually set a price for its shares above the stock's par or stated value. Amounts paid in excess of par value establish the corporation's initial surplus.[1] For example, suppose the new company must have at least $1 million capital and $500,000 surplus in order to be licensed in its state of domicile. Ignoring costs incurred in marketing stock, the incorpora-

Table 6-1

New Company Balance Sheet

Assets		Liabilities and Net Worth	
Cash	$1,500,000	Capital Paid Up Surplus Paid In	$1,000,000 500,000
Total Assets	$1,500,000	Total Liabilities and Net Worth	$1,500,000

tors can arrange the necessary financing by selling 100,000 shares of common stock with a $10 par value per share at an issue price of $15 per share. After the stock is issued, the insurer's beginning balance sheet would appear as shown in Table 6-1. There are several reasons why investors may be willing to purchase shares of stock at a price greater than its par value. The most general reason is that the par value of a company's stock does not necessarily reflect its inherent worth. Investors may believe that the economic prospects of the new company, the calibre of management, and its opportunities for profitable growth are so favorable that a price greater than the par value assigned to the stock is appropriate. The insurer's organizers may prefer as low a par value as permitted in order to facilitate widespread sale of the company's shares. Moreover, the concept of par value has little economic significance; it serves a legal purpose which may be worthwhile disclosing for small or incipient corporations because it assures creditors that, at a minimum, the par value has been paid into the company. Nevertheless, par value has little meaning except in the case of a recapitalization or liquidation.

Mutual and reciprocal insurers do not have capital stock but obtain their original financing from or through organizers whose entire contribution becomes paid-in surplus. The company frequently pays interest on this initial contribution, which is referred to as guarantee capital, and it may repay the organizers' initial contribution out of earnings during subsequent years. Repayments can be made *only* out of earnings. Some states allow the licensing of mutual and reciprocal insurers with lower paid-in surplus than the total capital and surplus required of a stock insurer. This seemingly illogical practice is explained in several ways. First, nonstock insurers that have only minimum surplus possess a limited power to assess their policyholders. Second, it is argued that application of higher initial net worth standards would effectively prohibit organizing an insurer as a mutual or reciprocal. Third, at least some nonstock insurers are truly cooperative ventures established to provide insurance at cost to a previously existing trade association or other well-defined sponsor. Because such "noncommercial" insurers usually do not incur the large start-up costs that commercial insurers must bear, a smaller initial capitalization may be justified.[2] Regardless of the merit, if any, in these assertions, a need for sufficient net worth applies equally to all insurance companies.

The amount of initial capital and surplus invested in new insurance organizations varies greatly among companies and from year to year. This is illustrated by the data in Table 6-2.[3] These eighty-three stock property and liability insurers began operations with an average capitalization of $3.4 million but the actual investment in individual insurers varied widely. For example, in 1977 a stock insurance company with capital of $150,000 and surplus of $75,000 was licensed in Texas to transact general casualty business; a New York domiciled reinsurer began operations during the same year with capital of $2 million and surplus of $21 million.

Continuing Functions Capital and surplus in a stock insurance company serve distinctly separate functions. If the company fails, capital acts as a guarantee fund to protect policyholders from loss. Minimum capital therefore must be maintained at all times; an impairment renders the company technically insolvent even though admitted assets may substantially exceed liabilities. Paid-in surplus does not remain whole after the company is formed. It provides funds to pay for organizational fees, development expenses, establishment of an agency force, and to meet loss settlement fluctuations. Substantial decreases in surplus may occur before the new company "turns the corner" and begins to replenish surplus from operating income. The company presumably may continue operations unless and until it exhausts its final dollar of surplus. For instance, a stock fire insurance company that has minimum initial capital of $100,000 and surplus of $50,000 can reduce its net worth to $100,000 without becoming technically insolvent.

Like stock companies, mutuals and reciprocals also are allowed to invade initial surplus. However, since surplus for these insurers must function as both a guarantee fund and as a source of working capital, surplus cannot be depleted below a prescribed level. This minimum surplus typically is the same as the smallest amount of capital allowed for a comparable stock insurance company. The insurance code of Pennsylvania, for instance, requires a mutual insurer writing nonassessable policies to maintain unimpaired surplus equal to the minimum required capital of a stock company authorized to transact the same class or classes of business. An assessment mutual must maintain unimpaired surplus of at least 50 percent of its initially required surplus.[4]

Table 6-2

Investments in New Insurance Organizations

Year	Number of Stock Companies Formed	Total Capitalization of New Stock Companies (in millions)	Average Capitalization Per Company (in millions)
1977	32	$ 91.7	$2.86
1976	34	37.5	1.10
1975	17	151.9	8.9
Totals	83	$281.1	$3.4

Capital and Surplus Expansion

The legal minimum capital and surplus levels required for new insurance companies also apply to seasoned insurers even though the premium volume, operating complexity, and management competency have increased and improved since operations began. Company management and state insurance regulating authorities nevertheless expect net worth to grow as the company becomes larger. As pointed out in Chapter 5, the relationship between premiums written-to-policyholders' surplus is used as a guide for judging whether capital and surplus are adequate in an expanding company. The fact that the relationship is, at best, a sliding scale is illustrated by the data in Table 6-3.[5] Even larger premiums written-to-policyholders' surplus ratios than those exhibited by these four companies have been shown by smaller insurers experiencing enlarged sales after suffering surplus losses due to cyclical earnings patterns. During periods of rapid sales expansion or when a company wishes to increase its market share, existing surplus may prove insufficient to support the desired growth. When this occurs, the insurer may need to alter its financial structure by increasing its equity base. This can be accomplished in several ways.

Traditionally, property and liability insurers have relied on internally generated profits for growth. However, retained earnings may be inadequate to sustain rapid upturns in premium volume caused by property value increases, higher liability coverages, and upward adjustments in premium rates. When internally generated funds are insufficient, the company must seek infusions of capital from existing owners or from the capital markets. A new issue of common stock is the most straightforward way to raise external equity capital but the cost of this instrument may be relatively high when compared to other alternatives and the potential for earnings and ownership dilution may displease existing stockholders. Many other financial instruments,

Table 6-3

Premiums to Surplus Ratios

Ratio of Premiums to Surplus		
Company	June 30, 1977	December 31, 1972
Aetna Life & Casualty	3.5:1	1.7:1
St. Paul Companies	3.8:1	1.7:1
Travelers	4.7:1	1.7:1
United States Fidelity & Guaranty	3.0:1	1.1:1

commonly used by noninsurance companies, also may be employed by insurers. This has not always been the case. For many years, the state of New York did not allow insurers freedom to include senior securities within their capital structure. Following publication of the *Report of the Special Committee on Insurance Holding Companies* in 1968, Section 76 of the *New York Insurance Code* was amended to allow insurers more flexibility in arranging their outside financing, subject to regulatory approval. Preferred stock, debentures, and other fixed income instruments may be issued directly by an insurer and the resulting funds can be included in policyholders' surplus accompanied by a footnote explanation. Alternatively, a holding company parent of an insurer can issue bonds or other senior instruments and funnel the proceeds to the insurer by purchasing more of its common stock.[6] Recent tax code changes have encouraged rapid expansion of premium volume by property and liability insurance company subsidiaries that can operate at a tax loss and provide their industrial company parent with a tax shelter. Therefore, the public financial markets may be more receptive to the idea of providing capital to an insurer that is posting significant underwriting losses on rapid sales gains if the securities are issued by a noninsurance holding company and funds are passed through to the insurer. The exact arrangements used by a particular company will depend on many factors but it can be assumed that management is attempting to minimize the corporation's weighted average cost of capital while simultaneously providing the capital infusion necessary for desired growth. The ability of the parent corporation to supply funds to a subsidiary insurance company should not be confused with the legal obligation to do so. The parent is not required to rescue a subsidiary in danger of financial collapse, although this often occurs.

METHODS OF MAINTAINING SOLVENCY

Minimum capital and surplus requirements are one way in which state legislatures and insurance regulators attempt to assure initial and continued solvency of insurance companies. Other methods include rate regulation, investment regulation, statutory accounting rules, financial reporting requirements, periodic examinations of insurance companies, and application of diagnostic tests to company financial data. Solvency surveillance through field examinations and the NAIC regulatory tests is described in this section.

Insurance Department Examinations

Insurance statutes of the various states require or permit the state's insurance commissioner to conduct periodic field examinations into the affairs of all insurance companies authorized to do business in the state. The commissioner usually is required to examine all domestic insurers at least once every three to five years and may initiate an examination whenever it is deemed expedient to do so. Authorized foreign and alien insurers also are examined periodically in conformance with the NAIC zone examinations described later in this section.

Purpose of Examinations State insurance department examinations serve several purposes. First, the examination strives to identify as early as possible those insurers that are experiencing financial trouble and/or engaging in unlawful and improper activities. Second, the examination seeks to develop information needed for appropriate regulatory action.[7] Examinations also confirm that the subject companies are operating and reporting in accordance with the uniform accounting instructions promulgated by the NAIC for use in completing the annual statement. The tangible product of an examination is the report on examination prepared by insurance department examiners. Some states, notably New York, require that the report on examination or a summary thereof be read at the first meeting of the insurer's board of directors following receipt of the report. A copy of the report on examination also must be furnished to each member of the board of directors. This requirement is intended to notify board members, including outside directors, of the company's activities and financial condition.[8] The examination therefore is helpful to the company as well as serving its regulator purpose. Company directors and regulatory officials can use the examination to safeguard the interests of policyholders and stockholders.

Examination Procedures State insurance department examiners are employees of the regulatory agency and typically are included in the state's civil service program. In some states, only a few examiners are employed but in the major insurance jurisdictions as many as 200 examiners may be included in the department's staff. It is estimated that over one-fourth of all insurance department personnel are examiners.[9]

Although they are state employees, or employees of private auditing firms, examiners conduct most of their work in insurance company home and branch offices. Facilities and supplies for the on-site examination are furnished by the subject insurer. In most states, all expenses associated with the examination are borne and paid by the insurer. The manner in which an examiner receives his or her salary varies among the states but the company being examined usually is billed by the state for charges associated with the examination; this includes the examiner's salary plus a "loading factor" to cover employee benefit costs and insurance department overhead.

An insurance company scheduled for examination often is requested to furnish selected information in advance of the examiners' visit. This information may include working papers from internal audits, reports from the company's independent public accountants, or other management information. Review of this material prior to company visitation allows the examination to focus on potential problem areas and thus reduces the time and cost involved. Examinations of large property and liability insurers may last as long as one year. This means that large insurers domiciled in states that require triennial examinations have examiners on their premises about one-third of the time. Close cooperation between insurance company employees and the examiners therefore is essential to expedite the progress of the examination and hold down the cost.

NAIC Zone Examinations To prevent duplication of examinations by the numerous insurance departments, the NAIC has divided the fifty-three separate regulatory jurisdictions into six zones. Jurisdictions assigned to each zone are shown in Table 6-4. One insurance commissioner in each zone is designated as the zone chairman. For all companies licensed in more than one zone or in more than three states in a single zone, the NAIC recommends an "Association" type of examination. This means that the examination follows the uniform procedures and reporting requirements outlined by the *NAIC Financial Condition Examiners' Handbook*. This is the type of examination applied to nearly all insurance companies.

Whether or not a particular company is examined by one state or more than one state depends upon the geographical scope of its operations and the volume of business done in each jurisdiction. If an insurer has annual direct premiums written of $1 million or more in a zone or if at least 20 percent of its writings, regardless of dollar amount, are in a zone, a representative from that zone shall be invited to participate in the examination. The insurance department of the

Table 6-4

NAIC Examination Zones*

Zone 1	Zone 2	Zone 3
Connecticut	Delaware	Alabama
Maine	District of Columbia	Florida
Massachusetts	Maryland	Georgia
New Hampshire	North Carolina	Kentucky
New Jersey	Ohio	Louisiana
New York	Pennsylvania	Missouri
Rhode Island	South Carolina	Mississippi
Vermont	Virginia	Puerto Rico
Virgin Islands	West Virginia	Tennessee
Zone 4	**Zone 5**	**Zone 6**
Illinois	Arkansas	Alaska
Indiana	Colorado	Arizona
Iowa	Kansas	California
Michigan	Nebraska	Hawaii
Minnesota	New Mexico	Idaho
North Dakota	Oklahoma	Montana
South Dakota	Texas	Nevada
Wisconsin	Wyoming	Oregon
		Utah
		Washington

*Reprinted from the National Association of Insurance Commissioners, *Proceedings*, annual.

company's state of domicile notifies the NAIC secretary when it proposes to examine a company. The NAIC secretary checks the premium volume shown in the company's most recent annual statement and notifies the chairman of each zone eligible for participation. The zone chairman designates one of the states within the zone to appoint an examiner as the zone representative on the examination team. If all states within the zone waive participation, the zone waives participation and is not represented. The examination team is headed by an examiner-in-charge from the domiciliary state and examiners representing each participating zone. The examiner-in-charge is responsible for outlining the examination program following the provisions of the *Examiners' Handbook*. Zone representatives may request investigation into specific areas of special interest to their state or members of their zone. Results are included in the report on examination.

The report on examination is prepared before the close of the examination and presented to the insurance company's officers for review and discussion. It contains summary financial statements from the most current annual statement along with an analysis of any specific changes resulting from the examination. Also included are a discussion of adverse findings, material changes in the financial statements, and other important regulatory information disclosed by the examination. In its current form, content of the report is predominantly critical in nature.

Critique of the Examination System   In recent years insurance regulators have reevaluated the procedures followed and purposes served by field examinations of insurance companies and the resulting report. The degree of overlap with examinations performed by inside auditors, independent public accountants, other state agencies, and the Internal Revenue Service has been recognized and attempts made to use these other examinations to help focus the attention of the financial condition examination. It has been suggested that every insurer required to complete an annual statement should be required to submit such statement to audit by an independent public accountant satisfactory to the commissioner of insurance.[10] A few states, such as Illinois and Massachusetts, have adopted rules requiring certain insurers to file annual audit reports prepared by independent certified public accountants. This permits the insurance departments to spend less time on financial verification and to target examination efforts on aspects of company operations that have the greatest impact on policyholders' surplus. The format of the report on examination has been changed to discourage ritualistic duplication of previous years' reports and to encourage disclosure of current company difficulties or unlawful and improper activities. Increased reliance on independent audits of insurance company financial statements represents a restructuring of regulatory procedures. Company examinations remain one of the most important phases of insurance supervision and solvency maintenance.

NAIC Regulatory Tests

In 1971, the NAIC developed a set of financial relationships or "tests" which were intended to provide diagnostic tools for the evaluation of insurance company strength. The tests were based on research conducted by personnel in several state insurance departments, especially in the California, Illinois, and Michigan departments. Initially, more than two dozen diagnostic tests were suggested but this number was reduced during subsequent years because of disagreements over the significance of some relationships and because of insufficient staffing within many insurance regulatory departments. During the first few years of the tests' development and use they were called "solidity" or "solvency" tests. However, because a direct measure of solvency was not provided by the diagnostic tools, a more general terminology has evolved. Since 1975 the two sets of separate but similar tests designed for property and liability insurance companies and life and health insurance companies have been called regulatory tests. A description of the tests applied to nonlife insurers is presented in this section. It is based on the NAIC publication, "Using the Early Warning System: NAIC Regulatory Tests for Property and Liability Insurers, 1976."

Purposes of the Tests The primary purpose of the regulatory tests is early identification of companies that may require close surveillance by insurance regulatory authorities. The tests signal the need for more thorough inquiry into the company's status and operations. They also may be helpful in suggesting what specific areas are in need of most immediate attention. Scheduling priorities for special on-site examinations can be based on the tests' results.

The regulatory tests are not meant to be a substitute for a field examination or a timely audit of the annual statement. They are only intended to supplement traditional forms of financial surveillance. The NAIC admonishes its members not to use results of the Early Warning System tests as the sole basis for key decisions—such as issuing or renewing a company's certificate of authority to conduct insurance operations within the state. In addition, it is recommended that test results be interpreted by knowledgeable and experienced examiners who have familiarized themselves with the company's annual statements. Despite these admonitions, 70 percent of the state insurance departments responding to a recent survey said the tests are used to determine whether companies should be granted authority to write insurance.[11]

Critics of the present solvency surveillance system have pointed out that use of the regulatory tests implies a failure on the part of state insurance departments to properly perform their traditional financial surveillance functions. It is noted that the regulatory tests are simply manipulations of data readily available in the annual statements filed with each state. The tests do not furnish additional raw data nor do they change the regulator's ability to exercise administrative powers. Therefore, this approach to improving financial surveillance is criticized as an added layer of regulation on a solvency maintenance system that is fundamentally deficient. Nevertheless, the regulatory tests do furnish a quick indication of the companies in need of more detailed examination, and they are helpful in directing the attention of examiners to specific areas of inquiry.

Mechanics of the System Each insurance company is requested or required to file its annual statement with a statistical agency designated by the NAIC to process the financial data and perform the regulatory tests. Exemptions from the filing requirement are granted to some insurers with geographically limited operations (e.g., single state companies, county mutuals, etc.). The statistical agency is paid a fee by the filing company to cover costs of the analysis. Results are reported to the insurance departments of each state in which the company operates. Two types of reports are provided. The first type is called a preliminary release; a series of preliminary releases is distributed periodically as test results become available. A second type of report, called a final release, is issued after test values are computed for substantially all companies. The final release updates the preliminary releases with amended results based on completed and revised data.

Two formats are used in the releases to set forth results of the regulatory tests. One exhibit lists companies in descending order according to the number of unsatisfactory statistical values their data produces. A second exhibit lists companies alphabetically with unsatisfactory results marked by an asterisk. If a predetermined number of unsatisfactory test values is generated by a particular company's information, the insurer is identified as a priority company and labeled with a "P" in the final release. Priority companies are those insurers most in need of closer than usual analysis.

Establishing criteria for test values is at the heart of this system. The ability of the regulatory tests to discriminate between companies that can receive normal supervision and those that require immediate careful scrutiny rests on the definition of normal and exceptional values. An unsatisfactory test result occurs whenever the value calculated for a particular company's data falls outside the "usual range" for that statistic. The usual range is defined in such a way as to include results expected from the majority of companies during a normal year. Because standards are set relative to industry operating results under normal conditions, greater numbers of companies are expected to fall outside the usual range in years marked by aberrant economic forces. For 1976 exceptional values were established in such a way as to assign approximately 15 percent of the companies a priority designation. Each insurer with four or more test results outside the usual range was classified as a priority company. For companies with some statistics outside the usual range but less than four exceptional values, the tests identify specific areas that should be investigated further during the normal examination process.

Nature and Interpretation of the Tests The 1976 Early Warning System for property and liability insurers included eleven tests which were classified into four groups, as follows:

1. Overall Tests
   Premiums-to-surplus
   Change in writings
   Surplus aid-to-surplus
2. Profitability Tests
   Two-year adjusted underwriting ratio
   Investment yield
   Change in surplus
3. Liquidity Tests
   Liabilities-to-liquid assets
   Agent's balances-to-surplus
4. Reserve Tests
   One-year reserve development-to-surplus
   Two-year reserve development-to-surplus
   Estimated current reserve deficiency-to-surplus

The calculation of each test is described below and the exceptional value criterion given. Table 6-5 presents results of the 1976 NAIC regulatory tests for 1,577 companies as of April 15, 1977.

Overall Tests

Premiums-to-Surplus. The ratio of premiums-to-surplus is considered a gauge of the company's insurance exposure; that is, as more insurance is written, surplus is exposed to greater chance of loss variations. This ratio shows the relationship between written premiums and unadjusted statutory net worth. A calculated value greater than 3-to-1 is considered unfavorable; that is, in order for an insurer's premiums-to-surplus ratio to be acceptable, the calculated value should be less than or equal to ($\leq$) 300 percent:

$$\frac{\text{Net Premiums Written}}{\text{Policyholders' Surplus}} \leq 300\%$$

For this test, only an upper limit or bound is established and all calculated values are forced to fall within a predetermined range. If policyholders' surplus is zero or negative, a value of 999 is assigned to the ratio. If policyholders' surplus is positive but net premiums written are negative, a value of zero is assigned. Negative net premiums written could result for an insurance company that cedes more business than it writes either directly or as a reinsurer. Using these rules for calculating test values, all test scores fall within the range of zero to 999.

Note that this test is more liberal than the 2-to-1 limit suggested by the second Kenney Rule discussed in Chapter 5. However, as this ratio's value approaches the 3-to-1 bench mark, regulators become interested in any mitigating relationships. For instance, a high test value for this ratio may be interpreted less severely in the presence of:

Table 6-5
1976 NAIC Property and Liability Regulatory Tests*

All Companies Percentiles	Prem to C&S	Chng in Writ	Surp Aid/ C&S	2 Yr Und Ratio	Inv Yld	Chng in C&S	Liab /Liq Asset	Agnt Bal/ C&S	1 Yr Res Devl	2 Yr Res Devl	Crnt Res Defic	Capital and Surplus	Earned Premium	Total Assets
Test	1	2	3	4	5	6	7	8	9	10	11			
Equal to or Over†	300	33	25	110	9.9	50	105	40	25	25	25			
Equal to or Under†		−33			4.0	−10								
Highest Value	999†	999†	999†	405†	9.9†	999†	999†	999†	999†	999†	999†	$2,105,547	$3,093,966	$5,106,257
99.0	865†	999†	110†	197†	9.2	999†	262†	168†	128†	248†	281†	342,095	590,221	1,370,100
98.0	645†	999†	67†	164†	8.3	678†	176†	120†	78†	161†	168†	179,838	317,112	755,814
97.0	547†	999†	51†	154†	7.7	210†	148†	102†	65†	119†	117†	116,869	233,053	449,836
95.0	434†	290†	34†	132†	7.2	95†	133†	77†	43†	76†	90†	65,163	139,090	314,698
92.5	392†	142†	24	122†	6.9	63†	118†	61†	31†	55†	54†	45,408	101,549	175,910
90.0	357†	108†	17	118†	6.8	49	110†	53†	24	42†	37†	35,411	66,977	123,181
85.0	316†	65†	10	114†	6.4	36	102	44†	16	27†	22	21,223	37,628	66,102
80.0	288	52†	7	111†	6.2	31	96	38	11	16	12	13,197	22,362	43,263
75.0	264	40†	4	109	6.0	26	91	31	7	11	7	9,634	16,029	30,802
50.0	148	19	0	102	5.3	13	72	12	0	0	0	3,105	3,223	7,514
25.0	38	2	0	96	4.6	5	35	0	−2	−1	−4	1,002	410	2,057
20.0	24	0	0	95	4.4	3	24	0	−4	−3	−7	754	163	1,531
15.0	11	0	0	92	4.1	0	15	0	−6	−6	−11	567	39	1,052
10.0	0	0	0	87	3.7†	−4	7	0	−10	−11	−17	380	0	605
7.5	0	−7	0	82	3.4†	−7	7	0	−13	−15	−24	295	0	456
5.0	0	−13	0	77	3.0†	−11†	3	0	−17	−22	−33	191	0	245
3.0	0	−23	0	65	2.3†	−17†	1	0	−26	−36	−56	107	0	156
2.0	0	−50†	0	58	1.7†	−23†	0	0	−41	−61	−89	75	0	105
1.0	0	−73†	0	41	1.0†	−38†	0	0	−99	−99	−99	37	0	52
Lowest Value	0	−99†	0	−35	0.0†	−99†	0	0	−99	−99	−99	−94,764	−49	0
Exceptional Companies	275	555	116	311	244	251	209	289	157	247	220			
Companies Having Results	1,577	1,577	1,577	1,356	1,577	1,577	1,577	1,577	1,577	1,577	1,577			
Percent Exceptional	17	35	7	23	15	16	13	18	10	16	14			

†Exceptional values.

*Reprinted with permission from National Association of Insurance Commissioners, 1977.

1. a lower premiums-to-surplus ratio for the group of affiliated insurance companies;
2. steadily increasing profits;
3. a low concentration of business in Schedule P lines of insurance;
4. adequate excess reinsurance;
5. a conservative and properly valued investment portfolio; and,
6. an adjustment for available surplus aid reinsurance (see discussion below).

The adequacy of surplus to absorb unexpected underwriting losses is evaluated more correctly by recognizing the interaction of these variables with the relationship between premiums and surplus. Of the 1,577 companies included in the 1976 NAIC regulatory tests results, 275 (or 17 percent) reported exceptional values for the premiums-to-surplus ratio.

Change in Writings. The rate of change in premiums written calculated in this ratio should not exceed ± 33 percent:

$$\frac{\text{Net Premiums Written}_t - \text{Net Premiums Written}_{t-1}}{\text{Net Premiums Written}_{t-1}} \leq 33\%$$

where the subscript t designates data for the current year and $t-1$ indicates data for the prior year. Large fluctuations in premiums usually signal instability in the company's underwriting operations. Expansion of operations into new product lines or new geographical areas, additions to the agency force, or increased production accompanying economic upturns may cause unusually large increases in premium volume. Changes attributable to causes such as these are not necessarily unfavorable. However, premium volume may be increased intentionally by a failing insurer that has been weakened with unanticipated losses. One way that this can be accomplished is to lower underwriting standards in an effort to increase cash flow. Clearly, such a precarious practice can hide fundamental difficulties only temporarily. Test values outside the usual range should prompt close examination of the insurer's liquidity and reserve adequacy.

The impact that an economic upturn accompanied by widespread rate increases has on this statistic is illustrated by the fact that 555, or 35 percent, of the companies showed exceptional change in writings ratio in 1976. None of the other tests produced as many values outside the usual range.

Surplus Aid-to-Surplus. Many types of reinsurance treaties provide surplus aid by allowing the primary insurer to transfer all or a portion of its unearned premium reserve requirement to the reinsurance company. In order for this type of surplus aid to be available, the reinsurer must be legally licensed to transact reinsurance in the state under consideration; that is, it must be an *admitted* reinsurance company. The reinsurer pays a commission to the ceding company to compensate it for acquisition expenses previously incurred. For purposes of this regulatory test, surplus aid is defined to consist of commissions on reinsurance ceded to nonaffiliated companies. Reinsurance transactions among affiliated companies are excluded so that the test will not be biased against members of fleets or group participating in reinsurance pooling arrangements.

To form the test ratio, surplus aid is divided by policyholders' surplus and expressed on a percentage basis. Values below 25 percent are interpreted as acceptable:

$$\frac{\text{Surplus Aid}}{\text{Surplus}} < 25\%$$

Surplus aid is not specifically reported in the annual statement. Therefore the numerator of this ratio must be estimated from available data. The following procedure is used:

$$\text{Surplus Aid} =$$

$$\left(\begin{array}{c} \text{Estimated Reinsurance} \\ \text{Commission Rate} \end{array} \right) \times \left(\begin{array}{c} \text{Unearned Premiums on} \\ \text{Reinsurance Ceded to Nonaffiliated} \end{array} \right)$$

A ceding commission rate is estimated by dividing the commission and brokerage fee on reinsurance ceded by reinsurance ceded premiums. Multiplying this commission rate by unearned premiums on reinsurance ceded to nonaffiliates produces the annual surplus aid figure. The denominator of the test ratio is surplus with regard to policyholders as given on the balance sheet.

The surplus aid-to-surplus ratio is an especially important regulatory test. Exceptionally large amounts of surplus aid are interpreted as an indication that the company's capitalization is not sufficient for the amount of direct insurance being written. The existence of significant surplus aid in the presence of inadequate surplus can distort results determined for some of the other regulatory tests. Consequently, several of the tests that include surplus in the calculation should be recomputed with surplus adjusted to remove surplus aid whenever an exceptional value is determined for this ratio.

In 1976, 116, or 7 percent, of the companies reported surplus aid-to-surplus ratios outside the acceptable range. This was the smallest number of exceptional values produced by any of the eleven regulatory tests.

Profitability Tests

Two-Year Adjusted Underwriting Ratio. This regulatory test is analogous to the combined ratio; it shows the relationship between losses plus expenses and premiums. Rather than being based on a single year's data, the current and prior years are considered together under the assumption that the longer observation period will mitigate fluctuations caused by interperiod revenue and cost allocations. The treatment given policyholder dividends and other income is a refinement of the combined ratio discussed earlier. Test values are considered exceptional if they equal or exceed 110 percent:

$$
\begin{array}{c}
\text{Two-Year Adjusted} \\
\text{Underwriting Ratio}
\end{array} =
$$

$$
\left[\begin{array}{c} \text{Two-Year Loss} \\ \text{Ratio} \end{array} + \begin{array}{c} \text{Two-Year Expense} \\ \text{Ratio} \end{array} \right] < 110\%
$$

The loss ratio component is calculated by adding losses, loss adjustment expenses, and policyholder dividends for the current and prior years and dividing the total by *premiums earned,* net of reinsurance, during the same periods. Underwriting expenses minus other income for the current and prior years are divided by *net premiums written* to form the expense ratio. Summing the two components gives a measurement of underwriting profit margin for the two-year period. Values less than 100 percent indicate underwriting profits and values in excess of 100 percent show underwriting losses.

One might question why the "usual" range of values extends beyond 100 percent. Two related explanations are given. First, this test makes no provision for investment income. Results of the next regulatory test, Investment Yield, must be considered along with underwriting profitability. Second, the purpose of the regulatory tests must be kept in mind. These tests are not designed to diagnose long-term operating problems but are meant to signal acute disorders that require immediate correction. Setting the exceptional value above 100 percent does not imply that insurance companies can successfully operate over long periods of time without underwriting profit so long as investment returns are available. Even at high premiums-to-surplus ratios a company could sustain underwriting losses within the usual range for several years before solvency would be threatened. For instance, if a company writing business steadily at a premiums-to-surplus ratio of 3-to-1 is experiencing a 9 percent underwriting loss, surplus would not be exhausted for more than three years even without investment income. Within this period corrective action could be instituted to halt the company's decline. The test ratio's two components can assisst in identifying where corrective measures are most appropriate—loss control, expense control, or both.

Because under- or over-reserving can distort operating results, the company's true underwriting position is not fully described by the two-year adjusted underwriting ratio. Values determined for this test should be related to the reserve development tests dicussed later in this section. Exceptional values for the reserve development tests recommend a recalculation of this test after elimination of the prior year's reserve development.

The aggregate underwriting loss recorded by the 1,577 companies included in the 1976 NAIC profitability report was $910,598,000. Although regulatory tests were made on data supplied by all 1,577 companies, only 1,356 two-year adjusted underwriting ratios were reported. Exceptional values were determined for 311, or 23 percent, of the companies. Less than half the insurers showed an underwriting profit.

Investment Yield. Investment earnings reflect the profitability and general quality of the company's investment portfolio. The investment yield ratio expresses net investment income as a percentage of the average amount of investment during the year. Calculated investment yields between 4.0 and 9.9 percent are considered to be within the usual range.

$$\text{Investment Yield} = \frac{\text{Net Investment Income}}{\text{Average Invested Assets}} \begin{array}{l} < 9.9\% \\ > 4.0\% \end{array}$$

Net investment income includes interest, dividends, and real estate income but not capital gains or losses whether realized or unrealized. The ratio's numerator therefore can be taken directly from the annual statement. On the other hand, the denominator must be calculated from annual statement data for the current and prior years. Invested assets are defined to be cash and other invested assets listed on the first seven lines of the statutory balance sheet plus accrued investment income minus borrowed money. The ratio's denominator is computed by adding invested assets at the end of the prior year to invested assets at the end of the current year, subtracting investment income for the current year, and dividing the net sum in half.

At first it may seem strange that an upper limit is placed on the usual range of values for this test. After all, a higher calculated yield means greater profits from investments. However, when investment returns are unusually large, the quality of portfolio assets becomes questionable. A suspicion arises that liquidity and safety of principal are being sacrificed in order to achieve an abnormally high current investment yield. Extremely high rates of return therefore trigger inquiry into the investment portfolio's composition and its valuation.

A low investment yield also may be symptomatic of serious problems in investment operations. For instance, unduly optimistic reliance on capital gains from speculative investments may be sacrificing current yield for potential appreciation. Low yields may be associated with investments made in securities of affiliated corporations or business ventures that are controlled by the insurance company's managers or owners. Imprudently large investments in home office facilities or other real estate may cause low current investment return and sacrifice liquidity as well.

The propriety of the insurer's investments should be judged in terms of the portfolio's liquidity, safety, and yield. Deficiencies in any one of these areas may be indicative of related problems in the others. Therefore, when the investment yield calculated for this regulatory test lies outside the usual range an in-depth analysis of the investment portfolio should be conducted. The types of invested assets owned by the insurance company can be determined from the annual statement. A study of the liquidity, safety, and yield characteristics of each investment category will pinpoint unfavorable holdings and help shape a corrective strategy.

Most of the 244 companies reporting exceptional value for the investment yield test in 1976 showed insufficient investment returns. Almost 85 percent of the companies had investment yield between 4.0 and 9.2 percent.

Change in Surplus. The two previous tests measured profitability of underwriting and investment operations individually. This test provides an overall measure of how much better or worse off the company is at the end of the current accounting period compared to the previous year-end. The general form of the test and the usual range of test values are as follows:

$$\frac{\text{Change In Surplus}}{\text{Ratio}} = \frac{\text{Change In Adjusted Surplus}}{\text{Adjusted Surplus Prior Year}} \quad \begin{array}{l} \geq -10\% \\ < +50\% \end{array}$$

The test is somewhat misnamed. Rather than being a ratio of the change in policyholders' surplus as listed in the annual statement, the test actually is based on *adjusted* surplus. An adjustment is made in the current and prior years' surplus for acquisition expenses. Although this adds some small degree of complexity to the calculation, it greatly increases the test's ability to discriminate between strong and weak companies.

Statutory surplus is adjusted for acquisition expenses subject to deferral under GAAP. Expenses included in the adjustment are agent's commissions, taxes, licenses and fees, and other underwriting costs associated with policy issue. The amount of expense adjustment is determined as follows:

$$\text{Expense Adjustment} = \left(\frac{\text{Unearned Premium}}{\text{Reserve}} \right) \times \left(\frac{\text{Acquisition Expenses}}{\text{Net Premiums Written}} \right)$$

Policyholders' surplus plus the expense adjustment for the prior year is subtracted from policyholders' surplus plus the expense adjustment for the current year. This difference equals the change in adjusted surplus that appears in the test ratio's numerator:

$$\text{Change In Adjusted Surplus} = \left(\begin{array}{c} \text{Current Year's} \\ \text{Surplus} \\ + \\ \text{Expense Adjustment} \end{array} \right) - \left(\begin{array}{c} \text{Prior Year's} \\ \text{Surplus} \\ + \\ \text{Expense Adjustment} \end{array} \right)$$

An increase in adjusted surplus greater than 50 percent would be very unusual for a company in sound financial condition. Although a growth in adjusted surplus of this magnitude may be possible for relatively small insurers, such a spectacular increase is interpreted as a sign of instability that may foreshadow insolvency. Large surplus increases also may be associated with changes in company management, control, or ownership. Further investigation is warranted when this ratio shows an excessive addition to adjusted surplus.

If the calculated ratio shows a decrease in adjusted surplus of more than 10 percent, additional analysis of operating results is advised. Dramatic declines in surplus most often will be accompanied by poor underwriting and/or investment results. The two-year adjusted underwriting ratio and the investment yield test will help identify the reason or reasons for surplus declines related to normal operations. Other factors, such as capital gains and losses, capital transactions, dividends to stockholders, changes in nonadmitted assets, changes in surplus aid from reinsurance, changes in utilization of unauthorized reinsurance, and changes in adjustments for foreign exchange also may explain an extraordinary drop in surplus.

Exceptional values for the change in surplus ratio were reported for 251, or 16 percent, of the 1,577 companies included in the 1976 NAIC regulatory tests. All classifications showed some companies outside the usual range. Small companies, those with premiums less than $1 million, accounted for almost one-third of the exceptional values. Two of the nation's largest insurers, each with premiums in excess of $500 million, had test values beyond the upper limit.

Liquidity Tests

Liabilities-to-Liquid Assets. This is the first of two liquidity tests. It shows liabilities as a percentage of liquid assets and defines the usual relationship to be less than 1.05-to-1.00:

$$\frac{\text{Liabilities to}}{\text{Liquid Assets}} = \frac{\text{Stated Liabilities}}{\text{Liquid Assets}} < 105\%$$

Several aspects of the ratio make it, at best, only a rough approximation of the insurer's ability to meet its obligations in a timely fashion. A portion of what is defined to be included in liquid assets may be less than totally realizable in the short-term. Liquid assets are defined for this test to include cash, invested assets, and accrued investment income minus investments in affiliated companies and excluding real estate investments in excess of 5 percent of liabilities. Because bonds are included in invested assets at amortized cost rather than at current market value, liquidity may be overstated. Questions may also be raised concerning the time required to convert real estate to cash and whether the balance sheet values will be realized upon conversion. The liquidity ratio does not deal with portfolio composition; consequently, an insurer conceivably could hold all its assets in cash and be judged less liquid than another company with a large bond portfolio that currently could not be liquidated at its full annual statement value. All these factors tend to overstate liquidity. On the other hand, companies that have large deposits with ceding reinsurers cannot include these funds in invested assets even though the related liability must be shown in the test ratio's numerator. This results in an understatement of liquidity for companies with substantial reinsurance commitments. In all cases, the accuracy of loss reserve estimates is directly related to the ratio's ability to correctly assess liquidity.

The primary rationale behind this test is the fact that a number of insurers threatened by insolvency experienced increasing liability-to-liquid asset ratios in years immediately prior to their ultimate demise. Therefore, test results should be observed over several years as well as compared to the exceptional value criterion.

In 1976, 209, or 13 percent, of the companies included in the NAIC report had exceptional liability-to-liquid assets ratios. A few insurers exhibited liabilities greater than two times liquid assets.

Agents' Balances-to-Surplus. A high ratio of agents' balances to policyholders' surplus often has been a harbinger of financial distress. Agents' balances frequently prove uncollectible in the event the company is liquidated. The ratio gives an indication of how dependent surplus is on an assets of questionable liquidity.

Data for this test can be taken directly from the annual statement. The calculation is made by dividing agents' balances in the course of collection by surplus. Values less than 40 percent are considered to be within the usual range.

$$\frac{\text{Ratio of Agents'}}{\text{Balances to Surplus}} = \frac{\substack{\text{Agents' Balances in} \\ \text{Course of Collection}}}{\text{Surplus}} < 40\%$$

It is suggested that the agents' balances account be analyzed closely if this test produces an unfavorable result. Balances more than ninety days old may have been included among admitted assets. A quick check can be made for what the approximate account balance should be. Since only the most recent ninety days' premiums are allowed to be included in the account, the balance can be estimated by finding one-quarter of the year's direct premiums written and reinsurance assumed, net of commissions. This calculation would give the maximum possible value for agents' balances if premium volume was evenly distributed throughout the year.

A relatively large number of insurers reported exceptional values for the ratio in 1976. There were 289 companies, slightly more than 18 percent, with more than 40 percent of their surplus invested in agents' balances. Only two other tests produced a greater number of exceptional values.

Reserve Tests

One-Year Reserve Development-to-Surplus. One of the best ways to examine a company's loss reserving practices is to compare the development of claims costs with the original liability for losses. Reserve development gives an indirect indication of management's attitude toward surplus adequacy. Except in periods when surplus is below a level desired by management, insurers have shown an inclination to overstate loss reserves. This has the effect of developing an equity in the loss reserves for the company through deferral of income recognition and related taxes.

As claims pass from an unpaid to paid status, the accuracy with which reserves were originally established can be gauged. The one-year reserve development-to-surplus ratio does this with the most recent data available. Current reserve balances on losses that were outstanding a year ago plus payments that have been made on these losses during the year can be compared to the reserves carried for these losses at the end of the prior year. The difference represents "reserve development" during the current year:

$$\text{Reserve Development} = A + B - C$$

where: A = reserves for losses incurred prior to the current year, B = payments made on losses incurred prior to the current year, and C = loss reserves reported in the prior year. If the prior year's reserve balance is more than currently reported reserves plus interim payments, reserve development is negative indicating that reserves were redundant. However, if the current reserve balances plus payments are greater than loss reserves reported at the end of the previous year, reserves were deficient.

The test ratio is constructed by dividing reserve development by the prior year's surplus. The resulting percentage indicates the extent by which the previous year's surplus was under- or over-stated through inaccurate reserve estimation given the benefit of one year's retrospective vision. Test values less than 25 percent are considered to fall within the usual range:

$$\begin{array}{c}\text{One-Year Reserve} \\ \text{Development-to-Surplus} \\ \text{Ratio}\end{array} = \frac{\text{One-Year Reserve Development}}{\text{Prior Year's Surplus}} < 25\%$$

Setting the usual range to include reserve deficiences of up to 25 percent of surplus is somewhat misleading. There is no implication that inadequate reserves are sanctioned. The criterion was selected because the test was able to distinquish financially sound from troubled companies. Any positive score for this test may cause concern over reserve adequacy. Calculated values approaching or exceeding the upper bound should prompt a detailed examination of reserves by line of business to see where deficiencies are occurring. An attempt also should be made to see whether deliberate underreserving has taken place.

One-half the companies reporting in 1976 had either sufficient or redundant reserves based on their one-year reserve development-to-surplus scores; that is, their test scores were zero or negative. The great majority of this group had overstated reserves by no more than 10 percent of the prior year's surplus. Reserve deficiencies, in terms of the test criterion, were reported by 157, or 10 percent, of the companies.

Two-Year Reserve Development-to-Surplus. This test is very similar to the previous ratio; it is based on reserves that have matured for two years rather than one year:

$$\text{Two-Year Reserve Development} = A + B - C$$

where: A = reserves for losses incurred prior to the preceding year, B = payments made on losses incurred prior to the preceding year, and C =

loss reserves reported in the second prior year. Again, a negative reserve development indicates overestimation of reserves has occurred during previous years while a positive score shows reserve deficiencies and overstatement of surplus. The extent to which prior reserve estimates missed the mark is shown relative to surplus at the end of the second prior year:

$$\text{Two-Year Reserve Development-to-Surplus Ratio} = \frac{\text{Two-Year Reserve Development}}{\text{Second Prior Year's Surplus}} < 25\%$$

The usual range for this ratio is the same as for the one-year reserve development test. Any significant positive score recommends additional examination of reserve adequacy.

One- and two-year reserve development tests can be used to determine whether intentional understatement of liabilities has been used to exaggerate surplus. Trends in the two reserve development ratios can be observed and the scores can be compared to one another. If a consistent record of positive scores emerges or if the two-year ratio is uniformly greater than the one-year test value, deliberate underestimation of reserves is probable. Additional reserve development tests, for periods longer than two years, can be conducted using Parts 2 and 3 of Schedule P. A consistent pattern of increasing reserve deficiencies after losses were incurred suggests intentional understatement of liabilities.

Estimated Current Reserve Deficiency-to-Surplus. Reserve development tests analyze how reserves established in prior years compare to payments actually made for losses plus current estimates of the remaining obligations. Although reserve development deals with how accurately claims liabilities were estimated during prior years, it also can be used to estimate the current adequacy of loss reserves and the related effect on surplus. The final NAIC regulatory test expresses the current estimated reserve deficiency or redundancy as a percentage of the current year's surplus. The estimated current reserve deficiency-to-surplus ratio is derived from results obtained in the two reserve development tests and therefore is somewhat more difficult to describe than previous tests. The basic relationship and critical value are:

$$\text{Estimated Current Reserve Deficiency-to-Surplus Ratio} = \frac{\text{Estimated Reserve Deficiency}}{\text{Surplus}} < 25\%$$

The denominator of the ratio is taken directly from the current annual statement but the numerator must be derived from annual statement data and the reserve development tests. A series of sequential relationships can be used to describe how the current estimated reserve deficiency is measured.

First, developed reserves for each of the two prior years must be calculated:

$$\begin{array}{c}\text{Developed Reserves} \\ \text{Prior Year}\end{array} = \begin{array}{c}\text{Stated Reserves} \\ \text{Prior Year}\end{array} \pm \begin{array}{c}\text{One-Year} \\ \text{Reserve Development}\end{array}$$

$$\begin{array}{c}\text{Developed Reserves} \\ \text{Second Prior Year}\end{array} = \begin{array}{c}\text{Stated Reserves} \\ \text{Second Prior Year}\end{array} \pm \begin{array}{c}\text{Two-Year Reserve} \\ \text{Development}\end{array}$$

Second, the relationship between developed reserves and net premiums earned in the two prior years is expressed in terms of a ratio:

$$\begin{array}{c}\text{Developed Reserves-to-} \\ \text{Premium Ratio, Prior Year}\end{array} = \frac{\text{Developed Reserves, Prior Year}}{\begin{array}{c}\text{Net Premium Earned} \\ \text{Prior Year}\end{array}}$$

$$\begin{array}{c}\text{Developed Reserves-to-} \\ \text{Premium Ratio, Second Prior Year}\end{array} = \frac{\begin{array}{c}\text{Developed Reserves,} \\ \text{Second Prior Year} \\ \text{Net Premium Earned}\end{array}}{\text{Second Prior Year}}$$

Third, the two developed reserves-to-premium ratios are averaged:

$$\begin{array}{c}\text{Average Developed} \\ \text{Reserve-to-} \\ \text{Premium Ratio}\end{array} =$$

$$\left(\frac{\begin{array}{c}\text{Developed Reserves-} \\ \text{to-Premium Ratio,} \\ \text{Prior Year}\end{array} + \begin{array}{c}\text{Developed Reserves-} \\ \text{to-Premium Ratio,} \\ \text{Second Prior Year}\end{array}}{2} \right)$$

Fourth, reserves required for the current year are estimated by multiplying the current year's net earned premium and the average ratio of developed reserves-to-premiums:

$$\text{Estimated Reserve Requirement} =$$

$$\left(\begin{array}{c} \text{Net Premium Earned} \\ \text{Current Year} \end{array} \right) \times \left(\begin{array}{c} \text{Average Ratio of Developed} \\ \text{Reserves-to-Premiums} \end{array} \right)$$

Fifth and finally, the estimated current reserve deficiency or redundancy is found by subtracting loss reserves carried in the current year's annual statement from the estimated reserve requirement:

$$\begin{array}{c} \text{Estimated Reserve Deficiency} \\ \text{or Redundancy} \end{array} = \left(\begin{array}{c} \text{Estimated} \\ \text{Required} \\ \text{Reserves} \end{array} \right) - \left(\begin{array}{c} \text{Stated Reserves,} \\ \text{Current Year} \end{array} \right)$$

Dividing the estimated reserve deficiency by stated surplus for the current year provides an estimate of how much surplus may be required to settle claims that have been incurred.

If the reserve development tests or the current estimated reserve deficiency indicates that surplus is significantly overstated, some of the regulatory tests described earlier should be recalculated using an adjusted surplus figure. For example, suppose an insurer's current annual statement reports surplus to be $1 million but the reserve development tests show that the company regularly underestimates loss reserves by 25 percent of surplus. Furthermore, the estimated current reserve deficiency to surplus ratio is 30 percent of surplus. All the earlier tests that included reported surplus should be performed again using an adjusted reserve figure of $700,000. In addition, the two-year adjusted underwriting ratio should be recalculated after the prior year's reserve development has been deducted from losses incurred. An insurer that would not be classified as a priority company on the basis of its original test scores might very well be reclassified as a problem company after adjusting surplus for reserve inadequacies.

THE SOLVENCY RECORD

The ability to precisely calculate an optimal capital and surplus level for new and continuing insurance companies would be beneficial to all parties concerned with their operation. Collective risk theory and the profit maximization calculus provide some guidance for setting net worth levels and making decisions involving alternative capital structures but these management tools are not without their limitations. Not even the shrewdest management can guarantee that unforeseeable contingencies will not destroy or severely reduce the financial capacity of the insurance company that it directs. Nor can government regulation be relied upon to prevent the occurrence of insurance company insolvencies. In the great majority of cases involving distressed insurers, efforts of regulatory agencies, and the collective action taken by other members of the industry have averted significant economic losses to policyholders. Nevertheless, the delays, uncertainty, and psychological trauma inflicted by failures of insurers recommend thoughtful consideration of insurance company financial strength.

Constructing an accurate record of solvency for the United States property and liability insurance industry is somewhat difficult. Available data sources often group together voluntary retirements, mergers, involuntary receiverships, rehabilitations, conservatorships, and liquidations. A diary of corporate changes is published annually by A. M. Best Company. In 1978, Best's ten-year summary of corporate changes included information on companies that exited the property and liability insurance industry; selected data are shown in Table 6-6. Figures developed in a United States Senate Antitrust and Monopoly Subcommittee study of high-risk automobile insurers indicated that during the 1958 to 1967 period, 110 property and liability insurance companies became insolvent. It appears that approximately 200 nonlife insurers have departed involuntarily from the marketplace during the most recent twenty-year period, an average of ten companies per year. Undoubtedly a number of the corporate changes listed as mergers also involved companies that could not sustain operations as independent entities. This continued incidence of company failures is disquieting to policyholders, insurance company management, and governmental bodies that oversee the industry.

A formalized mechanism for monitoring and reporting the economic impact of insolvencies has been established through creation of the National Committee on Insurance Guaranty Funds (NCIGF). According to the NCIGF, ongoing insurance companies were assessed approximately $147.5 million from November 1969 through December 1977 in order to meet the costs of insurers declared insolvent.[12] The assessments are equivalent to less than 0.04 percent of the total net premiums written by property and liability companies during these years. This indicates that insurance company failures have been concentrated among small insurers and have inflicted relatively small economic costs on the total industry. The industry's overall record however is of little solace to individuals personally affected by an insurance company collapse.

Table 6-6

Analysis of Property and Liability Company Retirements*

	Liquidated, Receivership, Rehabilitation, Conservatorship, Restraining Order, etc.	Mergers	Voluntary Retirements	Total
1968	5	26	9	40
1969	4	11	16	31
1970	13	27	6	46
1971	13	23	3	39
1972	6	21	10	37
1973	6	13	6	25
1974	5	21	9	35
1975	28	21	5	54
1976	3	15	8	27
1977	6	5	7	18
	89	183	79	352

*Reprinted with permission from "Corporate Changes—1977," *Best's Review*, Property/ Casualty Insurance Edition, March 1978, pp. 10.

Factors Leading to Insolvency

A variety of factors that precede delinquency proceedings have been identified through studies of insurance company failures. Some of the broadly defined causes are :

- Improper underwriting, reserving, and claims handling
- Inadequate expense controls
- Questionable investment practices
- Management dishonesty
- Abnormal transactions with agents, brokers, or reinsurers
- Excessive commissions or management allowances

These factors and others have been found repeatedly by researchers analyzing delinquent insurers. Management dishonesty, as manifested in questionable agency balances and possible falsification of cash and investments, was almost universally present in a group of defunct Texas insurers studied by Douglas G. Olson.[13] In a subsequent study of eight Pennsylvania companies that became insolvent, Professor Olson stated "the history of most of the companies reflected intentional management ineptness, bordering on fraudulent behavior, rather than impersonal market forces."[14] Low underwriting standards and questionable investments highlight the profile of substandard automobile insurance company failures developed by Campbell K. Evans.[15]

Examples of Insolvencies Although each company's pattern of distress is unique some common symptoms can be identified by scrutinizing its operations during the years immediately prior to its exiting the marketplace. A brief description of three insolvencies that occurred in the 1970s illustrates several characteristics of insurance companies headed for delinquency proceedings.

Signal Insurance Company[16] The first example focuses on Signal Insurance Company of Los Angeles. This company was incorporated under the laws of California, received its license and began business on December 28, 1962. Initial capitalization was provided by $1,018,573 of paid-up capital and $3,526,399 of contributed surplus. Surplus was augmented in 1963 through the sale of surplus notes (a form of subordinated debt classified as equity on the statutory balance sheet) that furnished $640,679. These notes were repaid by the close of 1965. Notes were issued again in 1971 and the proceeds used to increase surplus by $3 million. This series of notes obligated Signal to pay 6.75 percent annual interest to holders of the notes. A stock dividend was declared in 1972 to increase the corporation's permanent capital to $2 million. In the same year, $5 million was contributed to surplus through the issuance of additional surplus notes; this series required annual interest charges at the rate of 7.5 percent. At the close of 1972, Signal's policyholders' surplus stood at its all-time year-end high of $17,823,809; of this amount, approximately 45 percent was provided by debt that committed Signal to annual interest costs totaling $577,500.

Two other insurance companies became affiliated with Signal through acquisition and expansion. Imperial Insurance Company, originally organized as a reciprocal in California but subsequently converted to a stock company, became a wholly-owned subsidiary of Signal in October 1966. This acquisition was accomplished through Signal's purchase for cash of all outstanding capital stock of Imperial from that company's original sponsors. A foreign operation—Signal/Imperial Insurance Company, Limited, London, England—was established in 1974 as a wholly-owned subsidiary of Imperial. At the close of 1974, Signal was licensed in eighteen states, Imperial was licensed in all but ten states, and Signal/Imperial of London operated as a nonadmitted insurer.

Signal was a medium size, multiple line insurance company engaged primarily in automobile and miscellaneous liability lines, including medical malpractice insurance. The company also accepted significant amounts of reinsurance business. In 1974, 68 percent of Signal's direct premiums came from business written in California. Premium rates for directly written insurance were based on independent rate filings that typically deviated upward from manual rates. Although underwriting profits declined after reaching a highpoint in 1971, insurance operations were reported to have been profitable during each of the company's final six full years of operation. From 1962 through 1974, an aggregate underwriting profit of $2,756,000 was reported by Signal. Net investment income, exclusive of capital gains and losses, totaled $3,656,000 during the same period.

Imperial was a relatively small insurer confining its underwriting operations solely to workers' compensation until late 1967. Thereafter, facilities were broadened to include full multiple line underwriting at manual or standard premium rates. The company grew rapidly after 1969; the value of its assets surpassed that of its parent company's assets in 1973 and 1974. More than half of Imperial's directly written business in 1974 came from miscellaneous liability lines of insurance. Automobile insurance and workers' compensation premiums also represented significant portions of Imperial's total direct business. Insurance written in California and Arizona accounted for 72 percent of the company's 1974 total direct premiums. In the years Imperial was owned by Signal, 1967 through 1974, the subsidiary recorded cumulative underwriting losses of $383,000. During the same period, net investment income, exclusive of capital gains and losses, amounted to $8,258,000.

At least three factors contributed to the eventual collapse of Signal Insurance Company and its domestic subsidiary: (1) overinvestment in equity securities; (2) excessive expansion of premiums written; and (3) inadequate loss reserving practices. The most direct cause of the companies' insolvency was overinvestment in equity securities by both Signal and Imperial. This investment strategy, along with an above average relationship between premiums written-to-policyholders' surplus, exposed the companies to adverse fluctuations in underwriting and investment results. In 1973, Imperial reported an underwriting loss of $200,792 coupled with realized and unrealized investment losses of $4,421,762. The following year's premiums written-to-policyholders' surplus ratio jumped to 5.7-to-1 as surplus, depleted by two successive years' investment losses, was used to support a 32 percent increase in premium volume. Although Imperial reported an underwriting profit of $282,202 in 1974, this was dwarfed by a realized investment loss of $5,062,636 and an asset write-down of an additional $8,124,260. In 1975, the California insurance commissioner's office found that Imperial had not established adequate loss reserves and when the company's policyholders' surplus proved insufficient to effectuate the necessary reserve strengthening, Imperial was declared insolvent. Because Imperial was at that time the primary asset of Signal, the subsidiary company's collapse rendered Signal insolvent as well. A court ordered

Table 6-7

Financial Ratios

	Signal Insurance Company		
Year	Premiums Written to Policyholders' Surplus	Stocks as a Percent of Assets	Stocks as a Percent of Policyholders' Surplus
1970	147.1	14.2%	41.5%
1971	166.9	49.4%[†]	130.9%
1972	111.5	63.1%[†]	147.8%
1973	123.1	56.3%[†]	157.7%
1974	316.7[*]	37.6%[†]	193.3%

	Imperial Insurance Company		
Year	Premiums Written to Policyholders' Surplus	Stocks as a Percent of Assets	Stocks as a Percent of Policyholders' Surplus
1970	251.7	—	—
1971	328.8[*]	57.9%[†]	238.5%
1972	183.4	71.2%[†]	212.2%
1973	221.3	63.2%[†]	265.0%
1974	566.9[*]	40.9%[†]	365.9%

conservatorship was granted the California insurance commissioner effective September 24,1975.

Two of the factors which led to the demise of Signal and Imperial are reflected in the ratios listed in Table 6-7. An asterisk (*) indicates a premiums written-to-policyholders' surplus ratio outside the acceptable range of values set by the NAIC Early Warning System tests in 1976. A dagger (†) indicates an above industry average investment in equity securities. Both companies' excessive commitment to common and preferred stocks is more forcefully emphasized by relating the value of stocks to policyholders' surplus. Expressing stocks as a percentage of policyholders' surplus illustrates the companies' vulnerability to a decline in market value. The inverse in this percentage shows the degree by which the value of stocks can decline before policyholders' surplus is completely extinguished. For instance, in 1971, a 42 percent (1 ÷ 2.385) decline in the value of Imperial's stock portfolio would have wiped out the company's policyholders' surplus. By 1974, only a 27 percent decline was necessary to accomplish the same thing. Signal's precarious situation is demonstrated further by noting that at the end of 1974, the parent company's investment in Imperial represented 15.9 percent of its assets and 81.9 percent of its policyholders' surplus. Therefore, when Imperial went under, Signal was doomed.

The ratings given to Signal and Imperial by Best's during the final

Table 6-8
Best's Ratings*

Policyholder Rating		Financial Rating (category)	
Signal	Imperial	Signal	Imperial
Year			
1971 A (excellent)	A	AAAA ($15 to $20 million)	AA+ ($7.5 to 10 million)
1972 A (excellent)	A	AAAA	AAA+
1973 B+ (very good)	B+	AAAA	AAA+
1974 C+ (fairly good)	C+	AAA+	AA+

*Reprinted from *Best's Insurance Reports*, 1972-1975.

five full years the companies operated are listed in Table 6-8. As pointed out in Chapter 5, Best's assigns property and liability insurers policyholders' ratings (A+, excellent, to C, fair) based on industry averages using various information to measure overall performance. Before 1976, Best's also assigned a financial rating based on the size of the insurer's net resources. This rating consisted of at least two letters (AAAAA for the largest companies to CC for the smallest) in order to avoid confusion with the policyholders' surplus rating. Beginning in 1976, Best's changed from financial ratings denoted by multiple letters to financial categories represented by Roman numerals (Class XV for the largest companies to Class I for the smallest). Because Signal and Imperial exited the marketplace prior to the change, Best's old rating system is used. Note that although the policyholders' ratings classified the companies as fairly good at the close of 1974, this rating had declined for two consecutive years. Moreover, reduction of the financial rating indicates that Best's lowered its estimate of the companies' net financial resources. While the demise of Signal and Imperial was more precipitous than some delinquencies, insurers do not slide into financial distress overnight. In his study of insurers that had been involved in delinquency proceedings, Herbert S. Denenberg noted that "all the delinquent companies with their [Best's] ratings experienced a downward trend in their ratings prior to delinquency."[17] All parties with an interest in Signal and Imperial were given an obvious danger signal by the deterioration of the ratings assigned the companies by insurance reporting services.

La Salle National Insurance Company[18]   In December of 1966, Midland National Insurance Company and La Salle Casualty Company, both located in Chicago, merged to form La Salle National Insurance Company. La Salle National was a medium-size, multiple-line, stock insurer with reported policyholders' surplus of $2,728,836 at the end of 1966. It specialized in substandard automobile insurance written at rates

Table 6-9

Operating Ratios Reported for
La Salle National Insurance Company

Year	Loss Ratio	Expense Ratio	Combined Ratio
1966	61.2	36.5	97.7
1967	65.5	35.9	101.4
1968	78.4	34.6	113.0
1969	104.1	27.6	131.7
1970	86.8	23.7	110.5

that deviated upward by 20 to 100 percent from manual. The company experienced a history of significant underwriting losses due to poor underwriting standards, inept claims settlement procedures, excessive agency override commissions and management fees, and inadequate loss reserving practices.

The Illinois Director of Insurance, acting on information developed in the department's 1970 examination of La Salle National, began administrative action against the company in May 1970 in an effort to protect policyholders from further deterioration of the insurer's financial strength. A petition of complaint for conservation against La Salle National was filed in court approximately one year later. On December 28, 1971, an order of liquidation against La Salle National was entered by the circuit court of Cook County, Illinois. The last examination of the company, conducted during 1971, found that its liabilities exceeded assets resulting in a deficit policyholders' surplus of $5,910,958.

In contrast to the Signal Insurance Company case, La Salle National's financial weakness was not aggravated by investment losses. This company collapsed primarily because of mismanagement, especially in the areas of underwriting and claims administration. Table 6-9 contains loss, expense, and trade-basis combined ratios reported by La Salle National. A loss reserve deficiency of $800,000 for 1968 was discovered by the Illinois Insurance Department in its examination of the company's affairs for that year. This caused the combined ratio for 1968 to be increased from 113.0 to 124.7. Again in 1970, the Illinois Insurance Department found that loss reserves were understated by $4,468,000. The combined ratio for that year jumped from its reported value of 110.5 to 182.1.

Further evidence of the distress status of La Salle National is given by applying the NAIC Early Warning System tests to the company's reported financial data. The results for the final five full years of La

Table 6-10

La Salle National Insurance Company Test Results of NAIC Early Warning
System: Years 1963 Through 1970*

Test	1966	1967	1968	1969	1970
1. Premium to Surplus	227.5	999.0	999.0²	999.0²	619.6²
2. Change in Writings	4.0	229.8²	−9.9	−20.2	−33.3²
3. Surplus Aid	7.0	2.1	3.5	8.9	9.4
4.¹ Five Year Operating Ratio	97.4	97.4	103.1²	110.1²	108.4²
4a. One Year Operating Ratio	97.5	97.4	109.2²	129.6²	107.5²
5. Investment Yield	1.7	3.7	3.6	3.3	3.0
6. Change in Surplus	999.0²	−99.0²	−99.0²	−99.0²	+54.8²
7. Liabilities to Liquid Assets	107.1²	133.3²	135.9²	156.6²	102.7²
8. Agents Balance to Surplus	53.2²	56.2²	39.0	42.2²	43.1²
9. One Year Reserve Development	116.4²	27.7	111.2²	237.2²	71.2²
10. Two Year Reserve Development	98.0²	109.8²	56.7²	272.5²	201.3²
11. Estimated Current Reserve Deficiency	−109.4²	479.3²	476.0²	337.3²	20.7
Number of Failed Tests	6	6	8	9	9

1. Tests 4 and 4a have been replaced by a two-year adjusted underwriting ratio as explained earlier in this chapter.
2. These values are outside the acceptable range established for this test by the NAIC.

*Test data were provided by Dale Traxler of State Farm Mutual Automobile Insurance Company and continued in "History and Causes of the La Salle National Insurance Company Insolvency" (unpublished report to Illinois Insurance Guaranty Fund, October 15, 1976), p. 24.

Salle National's operations are shown in Table 6-10. Note that this company would have been assigned a priority status for further investigation in each year shown in the table if the Early Warning System had been in use at that time.

Several of the test statistics are especially noteworthy. The company consistently had a premiums written-to-policyholders surplus ratio far above industry norms. The high volume of new business exposed net worth to a magnification of losses from unprofitable underwriting. This rapid sales growth undoubtedly was a consequence of the Midland National and La Salle Casualty merger; nevertheless, the magnitude of the premium expansion by the survivor of a merger between two companies that historically posted poor and mediocre underwriting results was a signal of future difficulties. It is paradoxical

Table 6-11

Best's Ratings*

Year	Company	Policyholders' Rating	Financial Rating	
1966	La Salle Casualty	B (Good)	BBBB	($2.5—$3.75 million)
1966	Midland National	C+ (Fairly Good)	BBB	($1.0—$1.5 million)
1967	La Salle National	B	BBBB	
1968	La Salle National	C+	BBBB+	($3.75—$5.0 million)
1969	La Salle National	C+	BBB+	
1970	La Salle National	Omitted†	N/A	
1971	La Salle National	Omitted†	N/A	

N/A: not available.
†See explanation of Best's ratings in Chapter 5.

*Reprinted from *Best's Insurance Reports*, 1967–1972.

that a company which overutilized its surplus did not show significant use of surplus aid reinsurance. Relatively low surplus aid ratios are shown for La Salle National even though premium writings remained high. The critical values for the liabilities-to-liquid assets and agents' balance-to-surplus ratios reflect the impact of unprofitable underwriting on the company's cash flow and surplus position. Perhaps the most significant disclosure in Table 6-10 is provided by the reserve development tests. La Salle National's failure to establish adequate loss reserves proved to be a principal factor in the company's eventual insolvency.

The ratings given to La Salle National and its two predecessor corporations by Best's for 1966 through 1970 are listed in Table 6-11. Using hindsight, these ratings may be criticized when compared to results produced by the Early Warning System tests. It might be argued that using the term "fairly good" to describe a C+ rated company is misleading to those who rely on the reporting service. However, it must be recalled that these ratings attempt to reflect the company's relative position in the industry when compared to substantially all other insurers. Therefore, a C+ or C rating denotes a low-rated company. Once again, a deterioration of the policyholders' rating occurred prior to initiation of delinquency proceedings against the insurer.

Gateway Insurance Company[19] This company began operations in 1955 as a Pennsylvania stock insurer with combined capital and surplus of $150,000. Financial control of Gateway was transferred several times during the 1960s until controlling interest was acquired in 1968 by First Investment Security Corporation (later known as FISCO, Incorporated), of Philadelphia. The founder of FISCO, Incorporated, became president of Gateway and continued to control the Philadelphia-based general agency, Acme Assurance Agency, which he had organized in 1966. The general agency, which eventually operated in four states, played an important role in the affairs of Gateway.

In 1972, Gateway acquired the controlling interest of Colonial Assurance Company, also a Pennsylvania domiciled stock insurer which operated thereafter as a subsidiary of Gateway. FISCO, Incorporated, also controlled Prestige Casualty Company located in Skokie, Illinois, and its wholly-owned subsidiary Trans-World Assurance Company, Nashville, Tennessee. Operations of Prestige Casualty and Trans-World Assurance were independent from Gateway and Colonial.

Gateway restricted its underwriting activities to fire, extended coverage, and automobile physical damage insurance prior to 1971. In that year it expanded its operations to include general liability and full coverage automobile insurance. Business that Gateway's affiliated general agencies previously had placed with other insurance companies was insured directly or reinsured with Gateway beginning in 1971. As a result, net premiums written by the company jumped in that year by 1,138 percent over the previous year's level. In order to accommodate this rapid expansion of underwriting activity, Gateway's parent corporation, FISCO, augmented the insurer's capital and surplus by $2.2 million in 1970 and by $8.5 million in 1971. An additional surplus contribution of $4.9 million was made in 1972 as net premiums written recorded a 121 percent annual increase. These substantial increments made in Gateway's capitalization prevented the rapid upswing in premium volume from producing inordinately above-average premiums written-to-policyholders' surplus ratios.

In 1973, Gateway reappraised its loss reserves and established its liability for claims settlements and loss adjustment expenses at more than 189 percent of the previous year's reserve level. About one-half of the increase was attributable to an adjustment for reserve deficiencies in prior years. The company also reported net investment losses in 1973 of more than $3 million. As a result of the year's combined underwriting and investment losses, policyholders' surplus fell by more than $5 million to only 64.6 percent of its 1972 level. Operations of Gateway were suspended on July 12, 1974 by order of the Pennsylvania Insurance Department. Within six weeks thereafter an order of liquidation was entered against the insurer.

An analysis of some selected operating and financial data for Gateway during its final five full years of operation reveals several relationships that should have indicated future distress. These data are shown in Table 6-12. Although the change-in-writings' ratios developed by Gateway might be expected to have been accompanied by depressed underwriting results because of statutory expense allocations, the company reported underwriting gains in 1969 through 1972. A drop of almost 13 percent in the loss ratio for the year in which broad scale liability insurance operations were initiated (1971) also should have been suspect. Underwriting profits reported for these years of rapid sales growth ultimately were shown to have been an accounting illusion. Even though loss reserves almost doubled during the year, the company's auditors informed FISCO that Gateway had undervalued reserves by $4 million at the end of 1973.

Foreboding information also was disclosed in Gateway's balance sheet. The relative amount of assets represented by agents' balances was abnormally high, especially after 1970. In four of the five years shown in the table, the ratio of agents' balances-to-policyholders' surplus would have been outside the acceptable range of values established for the 1976 NAIC Early Warning System tests. Furthermore, when agents' balances are added to Gateway's investment in its subsidiary company, the sum of these two investments exceeds policyholders' surplus for 1972 and 1973. Severe underwriting losses suffered by the subsidiary insurance company in 1973 forced Gateway to lower its valuation of this investment by 30 percent between 1972 and 1973. Because Gateway's policyholders' surplus fell at an even sharper rate, the percentage of surplus represented by the affiliated company investment increased.

Another aspect of the Gateway case delivers a stinging indictment of how effectively state insurance regulation dealt with this particular potential delinquency. In commenting on this point, an industry authority observed the following:

> Early in 1974, an article appeared in the *Wall Street Journal* describing problems of a company named FISCO. This article was important because FISCO was the holding company for Gateway Insurance Company, and if FISCO was in trouble, probably, Gateway was also in trouble. Rumors about the financial difficulties of Gateway existed prior to the FISCO article. Many people in the industry felt that this article would force insurance department action. Unfortunately, the first official regulatory action took place on July 12, 1974, more than five months following the publication of the article. Obviously, the industry does not know what went on in the insurance departments of Pennsylvania, New Jersey, and Florida, the three departments directly affected by the Gateway problem; however, action was neither decisive nor swift.[20]

The Gateway case serves as an illustration of the fact that financial analysis and early detection of distress are not sufficient answers to the

Table 6-12
Comparative Data Reported for Gateway Insurance Company, 1969–1973*

Year	Premiums to Surplus Ratio	Change in Writings Ratio	Loss Ratio	Expense Ratio	Combined Ratio	Underwriting Profit or Loss	Investment in Affiliates-to-Surplus	Investment in Agents' Balance-to-Surplus
1969	2.33	1.97†	57.9	24.2	82.1	$ 85,000	—	51%†
1970	0.66	1.01†	60.0	21.3	81.3	142,000	—	17†
1971	2.09	11.38†	47.3	20.3	67.6	660,000	—	67†
1972	3.46	1.21†	60.0	31.9	91.9	862,000	35%	70†
1973	3.46	0.35†	122.0	−9.5	112.5	−6,175,000	38	91†

†Values exceed acceptable range set in 1976 NAIC Early Warning System tests.

*Reprinted from *Best's Insurance Reports,* 1970–1974.

insolvency threat. Financial diagnostics are meant to assist state insurance regulators to act effectively. But the ultimate responsibility to act is the regulator's. As Robert A. Bailey, former head actuary of the Michigan Insurance Department, stated, "... the regulator needs guts to prevent insolvency."[21]

In August of 1977, the Securities Exchange Commission filed a complaint accusing FISCO of underreporting losses in its insurance company subsidiaries. A federal grand jury indicted the president and vice president of the holding company in June of 1978, charging them with one count of conspiracy, twelve counts of mail fraud, and four counts of bank fraud. The indictments charged that the corporate officers had intentionally misled lenders, state insurance departments, public investors, and the SEC by holding down loss reserves and manipulating financial reports.[22]

INSURANCE GUARANTY MECHANISMS

Insurance guaranty associations designed to provide reparations to policyholders and third-party claimants of insolvent insurers have been established in forty-seven states, the District of Columbia, and Puerto Rico.[23] These funds do not directly guarantee the solvency of insurance companies. Rather, the guaranty associations reimburse entities that have a justifiable claim against an *insolvent* insurance company. The amount of reimbursement usually is subject to both a deductible and a maximum limit of liability. Not all insurers licensed in a particular jurisdiction have their obligations guaranteed by the association. Generally, the associations respond to insolvencies of insurers that write all direct lines of property and liability insurance but not to insolvencies involving insurance companies that write life and disability income insurance, annuities, fidelity and surety bonds, credit, mortgage guaranty, and ocean marine insurance. A handful of states have formed separate guaranty associations for life insurance companies. With a few notable exceptions, the state insurance guaranty associations were created in the early 1970s in an effort to forestall federal intervention in this area of state insurance regulation. A review of the federal interest in insurance guaranty mechanisms and the states' response to federal initiatives therefore helps explain the development and purpose of the current system.

Federal Proposals

Following an investigation of automobile insurance by the United

States Senate Antitrust and Monopoly Subcommittee of the Committee on the Judiciary, the late Senator Thomas J. Dodd proposed a Federal Motor Vehicle Insurance Guaranty Corporation (FMVIGC). Senator Dodd's initial bill (S. 3919, 89th Congress, 2d session) was introduced in 1966. It proposed a federal government remedy for unsatisfied claims against insolvent automobile insurance companies. Sponsors of the legislation had little hope for its early adoption but they believed it would stimulate consideration and discussion of problems posed by insurance company insolvencies. A second bill to establish a FMVIGC was introduced to the 90th Congress by Senator Dodd in 1967. Although Senator Dodd's bills were not enacted into law, they did cause the NAIC to begin an investigation of the appropriateness of federal intervention which, as might be expected, was quickly repudiated as being unnecessary.

In 1969, Senator Warren G. Magnuson sponsored a bill similar to, but more comprehensive than, those introduced earlier by Senator Dodd. The Magnuson bill sought to create a Federal Insurance Guaranty Corporation modeled after the Federal Deposit Insurance Corporation which insures deposits in commercial banks. Under the proposed legislation virtually all insurance companies would be compelled to pay an annual small percentage premium tax to the federal guaranty corporation. These funds, together with initial financing provided by a $50 million federal appropriation, would be used to pay claims against insurance companies that subsequently became insolvent. At least one other Senate bill and not fewer than five House of Representatives bills advocating a federal solvency guaranty plan were offered in the 91st Congress. This intense interest in insurance company solvency guaranty mechanisms forced a response from the states.

The NAIC Model Bill

The Magnuson bill threatened to preempt for the federal government much of the states' regulatory prerogative. Coupled with the bill's pre-assessment funding mechanism were proposals that would permit the federal guaranty agency broad financial examination powers, the ability to replace company officers in an effort to rehabilitate an insurer, and the responsibility to adjust and settle claims against insolvent insurers. Federal solvency supervision of this scope was seen as a major redefinition of which governmental level is primarily responsible for insurance regulation. The NAIC, individual state insurance commissioners, state legislators, and insurance industry members favoring continued state regulatory primacy launched an intense campaign to stave off this federal initiative by enacting guaranty fund laws at the state level.

In December of 1969, the NAIC's Special Committee on Automobile Insurance Problems presented the results of the study it had begun several years earlier. Based on this study, the NAIC concluded once again that federal legislation to guarantee insurance company solvency would be an unnecessarily wasteful imposition of a redundant federal system on an effective state regulatory structure. To achieve the goals sought by the federal proposals, the NAIC recommended adoption of state laws similar to the model bill it drafted. The NAIC's proposed legislation contains the following features:

1. An association of insurers admitted to each state is formed on a nonprofit basis to share obligations created by insolvent insurers. Membership in the association is compulsory.

2. The association is governed by a board of nine directors selected by member insurers and approved by the Insurance Commissioner.

3. The association will pay claims up to $300,000 with a $100 deductible. Workers' compensation claims are paid in full. In no case will claims against the association exceed those obligations of the insolvent insurer.

4. Members of the association are assessed for claims in proportion to the net premiums written by each member, but not to exceed 2% of their net premiums written in the preceding year. Any unpaid obligations in a given year will be held over to a subsequent year. The association may benefit from any reinsurance available to the insolvent insurer.

5. The association has the power to settle claims, borrow funds, sue or be sued, contract with others to carry out its functions, and in other ways act as an independent body. Being nonprofit, it is exempt, however, from state taxes.

6. The association has the right to join other creditors of the insolvent insurer in claiming recoveries resulting from bankruptcy proceedings.

7. The association has the duty to notify the Insurance Commissioner of any information which indicates a financially hazardous condition of any insurer operating in the state.[24]

There are several significant differences between the guaranty mechanism recommended by the NAIC and the federal proposals. The model bill espouses a post-insolvency assessment approach rather than a funded program. It imposes a mandatory deductible and places limits on the amount of recovery per claim (other than workers' compensation) while the Magnuson bill imposed no limits. Obligations that remain unsatisfied by one year's assessments are carried forward to subsequent years under the NAIC proposal. The intent of this provision is to prevent insolvency contributions from causing the domino effect that might occur if contributing insurers were substantially weakened by unlimited insolvency assessments. The "watchdog" provision, which requires notice to be given of suspected financial distress, makes the model bill approach something more than a strict "bail-out" mechanism. This safeguard encourages the guaranty fund to support other state regulatory measures designed to prevent insolvency.

State Guaranty Laws

Prior to 1969, only three states had enacted insurance company guaranty laws—New York in 1947, New Jersey in 1952, and Maryland in 1965. Within three years of the NAIC's introduction of a model bill, forty-seven states had enacted guaranty association legislation. Many of the laws are patterned after the model legislation but significant variations are found in the various statutes. For example, most states limit the annual assessment that can be charged an insurer by setting the maximum at 2 percent of its net premiums written in that state. However, some states place the limit at 1½ percent or 1 percent of premiums written or do not state a maximum percentage limit. While most guaranty laws obligate the association to return unutilized resources to contributing insurers, nine laws do not provide for such a refund. New York's guaranty plan, the earliest in existence, continues on a pre-insolvency funded basis although subsequent plans were either established on a post-insolvency assessment basis or were converted from pre- to post-funding. Coverage limits also vary among the separate associations. A deductible of $100 per claim is applied in the majority of states; but at least one state has a $50 deductible, another state imposes a $200 deductible, and ten plans do not involve deductible provisions. The single most common maximum coverage limit per claim is $300,000; lower limits exist in some states and at least one state, California, places a ceiling per claim at $500,000 (except for workers' compensation claims which are paid in full). One of the most significant differences among the plans is whether or not unearned premium claims qualify for reimbursement. In some states, notably New York, premiums collected but not earned at the time the insurer becomes insolvent do not become an obligation of the guaranty fund.

In addition to differences in the guaranty laws themselves, there are variations in related state statutes that affect how the plans operate. A few states have enacted so-called *early access* and *advanced priority* measures. Early access allows the guaranty association to gain immediate control of a delinquent insurance company's assets thereby protecting policyholders and others from the transfer of valuable resources to outside interests. By allowing the guaranty association quick access, the defunct company's assets can be used for the purpose intended—settlement of claims against the insurer. Advanced priority gives the plan a higher claim on an insolvent insurer's assets in liquidation than it would otherwise possess in the status of a general creditor. This should increase the likelihood that the association can return unutilized resources to contributing member companies after an insolvency case is settled.

Another operating characteristic that varies among the state plans arises from a basic public policy decision concerning who should bear the cost of insurance company insolvencies. Several states have enacted laws that grant insurers an offset against premium taxes for assessments paid to the guaranty fund. Premiun tax offset provisions are justified on the basis that members of the general public as well as policyholders are benefited by the guaranty of insurance obligations. Therefore, it is reasoned, public funds are the proper source of reparation payments. Moreover, the tax offset arrangements are believed to promote prevention of delinquencies because public funds are at stake. In effect, a state that allows a licensed insurance company to operate while in a hazardous financial condition is penalized through the loss of tax revenues if an insolvency results. Guaranty associations in states that grant tax offsets are not purely private sector mechanisms but are quasi-public solutions to the problems of insurance company insolvencies.

At least one state, Illinois, has enacted a statute that attempts to minimize losses resulting from an insolvency by requiring insurers to maintain "policyholder security accounts." The law (Section 155.09, Illinois Insurance Code) seeks to prevent undue investment in assets which may prove of little value if forced liquidation becomes necessary. Essentially this requirement compels member companies to cover their policyholder liabilities—unearned premium, loss, and loss adjustment expense reserves—with investments in marketable securities. A segregation of insurance company assets into policyholder security or custodial accounts has been suggested several times as an amendment to the guaranty association model bill but, as yet, has not been adopted by the NAIC.

The state solvency guaranty laws form a patchwork of legislation that overall has produced a checkered record of operational effectiveness. Generally favorable results are reported for promptness and adequacy of claims settlement. It is estimated that between 60 and 70 percent of all claims against delinquent companies are discharged within nine months after the insurer has become insolvent. Consumers have received payments from the associations that are approximately equal to their full economic loss whereas, prior to creation of these guaranty plans, reimbursements were ten to twenty cents on the dollar.[25] In terms of administrative efficiency, the overall record appears favorable. When an insolvency occurs, a member insurance company typically acts as the servicing agent for the guaranty association. This involves claims investigation, loss settlement, and a report to the plan on the final discharge of its obligations related to the liquidated insurer. Over the eight-year period prior to 1978, the guaranty plans collected $147.5 million through assessments from member companies and used nearly 99.5 percent for insolvency reparations; only about 0.5 percent was absorbed by administrative charges. In spite of this overall record of performance, a number of deficiencies exist in the present system. Criticism of the plans center around three major issues: (1) the associations' failure to have a significant impact on reducing the number of insolvencies; (2) the plans' suspected inability to handle a major company default; and (3) difficulties arising from the use of single-state guaranty plans for multiple-state insurance operations. These criticisms have lead to a number of suggested changes in the present system.

Proposed Changes

While a few states have enacted early access and advanced priority laws, the majority of guaranty associations do not have recourse to the insolvent insurer's assets until after covered losses and other obligations have been discharged. Thus, obligations incurred by the guaranty plan are settled on a *gross* rather than a *net* basis. [26] As an example, suppose a major insurer with $600 million in guaranteed liabilities was to become insolvent. Most guaranty plans would be forced to raise the entire $600 million or more by assessing member companies, even though the insolvent insurer's estate contained assets worth perhaps $580 million. Subsequent recoveries by the guaranty association from the bankrupt company's estate would be returned to contributing members but this would occur only after delays and administrative costs had been incurred. Proposed legislative changes would allow a court appointed liquidator to advance funds from the bankrupt company's marshaled assets to the guaranty plan. This has the effect of granting policyholders and other claimants a higher priority claim on the insolvent insurer's assets than possessed by other general creditors. Assessments by the association would be substantially reduced to an amount that would provide working capital and meet obligations on a net basis.

Several proposals have been made that either would drastically modify or completely replace the existing state insurance guaranty system. Under these proposals, attention would be focused primarily on solvency maintenance but when insolvencies did occur, attempts would be made to handle claims settlement more efficiently than is currently possible. A variety of plans has been suggested to fulfill these objectives. For instance, one proposal would require insurance companies to purchase insolvency reinsurance from a specially incorporated, private, nonprofit insurance organization.[27] Creation of a funded federal government insurance guaranty agency is a persisting alternative. Although diverse in many respects, these proposals share the common characteristic of advocating a centralized organization instead of individual state associations. A central guaranty mechanism could reduce the duplication of efforts and magnification of costs that result from separate single-state plans. Centralization would not restrict recovery to residents of a particular state as frequently occurs under the existing system. Also, by staffing a central organization with full-time, technically trained personnel, greater attention could be devoted to solvency surveillance and loss prevention.

Some Unresolved Questions

Intense discussions of the issues involved with establishing an insurance company guaranty system began in earnest when it appeared that the federal government was on the verge of exercising its legislative initiative in this area. The discussions raised a number of questions which remain unresolved. One very fundamental question deals with the fairness of assessing financially healthy insurance companies—and indirectly their policyholders—in order to bail out poorly managed or otherwise financially weak insurers. On one side of this issue, it can be asserted that claimants are the ones benefited by a guaranty system and that inept or dishonest management receives no direct subsidy. The alternative viewpoint argues that unless a company has the ultimate responsibility for its behavior and obligations, company management and the governmental authorities that oversee its operations cannot help but be less circumspect in performing their functions. This point of view was illustrated in a recently published insurance text:

> The existence of guaranty funds adds to the effective capacity of private insurance in that all insurers affected could conceivably be more liberal in their underwriting or could accept a larger ratio of premiums to surplus than would otherwise be the case. . . .

> Although guaranty funds are designed mainly to insure and help prevent insolvency, they have an effect on insurance capacity in that the resources of the entire insurance industry in given states may be marshalled to meet claims of bankrupt companies, if necessary. Thus, through the combination method, resources of strong insurers not fully utilized may be made available for losses elsewhere.[28]

Whether it is fair to use resources of "strong insurers" to subsidize weak companies is still a subject worthy of discussion. However, given the existence of the current guaranty system, questions of operational efficiency and equity now seem more appropriate.

The insurance industry traditionally has espoused the virtues of advance-premium funding for the insurance products it sells. Nevertheless, only one state solvency guaranty plan, New York, currently operates on a funded basis. Industry opposition to pre-insolvency assessment financing for guaranty plans reflects a general unwillingness to allow governmental authorities management and use of industry-supplied funds. This aversion springs out of a fear that custodial funds will be diverted from their intended use to support other public programs. The precedent set in New York adds substance to the industry's viewpoint. Early in 1976, the New York Property and Liability Insurance Security Fund had assets of approximately $240 million. Almost 98 percent of the funds were invested in obligations of various New York State agencies, including $114 million in the Housing Finance Agency and $90 million in the Project Finance Agency. The commitment of security fund money to state agency obligations caused concern that the guaranty fund may have lacked liquidity. In testimony before the New York State Senate Committee on Insurance, George M. Mulligan of the American Insurance Association stated: "We think it is important to ask at this time whether the current portfolio of this Security Fund is a deterrent against the Insurance Department's proper determination as to whether or not an insurer is insolvent."[29] The New York experience adds an additional dimension to the question of whether advance-funding should be preferred to post-insolvency assessments. It questions the propriety of complete governmental control over how assets of funded guaranty plans are invested and suggests that industry participation in investment decisions should be allowed.

Several other issues that are not encountered when post-insolvency funding is utilized arise under pre-insolvency assessment plans. One issue relates to the ownership and ultimate disposition of security plan assets. Does an insurer own a proportionate part of the assets in the fund and can it claim that amount if it elects to discontinue operations within that state? Another question concerns the equity of allowing newly licensed insurers to begin operations in an advance-funding jurisdiction during a period when no new assessments are being made to supplement the plan's assets. Should a "buy-in" provision whereby the new company reimburses guaranty fund members a proportionate share of their fund balances be used as a condition of licensure? These unsettled questions and the industry's overriding aversion to accumulating pools of money that might be subject to governmental takeover make conversion to pre-insolvency assessment plans highly unlikely.

Perhaps the most important question concerning solvency guaranty plans is whether they can, in fact, guarantee performance in a cyclical industry that has been chronically unprofitable. If it is assumed that an assessment of 2 percent of net premiums written by the property and liability insurance industry in 1976 could have been collected by existing guaranty plans, there would have been approximately $1.2 billion available to pay claims and meet administrative costs of insolvent companies.[30] For perspective, this figure is roughly equal to the combined loss and loss expense reserves of Continental Casualty and Government Employees Insurance Company at the end of 1976. If unearned premiums were added, the assessment would fall short by almost $562 million. The comparison is made in order to emphasize two points. First, settling claims without immediate access to assets of the insolvent insurer unduly challenges the capacity of solvency guaranty associations. Second, the guaranty plans, as currently constituted, are not designed to handle major insurance company insolvencies nor a series of medium-sized company failures. Over-reliance on the capabilities of the solvency guaranty plans therefore must be avoided.

Future of the Solvency Guaranty Mechanism

Pronouncements within the insurance industry indicate that there is less than complete satisfaction with the current approach being taken to guarantee insurance company financial performance. The enthusiasm of those groups which regarded enactment of state guaranty association laws a victory over federal intervention was short-lived. Significant problems continue to exist in regard to the operating effectiveness and capacity of state plans although the sharp rebound of underwriting profits in 1977 may have lessened the perceived urgency of dealing with solvency maintenance. Nevertheless, guaranteeing the financial ability of insurance company performance will be an integral part of the evolving insurance industry environment. The New York Insurance Department, in declaring that it is taking a new approach to the combined issues of competitive rating and financial stability, stated that:

> The legitimate need for improved market performance by insurers also make(s) it increasingly less appropriate to regard preservation of strong financial condition and prevention of insolvency as absolute goals of insurance regulation. Instead, our objectives with respect to financial condition must increasingly be balanced against their impact on other goals of insurance regulation.[31]

If there is to be a trade-off between pricing flexibility and solvency maintenance, an efficient, effective, and equitable guaranty mechanism should be in place.

SUMMARY

Security offered through insurance products is based on the financial health and vigor of the insurance company that provides coverage. Managers of insurance companies have the first-line responsibility for solvency maintenance and must operate the company in a manner that is consistent with achieving this objective. Company management is supported in this area by insurance regulation that traditionally has identified preservation of solvency as a central regulatory purpose. Techniques or regulatory tools designed to help assure the continued ability of insurance company financial performance include:

- Minimum Capitalization Standards
- Uniform Annual Statements
- NAIC Zone Examinations
- NAIC Early Warning System Reports
- Investment Portfolio Limitations
- State Insurance Department Surveillance
- State Insurance Department Conservation and Rehabilitation Efforts

In the event that a company does become insolvent, guaranty funds have been established to avoid losses to insureds and third parties that have a claim against an insolvent insurer.

Attention has been concentrated in this chapter on initial and continuing capitalization requirements and on the mechanism currently in use to guarantee obligations of insolvent insurers. The amount of capital and surplus relative to the volume of premiums being written clearly has an effect on the probability that an insurer will be able to keep its promises. However, an insurance company's optimal operating position cannot be reduced to a simple ratio of premiums written-to-policyholders' surplus. Many other factors—including underwriting and investment profitability, diversification of the investment portfolio, and adequacy of loss reserve estimates—are interrelated with the impact that volume and capitalization have on an insurer's probability of continued solvency.

The recent history of property and liability insurance company failures does not project the image of financial solidity that ought to be desired by the industry and its regulators. Consistent failure of ten or more companies each year creates a specter that haunts the industry whenever it attempts to gain operating flexibility—in pricing, for instance. Management and regulation for solvency are neither trivial endeavors nor easily accomplished tasks but some progress is being made toward improving the solvency record.

More than two hundred years ago, Adam Smith, in observing the insurance companies of his time, noted the need for adequate capitalization:

> The trade of insurance gives great security to the fortunes of private people, and by dividing among a great many that loss which would ruin an individual, makes it fall light and easy upon the whole society. In order to give this security, however, it is necessary that the insurers should have a very large capital. Before the establishment of the two joint stock companies for insurance in London, a list, it is said, was laid before the attorney-general, of one hundred and fifty private insurers who had failed in the course of a few years.[32]

Contemporary insurance regulation continues to rely on capital and surplus requirements as a standard that must be met if a particular insurance company is to be admitted or allowed to remain in the marketplace. The concept of maintaining solvency has been extended by establishing guaranty associations that have substantially reduced monetary losses to policyholders and third-party claimants. Improvements in the guaranty mechanism are being considered by state and federal government agencies. Because deductibles, limits placed on recoveries, and indirect costs of insolvencies force reparations to be less than complete, the guaranty mechanism should be considered a less than optimal solution. Loss prevention is the preferred answer to problems caused by insolvencies.

Chapter Notes

1. General accounting uses the term "capital-surplus" to refer to capital paid in excess of par value. Because the annual statement caption is "surplus paid-in," this terminology is used here. The two terms are synonymous.
2. The initial surplus requirements for reciprocal insurers are discussed in detail by Dennis F. Reinmuth, *The Regulation of Reciprocal Insurance Exchanges* (Homewood, IL: Richard D. Irwin, Inc., 1967).
3. "Corporate Changes—1977," *Best's Review Property/Casualty Insurance Edition*, (March 1978), pp. 10-12, 86.
4. *Pennsylvania Insurance Laws and Related Statutes*, Ch. 2, Sec. 205.
5. These data are based on property and liability operations only. "Insurance Companies Turn to Public Markets," *Business Week*, 24 October 1977, p. 98.
6. Several alternative approaches can be used to convey additional funds to an insurance company that operates within a conglomerate or congeneric. For example, International Telephone & Telegraph Corporation, parent of the Hartford Insurance Group, increased paid-in surplus of the insurance company group by contributing $100 million of assets to the insurers during 1977 and 1978. Assets transferred to the Hartford included various ITT properties and securities.
7. *Financial Condition Examiners Handbook* (Milwaukee, WI: National Association of Insurance Commissioners, 1976).
8. Some authorities believe that the current brief format of the report on examination is not as informative and useful as a management aid as was the longer form used prior to 1975. See: I. Murray Krowitz, "Field Examinations of Insurance Companies," *Best's Review Property/Casualty Insurance Edition* (June 1978), p. 36.
9. Robert A. Zelten, "Solvency Surveillance: The Problem and a Solution," *The Journal of Risk and Insurance*, Vol. XXXIX, No. 4 (December 1972), p. 576.
10. Ibid., p. 586.
11. "50% of States Say NAIC Solvency Tests Primary Lead to Problem Cos.," *The National Underwriter*, Property/Casualty Insurance Edition, 17 June 1977, p. 32.
12. "Report Insolvencies Cost $146 Million," *The National Underwriter*, Property/Casualty Insurance Edition, 17 February 1978, p. 1.
13. Douglas G. Olson, "Insolvencies Among High-Risk Automobile Insurance Companies" (unpublished Ph.D. dissertation, University of Pennsylvania, 1968).
14. U.S. Department of Transportation, *Insolvencies Among Automobile Insurers*, by Douglas G. Olson, Department of Transportation Automobile Insurance and Compensation Study (Washington, DC: Government Printing Office, 1970), p. 43.
15. Campbell K. Evans, "Basic Financial Differences of Substandard Automo-

bile Insurers," *The Journal of Risk and Insurance*, Vol. 35, No. 4 (December 1968), pp. 489-513.

16. Information in this section is derived from various issues of *Best's Insurance Reports Property/Liability Edition* and *Best's Review Property/Casualty Insurance Edition* (November 1975), p. 109.

17. Herbert S. Denenberg, "Is 'A-Plus' Really a Passing Grade?," *The Journal of Risk and Insurance*, Vol. 34, No. 3 (September 1967), p. 381.

18. References used in this section include various issues of *Best's Insurance Reports Property/Liability Edition* and a report prepared for the Illinois Insurance Guaranty Fund by Andrew F. Whitman and Alan Page, dated October 15, 1976.

19. References used in this section include various issues of *Best's Insurance Reports Property/Liability Edition, Best's Review Property/Casualty Insurance Edition,* and *The Wall Street Journal* (24 January 1974).

20. Jean C. Hiestand, "The Insurance Guaranty Funds and Their Implications for the Insurance Business," *CPCU Annals*, Vol. 30, No. 2 (June 1977), p. 115.

21. Mr. Bailey currently is Actuary and Director of the NAIC Data Base in the Milwaukee office of the NAIC. The quote is taken from James S. Trieschmann and George E. Pinches, "A Multivariate Model for Predicting Financially Distressed P-L Insurers," *The Journal of Risk and Insurance*, Vol. 40, No. 3 (September 1973), p. 338.

22. *Best's Review Property/Casualty Insurance Edition*, Vol. 79, No. 2 (June 1978), p. 6.

23. Harold C. Krogh, "Insurer Postinsolvency Funds: An Analysis of Operations," unpublished manuscript presented to the American Risk and Insurance Association (August 1977), p. 6.

24. *NAIC Proceedings*, 1970, Vol. I, p. 253.

25. Krogh, p. 6.

26. Hiestand, p. 115.

27. Armor H. Hank, " 'Permanent' Plan for Insolvency Woes," *The National Underwriter, Property & Casualty Insurance Edition* (August 19, 1977), p. 27.

28. Mark R. Greene and Oscar N. Serbein, *Risk Management: Text and Cases* (Reston, VA: Reston Publishing Company, 1978), pp. 384-385.

29. "Insolvency Law Deficiencies," *International Insurance Monitor* (July/August 1976), p. 10.

30. Net premiums written by property and liability insurance companies in 1976 are reported to have been $60,813,317,881; 2 percent of net premiums written equals $1,216,266,358. *Best's Aggregates and Averages*, (Oldwick, NJ: A. M. Best & Co., 1977) p. 1.

31. "Regulation of Financial Condition of Insurance Companies," New York Insurance Department (1974), p. 74.

32. Adam Smith, *An Inquiry into the Nature and Causes of the Wealth of Nations*, Book V, Chapter I, Part III, Modern Library edition (New York: Random House, 1937), p. 715.

Bibliography

Armor, H. Hank. "'Permanent' Plan for Insolvency Woes." *The National Underwriter* (Property/Casualty), 19 Aug. 1977, p. 27.

Auditing Standards and Procedures, Statement on Auditing Procedure No. 33. New York: American Institute of Certified Public Accountants, 1963.

Audits of Fire and Casualty Insurance Companies. New York: American Institute of Certified Public Accountants, 1966.

Automobile Insurance ... For Whose Benefit? NY: State of New York Insurance Department, 1970.

Beard, R. E.; Pentikainer, T.; and Pesonen, E. *Risk Theory.* London: Methuen, 1969.

Bernstein, Leopold A. *Financial Statement Analysis: Theory, Application, and Interpretation.* Rev. ed. Homewood, IL: Richard D. Irwin, 1978.

Best's Aggregates and Averages (Property/Liability). 36th Annual Ed. Oldwick, NJ: A. M. Best Co., 1975.

Best's Aggregates and Averages. Oldwick, NJ: A. M. Best Co., 1977.

Best's Insurance Reports (Property/Liability). Oldwick, NJ: A. M. Best Co.

Best's Review (Property/Casualty). Oldwick, NJ: A. M. Best Co.

Burch, Ernie. "Loss and Loss Expense Processing and Accounting." *Property-Liability Insurance Accounting*, p. 195.

Cootner, Paul H. and Holland, Daniel M. "Rate of Return and Business Risk." *The Bell Journal of Economics and Management Science*, Vol. 1, No. 2, Autumn 1970, pp. 211-226.

"Corporate Changes—1977." *Best's Review* (Property/Casualty), March 1978, pp. 10-12, 86.

Denenberg, Herbert S. "Is 'A-Plus' Really A Passing Grade?" *The Journal of Risk and Insurance*, Vol. 34, No. 3, September 1967, pp. 371-384.

Drake, Carl B., Jr. "What An Insurance Executive Expects From Management Reports." *Best's Review* (Property/Liability), May 1973, pp. 78-82.

Evans, Campbell K. "Basic Financial Differences of Substandard Automobile Insurers." *The Journal of Risk and Insurance*, Vol. 35, No. 4, December 1968, pp. 489-513.

329

"50% of States Say NAIC Solvency Tests Primary Lead to Problem Cos." *The National Underwriter* (Property/Casualty), 17 June 1977, p. 32.

Financial Condition Examiners Handbook. Milwaukee, WI: National Association of Insurance Commissioners, 1976.

Financial Reporting Trends, Fire and Casualty Insurance. New York: Ernst & Ernst, 1974.

Forbes, Stephen W. "Rates of Return in the Nonlife Insurance Industry." *The Journal of Risk and Insurance*, Vol. 38, No. 3, September 1971, pp. 409-442.

Greene, Mark R. and Serbein, Oscar N. *Risk Management: Text and Cases*. Reston, VA: Reston Publishing Co., 1978.

Hendriksen, Eldon S. *Accounting Theory*. Homewood, IL: Richard D. Irwin, 1965.

Hiestand, Jean C. "The Insurance Guaranty Funds and Their Implications for the Insurance Business." *CPCU Annals*, Vol. 30, No. 2, June 1977, p. 115.

Homer, Sydney and Leibowitz, Martin L. *Inside the Yield Book*. Englewood Cliffs, NJ: Prentice-Hall, 1972.

Huff, Gerald W. "Assets." *Property-Liability Insurance Accounting*. Ed. Robert W. Strain. Santa Monica, CA: Merritt Co., 1976.

"Industry Need to Double Capital." *The National Underwriter* (Property/Casualty), 1 July 1977, p. 1.

"Insolvency Law Deficiencies." International Insurance Monitor, July/August 1976, p. 10.

"Insurance Companies Turn to Public Markets." *Business Week*, 24 Oct. 1977, p. 98.

Kahane, Yehuda and Nye, David. "A Portfolio Approach to the Property-Liability Insurance Industry." *The Journal of Risk and Insurance*, Vol. 42, No. 4, December 1975, pp. 579-598.

Krogh, Harold C. "Insurer Postinsolvency Funds: An Analysis of Operations." Unpublished manuscript presented to the American Risk and Insurance Association, August 1977.

Krouse, Clement G. "Portfolio Balancing Corporate Assets and Liabilities with Special Application to Insurance Management." *Journal of Financial and Quantitative Analysis*, Vol. 6, 14 Sept. 1971.

Krowitz, I. Murray. "Field Examinations of Insurance Companies." *Best's Review* (Property/Casualty), June 1978, p. 36.

Lenrow, Gerald I. and Milo, Ralph. "The IRS Issues Its Position on Unpaid Losses." *Best's Review* (Property/Liability), March 1976, pp. 64-70.

McEnally, Richard W. and Tavis, Lee A. " 'Spatial Risk' and Return Relationships: A Reconsideration." *The Journal of Risk and Insurance*, Vol. 39, No. 3, September 1972, pp. 351-368.

Markle, John L. and Hofflander, A. E. "A Quadratic Programming Model of the Non-Life Insurer." *The Journal of Risk and Insurance*, Vol. 43, No. 1, March 1976, pp. 99-120.

Murphy, Robert J. "Reinsurance Accounting." *Property-Liability Insurance Accounting*, pp. 267-268.

NAIC Proceedings. Vol. 1. Milwaukee, WS: National Association of Insurance Commissioners, 1970.

Noback, Joseph C. *Life Insurance Accounting.* Homewood, IL: Richard D. Irwin, 1969.

Olson, Douglas G. *Insolvencies Among Automobile Insurers.* Department of Transportation Automobile Insurance and Compensation Study. Washington, D. C.: GPO, 1970.

———————. "Insolvencies Among High-Risk Automobile Insurance Companies." Ph.D. dissertation, Univ. of Pennsylvania, 1968.

Plotikin, Irving H. "Rates of Return in the Property and Liability Insurance Industry: A Comparative Analysis." *The Journal of Risk and Insurance,* Vol. 36, No. 2, June 1969, pp. 173-200.

Proposed Statement of Position on Accounting for Property and Liability Insurance Companies. New York: Accounting Standards Division of the American Institute of Certified Public Accountants (AICPA), 1977.

"Regulation of Financial Condition of Insurance Companies." New York: New York Insurance Department, 1974.

Reinmuth, Dennis F. *The Regulation of Reciprocal Insurance Exchanges.* Homewood, IL: Richard D. Irwin, 1967.

"Report Insolvencies Cost $146 Million." *The National Underwriter* (Property/Casualty), 17 Feb. 1978, p. 1.

Rosenbloom, Jerry S. *Automobile Liability Claims: Insurance Company Philosophies and Practices.* Homewood, IL: Richard D. Irwin, 1968.

Roy, Tapan S. and Witt, Robert Charles. "Leverage, Exposure Ratios and the Optimal Rate of Return on Capital for the Insurer." *The Journal of Risk and Insurance,* Vol. 43, No. 1, March 1976, pp. 53-72.

Salzmann, Ruth. "Estimated Liabilities for Losses and Loss Adjustment Expenses." *Property-Liability Insurance Accounting.* Ed. Robert W. Strain, Santa Monica, CA: Merrit Co., 1976.

Smith, Adam. *An Inquiry Into the Nature and Causes of the Wealth of Nations.* New York: Random House, 1937. Book 5. Chapter 1.

Sprouse, Robert T. and Moonitz, Maurice. *A Tentative Set of Broad Accounting Principles for Business Enterprises.* New York: American Institute of Certified Public Accountants, 1962.

Thompson, Howard E.; Matthews, John P.; and Li, Bob C. L. "Insurance Exposure and Investment Risks: An Analysis Using Chance-Constrained Programming." *Operations Research,* Vol. 22, September-October 1974, pp. 991-1007.

Trieschmann, James S. "Property-Liability Profits: A Comparative Study." *The Journal of Risk and Insurance,* Vol. 43, No. 1, March 1976, pp. 53-72.

Trieschmann, James S. and Pinches, George E. "A Multivariate Model for Predicting Financially Distressed P-L Insurers." *The Journal of Risk and Insurance,* Vol. 40, No. 3, September 1973, p. 338.

Whitman, Andrew F. and Page, Alan. Report prepared for the Illinois Insurance Guaranty Fund. 15 Oct. 1976.

Zelten, Robert A. "Solvency Surveillance: The Problem and a Solution." *The Journal of Risk and Insurance,* Vol. 39, No. 4, December 1972, p. 576.

Index

333

Appendix

Annual Statement
of the
Fire and Casualty
Companies

Note: In the case of reciprocal exchanges and other types of insurers using special terminology, the printed items and references in this blank, if not appropriately changed, shall be construed to apply to such insurers in respect to corresponding data and information as the context may require.

ANNUAL STATEMENT *

For the Year Ended December 31, 1976

OF THE CONDITION AND AFFAIRS OF THE

NAIC Group Code: _____   NAIC Company Code: _____

Organized under the Laws of the State of _____, made to the

INSURANCE DEPARTMENT OF THE STATE OF

PURSUANT TO THE LAWS THEREOF

Incorporated _____ Commenced Business _____

Home Office _____ , _____
(Street and Number)   (City or Town, State and Zip Code)

Mail Address _____ , _____
(Street and Number)   (City or Town, State and Zip Code)

Main Administrative Office _____
(Area Code)   (Telephone Number)

OFFICERS **

President _____

Secretary _____   Vice-Presidents

Treasurer _____

DIRECTORS OR TRUSTEES **

State of _____
County of _____ } ss

of the _____ President, _____ Secretary, _____ Treasurer*
of the _____ being duly sworn, each for himself deposes and says that they are the above described officers of the said insurer, and that on the thirty-first day of December last, all of the herein described assets were the absolute property of the said insurer, free and clear from any liens or claims thereon, except as herein stated, and that this annual statement, together with related exhibits, schedules and explanations herein contained, annexed or referred to are a full and true statement of all the assets and liabilities and of the condition and affairs of the said insurer as of the thirty-first day of December last, and of its income and deductions therefrom for the year ended on that date, according to the best of their information, knowledge and belief, respectively.

Subscribed and sworn to before me this

_____ day of _____, 1977   _____ President

_____   _____ Secretary

_____ Treasurer*

*or corresponding persons having charge of the accounts and finances of the insurer.
Note: In the case of United States Branches the affidavit must be amended to show that it covers the statement of the United States Branch. If the United States Manager of the Attorney-in-Fact of a Reciprocal Exchange or Lloyds Underwriters is a corporation the affidavit must be signed by two (or three) principal officers of the corporation or if a partnership by two (or three) of the principal members of the partnership.
**Show full name (initials not acceptable) and indicate by number sign (#) those officers and directors who did not occupy the indicated position in the previous annual statement.
Note: The pages identified by the symbol ⑤ in this annual statement were reproduced by the John S. Swift Company from master forms copyright 1976 by the John S. Swift Company, Incorporated.

*Reprinted with permission from *Annual Statement of the Fire and Casualty Companies*. Copyright 1976 by John S. Swift Company, Inc.

2   ANNUAL STATEMENT FOR THE YEAR 1976 OF THE .... Form 2

Write or Stamp Name

	(1) Current Year	(2) Previous Year
ASSETS		
1. Bonds (Schedule D) *		
2. Stocks (Schedule D): *		
2.1 Preferred stocks		
2.2 Common stocks		
3. Mortgage loans on real estate (Schedule B)		
4. Real estate (Schedule A):		
4.1 Properties occupied by the company (less $.............................encumbrances) . .		
4.2 Other properties (less $.............................encumbrances)		
5. Collateral loans (Schedule C)		
6. Cash on hand and on deposit (Exhibit 1)		
7. Other invested assets (Schedule BA)		
7a. Subtotals, cash and invested assets, sum of Items 1 to 7 inclusive		
8. Agents' balances or uncollected premiums (Exhibit 1):		
8.1 Premiums and agents' balances in course of collection		
8.2 Premiums, agents' balances and installments booked but deferred and not yet due . .		
9. Funds held by or deposited with ceding reinsurers (Exhibit 1)		
10. Bills receivable, taken for premiums (Exhibit 1)		
11. Reinsurance recoverable on loss payments (Exhibit 1)		
12. Federal income tax recoverable		
13.		
14. Interest, dividends and real estate income due and accrued (Part 1)		
15.		
16. .... •		
17.		
18.		
19.		
20.		
21.		
22. TOTALS (Per Exhibit 1, Col. 4)		

*State basis of valuation...

	(1) Current Year	(2) Previous Year
LIABILITIES, SURPLUS AND OTHER FUNDS		
1. Losses (Part 3A)		
2. Loss adjustment expenses (Part 3A)		
3. Contingent commissions and other similar charges . . .		
4. Other expenses (excluding taxes, licenses and fees)		
5. Taxes, licenses and fees (excluding federal and foreign income taxes) . .		
6. Federal and foreign income taxes (excluding deferred taxes)		
7.		
8. Borrowed money		
9. Interest, including $.........................on borrowed money		
10. Unearned premiums (Part 2B)		
11. Dividends declared and unpaid:		
(a) Stockholders		
(b) Policyholders		
12. Funds held by company under reinsurance treaties		
13. Amounts withheld or retained by company for account of others . . .		
14a. Unearned premiums on reinsurance in unauthorized companies . . . . $.........................		
14b. Reinsurance on paid losses $.........................and on unpaid losses		
$.........................due from unauthorized companies . . . . $.........................		
14c. Total . . . . $.........................		
15. Less funds held or retained by company for account of such unauthorized companies as per Schedule F, Part 2 . . . . $.........................		
16. Excess of statutory reserves over statement reserves (Schedule P, Parts 1A, 1B, 1C, 1D and Schedule K)		
17. Net adjustments in assets and liabilities due to foreign exchange rates		
18. Ceded reinsurance balances payable		
19.		
20.		
21.		
22.		
23. Total liabilities		
24. Special surplus funds:		
(a)		
(b)		
(c)		
25A. Capital paid up		
25B.		
26A. Gross paid in and contributed surplus		
26B. Unassigned funds (surplus)		
26C. Less treasury stock, at cost:		
(1) ....shares common (value included in Item 25A $.........................) . . .		
(2) ....shares preferred (value included in Item 25A $.........................) . . .		
27. Surplus as regards policyholders (Items 24 to 26B, less 26C)		
28. Totals		

Write or Stamp Name

	(1) Current Year	(2) Previous Year

UNDERWRITING AND INVESTMENT EXHIBIT
STATEMENT OF INCOME

UNDERWRITING INCOME

1. Premiums earned (Part 2) . . . .

DEDUCTIONS

2. Losses incurred (Part 3) . . . .
3. Loss expenses incurred (Part 4) . . . .
4. Other underwriting expenses incurred (Part 4) . . . .
5. ....
6. Total underwriting deductions . . . .
7. Net underwriting gain or loss (—) . . . .

INVESTMENT INCOME

8. Net investment income earned (Part 1) . . . .
9. Net realized capital gains or losses (—) (Part 1A) . . . .
9A. Net investment gain or loss (—) . . . .

OTHER INCOME

10. Net gain or loss (—) from agents' or premium balances charged off
 (amount recovered $_____ amount charged off $_____)
11. Finance and service charges not included in premiums . . . .
12. ....
13. ....
14. ....
15. ....
16. ....
17. Total other income . . . .
18. Net income before dividends to policyholders and before federal and foreign income taxes . . . . .
18A. Dividends to policyholders
18B. Net income, after dividends to policyholders but before federal and foreign income taxes . . . . . .
19. Federal and foreign income taxes incurred * . . . .
20. Net income . . . .

CAPITAL AND SURPLUS ACCOUNT

21. Surplus as regards policyholders, December 31, previous
 year . . . .

GAINS (+) AND LOSSES (—) IN SURPLUS

22. Net income (from Item 20) . . . .
23. Net unrealized capital gains or losses (Part 1A) . . . .
24. Change in non-admitted assets (Exhibit 2, Item 33, Col. 3) . . . . . .
25. Change in liability for unauthorized reinsurance . . . .
26. Change in foreign exchange adjustment . . . .
27. Change in excess of statutory reserves over statement reserves . . . . . .
28. Capital changes:
 (a) Paid in . . . .
 (b) Transferred from surplus (Stock Divd.) . . . .
 (c) Transferred to surplus . . . .
29. Surplus adjustments:
 (a) Paid in . . . .
 (b) Transferred to capital (Stock Divd.) . . . .
 (c) Transferred from capital . . . .
30. Net remittances from or to Home Office . . . .
31. Dividends to stockholders (cash) . . . .
32. Change in treasury stock . . . .
33. ....
34. ....
35. ....
36. ....
37. ....
38. ....
39. Change in surplus as regards policyholders for the year . . . .
40. Surplus as regards policyholders, December 31 current year . . . .

*Amount of federal income taxes incurred and available for recoupment in the event of future net losses: current year $_____ first preceding year $_____ second preceding year $_____. Amount of net losses carried forward and available to offset future net income subject to federal income taxes: current year $_____ first preceding year $_____ second preceding year $_____ third preceding year $_____ fourth preceding year $_____.

UNDERWRITING AND INVESTMENT EXHIBIT

PART 1—INTEREST, DIVIDENDS AND REAL ESTATE INCOME

(1)	(2) Schedule	(3) Collected During Year Less Paid For Accrued On Purchases	PAID IN ADVANCE		DUE AND ACCRUED‡		(8) Earned During Year (3) + (5) + (6) — + (4) — (7)
			(4) Current Year	(5) Previous Year	(6) Current Year	(7) Previous Year	
1. U. S. government bonds	D*						
1.1 Bonds exempt from U. S. tax . .	D*						
1.2 Other bonds (unaffiliated) . . .	D*						
1.3 Bonds of affiliates	D*						
2.1 Preferred stocks (unaffiliated) . .	D						
2.11 Preferred stocks of affiliates . .	D						
2.2 Common stocks (unaffiliated) . .	D						
2.21 Common stocks of affiliates . .	D						
3. Mortgage loans	B†						
4. Real estate	A§						
5. Collateral loans	C						
6. Cash on deposit	N						
7. Other invested assets	BA						
8. Options	D						
9.							
10. Totals							

DEDUCTIONS

11. Total investment expenses incurred (Item 22, Col. (3), Part 4) . . . .

12. Depreciation on real estate (for companies which depreciate annually on a formula basis) . . . . . .

13. ....

14. ....

15.   Total deductions . . . .

16. Net investment income earned (Line 10 minus Line 15 — to Item 8, Page 4) . . . .

* Includes $...................accrual of discount less $...................amortization of premium.

† Includes $...................accrual of discount less $...................amortization of premium.

§ Includes $...................for company's occupancy of its own buildings.

‡ Admitted items only. State basis of exclusions...................................

PART 1A—CAPITAL GAINS AND LOSSES ON INVESTMENTS

	(1) Profit on Sales or Maturity	(2) Loss on Sales or Maturity	(3) Increases by Adjustment in Book Value	(4) Decreases by Adjustment in Book Value	(5) Net Gain (+) or Loss (—) from Change in Difference Between Book and Admitted Values	(6) Total (Net of Cols. (1) to (5) incl.)
1. U. S. government bonds . .						
1.1 Bonds exempt from U. S. tax .						
1.2 Other bonds (unaffiliated) . .						
1.3 Bonds of affiliates						
2.1 Preferred stocks (unaffiliated) .						
2.11 Preferred stocks of affiliates .						
2.2 Common stocks (unaffiliated) .						
2.21 Common stocks of affiliates .						
3. Mortgage loans						
4. Real estate			‡			
5. Collateral loans						
6. Cash on hand and on deposit .						
7. Other invested assets						
8. Options						
9.						
10. Totals						

(Distribution of Item 10, Col. (6))

11. Net realized capital gains or losses* . . . .

12. Net unrealized capital gains or losses* . . . .

*Attach statement or memorandum explaining basis of division.

‡ Excluding $...................depreciation on real estate included in Part 1, Item 12.

Form 2

ANNUAL STATEMENT FOR THE YEAR 1976 OF THE ....

Write or Stamp Name

UNDERWRITING AND INVESTMENT EXHIBIT

PART 2—PREMIUMS EARNED

LINE OF BUSINESS	Net Premiums Written (1)	Unearned Premiums Dec. 31 Previous Year— per Col. 3, Last Year's Part 2 (2)	Unearned Premiums Dec. 31 Current Year— per Col. 7, Part 2B (3)	Premiums Earned During Year (4)	
1. Fire					1
2. Allied lines					2
3. Farmowners multiple peril					3
4. Homeowners multiple peril					4
5. Commercial multiple peril					5
8. Ocean marine					8
9. Inland marine					9
10.					10
11. Medical malpractice					11
12. Earthquake					12
14. Group accident and health					14
15. Other accident and health					15
16. Workmen's compensation					16
17. Other liability					17
19. Auto liability					19
21. Auto phys. damage					21
22. Aircraft (all perils)					22
23. Fidelity					23
24. Surety					24
25. Glass					25
26. Burglary and theft					26
27. Boiler and machinery					27
28. Credit					28
29. International					29
30. Reinsurance					30
31. TOTALS					31

PART 2A—PREMIUMS IN FORCE

In Force Dec. 31 Last Year Without Deducting Reinsurance (1)	Premiums Written or Renewed During Year per Cols. 1 and 2, Part 2C (2)	Excess of Original Premiums over Amount Received for Additional Premiums and Reinsurance (3)	Deduct Expirations and Excess of Original Premiums over Return Premiums on Cancellations (4)	In Force At End of Year (1) + (2) + (3) — (4) (5)	Deduct Reinsurance In Force (Schedule F) Authorized and Unauthorized Companies (6)	Net Premiums In Force (5) — (6) (7)	
							1
							2
							3
							4
							5
							8
							9
							10
							11
							12
							14
							15
							16
							17
							19
							21
							22
							23
							24
							25
							26
							27
							28
							29
							30
							31

Form 2

ANNUAL STATEMENT FOR THE YEAR 1976 OF THE ....

Write or Stamp Name

UNDERWRITING AND INVESTMENT EXHIBIT

PART 2B—RECAPITULATION OF ALL PREMIUMS

†Gross premiums (less reinsurance) and unearned premiums on all unexpired risks and reserve for return premiums under rate credit or retrospective rating plans based upon experience, viz.:

LINE OF BUSINESS	Running One Year or Less From Date of Policy		Running More Than One Year from Date of Policy		Advance Premiums (100%)	Reserve for Rate Credits and Retrospective Return Based on Experience	Total Reserve for Unearned Premiums (2)+(4)+(5)+(6)
	Premiums In Force (1)	Amount Unearned* (2)	Premiums In Force (3)	Amount Unearned* (4)	(5)	(6)	(7)
1. Fire	(c)						
2. Allied lines							
3. Farmowners multiple peril							
4. Homeowners multiple peril							
5. Commercial multiple peril							
8. Ocean marine							
9. Inland marine							
10.							
11. Medical malpractice							
12. Earthquake						(b)	
14. Group accident and health						(a)	
15. Other accident and health						(b)	
16. Workmen's compensation							
17. Other liability							
19. Auto liability							
21. Auto phys. damage							
22. Aircraft (all perils)							
23. Fidelity							
24. Surety							
25. Glass							
26. Burglary and theft							
27. Boiler and machinery							
28. Credit							
29. International							
30. Reinsurance							
31. **TOTALS**							

†By gross premiums is meant the aggregate of all the premiums written in the policies written or renewals in force.
Are they so returned in this statement? Answers: ....
*State here basis of computation used in each case. ....

(a) Additional reserve on non-cancellable accident and health policies.
(b) Including $ .... reserved for deferred maternity and other similar benefits.
(c) Including $ .... premium deposits on perpetual fire insurance risks.

PART 2C—PREMIUMS WRITTEN

	Gross Premiums (Less Return Premiums), Including Policy and Membership Fees, Written and Renewed During Year			
	Direct Business (1)	Reinsurance Assumed (2)	Reinsurance Ceded (3)	Net Premiums Written (1) + (2) — (3) (4)
1				
2				
3				
4				
5				
8				
9				
10				
11				
12				
14				
15				
16				
17				
19				
21				
22				
23				
24				
25				
26				
27				
28				
29				
30				
31				

7

Form 2

ANNUAL STATEMENT FOR THE YEAR 1976 OF THE _____

Write or Stamp Name

UNDERWRITING AND INVESTMENT EXHIBIT

PART 3—LOSSES PAID AND INCURRED

LINE OF BUSINESS	LOSSES PAID LESS SALVAGE			Net Losses Unpaid Current Year (Part 3A, Col. 5) (5)	Net Losses Unpaid Previous Year (6)	Losses Incurred Current Year (4) + (5) — (6) (7)	Ratio Losses Incurred (Col. 7, Part 3) to Premiums Earned (Col. 4, Part 2) (8)	
	Direct Business (1)	Reinsurance Assumed (2)	Reinsurance Recovered (3)	Net Payments (1) + (2) — (3) (4)				
1. Fire								1
2. Allied lines								2
3. Farmowners multiple peril								3
4. Homeowners multiple peril								4
5. Commercial multiple peril								5
8. Ocean marine								8
9. Inland marine								9
10.								10
11. Medical malpractice								11
12. Earthquake								12
14. Group accident and health								14
15. Other accident and health								15
16. Workmen's compensation								16
17. Other liability								17
19. Auto liability								19
21. Auto phys. damage								21
22. Aircraft (all perils)								22
23. Fidelity								23
24. Surety								24
25. Glass								25
26. Burglary and theft								26
27. Boiler and machinery								27
28. Credit								28
29. International								29
30. Reinsurance								30
31. TOTALS								31

Form 2   ANNUAL STATEMENT FOR THE YEAR 1976 OF THE ....
Write or Stamp Name

9

UNDERWRITING AND INVESTMENT EXHIBIT

PART 3A — UNPAID LOSSES AND LOSS ADJUSTMENT EXPENSES

LINE OF BUSINESS	Adjusted or in Process of Adjustment		(2) Deduct Reinsurance Recoverable from Authorized and Unauthorized Companies per Schedule F, Part 1A, Sec. 1, Col. 2	(3) Net Losses Excl. Incurred But Not Reported	(4) Incurred But Not Reported	(5) Net Losses Unpaid Excluding Loss Adjustment Expenses	(6) Unpaid Loss Adjustment Expenses
	(1a) Direct	(1b) Reinsurance Assumed per Schedule F, Part 1A, Sec. 2, Col. 2					
1. Fire							
2. Allied lines							
3. Farmowners multiple peril							
4. Homeowners multiple peril							
5. Commercial multiple peril							
8. Ocean marine							
9. Inland marine							
10.							
11. Medical malpractice							
12. Earthquake							
14. Group accident and health							
15. Other accident and health							
16. Workmen's compensation							
17. Other liability							
19. Auto. liability							
21. Auto. phys. damage							
22. Aircraft (all perils)							
23. Fidelity							
24. Surety							
25. Glass							
26. Burglary and theft							
27. Boiler and machinery							
28. Credit							
29. International							
30. Reinsurance							
31. TOTALS							

(a) Including $.................... for present value of life indemnity claims and $.................... reserved for deferred maternity and other similar benefits.

10   ANNUAL STATEMENT FOR THE YEAR 1976 OF THE ....   Form 2

Write or Stamp Name

UNDERWRITING AND INVESTMENT EXHIBIT

PART 4 — EXPENSES

	(1) LOSS ADJUSTMENT EXPENSES	(2) OTHER UNDERWRITING EXPENSES	(3) INVESTMENT EXPENSES	(4) TOTAL
1. Claim adjustment services:				
(a) Direct				
(b) Reinsurance assumed				
(c) Reinsurance ceded				
(d) Net claim adjustment services				
2. Commission and brokerage:				
(a) Direct				
(b) Reinsurance assumed				
(c) Reinsurance ceded				
(d) Contingent—net				
(e) Policy and membership fees				
(f) Net commission and brokerage				
3. Allowances to managers and agents				
4. Advertising				
5. Boards, bureaus and associations				
6. Surveys and underwriting reports				
7. Audit of assureds' records				
8. Salaries				
9. Employee relations and welfare				
10. Insurance				
11. Directors' fees				
12. Travel and travel items				
13. Rent and rent items				
14. Equipment				
15. Printing and stationery				
16. Postage, telephone and telegraph, exchange and express . . .				
17. Legal and auditing				
17a. Totals (Items 3 to 17)				
18. Taxes, licenses and fees:				
(a) State and local insurance taxes				
(b) Insurance department licenses and fees				
(c) Payroll taxes				
(d) All other (excluding federal and foreign income and real estate)				
(e) Total taxes, licenses and fees				
19. Real estate expenses				
20. Real estate taxes				
21. Miscellaneous (itemize):				
(a)				
(b)				
(c)				
22. Total expenses incurred				
23. Less unpaid expenses—current year				
24. Add unpaid expenses—previous year				
25. Total expenses paid				

Form 2   ANNUAL STATEMENT FOR THE YEAR 1976 OF THE ....

Write or Stamp Name

11

EXHIBIT 1 — ANALYSIS OF ASSETS

	(1) Ledger Assets	(2) Non-Ledger Including Excess of Market (or Amortized) Over Book Values	(3) Assets Not Admitted Including Excess of Book Over Market (or Amortized) Values	(4) Net Admitted Assets
1. Bonds (Schedule D)				
2. Stocks (Schedule D):				
2.1 Preferred stocks				
2.2 Common stocks				
3. Mortgage loans on real estate (Schedule B):				
(a) First liens				
(b) Other than first liens				
4. Real estate, less encumbrances (Schedule A) . . .				
5. Collateral loans (Schedule C)				
6. Cash on hand and on deposit:				
(a) Cash in company's office				
(b) Cash on deposit (Schedule N)				
7. Other invested assets (Schedule BA)				
8. Agents' balances or uncollected premiums (net as to commissions and dividends):				
8.1 Premiums and agents' balances in course of collection				
8.2 Premiums, agents' balances and installments booked but deferred and not yet due				
9. Funds held by or deposited with ceding reinsurers .				
10. Bills receivable, taken for premiums				
11. Reinsurance recoverable on loss payments (Schedule F, Part 1A, Col. 1)				
12. Federal income tax recoverable				
13.				
14. Interest, dividends and real estate income due and accrued				
15. Equipment, furniture and supplies			X X X	
16. Bills receivable, not taken for premiums			X X X	
17. Loans on personal security, endorsed or not . . .			X X X	
18.				
19.				
20.				
21a.				
21b.				
21c.				
21d.				
21e.				
21f.				
22. Totals				

EXHIBIT 2—ANALYSIS OF NON-ADMITTED ASSETS

Excluding Excess of Book over Market (or Amortized) Values and Item 14, Col. (3), Exhibit 1

	(1) End of Previous Year	(2) End of Current Year	(3) Change for Year Increase (—) or Decrease (+)
23. Company's stock owned			
24. Loans on company's stock			X X X X X
25. Deposits in suspended depositories, less estimated amount recoverable. .			
26. Agents' balances or uncollected premiums over three months due:			
26.1 Premiums and agents' balances in course of collection . . .			
26.2 Premiums, agents' balances and installments booked but deferred and not yet due			
27. Bills receivable, past due, taken for premiums			
28. Excess of bills receivable, not past due, taken for risks over the unearned premiums thereon			
29. Equipment, furniture and supplies			
30. Bills receivable, not taken for premiums			
31. Loans on personal security, endorsed or not			
32. Other assets not admitted (itemize):			
(a)			
(b)			
(c)			
(d)			
(e)			
(f)			
(g)			
(h)			
(i)			
(j)			
33. Total change (Col. 3) (Carry to Item 24, Page 4)	X X X X X	X X X X X	

EXHIBIT 3—RECONCILIATION OF LEDGER ASSETS

INCREASE IN LEDGER ASSETS

1. Net premiums written (Part 2, Col. (1)) . . . .
2. Interest, dividends and real estate income received (Part 1, Item 10, Col. (3)) . . . .
3. From sale or maturity of ledger assets (Part 1A, Col. (1)) . . . .
4. Other income items or increases, viz.:
    (a) Agents' balances previously charged off . . . .
    (b) Remittances from home office to U. S. branch (gross) . . . .
    (c) Funds held under reinsurance treaties (net) . . . .
    (d) Borrowed money (gross) . . . .
    (e) Amounts withheld or retained for account of others (net) . . . .
    (f) Ceded reinsurance balances . . . .
    (g) ....
    (h) ....
    (i) ....
    (j) ....
    (k) ....
    (l) ....
5. Adjustment in book value of ledger assets (Part 1A, Col. (3)) . . . .
6. Capital paid in . . . .
7. Surplus paid in . . . .
8.   Total (Items 1 to 7) . . . .

DECREASE IN LEDGER ASSETS

9. Net losses paid (Part 3, Col. (4)) . . . .
10. Expenses paid (Part 4, Item 25, Col. (4)) . . . .
11. From sale or maturity of ledger assets (Part 1A, Col. (2)) . . . .
12. Other disbursement items or decreases, viz.:
    (a) Agents' balances charged off . . . .
    (b) Remittances to home office from U. S. branch (gross) . . . .
    (c) Funds held under reinsurance treaties (net) . . . .
    (d) Borrowed money (gross) . . . . - . . . .
    (e) Amounts withheld or retained for account of others (net) . . . .
    (f) Ceded reinsurance balances . . . .
    (g) ....
    (h) ....
    (i) ....
    (j) ....
    (k) ....
    (l) ....
13. Adjustment in book value of ledger assets (Part 1A, Col. (4)) and depreciation (Item 12, Part 1) . . . .
14. Federal and foreign income taxes paid . . . .
15. Dividends paid stockholders . . . .
16. Dividends to policyholders on direct business, less $..................... dividends on reinsurance assumed or ceded (net) . . . . .
17. ....
18. ....
19.   Total (Items 9 to 18) . . . .

RECONCILIATION BETWEEN YEARS

20. Amount of ledger assets as per balance December 31 of previous year . . . .
21. Increase (+) or decrease (−) in ledger assets during the year (Item 8 minus Item 19) . . . .
22.   Balance = ledger assets December 31 of current year . . . .

GENERAL INTERROGATORIES — PART A

1. Have there been included in this statement proper reserves to cover liabilities which may have been actually incurred on or before December 31 but of which no notice was received at the home office until subsequently? ANSWER:........
2. Does the company issue both participating and non-participating policies? ANSWER:........ If so, state the amount of net premiums in force on both participating and non-participating policies. ANSWER:........
3. (Mutual Companies and Reciprocal Exchanges only)
   (a) Does company issue assessable policies? ANSWER:........ (b) Does company issue non-assessable policies? ANSWER:........
   (c) If assessable policies are issued, what is the extent of the contingent liability of the policyholders? ANSWER:........
   (d) Total amount of assessments laid or ordered to be laid during the year on deposit notes or contingent premiums, $........
   (e) State total amount of advances to surplus not repaid, $........
4. (Reciprocal Exchanges only)
   (a) Does the Exchange appoint local agents? ANSWER:........ If so, is the commission paid out of Attorney-in-Facts' compensation or as a direct expense of the Exchange? ANSWER:........
   (b) What expenses of the Exchange are not paid out of the compensation of the Attorney-in-Fact? ANSWER:........
   (c) Has any Attorney-in-Fact compensation, contingent on fulfillment of certain conditions, been deferred? ANSWER:........ If so, give full information.
5. What interest, direct or indirect, has this company in the capital stock of any other insurance company? ANSWER:........
6. Is the company directly or indirectly owned or controlled by any other company, corporation, group of companies, partnership or individual? ANSWER:
   If so, give full particulars........
7.   CAPITAL STOCK OF THIS COMPANY

CLASS	Number Shares Authorized	Number Shares Outstanding	Par Value Per Share	Redemption Price If Callable	Is Dividend Rate Limited?	Are Dividends Cumulative?
Preferred						
Common				XXXX	XXXX	XXXX

8. If company has outstanding bonds, debentures, guaranty capital notes, etc., furnish pertinent information concerning redemption price, interest features, etc. ANSWER:........
8a. Does the company have a plan or program for granting to agents, brokers, employees or others any options, warrants or rights to purchase stock of the company or its parents, subsidiaries or affiliates, other than options, warrants or rights issued to all stockholders on a pro rata basis? ANSWER:........
   If the answer is in the affirmative, attach a statement providing the information required by the Instructions for this General Interrogatory.
9. Does the company own any securities of a real estate holding company or otherwise hold real estate indirectly? ANSWER:........
   If so, explain........
   ....Name of real estate holding company........
   Number of parcels involved........Total book value $........
10. If reporting company is a stock company, has it filed Schedule SIS with the Insurance Commissioner of its domiciliary state for the year covered by this Annual Statement? ANSWER:........ If answer is "no," explain in detail in separate memorandum to the Insurance Commissioner of domiciliary state.
10a. Is the company a member of an insurance Holding Company System consisting of two or more affiliated persons, one or more of which is an insurer? ANSWER:........
10b. If the answer to General Interrogatory 10a is yes, did the company register and file with its domiciliary State Insurance Commissioner, Director or Superintendent, or with such regulatory official of the State of domicile of the principal insurer in the Holding Company System, a registration statement providing disclosure substantially similar to the standards adopted by the National Association of Insurance Commissioners in its Model Insurance Holding Company System Regulatory Act and model regulations pertaining thereto, or is the company subject to standards and disclosure requirements substantially similar to those required by such Act and regulations? ANSWER:........
   ....State regulating........
11. Total amount loaned during the year to directors or other officers, $........; to stockholders not officers, $........
   Total amount of loans outstanding at end of year to directors or other officers, $........; to stockholders not officers, $........
12. Did any person while an officer, director or trustee of the company receive directly or indirectly, during the period covered by this statement, any commission on the business transactions of the company? ANSWER:........
12a. Did any person while an officer, director, trustee or employee receive directly or indirectly, during the period covered by this statement, any compensation in addition to his regular compensation on account of the reinsurance transactions of the company? ANSWER:........
12b. Has the company an established procedure for disclosure to its board of directors or trustees of any material interest or affiliation on the part of any of its officers, directors, trustees, or responsible employees which is in or is likely to conflict with the official duties of such person? ANSWER:........
12c. Except for retirement plans generally applicable to its staff employees and agents and contracts with its agents for the payment of commissions, has the company any agreement with any person whereby it agrees that for any service rendered or to be rendered he shall receive, directly or indirectly, any salary, compensation or emolument that will extend beyond a period of 12 months from the date of the agreement? ANSWER:........
13. What amount of installment notes is owned and now held by the company? ANSWER:........
14. Have any of these notes been hypothecated, sold or used in any manner as security for money loaned within the past year?........If so, what amount? ANSWER:........
15. Largest net aggregate amount insured in any one risk (excluding workmen's compensation). ANSWER:........
16. What provision has this company made to protect itself from an excessive loss in the event of a catastrophe under a workmen's compensation contract issued without limit of loss? ANSWER:........
17. Has this company guaranteed any financed premium accounts? ANSWER:........ If so, give full information........
18. Has this company reinsured any risk with any other company and agreed to release such company from liability, in whole or in part, from any loss that may occur on the risk, or portion thereof, reinsured? ANSWER:........
   If so, give full information........
19. If the company has assumed risks from another company, there should be charged on account of such reinsurances a reserve equal to that which the original company would have been required to charge had it retained the risks. Has this been done? ANSWER:........
20. Has this company guaranteed policies issued by any other company and now in force? ANSWER:........
   If so, give full information........
21. Were all the stocks, bonds and other securities owned December 31 of current year, in the actual possession of the company on said date, except as shown by the schedules of special and other deposits? ANSWER:........
   If not, give full and complete information relating thereto:........
21a. Does the company own any investments in letter stock or other restricted securities? ANSWER:........
   If yes, are they identified by appropriate symbol or otherwise in Schedule D? ANSWER:........
21b. Have all private placement investments which were the subject of renegotiation or modification of their terms during the year been disclosed to the Valuation of Securities office of the NAIC, with full details as to the provisions renegotiated or modified? ANSWER:........
21c. Have filings been made with the Valuation of Securities office of the NAIC in connection with acquisition and disposition of securities as required by Section 8 of the Valuation Procedures and Instructions for Bonds and Stocks? ANSWER:........
22. Were any of the stocks, bonds or other assets of the company loaned, placed under option agreement, or otherwise made available for use by another person during the year covered by this statement? ANSWER:........
   If yes, give full and complete information relating thereto........
23. State as of what date the latest examination of the company was made or is being made, and by what department or departments. ANSWER:........
24. Has any change been made during the year of this statement in the charter, by-laws, articles of incorporation, or deed of settlement of the company? ANSWER:........ If so, when?........ If not previously filed, furnish herewith a certified copy of the instrument as amended.
25a. In what states, territories or foreign countries is the company (or United States branch) authorized to transact business? ANSWER:........
25b. Has any direct new business been solicited or written in any state where the company was not licensed? ANSWER: Yes........ No........ If answer is "yes," explain........
26. Is the purchase or sale of all investments of the company passed upon either by the board of directors or a subordinate committee thereof? ANSWER:........
27. Does the company keep a complete permanent record of the proceedings of its board of directors and all subordinate committees thereof? ANSWER:........
28. Have the instructions accompanying the blank furnished by this Department been followed in every detail? ANSWER:........
(Only United States branches of foreign companies need answer interrogatories 29 and 30):
29. What changes have been made during the year in the United States manager or the United States trustees of the company? ANSWER:........
30. Does this statement contain all business transacted for the company through its United States branch, on risks wherever located? ANSWER:........
30a. Are any of the liabilities for unpaid losses and unpaid loss adjustment expenses discounted to present value at a rate of interest greater than zero? ANSWER:........ If so, state maximum rate of interest used:........% and the aggregate amount of discount: $........

GENERAL INTERROGATORIES — PART A

31. Ceded Reinsurance Report

SECTION 1. Annual Report of Reinsurance Transactions (including facultative and pooling transactions)

1. What is the maximum amount of return commission which would have been due reinsurers if they or you had cancelled all of your company's reinsurance or if you or a receiver had cancelled all of your company's direct business and reinsurance assumed as of the end of the period covered by this Annual Statement, with the return of the unearned premium reserve? Intercompany pooling agreement:.., All other reinsurance:........................, Total:........................

2. What would be the amount of the reduction in surplus as shown on this Annual Statement if adjustments were made to reflect the full amount described in Question 1? Intercompany pooling agreement:........................, All other reinsurance:........................, Total:........................

3. On the basis of loss experience to date, have you accrued earned additional premiums which would be payable or return reinsurance commissions which would be refundable in the future if the reinsurer or you cancelled all of your company's reinsurance as of the end of the period covered by this Annual Statement? Answer:........................ If you have not so accrued, what would be the amount of such additional premium or return commission? Intercompany pooling agreement:........................, All other reinsurance:........................, Total:........................

4. What would be the amount of the reduction in surplus as of the end of the period covered by this Annual Statement if adjustments were made to reflect the full amount described in Question 3? Intercompany pooling agreement:........................, All other reinsurance:........................, Total:........................

5. What would be the percentage reduction in surplus as of the end of the period covered by this Annual Statement from the combined effects of the amounts described in Questions 2 and 4? Intercompany pooling agreement:........................, All other reinsurance:........................, Total:........................

6. What is the amount of additional reinsurance premiums, computed at the maximum level provided by the reinsurance contracts, in excess of amounts previously paid and presently accrued (including as accrued the amount shown in response to Question 3) on retrospective adjustment periods covering the most recent three years? Intercompany pooling agreement:........................, All other reinsurance:........................, Total:........................

7. What is the amount of return reinsurance commission, computed at the minimum level provided by the reinsurance contracts, in excess of amounts previously paid and presently accrued (including as accrued the amount shown in response to Question 3) on retrospective adjustment periods covering the most recent three years? Intercompany pooling agreement:........................, All other reinsurance:........................, Total:........................

8. What would be the percentage reduction in surplus as of the end of the period covered by this Annual Statement from the combined effects of the amounts described in Questions 6 and 7? Intercompany pooling agreement:........................, All other reinsurance:........................, Total:........................

9. What would be the percentage reduction in surplus as of the end of the period covered by this Annual Statement from the combined effects of the amounts described in Questions 2, 4, 6 and 7? Intercompany pooling agreement:........................, All other reinsurance:........................, Total:........................

SECTION 2. Supplementary Report of Reinsurance Transactions

Whenever the company enters into a new reinsurance contract or alters the terms of any existing ceded reinsurance contract, during the year following the date of this Annual Statement, it shall answer the questions set forth in Section 1 as of the effective date of such new or altered contracts. If the answer to Question 5 shows a reduction in the then current surplus of 30% or more, it shall report such fact within 15 days after the date of such new contract or alteration to each Regulatory Authority with which this Annual Statement was filed.

SECTION 3. Requirements for Reinsurance Credit

Whenever the answer to Question 5 shows a reduction in surplus of 30% or more, or whenever the answer to Question 8 shows a reduction in surplus of 50% or more, or whenever the answer to Question 9 shows a reduction in surplus of 60% or more the company shall not take credit for its ceded reinsurance unless:

    A. The company shall file in respect of each reinsurer separately as of the end of each calendar quarter, a statement of balances which shall include cash balances, unearned premium reserves, loss reserves and accruals for retrospective adjustments. Such statement shall be certified by the reinsurer and filed by the company within 45 days after the end of each calendar quarter with each Regulatory Authority with which the Annual Statement is filed; and,

    B. Its reinsurance contract provides that in the event of termination the reinsurer shall continue to be obligated, with respect to business in force, for 90 days or until the earliest date thereafter as of which such original business may be terminated, but in no event more than 12 months; and,

    C. In the event of insolvency of the company, the reinsurer shall be entitled to recoup unearned ceding commission only to the extent that original commissions and taxes are recouped by the company; and,

    D. The company submits all reinsurance contracts in force and thereafter negotiated to each Regulatory Authority with which the Annual Statement is filed; and,

    E. The reinsurance agreements for which credit is claimed by the company contain provisions protecting the company from an element of risk from ultimate underwriting loss; or,

    F. The reduction is attributable to a reinsurance pooling agreement between affiliated companies which has been approved by the insurance regulatory authority in the company's domiciliary state.

Consistent with the purpose of this report, the Regulatory Authority (ies) in appropriate cases may waive one or more of these instructions.

Instructions for Completing Ceded Reinsurance Report

Question   1. This amount should be computed by applying the fixed or provisional commission rates for each treaty to the unearned premium reserve for each such treaty. For this calculation, it shall be assumed that all reinsurance is entirely cancelled, with return of unearned premium and commission.

Question   2. The amount determined in response to Question 1 should be reduced to reflect applicable income taxes and unearned premium reserves ceded to unauthorized companies, if any.

Question   3. The amount determined in response to this question should be based on loss experience to date reflecting amounts claimed as reinsurance recoverable on paid and unpaid losses as set forth in Schedule F, Part 1A, Section 1.

Question   4. The amount determined in response to Question 3 should be adjusted to reflect applicable income taxes.

Question   5. Divide the sum of the answers to Questions 2 and 4 by Surplus As Regards Policyholders as shown on Page 3, Line 27 of this Annual Statement.

Questions 6 and 7. These instructions apply to retrospective rated contracts and sliding scale commission contracts.

The amounts below should be computed separately for each retrospective adjustment period which is currently in force or which was in force during the most recent three years:

    (a) In regard to retrospective adjustment periods which commenced within the most recent three years and ended during this period, the amount should be computed at the maximum level provided by the reinsurance contracts less amounts previously paid to reinsurers and less amounts presently accrued (including as accrued the amount shown in response to Question 3).

    (b) In regard to retrospective adjustment periods which commenced prior to the most recent three years and which ended during this period, the amount should be determined as in (a) above, but should be pro rata reduced for the period of time of the retrospective adjustment period which is prior to the most recent three-year period.

    (c) In regard to retrospective adjustment periods which commenced within the most recent three years but will end after this period, the amount should be computed at the maximum level provided by the reinsurance contracts on the basis of inception to statement date premium data. Otherwise, with this exception the instructions in (a) above should be followed.

    (d) In regard to retrospective adjustment periods which commenced prior to the most recent three years and which will end after this period, the amount should be determined at the maximum level provided by the reinsurance contracts on the basis of inception to statement date premium data. This amount should be pro rata reduced for the period of time of the retrospective adjustment period which is prior to the most recent three-year period. Otherwise, with these exceptions the instructions in (a) above should be followed.

Question   8. Divide the sum of the amounts determined as answers to Questions 6 and 7, less applicable income taxes by Surplus As Regards Policyholders as shown on Page 3, Line 27 of this Annual Statement.

Question   9. Divide the sum of the answers to Questions 2, 4, 6 and 7 (adjusted by applicable income taxes) by Surplus As Regards Policyholders as shown on Page 3, Line 27 of this Annual Statement.

Form 2   ANNUAL STATEMENT FOR THE YEAR 1976 OF THE 13B

Write or Stamp Name

GENERAL INTERROGATORIES — PART B

CONTINGENT LIABILITIES

Report Briefly the Nature of Contingent Liabilities Which May Materially Affect Financial Position or Results of Operations. *

Report the Date Incurred or Discovered, the Nature of the Contingent Liability, Contract, Arrangement or Commitment, the Amount or Amounts, if Known, the Status as of the Annual Statement Date and All Other Information Necessary for a Full Disclosure.

Has the company committed any surplus funds to reserves for contingent liabilities or arrangements mentioned above? ANSWER: .... If so, has the reserve been reported as a special surplus funds reserve on page three of the annual statement? ANSWER: ....

Has the company followed instructions for reporting any unreimbursed expenditures on behalf of the company by its parent, its affiliates or subsidiaries? ANSWER: ....

FEDERAL INCOME TAX ALLOCATION

1. Is the company's federal income tax return consolidated with those of any other entity or entities? ANSWER: ....

2. If the answer to Question 1 is yes, list the names of the entities with whom the company's federal income tax return is consolidated for the current year.

3. If the company's federal income tax return is consolidated with those of any other entity or entities, does it have a written agreement, approved by its Board of Directors, setting forth the manner in which the total consolidated federal income tax for all entities is allocated to each entity which is a party to the consolidation? ANSWER: ....

4. If the answer to Question 3 is no, give an explanation why such agreement has not been executed and also describe the method of allocation setting forth the manner in which the company has an enforceable right to recoup federal income taxes in the event of future net losses or to recoup its net losses carried forward as an offset to future net income subject to federal income taxes.

5. If the answer to Question 3 is yes, describe the method of allocation setting forth the manner in which the company has an enforceable right to recoup federal income taxes in the event of future net losses which it may incur or to recoup its net losses carried forward as an offset to future net income.

*Including but not limited to notes receivable discounted, accounts and agents' balances assigned, accommodation paper, lawsuits, additional taxes, guarantees of liabilities of other companies, establishment of compensating balances, long-term contracts and lease agreements, loan take-out agreements and indemnification agreements. Include also deferred expense contracts and arrangements between parents, subsidiaries or affiliates.

EXHIBIT OF PREMIUMS AND LOSSES

BUSINESS IN THE STATE OF   **DURING THE YEAR**

(1) LINE OF BUSINESS	GROSS PREMIUMS, INCLUDING POLICY AND MEMBERSHIP FEES, LESS RETURN PREMIUMS AND PREMIUMS ON POLICIES NOT TAKEN		(4) DIVIDENDS PAID OR CREDITED TO POLICYHOLDERS ON DIRECT BUSINESS	(5) DIRECT LOSSES PAID (deducting salvage)	(6) DIRECT LOSSES INCURRED
	(2) DIRECT PREMIUMS WRITTEN	(3) DIRECT PREMIUMS EARNED*			
1. Fire					
2. Allied lines					
3. Farmowners multiple peril . . .					
4. Homeowners multiple peril . . .					
5. Commercial multiple peril . . .					
8. Ocean marine					
9. Inland marine					
10.					
11. Medical malpractice					
12. Earthquake					
14. Group accident and health . . . 15.1 Credit A & H (Group and Individual)ᵃ					
15.2 Collectively renewable A & H . .					
15.3 Non-cancellable A & H					
15.4 Guaranteed renewable A & H . . 15.5 Non-renewable for stated reasons only					
15.6 Other accident only					
15.7 All other A & H					
16. Workmen's compensation . . .					
17. Other liability . . . . . . 19.1 Private passenger auto no-fault (personal injury protection)†† .					
19.2 Other private passenger auto liability					
19.3 Commercial auto no-fault (personal injury protection)†† .					
19.4 Other commercial auto liability 21.1 Private passenger auto physical damage					
21.2 Commercial auto physical damage					
22. Aircraft (all perils)					
23. Fidelity					
24. Surety					
25. Glass					
26. Burglary and theft					
27. Boiler and machinery					
28. Credit					
29.					
30.					
31. TOTALS†					

Finance and service charges not included in Lines 1 to 31: $...

*Direct premiums earned may be estimated by formula on the basis of country-wide ratios for the respective lines of business except where adjustments are required to recognize special situations.
ᵃ Business not exceeding 120 months duration.
†To agree with Schedule T.
††As defined by state concerned.

CREDIT ACCIDENT AND HEALTH INSURANCE
(Included in the Above Exhibit)

To be submitted not later than April 1.

	(1) DIRECT PREMIUMS (Excluding Reinsurance Accepted and without Deduction of Reinsurance Ceded)	(2) DIRECT PREMIUMS EARNED** (prior to Dividends and Retrospective Rate Credits Paid or Credited)	(3) DIVIDENDS PAID OR CREDITED ON DIRECT BUSINESS	(4) DIRECT LOSSES PAID	(5) DIRECT LOSSES INCURRED**
32a. Group A & H Policies — Loans of 60 or LESS months' duration .					
32b. Group A & H Policies — Loans of GREATER THAN 60 MONTHS' DURATION BUT NOT GREATER THAN 120 MONTHS					
33. Other A & H Policies					
34. Totals (Lines 32 + 33)					

**The figures shown in these columns should be consistent with the corresponding figures in the Credit Life and Accident and Health Exhibit.

Form 29   ANNUAL STATEMENT FOR THE YEAR 1976 OF THE **15**

Write or Stamp Name

Note.—In case the following schedules do not afford sufficient space, companies may furnish them on separate forms, provided the same are upon paper of like size and arrangements and contain the information asked for herein and have the name of the company printed or stamped at the top thereof.

SPECIAL DEPOSIT SCHEDULE

Showing all deposits or investments NOT held for the protection of ALL the policyholders of the Company

(1) WHERE DEPOSITED	(2) DESCRIPTION AND PURPOSE OF DEPOSIT (Indicating literal form of registration of Securities)	(3) PAR VALUE	(4) STATEMENT VALUE	(5) MARKET VALUE
	Totals			

SCHEDULE OF ALL OTHER DEPOSITS

Showing all deposits made with any Government, Province, State, District, County, Municipality, Corporation, firm or individual, except those shown in Schedule N, and those shown in "Special Deposit Schedule" above

(1) WHERE DEPOSITED	(2) DESCRIPTION AND PURPOSE OF DEPOSIT (Indicating literal form of registration of Securities)	(3) PAR VALUE	(4) STATEMENT VALUE	(5) MARKET VALUE
	Totals			

Write or Stamp Name

SCHEDULE OF EXAMINATION FEES AND EXPENSES

(1) TYPE OF EXAM (a)	(2) STATE INITIATING EXAM (b)	(3) STATES PARTICIPATING (b)	(4) DATE BEGUN	(5) DATE COMPLETED	(6) DATE REPORT PUBLISHED	FEES AND EXPENSES INCURRED IN CURRENT YEAR		(9) OFFSETTING CREDITS, IF ANY
						(7) AMOUNT (c)	(8) STATE (b)	
					Total	-		

(a) "M" for marketing conduct, "F" for financial condition, describe others
(b) Use 2 digit post office abbreviation
(c) Show amount paid to each state (or representatives thereof) separately. The total amount plus $...................................... for other state insurance department licenses and fees should agree with Page 10, Column 4, Item 18(b).

Form 39

ANNUAL STATEMENT FOR THE YEAR 1976 OF THE ....

Write or Stamp Name

SCHEDULE A—Part 1

Showing All Real Estate OWNED December 31 of Current Year, the Cost, Book and Market Value thereof, the Nature and Amount of all Liens and Encumbrances thereon, including Interest Due and Accrued, etc.

NO.	(2) DATE ACQUIRED	(3) NAME OF VENDOR	QUANTITY, DIMENSIONS AND LOCATION OF LANDS; SIZE AND DESCRIPTION OF BUILDINGS (Nature of encumbrances, if any, including interest due and accrued)	(4) AMOUNT OF ENCUMBRANCES	(5) *ACTUAL COST	(6) BOOK VALUE LESS ENCUMBRANCES	(7) †MARKET VALUE LESS ENCUMBRANCES	(8) INCREASE BY ADJUSTMENT BOOK VALUE DURING YEAR	(9) DECREASE BY ADJUSTMENT BOOK VALUE DURING YEAR	(10) GROSS INCOME LESS INTEREST ON ENCUMBRANCES	(11) EXPENDED FOR TAXES, REPAIRS AND EXPENSES	(12) NET INCOME	RENTAL VALUE OF SPACE OCCUPIED BY		(15) YEAR OF LAST APPRAISAL
													(13) Company	(14) Parents, Subsidiaries and Affiliates	
Totals															

*Including cost of acquiring title, and, if the property was acquired by foreclosure, such acts shall include the amounts expended for taxes, repairs and improvements prior to the date on which the company acquired title.   †State basis on which market value was determined.

CLASSIFICATION

Showing the total amount of Real Estate owned in each State and Foreign Country

STATE	MARKET VALUE	STATE	MARKET VALUE	STATE	MARKET VALUE	FOREIGN COUNTRY	MARKET VALUE
						Total	

ANNUAL STATEMENT FOR THE YEAR 1976 OF THE ....

....
Write or Stamp Name

SCHEDULE A—Part 2

Showing All Real Estate ACQUIRED During the Year and Showing also Amounts Expended for Additions and Permanent Improvements Made During said Year to ALL Real Estate

No	(1) QUANTITY, DIMENSIONS AND LOCATION OF LANDS, SIZE AND DESCRIPTION OF BUILDINGS (OR) NATURE OF ADDITIONS AND PERMANENT IMPROVEMENTS MADE DURING THE YEAR (Nature of encumbrances, if any)	(2) DATE ACQUIRED	(3) HOW ACQUIRED	(4) NAME OF VENDOR	(5) COST TO COMPANY DURING THE YEAR	(6) AMOUNT EXPENDED FOR ADDITIONS AND PERMANENT NEW IMPROVEMENTS DURING THE YEAR	(7) BOOK VALUE DECEMBER 31 OF CURRENT YEAR LESS ENCUMBRANCES

Totals

SCHEDULE A—Part 3

Showing All Real Estate SOLD or Otherwise Disposed of During the Year Including Payments During the Year on "Sales under Contract"

No	(1) QUANTITY, DIMENSIONS AND LOCATION OF LANDS, SIZE AND DESCRIPTION (Nature of encumbrances, if any)	(2) DATE SOLD	(3) NAME OF PURCHASER	(4) †COST TO COMPANY	(5) INCREASE BY ADJUSTMENT IN BOOK VALUE DURING THE YEAR	(6) DECREASE BY ADJUSTMENT IN BOOK VALUE DURING THE YEAR	(7) ††BOOK VALUE AT DATE OF SALE LESS ENCUMBRANCES	(8) AMOUNT RECEIVED INCLUDING PAYMENTS ON SALES UNDER CONTRACT	(9) PROFIT ON SALE	(10) LOSS ON SALE	(11) GROSS INCOME DURING THE YEAR LESS INTEREST ON ENCUMBRANCES	(12) EXPENDITURE FOR TAXES, REPAIRS AND EXPENSES DURING THE YEAR

Totals

SCHEDULE A—Verification Between Years

Book value, December 31, previous year (Item 4, Col. (1), Exhibit 1) . . . .

Current year:—

Increase by adjustment: Totals, Part 1, Col. (8) . . . .

Totals, Part 3, Col. (5) . . . .

Cost of acquired, Part 2, Col. (5) . . . .

Cost of additions and permanent improvements, Part 2, Col. (6) . . . .

Profit on sales, Part 3, Col. (9) . . . .

Total . . . .

Less:—

Decrease by adjustment: Totals, Part 1, Col. (9) . . . .

Totals, Part 3, Col. (6) . . . .

Received on sales, Part 3, Col. (8) . . . .

Loss on sales, Part 3, Col. (10) . . . .

Book value, December 31, current year (Item 4, Col. (1), Exhibit 1)

†Including cost of acquiring title, and, if the property was acquired by foreclosure, such costs shall include the amounts expended for taxes, repairs, and improvements prior to the date on which the company acquired title. In reporting sales under contract, include payments received during the current year only.
†Include payments on "Sales under contract, include payments received during current year only, until book value per Part 1 is exhausted.
††In case of sales under contract, include payments received during current year only, until book value per Part 1 is exhausted.

Form 2

ANNUAL STATEMENT FOR THE YEAR 1976 OF THE

....
Write or Stamp Name

SCHEDULE B

Showing all MORTGAGES OWNED December 31 of Current Year, and all Mortgage Loans Made, Increased, Discharged, Reduced or Disposed of During the Year

Indicate by symbols FHA and VA if loans are so insured. All such FHA and VA insured loans not in process of foreclosure may be summarized by year and state of issue and combined values may be shown for land and buildings.

NUMBER (1)	DATE		RECORD OF MORTGAGE				PRINCIPAL				INTEREST						VALUE OF LANDS MORTGAGED (18)	VALUE OF BUILDINGS (19)	AMOUNT OF FIRE INSURANCE HELD BY COMPANY ON THE BUILDINGS (20)	LOCATION AND DESCRIPTION (State if this mortgage is being foreclosed, or if there are any prior liens. State name of mortgagor if mortgagor is a parent, subsidiary, affiliate, officer or director.) (21)
	Year Given (2)	Year Due (3)	State (4)	County (5)	Book (6)	Page (7)	Amount Unpaid Dec. 31 of Previous Year (8)	Amount Loaned During Year (9)	Amount Paid on Account or in Full During Year (10)	Amount Unpaid Dec. 31 of Current Year (11)	Rate Due (12)	Rate of (13)	Amount Past Due Dec. 31 of Current Year (14)	Amt. Accrued Dec. 31 of Current Year (15)	Gross Am't Rec'd During Year (16)	Paid for Accrued Interest on Mortgages Acquired During Year (17)				

Totals

(A) Including all mortgages "purchased" or otherwise acquired during the year and all increases during the year or loans outstanding December 31 of previous year.

(B) Including mortgages under which Company has secured title and possession by foreclosure.

CLASSIFICATION

Showing the Total Amount of Mortgage Loans on Real Estate in Each State and Foreign Country

STATE	AMOUNT	STATE	AMOUNT	STATE	AMOUNT	FOREIGN COUNTRY	AMOUNT
						Total	

NOTE: Any casualty company having a majority of its premium volume derived from non-cancellable accident and health policies, may report on Schedule B forms of the Life Blank in lieu of this schedule.

19

Form 2

ANNUAL STATEMENT FOR THE YEAR 1976 OF THE ....

SCHEDULE B A — PART 1

Showing Other Invested Assets OWNED December 31, Current Year

Write or Stamp Name

(1) NUMBER OF UNITS AND DESCRIPTION*	(2) YEAR ACQUIRED	(3) LESSEE OR LOCATION	(4) AMOUNT OF ENCUMBRANCES	(5) COST TO COMPANY	(6) BOOK VALUE AT DECEMBER 31, LESS ENCUMBRANCES	(7) STATEMENT VALUE AT DECEMBER 31	(8) MARKET OR INVESTMENT VALUE AT DECEMBER 31, LESS ENCUMBRANCES	(9) ADDITIONS TO (+) OR REDUCTIONS IN (—) INVESTMENT†	(10) DECREASE (—) OR INCREASE (+) BY ADJUSTMENT IN BOOK VALUE DURING YEAR‡	(11) GROSS INCOME RECEIVED DURING YEAR‡	(12) NET INCOME RECEIVED DURING YEAR §	(13) AMOUNTS ACCRUED AT DECEMBER 31 §§	(14) AMOUNTS PAST DUE AT DECEMBER 31 §§

Grand Totals

*Give detailed description of investment and underlying security. (Footnotes may be used to describe leases for each class in the aggregate.)
Indicate statutory category of investment, i.e., real estate, mortgage, security or other. Include in this Schedule, showing subtotals by class and grand total for all classes: (1) All loans on or investments in oil and gas production payments except those listed in Schedule D, Part 1; (2) All Transportation Equipment; (3) Timber Deeds; (4) Mineral Rights carried as admitted assets; (5) Motor Vehicle Trust Certificates; (6) Any other class of ADMITTED investment not clearly includable in other statement schedules.

†Include additional investments made, or portion of investment repaid.
‡Include depreciation on real estate and transportation equipment, etc., amortization of premium and accrual of discount if applicable.
§After appropriate reduction for interest paid to manufacturer during year and depletion and amortization of mineral rights.
§§After appropriate reduction for due and accrued interest payable to manufacturers.

SCHEDULE B A — VERIFICATION BETWEEN YEARS

1. Book value of other invested assets, Exhibit 1, Line 7, previous year . . . . _____
2. Cost of acquisitions during year:
   (a) Column 5, Part 2 . . . . _____
   (b) Column 9, Part 1 . . . . _____
   (c) Column 7, Part 3 . . . . _____
3. Increase by adjustment during year:
   (a) Column 10, Part 1 . . . . _____
   (b) Column 8, Part 3 . . . . _____
4. Profit on disposition, Column 9, Part 3 . . . . _____
5. Total . . . . _____

6. Deduct consideration on disposition, Column 5, Part 3 . . . . _____
7. Reductions in investment during year:
   (a) Column 9, Part 1 . . . . _____
   (b) Column 7, Part 3 . . . . _____
8. Decrease by adjustment during year:
   (a) Column 10, Part 1 . . . . _____
   (b) Column 8, Part 3 . . . . _____
9. Loss on disposition, Column 10, Part 3 . . . . _____
10. Book value of other invested assets, Exhibit 1, Line 7, current year . . . . _____

Cash payments on account of capital, e.g. depletion and amortization of mineral rights.

Form 2

ANNUAL STATEMENT FOR THE YEAR 1976 OF THE _____

Write or Stamp Name

SCHEDULE B A – PART 2

Showing Other Invested Assets ACQUIRED During Current Year

(1) NUMBER of UNITS AND DESCRIPTION*	(2) DATE ACQUIRED	(3) LESSEE OR LOCATION	(4) COST TO COMPANY	(5) CONSIDERATION PAID DURING CURRENT YEAR	(6) NAME OF VENDOR
Grand Totals					

SCHEDULE B A – PART 3

Showing Other Invested Assets DISPOSED of During Current Year

(1) NUMBER of UNITS AND DESCRIPTION*	(2) DATE DISPOSED OF	(3) LESSEE OR LOCATION	(4) NAME OF PURCHASER OR NATURE OF DISPOSITION	(5) CONSIDERATION	(6) BOOK VALUE AT DATE OF SALE	(7) ADDITIONS TO (+) OR REDUCTIONS IN (—) INVESTMENT	(8) DECREASE (—) OR INCREASE (+) BY ADJUSTMENT IN BOOK VALUE DURING YEAR	(9) PROFIT ON SALE	(10) LOSS ON SALE	(11) NET INCOME
Grand Totals										

*Include in this Schedule, showing subtotals by class and grand total for all classes: (1) All loans on or investments in oil and gas production payments except those listed in Schedule D, Part 1 (2) All Transportation Equipment; (3) Timber Deeds; (4) Mineral Rights carried as admitted assets; (5) Motor Vehicle Trust Certificates; (6) Any other class of ADMITTED investment not clearly includable in other statement schedules.

21

Form 249

22

ANNUAL STATEMENT FOR THE YEAR 1976 OF THE _____

Write or Stamp Name

SCHEDULE C — Part 1

Showing All Collateral Loans IN FORCE December 31 of Current Year

(1) NO.	(2) DESCRIPTION OF SECURITIES HELD AS COLLATERAL DECEMBER 31 OF CURRENT YEAR (Give in this column the number of shares of each block of stock and rate of interest and year of maturity of each bond held as collateral)	(3) PAR VALUE	(4) RATE USED TO OBTAIN MARKET VALUE	(5) MARKET VALUE DEC. 31 OF CURRENT YEAR	(6) AMOUNT LOANED THEREON	(7) DATE OF LOAN	(8) MATURITY OF LOAN	(9) Rate on Loan	INTEREST (10) Amount Past Due Dec. 31 of Current Year	(11) Amount Accrued Dec. 31 of Current Year	(12) Amount Received During Year	(13) NAME OF ACTUAL BORROWER (State if the borrower is a parent, subsidiary, affiliate, officer or director)
Totals			x x x			x x x	x x x	x x x				

SCHEDULE C — Part 2

Showing All Collateral Loans MADE During the Year

(1) NO.	(2) DESCRIPTION OF SECURITY ACCEPTED AS COLLATERAL WHEN LOAN WAS MADE	(3) PAR VALUE	(4) RATE USED TO OBTAIN MARKET VALUE	(5) MARKET VALUE AT DATE OF LOAN	(6) AMOUNT LOANED THEREON	(7) DATE OF LOAN	(8) MATURITY OF LOAN	(9) RATE OF INTEREST ON LOAN	(10) NAME OF ACTUAL BORROWER (State if the borrower is a parent, subsidiary, affiliate, officer or director)
Totals			x x x			x x x	x x x	x x x	

ANNUAL STATEMENT FOR THE YEAR 1976 OF THE _____

Write or Stamp Name

SCHEDULE C — Part 3

Showing All Collateral Loans DISCHARGED in Whole or in Part During the Year

(1) NO. Indicate partial payments by the letter "P"	(2) DESCRIPTION OF COLLATERAL RELEASED WHEN LOAN WAS DISCHARGED. (In case of partial payments enter collateral released only)	(3) PAR VALUE	(4) RATE USED TO OBTAIN MARKET VALUE	(5) MARKET VALUE AT DATE OF DISCHARGE	(6) AMOUNT OF LOAN REPAID	(7) DATE OF LOAN	(8) DATE OF REPAYMENT	(9) Rate on Loan	INTEREST (10) Amount Received During Year	(11) NAME OF ACTUAL BORROWER (State if the borrower is a parent, subsidiary, affiliate, officer or director)
Totals			x x x		x x x	x x x	x x x	x x x	x x x	

SCHEDULE C — Part 4

Showing All Substitutions of Collateral During the Year

(1) NO. (To Correspond with No. Shown in Parts 1, 2 and 3)	(2) AMOUNT OF LOAN Col. (6) of Parts 1, 2 or 3	COLLATERAL SUBSTITUTED				COLLATERAL RELEASED			
		(3) Description	(4) Date	(5) Par Value	(6) Market Value	(7) Description	(8) Date	(9) Par Value	(10) Market Value
Totals		x x x	x x x	x x x		x x x	x x x		x x x

23

SCHEDULE D—SUMMARY BY COUNTRY
Bonds and Stocks OWNED December 31 of Current Year

(1) DESCRIPTION		(2) BOOK VALUE	(3) †MARKET VALUE (Excluding accrued interest)	(4) ACTUAL COST (Excluding accrued interest)	(5) PAR VALUE OF BONDS	(6) *AMORTIZED OR INVESTMENT VALUE
BONDS Governments (Including all obligations guaranteed by governments)	1. United States					
	2. Canada					
	3. Other Countries					
	4. Totals					
States, Territories and Possessions (Direct and guaranteed)	5. United States					
	6. Canada					
	7. Other Countries					
	8. Totals					
Political Subdivisions of States, Territories and Possessions (Direct and guaranteed)	9. United States					
	10. Canada					
	11. Other Countries					
	12. Totals					
Special revenue and special assessment obligations and all non-guaranteed obligations of agencies and authorities of governments and their political subdivisions	13. United States					
	14. Canada					
	15. Other Countries					
	16. Totals					
Railroads (unaffiliated)	17. United States					
	18. Canada					
	19. Other Countries					
	20. Totals					
Public Utilities (unaffiliated)	21. United States					
	22. Canada					
	23. Other Countries					
	24. Totals					
Industrial and Miscellaneous (unaffiliated)	25. United States					
	26. Canada					
	27. Other Countries					
	28. Totals					
Parents, Subsidiaries and Affiliates	29. Totals					
	30. Total Bonds					
PREFERRED STOCKS Railroads (unaffiliated)	31. United States					
	32. Canada					
	33. Other Countries					
	34. Totals					
Public Utilities (unaffiliated)	35. United States					
	36. Canada					
	37. Other Countries					
	38. Totals					
Banks, Trust and Insurance Companies (unaffiliated)	39. United States					
	40. Canada					
	41. Other Countries					
	42. Totals					
Industrial and Miscellaneous (unaffiliated)	43. United States					
	44. Canada					
	45. Other Countries					
	46. Totals					
Parents, Subsidiaries and Affiliates	47. Totals					
	48. Total Preferred Stocks					
COMMON STOCKS Railroads (unaffiliated)	49. United States					
	50. Canada					
	51. Other Countries					
	52. Totals					
Public Utilities (unaffiliated)	53. United States					
	54. Canada					
	55. Other Countries					
	56. Totals					
Banks, Trust and Insurance Companies (unaffiliated)	57. United States					
	58. Canada					
	59. Other Countries					
	60. Totals					
Industrial and Miscellaneous (unaffiliated)	61. United States					
	62. Canada					
	63. Other Countries					
	64. Totals					
Parents, Subsidiaries and Affiliates	65. Totals					
	66. Total Common Stocks					
	67. Total Stocks					
	68. Total Bonds and Stocks					

† For certain bonds, values other than actual market may appear in this column (See Schedule D. Part 1, for details). *Companies, societies, and associations which do not amortize their bonds should leave this column blank.

The aggregate value of bonds which are valued at other than actual market is $ ....

SCHEDULE D—Verification Between Years

1. Book value of bonds and stocks, per Items 1 and 2, Col. 1, Exhibit 1, previous year . . . . _____

2. Cost of bonds and stocks acquired, Col. 5, Part 3 . . _____

3. Increase by adjustment in book value:
   (a) Col. 10, Part 1 . . . . _____
   (b) Col. 9, Part 2, Sec. 1 . . _____
   (c) Col. 8, Part 2, Sec. 2 . . _____
   (d) Col. 9, Part 4 . . . . _____

4. Profit on disposal of bonds and stocks, Col. 11, Part 4 _____

5. Total . . . . _____

6. Deduct consideration for bonds and stocks disposed of, Col. 5, Part 4 . . . . _____

7. Decrease by adjustment in book value:
   (a) Col. 11, Part 1 . . . . _____
   (b) Col. 10, Part 2, Sec. 1 . _____
   (c) Col. 9, Part 2, Sec. 2 . . _____
   (d) Col. 10, Part 4 . . . . _____

8. Loss on disposal of bonds and stocks, Col. 12, Part 4 . . . . _____

9. Book value of bonds and stocks, per Items 1 and 2, Col. 1, Exhibit 1, current year . . . . _____

Form 210

ANNUAL STATEMENT FOR THE YEAR 1976 OF THE ....

Write or Stamp Name

SCHEDULE D — Part 1

Showing all BONDS Owned December 31 of Current Year

Bonds to be grouped in the following manner and each group arranged alphabetically.
(The *italic* lettering in Groups 2, 3 and 4 should be alphabetical (See No.*)
1. Governments (including all obligations guaranteed by governments.
2. *States, Territories and Possessions (direct and guaranteed)*
3. *Political Subdivisions of States, Territories and Possessions (direct and guaranteed)*
4. *Special revenue and special assessment obligations and all non-guaranteed obligations of agencies and authorities of governments and their political subdivisions.*
5. Railroads—*unaffiliated*
6. Public Utilities—*unaffiliated*
7. Industrial and Miscellaneous (unaffiliated)
8. Parents, Subsidiaries and Affiliates.

Show sub-totals for each group.

Supplemental columns for data concerning Amortization.   SEE NOTE

(1) DESCRIPTION	(2) INTEREST		(3) DATE OF				(4) BOOK VALUE	PAR VALUE	Rate Used to Obtain Market Value	†Market VALUE (excluding accrued interest)	ACTUAL COST (excluding accrued interest)	INTEREST		(10) Increase by Adjustment in Book Value During Year	(11) Decrease by Adjustment in Book Value During Year	(12) Amount of Interest due and accrued Dec. 31, current year, on bonds in default as to principal or interest	(13) NAIC Designation	(14) Year Acquired	(15) Effective Rate of Interest at Which Purchase Was Made	(16) Amortized or Investment Value Dec. 31 of Current Year	(17) Increase in Amortized Value During Year	(18) Decrease in Amortized Value During Year
	Rate of	How Paid	Maturity		†Option							(9.1) Amount Due and Accrued Dec. 31 of Current Year on bonds in default	(9.2) Gross Am't Received During Year									
CUSIP Identification			Year	Months	Year	Call Price																

Give complete and accurate description of all bonds owned, including the location of all inter railway and miscellaneous Companies. If bonds are "serial" issues give amount maturing each year.

††Where amortized value or any value other than the market value published in the NAIC Valuation of Securities Manual is entered in Column 7, insert a symbol alongside of the amount reported.
*Insert initial letters of months in which interest is payable.
**Where a bond is payable in a foreign currency the par value and purchase price in that currency should be included as a part of the description.
***May be left blank if no CUSIP identification number is listed in the NAIC Valuation of Securities Manual.

§Perpetual bonds, bonds in default as to principal or interest and bonds not amply secured, are to be entered in this column at market value. Companies which use "Amortized" as "Book Value" may omit entering figures in these columns, and provide the following footnote:
"The increases and decreases in amortized values are the same as those shown in volumns for 'Increase' and 'Decrease by Adjustment in Book Value,' excepting as otherwise indicated."

†Insert the NAIC designation for each security printed in the NAIC Valuation of Securities Manual.

NOTE—This supplemental information, required of all Companies which amortize their bonds, is not to be used as a substitute for the information required in the preceding columns but in addition thereto. Show year-end call price pertaining to option, if any, on which amortization is based. On bonds purchased at a premium, the maturity date or call feature producing lowest amortized value should be used.

Form 29

ANNUAL STATEMENT FOR THE YEAR 1976 OF THE .... Write or Stamp Name

SCHEDULE D—Part 2—Section 1

Stocks to be grouped in following order and each group arranged alphabetically:
Railroads. (unaffiliated)
Public Utilities. (unaffiliated)
Banks, Trust and Insurance Companies. (unaffiliated)
Industrial and Miscellaneous. (unaffiliated)
Parents, Subsidiaries and Affiliates.

Showing all PREFERRED STOCKS Owned December 31 of Current Year

Show sub-totals for each group.

CUSIP Identification ***	(1) DESCRIPTION Give complete and accurate description of all preferred stocks owned, including redeemable options, if any, and location of all street railway, bank, trust and miscellaneous companies.	(2) NO. OF SHARES	(3) PAR VALUE PER SHARE	(4) BOOK VALUE	(5) RATE PER SHARE USED TO OBTAIN MARKET VALUE	(6) MARKET VALUE	(7) ACTUAL COST	DIVIDENDS		(8) INCREASE BY ADJUSTMENT IN BOOK VALUE DURING YEAR	(9) DECREASE BY ADJUSTMENT IN BOOK VALUE DURING YEAR	(11) §NAIC DESIG-NATION	(12) YEAR ACQUIRED
								(8.1) DECLARED BUT UNPAID	(8.2) AMOUNT RECEIVED DURING YEAR				

Total Preferred Stocks

SCHEDULE D—Part 2—Section 2

Stocks to be grouped in following order and each group arranged alphabetically:
Railroads. (unaffiliated)
Public Utilities. (unaffiliated)
Banks, Trust and Insurance Companies. (unaffiliated)
Industrial and Miscellaneous. (unaffiliated)
Parents, Subsidiaries and Affiliates.

Showing all COMMON STOCKS Owned December 31 of Current Year

Show sub-totals for each group.

CUSIP Identification ***	(1) DESCRIPTION Give complete and accurate description of all common stocks owned, including redeemable options, if any, and addresses (City and State) of all street railway, banks, trust and insurance companies, savings and loan or building and loan association and miscellaneous companies.	(2) NO. OF SHARES	(3) BOOK VALUE	(4) RATE PER SHARE USED TO OBTAIN MARKET VALUE	(5) MARKET VALUE	(6) ACTUAL COST	DIVIDENDS		(7) INCREASE BY ADJUSTMENT IN BOOK VALUE DURING YEAR	(8) DECREASE BY ADJUSTMENT IN BOOK VALUE DURING YEAR	(10) §NAIC DESIG-NATION	(11) YEAR ACQUIRED
							(7.1) DECLARED BUT UNPAID	(7.2) AMOUNT RECEIVED DURING YEAR				

Total Common Stocks

Total Preferred and Common Stocks

NOTES: Complete information must be furnished in connection with any holding of preferred or common stock on the statement date which is optioned or restricted in any way as to its sale by the insurer.
Identify all such securities by the symbol "R" to be inserted beside the figure shown as the rate per share to obtain market value.
Transferable shares only, of Savings and Loan or Building and Loan Associations to be reported herein.

***May be left blank if no CUSIP identification number is listed in the NAIC Valuation of Securities Manual.
§Insert the NAIC designation for such security printed in the NAIC Valuation of Securities Manual.

Form 249

ANNUAL STATEMENT FOR THE YEAR 1975 OF THE

_____
Write or Stamp Name

SCHEDULE D—Part 3

Showing all Bonds and Stocks ACQUIRED During Year

Bonds, preferred stocks and common stocks to be grouped separately
showing sub-totals for each group.

(1) DESCRIPTION‡		(2) DATE ACQUIRED*	(3) NAME OF VENDOR*	(4) NO. OF SHARES OF STOCK	(5) ACTUAL COST (Excluding Accrued Interest and Dividends)	(6) PAR VALUE OF BONDS	(7) PAID FOR ACCRUED INTEREST AND DIVIDENDS
CUSIP Identification ***	Give complete and accurate description of each bond and stock, including location of all street railway, bank, trust and miscellaneous companies.††						

‡Enter as a summary item the totals of Columns 6, 7 and 36 of Part 5. All bonds and stocks acquired and fully dispose of during the year are not to be itemized in this Part.

Totals ... X X X

SCHEDULE D—Part 4

Showing all Bonds and Stocks SOLD, REDEEMED or Otherwise DISPOSED OF During Year

Bonds, preferred stocks and common stocks to be grouped separately
showing sub-totals for each group.

(1) DESCRIPTION‡		(2) DISPOSAL DATE**	(3) NAME OF PURCHASER (If matured or called under redemption option, so state and give price at which called.)	(4) PAR VALUE OF BONDS	(5) NO. OF SHARES OF STOCK	(6) CONSIDERATION (Excluding Accrued Interest and Dividends)	(7) ACTUAL COST (Excluding Accrued Interest and Dividends)	(8) BOOK VALUE AT DISPOSAL DATE	(9) INCREASE BY ADJUSTMENT IN BOOK VALUE DURING YEAR	(10) DECREASE BY ADJUSTMENT IN BOOK VALUE DURING YEAR	(11) PROFIT ON DISPOSAL	(12) LOSS ON DISPOSAL	(13) INTEREST ON BONDS RECEIVED DURING YEAR†	(14) DIVIDENDS ON STOCKS RECEIVED DURING YEAR†
CUSIP Identification ***	Give complete and accurate description of each bond and stock, including location of all street railway, bank, trust and miscellaneous companies.††													

‡Enter as a summary item the totals of Columns 6 to 34 of Part 5. All bonds and stocks acquired and fully disposed of during the year are not to be itemized in this Part.

Totals ... X X X

SCHEDULE D—Part 5

Showing all Bonds and Stocks ACQUIRED During the Current Year and Fully DISPOSED OF During the Current Year

Bonds, preferred stocks and common stocks to be grouped separately
showing sub-totals for each group.

(1) DESCRIPTION‡		(2) DATE ACQUIRED *	(3) NAME OF VENDOR*	(4) PAR VALUE (BONDS) OR NUMBER OF SHARES (STOCKS)	(5) NAME OF PURCHASER (If matured or called under redemption option, so state and give price at which called.)	(6) DISPOSAL DATE**	(7) COST TO COMPANY (Excluding Accrued Interest and Dividends)	(8) CONSIDERATION (Excluding Accrued Interest and Dividends)	(9) BOOK VALUE AT DISPOSAL DATE	(10) INCREASE BY ADJUSTMENT IN BOOK VALUE DURING YEAR	(11) DECREASE BY ADJUSTMENT IN BOOK VALUE DURING YEAR	(12) PROFIT ON DISPOSAL	(13) LOSS ON DISPOSAL	(14) INTEREST AND DIVIDENDS RECEIVED DURING YEAR	(15) PAID FOR ACCRUED INTEREST AND DIVIDENDS
CUSIP Identification ***	Give complete and accurate description of each bond and stock, including location of all street railway, bank, trust and miscellaneous companies.††														

Grand Totals ... X X X

*The items with reference to each issue of bonds and stocks acquired at public offerings may be totaled in one line use the word "Various" inserted in Columns 2 and 3.
**Companies may at their option summarize all bonds of the same issue called, matured or redeemed during the year use; omit disposal dates.
***May be left blank if no CUSIP identification number is listed in the NAIC Valuation of Securities Manual.
†Including accrued interest and dividends received and stocks and bonds disposed of.
††† bonds are serial issues give amounts maturing each year.

27

SCHEDULE D—Part 6—Section 1

Questionnaire Relating to the Valuation of Shares of Certain Subsidiary, Controlled or Affiliated Companies

(1) Name of Subsidiary, Controlled or Affiliated Company	(2) Do Insurer's Admitted Assets Include Intangible Assets Connected with Holding of Such Company's Stock?	(3) If Yes, Amount of Such Intangible Assets	Common Stock of Such Company Owned by Insurer on Statement Date	
			(4) No. of Shares	(5) % of Outstanding
Total				

Amount of Insurer's Capital and Surplus (Page 3, Line 27 of previous year's statement filed by the insurer with its domiciliary insurance department): $...............................

SCHEDULE D—Part 6—Section 2

(1) Name of Lower-tier Company	(2) Name of Company Listed in Section 1 which controls Lower-tier Company	(3) Amount of Intangible Assets Included in Amount Shown in Column (3), Section 1	Common Stock of Lower-tier Company Owned Indirectly by Insurer on Statement Date	
			(4) No. of Shares	(5) % of Outstanding
Total				

Instructions:

SECTION 1

Column (1): List each subsidiary, controlled or affiliated company, securities of which are directly owned by an insurer (SCA Company) for which a Form SUB filing is required under Section 4 (B) of the NAIC Valuation Procedures, and which SCA Company was acquired through purchase or formation, or to which purchased assets have been transferred.

Column (2): State whether the admitted assets shown by the insurer in this statement include, through the carrying value of common stock of the SCA Company valued under Section 4 (B) of the NAIC Valuation Procedures, intangible assets arising out of the purchase of such common stock by the insurer or the purchase by the SCA Company of common stock of a lower-tier company controlled by the SCA Company. For purposes of this questionnaire, intangible assets at purchase shall be defined as the excess of the purchase price over the tangible net worth (total assets less intangible assets and total liabilities) represented by such shares, as recorded immediately prior to the date of purchase on the books of the company whose stock was purchased.

Column (3): If the answer in Column (2) is "Yes", give the amount of intangible assets involved. The intangible assets shown for the SCA Company must include any intangible assets which are included in the SCA Company's carrying value of the common stock of one or more lower-tier companies controlled by the SCA Company. In all cases the current intangible assets equal the intangible assets at purchase, as defined above, minus any write-off thereof between the date of purchase and the statement date. If the answer in Column (2) is "No", state "N/A" in Column (3).

Columns (4) and (5): State the number of shares of common stock of the SCA Company owned by the insurer on the statement date, and the percent owned of the outstanding shares of the same class.

SECTION 2

Column (1): List each company which is controlled by an SCA Company by means of a holding of a control block of the outstanding common stock, either directly or through one or more intervening companies which are also so controlled. Do not include companies which are themselves SCA Companies listed in Section 1.

Column (2): If more than one SCA Company controls the lower-tier company, list each such SCA Company and complete Columns (3)—(5) separately for each.

Column (3): As explained in the Instructions for Section 1, this amount is based on the intangible assets at purchase of the stock of the lower-tier company, reduced by any subsequent write-off. The amount shown is also based on the proportionate ownership of the lower-tier company by the reporting insurer.

Columns (4) and (5): These figures represent the proportionate ownership by the reporting insurer through the particular SCA Company.

Form 249

Stocks to be grouped in the following order and each group arranged alphabetically:
Railroads
Public Utilities
Banks, Trust and Insurance Companies
Industrial and Miscellaneous

ANNUAL STATEMENT FOR THE YEAR 1975 OF THE _____ Write or Stamp Name

SCHEDULE D – PART 7 – SECTION 1

Showing Options in Force December 31st of Current Year

DESCRIPTION (1) Give complete description of security	NO. OF SHARES OPTIONED (2)	XX (3)	DATE OPTIONED (4)	EXPIRATION DATE (5)	CONSIDERATION FOR OPTIONS (6)	EXERCISE PRICE (7)	MARKET VALUE OF STOCK	
							Rate (8)	Value (9)
CUSIP Identification*								
Totals	X X X		X X X	X X X				

SCHEDULE D – PART 7 – SECTION 2

Showing Options Issued During the Current Year

DESCRIPTION (1) Give complete description of security	NO. OF SHARES OPTIONED (2)	XX (3)	DATE OPTIONED (4)	EXPIRATION DATE (5)	EXERCISE PRICE (6)	TOTAL CONSIDERATION FOR THE OPTIONS (7)
CUSIP Identification*						
Totals	X X X		X X X	X X X		

*CUSIP identification number of stock optioned if detailed in NAIC Valuation of Securities Manual.

XX Did Company own underlying stock at time option was sold? Answer "yes" or "no" for each entry.

Form 249

ANNUAL STATEMENT FOR THE YEAR 1976 OF THE _____ Write or Stamp Name

Stocks to be grouped in the following order and each group arranged alphabetically:
Railroads
Public Utilities
Banks, Trust and Insurance Companies
Industrial and Miscellaneous

SCHEDULE D—PART 7—SECTION 3
Showing Options Exercised During the Current Year

(1) DESCRIPTION CUSIP Identification* Give complete description of security	(2) NO. OF SHARES EXERCISED	(3) XX	(4) DATE ISSUED	(5) DATE EXERCISED	(6) BOOK VALUE OF SHARES AT EXERCISE	(7) CONSIDERATION FOR OPTIONS EXERCISED	(8) CONSIDERATION ON SALE OF STOCK	(9) PROFIT ON SALE (Including Received for Options)	(10) LOSS ON SALE (Including Received for Options)
Totals	X X X		X X X	X X X					

SCHEDULE D—PART 7—SECTION 4
Showing Options Terminated by Closing Purchase Transactions During Current Year

(1) DESCRIPTION CUSIP Identification* Give complete description of security	(2) NO. OF SHARES OPTIONED	(3) XX	(4) DATE OPTIONS SOLD	(5) CONSIDERATION FOR SALE OF OPTIONS	(6) NO. OF OPTIONED SHARES TERMINATED	(7) DATE OPTIONS TERMINATED	(8) COST OF TERMINATING OPTIONS	(9) NET GAIN OR LOSS TO INVESTMENT INCOME COLS. (5)-(8)
Totals	X X X		X X X					

*CUSIP identification number of stock optioned if detailed in NAIC Valuation of Securities Manual.

XX Did Company own underlying stock at time option was sold? Answer "yes" or "no" for each entry.

Form 249

Stocks to be grouped in the following order and each group arranged alphabetically:
Railroads
Public Utilities
Banks, Trust and Insurance Companies
Industrial and Miscellaneous

ANNUAL STATEMENT FOR THE YEAR 1976 OF THE ....

Write or Stamp Name

SCHEDULE D—PART 7—SECTION 5
Showing Options Expired During Current Year

(1) DESCRIPTION Give complete description of security	(2) NO. OF OPTIONED SHARES EXPIRED	(3) XX	(4) ● DATE ISSUED	(5) DATE EXPIRED	(6) CONSIDERATION FOR SALE OF OPTIONS EXPIRED
CUSIP Identification*					
Totals	X X X		X X X	X X X	

*CUSIP identification number of stock optioned if detailed in NAIC Valuation of Securities Manual.

XX Did Company own underlying stock at time option was sold? Answer "yes" or "no" for each entry.

SCHEDULE D—PART 7—RECAPITULATION

	CONSIDERATION FOR OPTIONS
1. Options in force 12/31 of Previous Year	....
2. Options issued Current Year	....
3. Total (Line 1 plus Line 2)	....
4. Options exercised Current Year	....
5. Options expired Current Year	....
6. Options terminated by purchase Current Year	....
7. Total (Line 4 plus Line 5 plus Line 6)	....
8. Options in force 12/31 Current Year (Line 3 minus Line 7)	....

SCHEDULE F—Part 1A—Section 1
Ceded Reinsurance as of December 31, Current Year

NAME OF REINSURER (Affiliates and non-affiliates to be grouped separately showing sub-totals for each group.)	LOCATION	(1) REINSURANCE RECOVERABLE ON PAID LOSSES	(2) REINSURANCE RECOVERABLE ON UNPAID LOSSES	(3) PREMIUMS IN FORCE	(4) UNEARNED PREMIUMS (Estimated)
	Totals				

SCHEDULE F—Part 1A—Section 2
Assumed Reinsurance as of December 31, Current Year
(To be filed not later than April 1)

NAME OF REINSURED (Affiliates and non-affiliates to be grouped separately showing sub-totals for each group.)	LOCATION	(1) REINSURANCE PAYABLE ON PAID LOSSES	(2) REINSURANCE PAYABLE ON UNPAID LOSSES	(4) UNEARNED PREMIUMS (Estimated)
	Totals			

SCHEDULE F—Part 1B

Portfolio Reinsurance Effected or Cancelled (-) during Current Year

NAME OF COMPANY	(1) DATE OF CONTRACT	(2) AMOUNT OF ORIGINAL PREMIUMS	(3) AMOUNT OF REINSURANCE PREMIUMS
(a) Reinsurance Ceded			
Total Reinsurance Ceded by Portfolio			
(b) Reinsurance Assumed			
Total Reinsurance Assumed by Portfolio			

SCHEDULE F—Part 2

Funds Withheld on Account of Reinsurance in Unauthorized Companies as of December 31, Current Year

NAME OF REINSURER	(1) UNEARNED PREMIUMS (Debit)	(2) PAID AND UNPAID LOSSES RECOVERABLE (Debit)	(3) TOTAL (1) + (2)	(4) DEPOSITS BY AND FUNDS WITHHELD FROM REINSURERS (Credit)	(5) MISCELLANEOUS BALANCES (Credit)	(6) SUM OF (4) + (5) BUT NOT IN EXCESS OF (3)
Totals						

SCHEDULE G

Showing Net Losses Paid on Fidelity and Surety claims that were undisposed of December 31st of the following years, as compared with Estimated Liability per Annual Statement of the respective years and at end of Current Year.

NET LOSSES UNPAID DECEMBER 31ST PER ANNUAL STATEMENT FOR EACH OF THE FOLLOWING YEARS (EXCLUDE RESERVES FOR CLAIMS INCURRED BUT NOT REPORTED) VIZ: (1) (2)		TOTAL AMOUNT PAID TO DATE SINCE DECEMBER 31 OF YEAR IN COLUMN (1) (3)	ESTIMATED LIABILITY DECEMBER 31ST CURRENT YEAR (4)	TOTAL (3) + (4) (5)	INCREASE OR (—) DECREASE ESTIMATED LIABILITY (5) — (2) (6)
1969	FIDELITY				
	SURETY				
1970	FIDELITY				
	SURETY				
1971	FIDELITY				
	SURETY				
1972	FIDELITY				
	SURETY				
1973	FIDELITY				
	SURETY				
1974	FIDELITY				
	SURETY				
1975	FIDELITY				
	SURETY				

SCHEDULE K

Computation of Excess of Statutory Reserve over Statement Reserves — Credit

1. Net unpaid losses on policies expired prior to October 1, current year . . . .
2. Reserve for losses on policies expired in October, November and December, current year:
    (a) Net premiums written on such policies . . . .
    (b) 50% of (a) . . . .
    (c) Net losses paid under such policies . . . .
    (d) Difference (b) — (c) . . . .
    (e) Net losses unpaid under such policies . . . .
    (f) Difference (d) — (e), show zero if negative . . . .
3. Reserve for accrued losses on policies in force December 31, current year:
    (a) Net premiums earned under such policies . . . .
    (b) 50% of (a) . . . . : . . . . .
    (c) Net losses paid under such policies . . . .
    (d) Difference (b) — (c) . . . .
    (e) Net losses unpaid under such policies . . . .
    (f) Difference (d) — (e), show zero if negative . . . .

4. Excess of Statutory Reserve over Statement Reserves 2(f) + 3(f) . . . .

Note: Sum of 1 + 2(e) + 3(e) should equal Page 9, Column 5, Item 28.

ANNUAL STATEMENT FOR THE YEAR 1976 OF THE _____

SCHEDULE H — ACCIDENT AND HEALTH EXHIBIT (To be filed not later than April 1)

Write or Stamp Name

PART 1. Premiums in Force

	(1) TOTAL		(2) GROUP ACCIDENT and HEALTH		(3) CREDIT* (Group and Individual)		(4) COLLECTIVELY RENEWABLE		OTHER INDIVIDUAL POLICIES							
									(5) NON-CANCELABLE		(6) GUARANTEED RENEWABLE		(7) NON-RENEWABLE FOR STATED REASONS ONLY		(8) OTHER ACCIDENT ONLY		(9) ALL OTHER	
	Amount	%†	Amount	%†	Amount	%†	Amount	%†	Amount	%†	Amount	%†	Amount	%†	Amount	%†	Amount	%†

1. Premiums in force, Dec. 31, previous year
2. Premiums paid in advance, Dec. 31, previous year
3. Premiums written or renewed during year:
4. Excess of original premiums over reinsurance assumed
5. Expirations and excess of original premiums over return premiums on cancellations
6. Premiums paid in advance, Dec. 31, current year
7. Premiums in force, Dec. 31, current year
8. Deduct reinsurance ceded premiums in force
9. Net premiums in force, Dec. 31, current year

PART 2. Analysis of Underwriting Operations

10. Premiums written: a. Direct
    b. Reinsurance assumed
    c. Reinsurance ceded
    d. Net
11. Increase in advance premiums and active life reserve
12. Premiums earned: a. Direct
    b. Reinsurance assumed
    c. Reinsurance ceded
    d. Net
13. Benefits of current year
14. Increase in claim reserves
15. Incurred claims: a. Direct
    b. Reinsurance assumed
    c. Reinsurance ceded
    d. Net
16. **Commissions: a. Direct
    b. Reinsurance assumed
    c. Reinsurance ceded
    d. Net
17. General insurance expense
18. Taxes, licenses and fees
19. Total expenses incurred
20. Gain from underwriting before dividends
21. Dividends to policyholders
22. Gain from underwriting after dividends

PART 3. Aggregate Reserve for Accident and Health Policies

A. ACTIVE LIFE RESERVE
1. Unearned premium reserve
2. Additional reserves§
3. Reserve for future contingent benefits (deferred maternity and other similar benefits)
4. Reserve for rate credits
5. TOTALS (Gross)
6. Reinsurance ceded
7. TOTALS (Net)

B. CLAIM RESERVE
1. Present value of amounts not yet due on claims§§
2. Reserve for future contingent benefits (deferred maternity and other similar benefits)
3. TOTALS (Gross)
4. Reinsurance ceded
5. TOTALS (Net)
C. GRAND TOTALS (Net)

Line 15d + Line 11; Column (4) .... %; Column (5) .... %; Column (6) .... %; Column (7) .... %; Column (8) .... %.
Line 15d .... Enter any for Lines 15d, 16d and 17 to 22 inclusive, in each of the columns of the Exhibit the percentage of the amounts of the same lines to the premiums earned entered in the columns of Line 12d.
‡ Attach statement as to basis, in calculating this reserve, specifying reserve, interest rates and methods.
§Estimate not exceeding 123 months duration.
§§Includes reserves for unearned benefits on incurred but unreported claims. Accrued benefits should be reported on Page 9, Part 3A.

* Includes 3 _____
** _____ reported as "Policy, membership and other fees retained by agents".
§§Includes reserves for unearned benefits on incurred but unreported claims. Accrued benefits should be reported on Page 9, Part 3A.

SCHEDULE M—PART 1

Showing all direct or indirect payments of more than $100 (exclusive of expenses paid in connection with settlement of losses, claims and salvage under policy contracts) in connection with any matter, measure or proceeding before legislative bodies, officers or departments of government during the year, excluding company's share of such expenditures made by organizations listed in Part 4 below.

(1) PAYEE		(2) AMOUNT PAID	(3) MATTER, MEASURE OR PROCEEDING	(4) BY WHOM AUTHORIZED
NAME	ADDRESS			

SCHEDULE M—PART 2

Showing all payments (other than salary, compensation, emoluments and dividends) to or on behalf of any officer, director or employee which exceeded $1,000 or amounted in the aggregate to more than $10,000 during the year. (Excluding reimbursement of expenditures for transportation, board and lodging of Company Auditors, Inspectors, Claims Investigators and Adjusters, and Special Agents, and excluding payments listed in Part 1.)

(1) NAME OF PAYEE AND TITLE OF POSITION	(2) AMOUNT PAID	(3) OCCASSION OF EXPENSE	(4) BY WHOM AUTHORIZED

SCHEDULE M—PART 3

Showing all payments for legal expenses which exceeded $500 or aggregated more than $5,000 during the year, exclusive of payments in connection with settlement of losses, claims and salvage under policy contracts. (Excluding payments listed in Part 1.)

(1) PAYEE		(2)	(3)	(4)
NAME	ADDRESS	AMOUNT PAID	OCCASION OF EXPENSE	BY WHOM AUTHORIZED

SCHEDULE M—PART 4

Showing all payments in excess of $1,000 to each Trade Association, Service Organization, Statistical, Actuarial or Rating Bureau during the year. (A service organization is defined as every person, partnership, association or corporation who or which formulates rules, establishes standards, or assists in the making of rates, rules, or standards for the information or benefit of insurers or rating organizations.)

(1) PAYEE		(2)	(3)	(4)
NAME	ADDRESS	AMOUNT PAID	OCCASION OF EXPENSE	BY WHOM AUTHORIZED

SCHEDULE N

Showing all Banks, Trust Companies, Savings and Loan and Building and Loan Associations in which deposits were maintained by the company at any time during the
year and the balances, if any (according to Company's records) on December 31, of the current year. Exclude balances represented by a negotiable instrument.

(1) DEPOSITORY* (Give Full Name and Location. State if depository is a parent, subsidiary or affiliate.) Show rate of interest and maturity date in the case of certificates of deposit or time deposits maturing more than one year from statement date.	(2) AMOUNT OF INTEREST RECEIVED DURING YEAR	(3) AMOUNT OF INTEREST ACCRUED DECEMBER 31 OF CURRENT YEAR	(4) BALANCE
OPEN DEPOSITORIES			
Totals—Open Depositories			
SUSPENDED DEPOSITORIES			
Totals—Suspended Depositories			
Grand Totals—All Depositories			

TOTALS OF DEPOSITORY BALANCES ON THE LAST DAY OF EACH MONTH DURING THE CURRENT YEAR

JANUARY		APRIL		JULY		OCTOBER	
FEBRUARY		MAY		AUGUST		NOVEMBER	
MARCH		JUNE		SEPTEMBER		DECEMBER	

*In each case where the depository is not incorporated and subject to governmental supervision, the word "PRIVATE" in capitals and in parentheses, thus—(PRIVATE), should be inserted to
the left of the name of the depository. Any deposit in a suspended depository which is taken credit for should have a star placed opposite the amount in the schedule.

Deposits in federally insured depositories not exceeding the insured amount may be combined and reported opposite the caption "Deposits in (insert number) depositories which do not exceed
the Federally insured amount in any one depository".

Negotiable certificates of deposit to be reported in Schedule D.

ANNUAL STATEMENT FOR THE YEAR 1976 OF THE _____

Write or Stamp Name

SCHEDULE O – PART 1 – LOSS DEVELOPMENT
(000 omitted)

(1)	(2)	(3)	(4)	(5)	(6)	(7)	(8)	(9)	(10)	(11)	(12)	(13)	(14)	(15)	(16)	(17)	(18) (19)
	Losses paid during the year, net salvage and reinsurance received thereon during the year (a)			Salvage and reinsurance received in the current year			Total (Col. 2 + 3 + 4 – 5 – 6 + 7) net disbursements (Col. 4 Part 3	Losses paid during 1976 on losses incurred prior to 1976, (Col. 3 + 4, Sch. O, 1975)	Losses unpaid December 31 of current year			Total, per Col. 8, Part 3A (Col. 10 + 11 + 12) (b)	Development		Estimated liability on unpaid losses		Change in such estimated liability
	On losses incurred during 1976	On losses incurred during 1975	On losses incurred prior to 1975	On losses incurred and paid during 1975	On losses incurred prior to 1976 paid during 1976	On losses paid prior to 1976			On losses incurred during 1976	On losses incurred during 1975	On losses incurred prior to 1975		On losses incurred prior to 1975 + 4 + 11 + 12)	On losses incurred prior to 1976 – 6 + 9 + 12)	Dec. 31, 1975 per Col. 8 Part 3A, 1975 (b)	Dec. 31, 1974 per Col. 5 Part 3A, 1974 (b)	Dec. 31, 1975 (Col. 14 less Col. 16)	Dec. 31, 1974 (Col. 15 less Col. 17)
1. Fire																	
2. Allied lines																	
9. Inland marine																	
10.																	
12. Earthquake																	
14. Group accident and health																	
15. Other accident and health																	
21. Auto phys. damage																	
23. Fidelity																	
24. Surety																	
25. Glass																	
26. Burglary and theft																	
28. Credit																	
29. International																	
30. Reinsurance																	
31. TOTALS																	

Exclude reserves for Fidelity and Surety losses incurred but not reported.

(a) Salvage and reinsurance as used in Columns 2, 3 and 4 include (1) received in cash, and (2) reinsurance recoverable (charged during year of statement) if carried as a ledger asset, and as used in Column 6, 9 and 7 include (1) received in cash and not carried as a ledger asset and not carried as a ledger asset in previous statement, and (2) reinsurance recoverable (charged during year of statement) if carried as a ledger asset.

(b) Fidelity and Surety reserve reserves obtained from Column 3 Lines 23 and 24, Part 3A.

SCHEDULE O – PART 2 – LOSS EXPENSE DEVELOPMENT
(000 omitted)

(1)	(2)	(3)	(4)	(5)	(6)	(7)	(8)	(9)	(10)	(11)	(12)	(13)	(14)	(15)	(16)	(17)	(18) (19)
	Allocated loss expense payments during the year			Unallocated loss expense payments during the year (a)			Total (Col. 2 + 3 + 4 + 5 + 6 + 7) net disbursements (b)	Loss expenses paid during 1975 on losses incurred prior to 1975, (Col. 3 + 4 + 6 + 7, Schedule O, Part 2 1975)	Unpaid loss adjustment expenses December 31 of current year			Total per Col. 8 Part 3A (Col. 10 + 11 + 12)	Development		Estimated liability on unpaid loss adjustment expenses		Change in such estimated liability
	On losses incurred during 1976	On losses incurred during 1975	On losses incurred prior to 1975	On losses incurred during 1976	On losses incurred during 1975	On losses incurred prior to 1975			On losses incurred during 1976	On losses incurred during 1975	On losses incurred prior to 1975		On losses incurred prior to 1975 (Col. 3 + 4 + 6 + 7 + 11 + 12)	On losses incurred prior to 1976 (Col. 4 + 7 + 9 + 12)	Dec. 31 1975 per Col. 6 Part 3A, 1975	Dec. 31 1974 per Col. 6 Part 3A, 1974	Dec. 31, 1975 (Col. 14 less Col. 16)	Dec. 31, 1974 (Col. 15 less Col. 17)
1. Fire																	
2. Allied lines																	
9. Inland marine																	
10.																	
12. Earthquake																	
14. Group accident and health																	
15. Other accident and health																	
21. Auto phys. damage																	
23. Fidelity																	
24. Surety																	
25. Glass																	
26. Burglary and theft																	
28. Credit																	
29. International																	
30. Reinsurance																	
31. TOTALS																	

(a) See Schedule P—Part 1F footnote (e) for method of distribution.

(b) Net disbursements, when considered with current year loss expense payments included in Cols. 4 & 5, Schedule P—Part 1—Summary, should agree with Col. 1, Line 35, Part 4.

NOTE: In Part 2 only, omit Columns 6, 15 and 19 for the 1976 reporting year only.

ANNUAL STATEMENT FOR THE YEAR 1976 OF THE ....

Write or Stamp Name

SCHEDULE O – PART 3 – SUMMARY – LOSS AND LOSS EXPENSE

(000 omitted)

(1) Years in Which Premiums Were Earned and Losses Were Incurred	(2) Premiums Earned	(3) Loss Payments (b)	(3a) Salvage Received After Year of Claim Payment (c)	(d) LOSS EXPENSE PAYMENTS				(6) Loss and Loss Expense Payments (Excluding Salvage Received After Year of Claim Payment) (3 + 4 + 5)	(7) Ratio 6 ÷ 2 %	(8)	(9) (e) Losses Unpaid	(10) (d) (e) Loss Expense Unpaid	(11) Total Losses and Loss Expense Incurred (Excluding Salvage Received After Year of Claim Payment) (6 + 9 + 10)	(12) Ratio 11 ÷ 2 %
				(4) Allocated	(4a) Ratio 4 ÷ 3 %	(5) (g) Unallocated	(5a) Ratio 5 ÷ 3 %							
1 Prior to 1975														
2 1975														
3 1976														
4 TOTALS														

(b) Include amounts reportable in Cols. 2, 3 and 4 of Schedule O—Part 1.

(c) Include amounts reportable in Cols. 5, 6 and 7 of Schedule O—Part 1.

(g) The unallocated loss expense payments paid during the most recent calendar year should be distributed to the various years in which losses were incurred as follows: (1) 45% to the most recent year, and (3) the balance to all years, including the most recent. If the distribution in (1) or (2) produce an accumulated distribution to such year in excess of 10% of the premiums earned for such year, disregarding all distributions made under (3), such accumulated distribution should be limited to 10% of premiums earned and the balance distributed in accordance with (3). Are they so reported in this statement? ANSWER..............

(d) The term "loss expense" includes all payments for legal expenses, including attorney's and witness fees and court costs, salaries and expenses of investigators, adjusters and field men, rents, stationery, telegraph and telephone charges, postage, salaries and expenses of office employees, home office expenses and all other payments under or on account of such losses, whether the payments are allocated to specific claims or are unallocated. Are they so reported in this statement? Answer:

(e) Include due provision for incurred but not reported items except on fidelity and surety reserves.

ANNUAL STATEMENT FOR THE YEAR 1976 OF THE _____

Write or Stamp Name

SCHEDULE P—PART 1—SUMMARY

(1) Years in Which Premiums Were Earned and Losses Were Incurred	(2) Premiums Earned	(3) Loss Payments	(d) LOSS EXPENSE PAYMENTS			(5) Loss and Loss Expense Payments (3+4+6)	(7) Ratio 6÷2 %	(8) Number of Claims Outstanding	(e) Losses Unpaid	(9) (e) Loss Expense Unpaid	(11) Total Losses and Loss Expense Incurred (6+8+9+10)	(12) Ratio 11÷2 %
			(x) Allocated	(g) Unallocated	(4a) Ratio 5÷3 %					(d) (e)		
1 Prior to 1975												
2 1975												
3 1976												
4 TOTALS												

SCHEDULE P—PART 1A—AUTO LIABILITY†

1 Prior to 1969												
2 1969												
3 1970												
4 1971												
5 1972												
6 1973												
7 1974												
8 1975												
9 1976												
10 TOTALS												

COMPUTATION OF EXCESS OF STATUTORY RESERVE OVER STATEMENT RESERVES—AUTO LIABILITY

1976 $_____ 1975 $_____ 1974 $_____ Total $_____ Calculation Method_____ % of Column 2, less Column 11, if negative enter zero. See Note a.

SCHEDULE P—PART 1B—OTHER LIABILITY†

1 Prior to 1969												
2 1969												
3 1970												
4 1971												
5 1972												
6 1973												
7 1974												
8 1975												
9 1976												
10 TOTALS												

COMPUTATION OF EXCESS OF STATUTORY RESERVE OVER STATEMENT RESERVES—OTHER LIABILITY

1976 $_____ 1975 $_____ 1974 $_____ Total $_____ Calculation Method_____ % of Column 2, less Column 11, if negative enter zero. See Note a.

See Schedule P—Part 1F for footnotes.

ANNUAL STATEMENT FOR THE YEAR 1976 OF THE

_____

Write or Stamp Name

SCHEDULE P — PART 1C — MEDICAL MALPRACTICE

(1) Years in Which Premiums Were Earned and Losses Were Incurred	(2) Premiums Earned	(3) Loss Payments	(d) LOSS EXPENSE PAYMENTS		(5a) Ratio 5÷3 %	(6) Loss and Loss Expense Payments (3+4+4+5)	(7) Ratio 6÷2 %	(8) Number of Claims Outstanding	(9) (e) (f) Losses Unpaid	(10) (d) (e) Loss Expense Unpaid	(11) Total Losses and Loss Expense Incurred (6+9+10)	(12) Ratio 11÷2 %
			(4) Allocated	(4a) Ratio 4÷3 %	(5) (g) Unallocated							
1 Prior to 1975												
2 1975												
3 1976												
4 TOTALS												

COMPUTATION OF EXCESS OF STATUTORY RESERVE OVER STATEMENT RESERVES — MEDICAL MALPRACTICE

1976 $ .... 1975 $ .... Calculation Method— .... % of Column 2, less Column 11, if negative enter zero. See Note a.

SCHEDULE P — PART 1D — WORKMEN'S COMPENSATION

1 Prior to 1969												
2 1969												
3 1970												
4 1971												
5 1972												
6 1973												
7 1974												
8 1975												
9 1976												
10 TOTALS												

COMPUTATION OF EXCESS OF STATUTORY RESERVE OVER STATEMENT RESERVES — WORKMEN'S COMPENSATION

1976 $ .... 1975 $ .... 1974 $ .... Total $ .... Calculation Method— .... % of Column 2, less Column 11, if negative enter zero. See Note a.

SCHEDULE P — PART 1E — FARMOWNERS MULTIPLE PERIL, HOMEOWNERS MULTIPLE PERIL, COMMERCIAL MULTIPLE PERIL, OCEAN MARINE, AIRCRAFT (ALL PERILS) AND BOILER AND MACHINERY

1 Prior to 1973												
2 1973												
3 1974												
4 1975												
5 1976												
6 TOTALS												

See Schedule P — Part 1F for footnotes.

ANNUAL STATEMENT FOR THE YEAR 1976 OF THE ....

Write or Stamp Name

SCHEDULE P – PART 1F – INCURRED BUT NOT REPORTED LOSSES

(1) Years in Which Losses Were Incurred	(b) INCURRED BUT NOT REPORTED LOSSES UNPAID INCLUDED IN COLUMN 9 OF:					(i) ONE YEAR DEVELOPMENT OF IBNR LOSSES INCLUDED IN COLUMNS 3 AND 9 OF:				
	(2) Part 1A	(3) Part 1B	(4) Part 1C	(5) Part 1D	(6) Part 1E	(7) Part 1A	(8) Part 1B	(9) Part 1C	(10) Part 1D	(11) Part 1E
1 Prior to 1969										
2 1969										
3 1970										
4 1971										
5 1972										
6 1973										
7 1974										
8 1975										
9 1976										
10 Totals										

Footnotes:

(a) The percentage used should be 60% if fewer than 3 of the 5 years immediately prior to the most recent 3 years have at least $1,000,000 reported in Column 2, and in any event, use 60% for years prior to 1970. In other cases the percentage used should be the lower ratio reported in Column 12, for any of the 5 years immediately prior to the most recent 3 years which has at least $1,000,000 reported in Column 2, but not less than 60%; nor more than 75%. Round percentage to nearest tenth of one percent. Indicate percentage used. (In Schedule o P—Part 1D substitute 60% for 60%.)

(d) The term "loss expense" includes all payments for legal expenses, including attorney's and witness fees and court costs, salaries and expenses of investigators, adjusters and field men, rents, stationery, telegraph and telephone charges, postage, salaries and expenses of office employees, home office expenses and all other payments under or on account of such injuries, whether the payments are allocated to specific claims or are unallocated. Are they so reported in this statement? Answer: ....

(e) Include due provision for incurred but not reported items.

(f) State maximum rate of interest used in determining present values of future workmen's compensation payments: ....%.

(g) The unallocated loss expense payments paid during the most recent calendar year should be distributed to the various years in which losses were incurred as follows: (1) 45% to the most recent year, (2) 5% to the next most recent year, and (3) the balance to all years, including the most recent, in proportion to the amount of loss payments paid for each year during the most recent calendar year. If the distribution in (1) or (2) produces an accumulated distribution in such year in excess of 10% of the premiums earned for such year, disregarding all distributions made under (3), such accumulated distribution should be limited to 10% of premiums earned and the balance distributed in accordance with (3). Are they so reported in this statement?
Answer: ....

(h) Totals on Line 10 to agree with the reserve shown on Page 9 Column 4 of this statement. The IBNR reserve estimates in Columns 2 through 6 should be sufficient to cover claims which may be reopened in future periods.

(i) Include payments and reserves in respect to losses incurred more than one year prior to the date of this statement and reported during the current year.

*Includes only Bodily Injury Liability prior to 1971.

SCHEDULE P – PART 2 – SUMMARY (d)

(1) Years in Which Losses Were Incurred	(a) INCURRED LOSSES AND LOSS EXPENSE REPORTED AT END OF YEAR (000 OMITTED)						(b) INCURRED LOSS AND LOSS EXPENSE RATIO REPORTED					
	(2) 1971	(3) 1972	(4) 1973	(5) 1974	(6) 1975	(7) 1976	(8) 1971	(9) 1972	(10) 1973	(11) 1974	(12) 1975	(13) 1976
1 Prior to 1971							X X X	X X X	X X X	X X X	X X X	X X X
2 1971												
3 Cumulative Total							X X X	X X X	X X X	X X X	X X X	X X X
4 1972	X X X						X X X					
5 Cumulative Total	X X X						X X X	X X X	X X X	X X X	X X X	X X X
6 1973	X X X	X X X					X X X	X X X				
7 Cumulative Total	X X X	X X X					X X X	X X X	X X X	X X X	X'X X	X X X
8 1974	X X X	X X X	X X X				X X X	X X X	X X X			
9 Cumulative Total	X X X	X X X	X X X				X X X	X X X	X X X	X X X	X X X	X X X
10 1975	X X X	X X X	X X X	X X X			X X X	X X X	X X X	X X X		
11 Cumulative Total	X X X	X X X	X X X	X X X			X X X	X X X	X X X	X X X	X X X	X X X
12 1976	X X X	X X X	X X X	X X X	X X X		X X X	X X X	X X X	X X X	X X X	

SCHEDULE P – PART 2A – AUTO LIABILITY†

(1) Years in Which Losses Were Incurred	(2) 1971	(3) 1972	(4) 1973	(5) 1974	(6) 1975	(7) 1976	(8) 1971	(9) 1972	(10) 1973	(11) 1974	(12) 1975	(13) 1976
1 Prior to 1971							X X X	X X X	X X X	X X X	X X X	X X X
2 1971												
3 Cumulative Total							X X X	X X X	X X X	X X X	X X X	X X X
4 1972	X X X						X X X					
5 Cumulative Total	X X X						X X X	X X X	X X X	X X X	X X X	X X X
6 1973	X X X	X X X					X X X	X X X				
7 Cumulative Total	X X X	X X X					X X X	X X X	X X X	X X X	X X X	X X X
8 1974	X X X	X X X	X X X				X X X	X X X	X X X			
9 Cumulative Total	X X X	X X X	X X X				X X X	X X X	X X X	X X X	X X X	X X X
10 1975	X X X	X X X	X X X	X X X			X X X	X X X	X X X	X X X		
11 Cumulative Total	X X X	X X X	X X X	X X X			X X X	X X X	X X X	X X X	X X X	X X X
12 1976	X X X	X X X	X X X	X X X	X X X		X X X	X X X	X X X	X X X	X X X	

SCHEDULE P – PART 2B – OTHER LIABILITY†

(1) Years in Which Losses Were Incurred	(2) 1971	(3) 1972	(4) 1973	(5) 1974	(6) 1975	(7) 1976	(8) 1971	(9) 1972	(10) 1973	(11) 1974	(12) 1975	(13) 1976
1 Prior to 1971							X X X	X X X	X X X	X X X	X X X	X X X
2 1971												
3 Cumulative Total							X X X	X X X	X X X	X X X	X X X	X X X
4 1972	X X X						X X X					
5 Cumulative Total	X X X						X X X	X X X	X X X	X X X	X X X	X X X
6 1973	X X X	X X X					X X X	X X X				
7 Cumulative Total	X X X	X X X					X X X	X X X	X X X	X X X	X X X	X X X
8 1974	X X X	X X X	X X X				X X X	X X X	X X X			
9 Cumulative Total	X X X	X X X	X X X				X X X	X X X	X X X	X X X	X X X	X X X
10 1975	X X X	X X X	X X X	X X X			X X X	X X X	X X X	X X X		
11 Cumulative Total	X X X	X X X	X X X	X X X			X X X	X X X	X X X	X X X	X X X	X X X
12 1976	X X X	X X X	X X X	X X X	X X X		X X X	X X X	X X X	X X X	X X X	

SCHEDULE P – PART 2C – MEDICAL MALPRACTICE (d)

(1) Years in Which Losses Were Incurred	(2) 1971	(3) 1972	(4) 1973	(5) 1974	(6) 1975	(7) 1976	(8) 1971	(9) 1972	(10) 1973	(11) 1974	(12) 1975	(13) 1976
1 Prior to 1971							X X X	X X X	X X X	X X X	X X X	X X X
2 1971												
3 Cumulative Total							X X X	X X X	X X X	X X X	X X X	X X X
4 1972	X X X						X X X					
5 Cumulative Total	X X X						X X X	X X X	X X X	X X X	X X X	X X X
6 1973	X X X	X X X					X X X	X X X				
7 Cumulative Total	X X X	X X X					X X X	X X X	X X X	X X X	X X X	X X X
8 1974	X X X	X X X	X X X				X X X	X X X	X X X			
9 Cumulative Total	X X X	X X X	X X X				X X X	X X X	X X X	X X X	X X X	X X X
10 1975	X X X	X X X	X X X	X X X			X X X	X X X	X X X	X X X		
11 Cumulative Total	X X X	X X X	X X X	X X X			X X X	X X X	X X X	X X X	X X X	X X X
12 1976	X X X	X X X	X X X	X X X	X X X		X X X	X X X	X X X	X X X	X X X	

See Schedule P—Part 2E for footnotes.

Form 2   ANNUAL STATEMENT FOR THE YEAR 1976 OF THE 45

Write or Stamp Name

SCHEDULE P – PART 2D – WORKMEN'S COMPENSATION

(1) Years in Which Losses Were Incurred	(a) INCURRED LOSSES AND LOSS EXPENSE REPORTED AT END OF YEAR (000 OMITTED)						(b) INCURRED LOSS AND LOSS EXPENSE RATIO REPORTED					
	(2) 1971	(3) 1972	(4) 1973	(5) 1974	(6) 1975	(7) 1976	(8) 1971	(9) 1972	(10) 1973	(11) 1974	(12) 1975	(13) 1976
1 Prior to 1971							X X X	X X X	X X X	X X X	X X X	X X X
2 1971												
3 Cumulative Total							X X X	X X X	X X X	X X X	X X X	X X X
4 1972	X X X						X X X					
5 Cumulative Total	X X X						X X X	X X X	X X X	X X X	X X X	X X X
6 1973	X X X	X X X					X X X	X X X				
7 Cumulative Total	X X X	X X X					X X X	X X X	X X X	X X X	X X X	X X X
8 1974	X X X	X X X	X X X				X X X	X X X	X X X			
9 Cumulative Total	X X X	X X X	X X X				X X X	X X X	X X X	X X X	X X X	X X X
10 1975	X X X	X X X	X X X	X X X			X X X	X X X	X X X	X X X		
11 Cumulative Total	X X X	X X X	X X X	X X X			X X X	X X X	X X X	X X X	X X X	X X X
12 1976	X X X	X X X	X X X	X X X	X X X		X X X	X X X	X X X	X X X	X X X	

SCHEDULE P – PART 2E – FARMOWNERS MULTIPLE PERIL, HOMEOWNERS MULTIPLE PERIL, COMMERCIAL MULTIPLE PERIL, OCEAN MARINE, AIRCRAFT (ALL PERILS) AND BOILER AND MACHINERY (c)

(1) Years in Which Losses Were Incurred	(2) 1971	(3) 1972	(4) 1973	(5) 1974	(6) 1975	(7) 1976	(8) 1971	(9) 1972	(10) 1973	(11) 1974	(12) 1975	(13) 1976
1 Prior to 1971							X X X	X X X	X X X	X X X	X X X	X X X
2 1971												
3 Cumulative Total							X X X	X X X	X X X	X X X	X X X	X X X
4 1972	X X X						X X X					
5 Cumulative Total	X X X						X X X	X X X	X X X	X X X	X X X	X X X
6 1973	X X X	X X X					X X X	X X X				
7 Cumulative Total	X X X	X X X					X X X	X X X	X X X	X X X	X X X	X X X
8 1974	X X X	X X X	X X X				X X X	X X X	X X X			
9 Cumulative Total	X X X	X X X	X X X				X X X	X X X	X X X	X X X	X X X	X X X
10 1975	X X X	X X X	X X X	X X X			X X X	X X X	X X X	X X X		
11 Cumulative Total	X X X	X X X	X X X	X X X			X X X	X X X	X X X	X X X	X X X	X X X
12 1976	X X X	X X X	X X X	X X X	X X X		X X X	X X X	X X X	X X X	X X X	

(a) From Schedule P—Part 1, Column 11. Use corresponding column for annual statements prior to 1973.
(b) From Schedule P—Part 1, Column 12. Use corresponding column for annual statements prior to 1973
(c) Completion of data for years prior to 1973 is optional.
(d) Completion of data for years prior to 1975 is optional.
†Includes only Bodily Injury Liability prior to 1971.

46   Form 2   ANNUAL STATEMENT FOR THE YEAR 1976 OF THE ....

Write or Stamp Name

SCHEDULE P—PART 3—SUMMARY (d)
Calendar Year Premiums Earned, Accident Year Loss and Loss Expense Incurred

	DOLLARS (000 omitted)							PERCENTAGES						
	(1) 1970	(2) 1971	(3) 1972	(4) 1973	(5) 1974	(6) 1975	(7) 1976	(8) 1970	(9) 1971	(10) 1972	(11) 1973	(12) 1974	(13) 1975	(14) 1976
	Summary Data from Schedule P—Part 1—Summary													
1 Premiums Earned														
2 Loss & Loss Exp. Inc'd.								100.0	100.0	100.0	100.0	100.0	100.0	100.0
	Loss & Loss Expense through 1 year													
3 Paid														
4 Reserve (2)—(3)														
	Loss & Loss Expense through 2 years													
5 Paid							X X							X X
6 Reserve (2)—(5)							X X							X X
	Loss & Loss Expense through 3 years													
7 Paid						X X	X X						X X	X X
8 Reserve (2)—(7)						X X	X X						X X	X X
	Loss & Loss Expense through 4 years													
9 Paid					X X	X X	X X					X X	X X	X X
10 Reserve (2)—(9)					X X	X X	X X					X X	X X	X X
	Loss & Loss Expense through 5 years													
11 Paid				X X	X X	X X	X X				X X	X X	X X	X X
12 Reserve (2)—(11)				X X	X X	X X	X X				X X	X X	X X	X X

SCHEDULE P—PART 3A—AUTO LIABILITY†
Calendar Year Premiums Earned, Accident Year Loss and Loss Expense Incurred

	DOLLARS (000 omitted)							PERCENTAGES						
	(1) 1970	(2) 1971	(3) 1972	(4) 1973	(5) 1974	(6) 1975	(7) 1976	(8) 1970	(9) 1971	(10) 1972	(11) 1973	(12) 1974	(13) 1975	(14) 1976
	Summary Data from Schedule P—Part 1A													
1 Premiums Earned														
2 Loss & Loss Exp. Inc'd.								100.0	100.0	100.0	100.0	100.0	100.0	100.0
	Loss & Loss Expense through 1 year													
3 Paid														
4 Reserve (2)—(3)														
	Loss & Loss Expense through 2 years													
5 Paid							X X							X X
6 Reserve (2)—(5)							X X							X X
	Loss & Loss Expense through 3 years													
7 Paid						X X	X X						X X	X X
8 Reserve (2)—(7)						X X	X X						X X	X X
	Loss & Loss Expense through 4 years													
9 Paid					X X	X X	X X					X X	X X	X X
10 Reserve (2)—(9)					X X	X X	X X					X X	X X	X X
	Loss & Loss Expense through 5 years													
11 Paid				X X	X X	X X	X X				X X	X X	X X	X X
12 Reserve (2)—(11)				X X	X X	X X	X X				X X	X X	X X	X X

SCHEDULE P—PART 3B—OTHER LIABILITY†
Calendar Year Premiums Earned, Accident Year Loss and Loss Expense Incurred

	DOLLARS (000 omitted)							PERCENTAGES						
	(1) 1970	(2) 1971	(3) 1972	(4) 1973	(5) 1974	(6) 1975	(7) 1976	(8) 1970	(9) 1971	(10) 1972	(11) 1973	(12) 1974	(13) 1975	(14) 1976
	Summary Data from Schedule P—Part 1B													
1 Premiums Earned														
2 Loss & Loss Exp. Inc'd.								100.0	100.0	100.0	100.0	100.0	100.0	100.0
	Loss & Loss Expense through 1 year													
3 Paid														
4 Reserve (2)—(3)														
	Loss & Loss Expense through 2 years													
5 Paid							X X							X X
6 Reserve (2)—(5)							X X							X X
	Loss & Loss Expense through 3 years													
7 Paid						X X	X X						X X	X X
8 Reserve (2)—(7)						X X	X X						X X	X X
	Loss & Loss Expense through 4 years													
9 Paid					X X	X X	X X					X X	X X	X X
10 Reserve (2)—(9)					X X	X X	X X					X X	X X	X X
	Loss & Loss Expense through 5 years													
11 Paid				X X	X X	X X	X X				X X	X X	X X	X X
12 Reserve (2)—(11)				X X	X X	X X	X X				X X	X X	X X	X X

SCHEDULE P – PART 3C – MEDICAL MALPRACTICE (d)
Calendar Year Premiums Earned, Accident Year Loss and Loss Expense Incurred

	DOLLARS (000 omitted)							PERCENTAGES						
	(1) 1970	(2) 1971	(3) 1972	(4) 1973	(5) 1974	(6) 1975	(7) 1976	(8) 1970	(8) 1971	(10) 1972	(11) 1973	(12) 1974	(13) 1975	(14) 1976
	Summary Data from Schedule P—Part 1C													
1 Premiums Earned								100.0	100.0	100.0	100.0	100.0	100.0	100.0
2 Loss & Loss Exp. Inc'd.														
	Loss & Loss Expense through 1 year													
3 Paid														
4 Reserve (2)—(3)														
	Loss & Loss Expense through 2 years													
5 Paid							X X							X X
6 Reserve (2)—(5)							X X							X X
	Loss & Loss Expense through 3 years													
7 Paid						X X	X X						X X	X X
8 Reserve (2)—(7)						X X	X X						X X	X X
	Loss & Loss Expense through 4 years													
9 Paid					X X	X X	X X					X X	X X	X X
10 Reserve (2)—(9)					X X	X X	X X					X X	X X	X X
	Loss & Loss Expense through 5 years													
11 Paid				X X	X X	X X	X X				X X	X X	X X	X X
12 Reserve (2)—(11)				X X	X X	X X	X X				X X	X X	X X	X X

SCHEDULE P – PART 3D – WORKMEN'S COMPENSATION
Calendar Year Premiums Earned, Accident Year Loss and Loss Expense Incurred

	DOLLARS (000 omitted)							PERCENTAGES						
	(1) 1970	(2) 1971	(3) 1972	(4) 1973	(5) 1974	(6) 1975	(7) 1976	(8) 1970	(9) 1971	(10) 1972	(11) 1973	(12) 1974	(13) 1975	(14) 1976
	Summary Data from Schedule P—Part 1D													
1 Premiums Earned								100.0	100.0	100.0	100.0	100.0	100.0	100.0
2 Loss & Loss Exp. Inc'd.														
	Loss & Loss Expense through 1 year													
3 Paid														
4 Reserve (2)—(3)														
	Loss & Loss Expense through 2 years													
5 Paid							X X							X X
6 Reserve (2)—(5)							X X							X X
	Loss & Loss Expense through 3 years													
7 Paid						X X	X X						X X	X X
8 Reserve (2)—(7)						X X	X X						X X	X X
	Loss & Loss Expense through 4 years													
9 Paid					X X	X X	X X					X X	X X	X X
10 Reserve (2)—(9)					X X	X X	X X					X X	X X	X X
	Loss & Loss Expense through 5 years													
11 Paid				X X	X X	X X	X X				X X	X X	X X	X X
12 Reserve (2)—(11)				X X	X X	X X	X X				X X	X X	X X	X X

SCHEDULE P – PART 3E – FARMOWNERS MULTIPLE PERIL, HOMEOWNERS MULTIPLE PERIL, COMMERCIAL MULTIPLE PERIL, OCEAN MARINE, AIRCRAFT (ALL PERILS) AND BOILER AND MACHINERY (e)
Calendar Year Premiums Earned, Accident Year Loss and Loss Expense Incurred

	DOLLARS (000 omitted)							PERCENTAGES						
	(1) 1970	(2) 1971	(3) 1972	(4) 1973	(5) 1974	(6) 1975	(7) 1976	(8) 1970	(9) 1971	(10) 1972	(11) 1973	(12) 1974	(13) 1975	(14) 1976
	Summary Data from Schedule P—Part 1E													
1 Premiums Earned								100.0	100.0	100.0	100.0	100.0	100.0	100.0
2 Loss & Loss Exp. Inc'd.														
	Loss & Loss Expense through 1 year													
3 Paid														
4 Reserve (2)—(3)														
	Loss & Loss Expense through 2 years													
5 Paid							X X							X X
6 Reserve (2)—(5)							X X							X X
	Loss & Loss Expense through 3 years													
7 Paid						X X	X X						X X	X X
8 Reserve (2)—(7)						X X	X A						X X	X X
	Loss & Loss Expense through 4 years													
9 Paid					X X	X X	X X					X X	X X	X X
10 Reserve (2)—(9)					X X	X X	X X					X X	X X	X X
	Loss & Loss Expense through 5 years													
11 Paid				X X	X X	X X	X X				X X	X X	X X	X X
12 Reserve (2)—(11)				X X	X X	X X	X X.				X X	X X	X X	X X

(c) Completion of data for years prior to 1973 is optional.
(c) Completion of data for years prior to 1975 is optional.
†Includes only Bodily Injury Liability prior to 1971.

Note: Item 2 is taken from this year's Schedule P—Part 1 and is consequently updated each year. Items 3, 5, 7, 9 and 11 are taken from the Schedule P—Part 1 (or corresponding Part for years prior to 1975) of the year indicated by the heading immediately above each item, and consequently do not change after once being entered.

Form 249

ANNUAL STATEMENT FOR THE YEAR 1976 OF THE

Write or Stamp Name

SCHEDULE X—Part 1—UNLISTED ASSETS

Showing all property owned by or in which the Company had any interest, on December 31 of current year, which is not entered on any other schedule and which is not included in the financial statement for the current year

DESCRIPTION (1)	FROM WHOM ACQUIRED (2)	DATE WHEN ACQUIRED (3)	DATE WHEN CHARGED OFF FROM STATEMENT (4)	PAR VALUE (5)	ACTUAL COST (6)	BOOK VALUE WHEN CHARGED OFF (7)	MARKET VALUE DECEMBER 31 OF CURRENT YEAR (8)	GROSS INCOME THEREFROM DURING YEAR (9)	OUTLAYS MADE DURING YEAR (10)	REASONS FOR NOT CARRYING PROPERTY ON BOOKS (11)

Totals

SCHEDULE X—Part 2

Showing all property acquired or transferred to Schedule X, Part 1, during the year except that shown in Schedules A, B, BA, C and D and except furniture, fixtures and supplies

DESCRIPTION (1)	DATE OF ACQUISITION (2)	FROM WHOM ACQUIRED (3)	PAR VALUE (4)	ACTUAL COST (5)

Totals

SCHEDULE X—Part 3

Showing all property sold or transferred from Schedule X, Part 1, during the year except that shown in Schedules A, B, BA, C and D

DESCRIPTION (1)	DATE OF ACQUISITION (2)	FROM WHOM ACQUIRED (3)	PAR VALUE (4)	ACTUAL COST (5)	DATE OF SALE (6)	TO WHOM SOLD (7)	CONSIDERATION (8)	GROSS INCOME THEREFROM DURING YEAR (9)	OUTLAY THEREON DURING YEAR OTHER THAN COST (10)

Totals

*Companies should limit entries in this schedule to items transferred from asset accounts.

ANNUAL STATEMENT FOR THE YEAR 1976 OF THE ....

Write or Stamp Name

SCHEDULE Y — TRANSACTIONS WITH AFFILIATES

PART 1. *Transactions by the company and any affiliated insurer with any affiliate. Non-insurance transactions involving less than 1/2 of 1% of the total assets of the largest affiliated insurer may be omitted. Exclude cost allocation transactions based upon generally accepted accounting principles, and reinsurance transactions.*

(1) DATE OF TRANSACTION	(2) EXPLANATION OF TRANSACTION	(3) NAME OF INSURER	(4) NAME OF AFFILIATE	ASSETS RECEIVED BY INSURER		ASSETS TRANSFERRED BY INSURER	
				(5) STATEMENT VALUE	(6) DESCRIPTION	(7) STATEMENT VALUE	(8) DESCRIPTION

PART 2. *Guarantees or undertakings for the benefit of an affiliate which result in a contingent exposure of the Company's or any affiliated insurer's assets to liability. List and describe:*

PART 3. *Management and service contracts and all cost sharing arrangements, other than cost allocation arrangements based upon generally accepted accounting principles, involving the Company or any affiliated insurer. List and describe:*

PART 4. *Organizational Chart. Attach a chart or listing presenting the identities of and interrelationships among all affiliated insurers and all other affiliates, identifying all insurers as such. No non-insurer affiliate need be shown if its total assets are less than 1/2 of 1% of the total assets of the largest affiliated insurer.*

NOTE: All members of a Holding Company Group shall prepare a common Schedule for inclusion in each of the individual annual statements and the consolidated Fire and Casualty Annual Statement of the Group.

SCHEDULE T—EXHIBIT OF PREMIUMS WRITTEN
Allocated by States and Territories

(1) STATES, ETC.	GROSS PREMIUMS, INCLUDING POLICY AND MEMBERSHIP FEES, LESS RETURN PREMIUMS AND PREMIUMS ON POLICIES NOT TAKEN		(4) DIVIDENDS PAID OR CREDITED TO POLICYHOLDERS ON DIRECT BUSINESS	(5) DIRECT LOSSES PAID (DEDUCTING SALVAGE)	(6) DIRECT LOSSES INCURRED	(7) DIRECT LOSSES UNPAID	(8) FINANCE AND SERVICE CHARGES NOT INCLUDED IN PREMIUMS
	(2) DIRECT PREMIUMS WRITTEN	(3) DIRECT PREMIUMS EARNED					
1 Alabama							
2 Alaska							
3 Arizona							
4 Arkansas							
5 California							
6 Colorado							
7 Connecticut							
8 Delaware							
9 Dist. Columbia							
10 Florida							
11 Georgia							
12 Hawaii							
13 Idaho							
14 Illinois							
15 Indiana							
16 Iowa							
17 Kansas							
18 Kentucky							
19 Louisiana							
20 Maine							
21 Maryland							
22 Massachusetts							
23 Michigan							
24 Minnesota							
25 Mississippi							
26 Missouri							
27 Montana							
28 Nebraska							
29 Nevada							
30 New Hampshire							
31 New Jersey							
32 New Mexico							
33 New York							
34 No. Carolina							
35 No. Dakota							
36 Ohio							
37 Oklahoma							
38 Oregon							
39 Pennsylvania							
40 Rhode Island							
41 So. Carolina							
42 So. Dakota							
43 Tennessee							
44 Texas							
45 Utah							
46 Vermont							
47 Virginia							
48 Washington							
49 West Virginia							
50 Wisconsin							
51 Wyoming							
52 Guam							
53 Puerto Rico							
54 U. S. Virgin Is.							
55 Canada							
56 Mexico							
57 Philippine Is.							
58 Other foreign (Itemize)							
98 *Totals							

Explanation of Basis of Allocation of Premiums by States, etc.

*Total for Column (2) to agree with the total of Column (1) in Part 2C, Page 7. Total for Column (5) to agree with the total of Column (1) in Part 3, Page 8.   Total for Column (6) to agree with the sum of totals for Columns (5)
Total for Column (7) to agree with the total of Column (1a) in Part 3A, Page 9. Total for Column (8) to agree with Item 11, Page 4.   and (7) less the total for Column (7) in the previous annual statement.

1976

INSTRUCTIONS

For Completing Fire and Casualty Annual Statement Blank

FOREWORD

Titles of the various statement items and lines are in general self-explanatory and as such constitute instructions. Specific further instructions are prescribed for items and lines about which there might be some question as to content. Any entry for which no specific instruction has been given should be made in accordance with sound insurance accounting principles and in a manner consistent with related items and lines covered by specific instructions.

Instructions for completing schedules and exhibits appearing therein and the Instructions for Uniform Classifications of Expenses of Fire and Marine and Casualty and Surety Insurers are not repeated here.

GENERAL

1. Date of filing: The statement is required to be filed on or before March 1st, unless otherwise provided by statute.
2. The name of the company must be plainly written or stamped at the top of all pages, exhibits and schedules (and duplicate schedules) and also upon all inserted schedules and loose sheets.
3. Printed statements or copies produced by some duplicating process, in lieu of handwritten or typewritten statements on the actual blanks furnished by this Department, will be accepted if (1) bound in covers similar in color to the blanks furnished by this Department; (2) printed or duplicated by a process resulting in permanent black characters on a good grade of paper of light color; (3) such statements and all supporting schedules contain all the information required, with the same headings and footnotes, and are of the same size and arrangement, page for page, column for column, and line for line, as in the blanks supplied by this Department, unless the company is otherwise instructed.
4. Blank schedules will not be accepted as meaning anything. If no entries are to be made, write "None" or "Nothing" across the schedule in question.

5. Check marks will not be accepted as answers to interrogatories.
6. Any item which cannot be readily classified under one of the printed items should be entered as a special item.
7. If the annual statement and schedules do not contain the information asked for in the blank or are not prepared in accordance with these Instructions, they will not be accepted.
8. For all items that are supported by exhibits, see the instructions for such exhibits.
9. Report all amounts in whole dollars only. Do not report any cents. Either round the amounts shown to the nearest dollar or simply drop the cents. If cents are dropped, state in a footnote on page 2 that the failure of the items to add to the totals shown throughout the statement is due to the dropping of cents.
10. The company in completing the annual statement should not change the page numbers in the association blank. If extra pages are needed, use decimals after the page number like 32.1, 32.2, etc. If pages are doubled up, double up the page numbers also. For example, if Pages 32, 33 and 34 are shown on the same page, show all three page numbers at the top of the page like 32, 33, 34.

ASSETS—PAGE 2 AND SUPPORTING SCHEDULES

Each class of assets should be entered on Page 2 at its statement value. This value for real estate, bonds, stocks, and the amount loaned on mortgages and collateral securities must in all cases prove with the corresponding value for the preceding year after taking into consideration the items affecting them as shown in Part 1A and the corresponding schedules. (See also the instructions for Exhibit 1.)

The space at the foot of Page 2 is provided for a statement of the valuation bases for bonds, stocks, etc., and for comments upon items or transactions that are unusual or not self-explanatory or that might otherwise be misunderstood.

Companies should report all bonds and stocks owned or held as collateral for loans at the rates promulgated by the National Association of Insurance Commissioners.

The determination of market values of bonds and stocks not quoted in the stock exchange sheets or in lists published by large stock and bond houses will be materially expedited if each insurance company owning or loaning on any such security will send to the Valuation of Securities Subcommittee, N. A. I. C., 67 Wall Street, New York, New

York 10005, a copy of the financial statement of the issuing corporation for the most recent fiscal year as soon as possible after the end of the calendar year.

Exchanges of assets are required to be identified in the schedules by the abbreviation "ex" followed by a numeral in parentheses after a description of the asset disposed of and the asset acquired.

Assets such as those listed in Exhibit 2 are not acceptable assets and should not be entered on this page of the statement.

A "person" is an individual, corporation, or any other legal entity. A "parent" is any person that, directly or indirectly, owns or controls the insurer. A "subsidiary" is any person that is, directly or indirectly, owned or controlled by the insurer. An "affiliate" is any person that is, directly or indirectly, owned or controlled by the same person or by the same group of persons, that, directly or indirectly, own or control the insurer. The term "affiliate" includes parents and subsidiaries. Control shall be presumed to exist if a person, directly or indirectly, owns, controls, holds with the power to vote or holds proxies, representing 10% or more of the voting securities of any other person.

LIABILITIES, SURPLUS AND OTHER FUNDS—PAGE 3

ITEM 5—TAXES, LICENSES AND FEES

Exclude: Any amounts withheld or retained by the Company acting as agents for others. (See instructions for Item 13.)

ITEM 11—DIVIDENDS DECLARED AND UNPAID:

(b) Policyholders

Exclude: Dividends on uncollected premiums. (See Exhibit 1, Item 8.)

ITEM 13—AMOUNT WITHHELD OR RETAINED BY COMPANY FOR ACCOUNT OF OTHERS

Include employees' Old Age and Unemployment Contributions, withholding for purchase of Savings Bonds, taxes withheld at source, as well as amounts held in escrow for payment of taxes, insurance, etc., under F. H. A. or other mortgage loans.

If, however, a company has separate bank accounts for exclusive use in connection with employee bond purchases or escrow F. H. A. payments or other amounts withheld or retained in a similar manner, the related assets should be shown separately in Exhibit 1, Page 11, and extended at zero value, unless such assets are income producing for the company, in which case they should be shown both as assets and liabilities in the statement.

ITEM 14a—UNEARNED PREMIUMS ON REINSURANCE IN UNAUTHORIZED COMPANIES

Include: Total of amounts in Col. 4 of Schedule F, Part 1A, Section 1 for unauthorized companies.

ITEM 14b—REINSURANCE ON PAID AND UNPAID LOSSES DUE FROM UNAUTHORIZED COMPANIES

Include: Total of amounts in Cols. 1 and 2 of Schedule F, Part 1A, Section 1 for unauthorized companies.

ITEM 16—EXCESS OF STATUTORY RESERVES OVER STATEMENT RESERVES (Schedule P—Parts 1A, 1B, 1C, 1D and Schedule K)

Enter from Schedule P—Parts 1A, 1B, 1C, 1D and Schedule K the excess reserves as calculated in accordance with the computation method instructions included at the bottom of Schedule P—Parts 1A, 1B, 1C, 1D and Schedule K.

ITEM 17—NET ADJUSTMENTS IN ASSETS AND LIABILITIES DUE TO FOREIGN EXCHANGE RATES

Apply the appropriate exchange differential to the excess, if any, of foreign currency assets over foreign currency liabilities. Do not report negative amounts in this item.

ITEMS 19-22—

These lines are for other liability items not specifically provided for and may be ledger or non-ledger.

Include: Interest paid in advance on mortgage loans.
Rents paid in advance.

Exclude: All voluntary and general contingency reserves and other special surplus funds not in the nature of liabilities.

Any unreimbursed expenditure on behalf of the Company by a parent, its affiliates or subsidiaries should be reported as a liability in the annual statement on this line.

ITEM 24—SPECIAL SURPLUS FUNDS

Enter only voluntary and general contingency reserves and other special surplus funds not in the nature of liabilities.

LIABILITIES, SURPLUS, AND OTHER FUNDS—PAGE 3 (Continued)

ITEM 25B—

Enter the amount of guaranty fund notes, contribution certificates, surplus notes, debenture notes, statutory deposits of alien insurers or similar funds other than capital stock, with appropriate description. Furnish pertinent information concerning conditions of repayment, redemption price and interest features, in answer to Question 8 on Page 13.

ITEM 26A—GROSS PAID IN AND CONTRIBUTED SURPLUS

This item should be the gross amount of paid in and contributed surplus without reduction on account of commissions or other expenses in connection with such transactions, but reduced by any distribution declared and paid as a return of such surplus.

ITEM 26C—TREASURY STOCK

Include number of shares, description, value included in Item 25A and cost of treasury stock acquired using Cost Method of accounting.

UNDERWRITING AND INVESTMENT EXHIBIT

STATEMENT OF INCOME—PAGE 4

This statement and the Capital and Surplus Account should be completed on the accrual, i.e., earned and incurred basis. Certain items may be either positive or negative, and should be entered accordingly. The various investment items of Interest, Rent, Profit and Loss, Depreciation, Appreciation, etc., appearing in the Parts supporting this statement of income must check with the data relating to the same transactions as set forth in the appropriate schedules. Profit and loss items must be itemized. The lists of items to be included in the various lines and supporting Parts are not intended to exclude analogous items which are omitted from the lists.

ITEM 12—(Write-in)

Premiums for life insurance on employees (less $ .... increase in cash values).

NOTE: Use this item only where the Company is beneficiary.

ITEMS 12-16—

Include: Checks cancelled because of non-presentation for payment, not included elsewhere.
Receipts from Schedule X assets, other than interest, divi-

dends and real estate income, and other than capital gains on investments.
Other sundry receipts and adjustments not reported elsewhere.

If the amount of any one type of item included in these lines represents more than 25% of the total for these lines, it should be identified separately.

ITEM 18A—DIVIDENDS TO POLICYHOLDERS

This item is the amount in Exhibit 3, Item 16, plus Item 11(b) on Page 3 of current year's statement, less Item 11(b) on Page 3 of prior year's statement.

ITEM 19—FEDERAL AND FOREIGN INCOME TAXES INCURRED

The amount of this item equals Item 14 of Exhibit 3, adjusted for reserves in Item 6 on Page 3 of the current and prior years' statements, and recoverables in Item 12 on Page 2 of current and prior years' statements.

CAPITAL AND SURPLUS ACCOUNT—PAGE 4

ITEM 25—CHANGE IN LIABILITY FOR UNAUTHORIZED REINSURANCE

This represents difference in Item 15 on Page 3 of current and prior years' statements.

ITEM 27—CHANGE IN EXCESS OF STATUTORY RESERVES OVER STATEMENT RESERVES

This item represents the difference in Item 16, Page 3 of current and prior years' statements.

ITEM 32—CHANGE IN TREASURY STOCK

Include: Change between years in ownership of treasury stock at cost.

ITEMS 33-38—

Include: Extraordinary amounts of taxes (including interest) and expenses relating to prior years.
Net proceeds from life insurance on employees.
Interest paid on contributions made to surplus (Surplus Notes).

PART 1—INTEREST, DIVIDENDS AND REAL ESTATE INCOME—PAGE 5

Exclude from Column 6 any investment income overdue more than a certain period but not greater than the period specified by law, regulation or ruling.

ITEMS 1-1.3—BONDS

Interest due and accrued on bonds in default as to principal or interest is to be excluded from Cols. 6 and 7. The market value of such bonds includes such interest.

If bonds are carried at amortized values, the amounts of yearly accrual of discount and of amortization of premium may be reflected in Part 1 or in Part 1A. If such amounts are included in Part 1, Column 3 of this item should agree with Schedule D.

ITEMS 2.1, 2.11, 2.2 AND 2.21—STOCKS

Include: Dividends on stocks declared to be ex-dividend on or prior to December 31 where said dividend is payable on or after January 1 of the following year.

ITEM 3—MORTGAGE LOANS

Include: Income from property for which the transfer or legal title is awaiting expiration of redemption or moratorium period.

Deduct: Outgo on such property unless capitalized or shown in Part 4.

Servicing fees paid to correspondents and others unless included in Part 4.

ITEM 4—REAL ESTATE

Include: Income from ownership of properties per Schedule A. Adequate rent for company's occupancy, in whole or in part, of its own buildings, and for space therein occupied by agencies.

Deduct: Interest on encumbrances.

Exclude: Reimbursements of amounts previously capitalized; such amounts should normally be credited to the item to which the expenditure was charged originally.

ITEM 9—

Any paid interest items included in this line should be preceded by a minus sign or by the word "minus".

ITEM 10—TOTALS

The total of Column 6 should agree with Item 14, Column 4 of Exhibit 1.

ITEMS 13-14—

Include: Interest on borrowed money on an incurred basis, with appropriate designation.

PART 1A—CAPITAL GAINS AND LOSSES ON INVESTMENTS—PAGE 5

Enter gains and losses separately in Columns 1 to 4. Gains and losses may be offset against each other only where they apply to the same bond issue, property, etc. "Increase in Book Value" and "Decrease in Book Value" should not include amounts due to accrual of discount or amortization of premium or depreciation on real estate if these items are reported in Part 1.

ITEMS 1-1.3—BONDS

The amounts to be shown in Columns 3 and 4 will depend on whether the Company values bonds on the amortized basis and if so, whether it reflects the accrual of discount and amortization of premium in Part 1, Column 3. If such items are reflected in Part 1, the amount in Column 3 of Part 1A should agree with the differences between the totals of Columns 10 and 17, Schedule D, Part 1, plus the total of the bond

portion of Column 9, Schedule D, Part 4, excluding accrual of discount. The amount in Column 4 should similarly agree with Schedule D.

ITEMS 2.1, 2.11, 2.2 AND 2.21—STOCKS

Include: In Column 5 the net change in the deduction for Company's stock owned. (See Exhibit 2, Line 23.)

Exclude: Proceeds of sale of rights, etc. (Reduce stock asset accordingly.)

ITEM 3—MORTGAGE LOANS

Include: In Column 1 bonuses (acceleration fees) received on prepayment of mortgage loans.

PART 1A—CAPITAL GAINS AND LOSSES ON INVESTMENTS—PAGE 5 (Continued)

ITEM 6—CASH ON HAND AND ON DEPOSIT
  Include: Gains or losses arising from the transfer of funds to or from other countries.
  In Column 5 the net change in deduction for deposits in suspended depositories.

ITEM 9—
  Include: Capital gains from investments previously charged off.

PARTS 2, 2A, 2B, 2C, 3, 3A AND PAGE 14—PREMIUMS AND LOSSES

ITEM 2—ALLIED LINES
  Include: Extended coverage; tornado, windstorm and hail; sprinkler and water damage; explosion, riot and civil commotion; growing crops; flood; rain; and damage from aircraft and vehicle.

ITEM 5—COMMERCIAL MULTIPLE PERIL
  Include: Multiple Peril policies (other than farmowners, homeowners and automobile policies) which include coverage for liability other than Auto.

ITEM 11—MEDICAL MALPRACTICE
  Include: The medical malpractice portion of any policy for which the premiums for medical malpractice are separately stated. Include all indivisible premium policies for which at least one half of the premium is for medical malpractice coverage. Medical malpractice is insurance of persons lawfully engaged in the practice of medicine, surgery, dentistry, nursing, dispensing drugs or medicines, or other health care services, and persons lawfully engaged in the operation of hospitals, sanitoriums, nursing homes, and other health care institutions, against loss, expense and liability resulting from errors, omissions, or neglect in the performance of professional service. It does not include insurance of persons engaged in the care and treatment of animals.

ITEM 15—OTHER ACCIDENT AND HEALTH
  Include: Credit Accident and Health (Group and Individual).

ITEM 17—OTHER LIABILITY
  Include: Physical damage other than auto and aircraft.

ITEM 19—AUTO LIABILITY
  Include: All automobile coverages except auto physical damage.

ITEMS 19.1, 19.2, 21.1 and 21.2—PRIVATE PASSENGER AND COMMERCIAL AUTOMOBILE
  19.1 and 21.1, Private passenger automobile, include all other automobile policies.
  19.2 and 21.2, Commercial automobile, include all automobile policies that include 5 or more automobiles or that include any commercial automobiles.

ITEM 29—International includes business transacted outside of the United States and its territories and possessions. International business which includes only one line of business or for which accurate detail is available for each line of business included, shall be excluded from this line and included in such other line or lines.

ITEM 30—Reinsurance which includes only one line of business or for which accurate detail is available for each line of business included, shall be excluded from this line and included in such other line or lines.

PART 2A—PREMIUMS IN FORCE—PAGE 6

Columns 2 and 4 should include additional premiums resulting from audits and all other premium transactions on expired policies.

Deductions of reinsurance ceded in Column 6 should be made on the basis of original premiums and original terms except in the case of excess loss or catastrophe reinsurance which should be deducted only on the basis of actual reinsurance premiums and actual reinsurance terms.

Annual instalments on term business may be set up in Part 2A as they become due or as if the entire term premium were prepaid.

PART 2B—RECAPITULATION OF ALL PREMIUMS—PAGE 7

Column 1 plus Column 3 plus Column 5 should agree with Column 7 of Part 2A.

Premium deposits on perpetual fire insurance risks should be charged as a liability to the extent of at least 90% of the gross amount of such deposit.

The reserve for rate credits and retrospective returns based on experience, Column 6, may be computed for each policy year by application of a flat percentage to the retrospective standard or subject earned premiums. The percentage should be based on the individual company's experience.

FOOTNOTE (b)—RESERVE FOR DEFERRED MATERNITY AND OTHER SIMILAR BENEFITS

A reserve must be carried in this Part or in Part 3A for any policy which provides for the extension of benefits after termination of the policy or of any insurance thereunder. Such benefits, which actually accrue and are payable at some future date, are predicated on a condition or actual disability which exists at the termination of the insurance and which is usually not known to the insurance company. These benefits are normally provided by contract provision but may be payable as a result of court decisions or of departmental rulings.

An example of the type of benefit for which this reserve must be carried is the coverage for hospital confinement due to maternity under a Group Hospital Expense policy where the hospitalization begins within a period, usually nine months, after the termination of an employee's insurance. Another example of the type of benefit for which a reserve may be set up is the coverage under a Group Hospital Expense policy for hospital confinement, due to causes other than maternity after the termination of an employee's insurance but prior to the expiration of a stated period. These examples are illustrative only and are not intended to limit the reserve to the benefits described. Some individual accident and health policies may also provide benefits similar to those under the "Extension of Benefits" section of a group policy.

A separate computation may be made of the reserve for deferred maternity benefits and of that for other extended benefits under group insurance policies. A further breakdown may be made, in the computation of the reserve, according to benefits for employee's hospitalization, those for dependent's hospitalization, medical and surgical benefits for employees, and medical and surgical benefits for dependents. Claims according to past experience for each of these classes can be related to the corresponding exposure and the resulting ratio applied to the current exposure to obtain the reserve for each such class.

The following is a theoretical illustration of the method referred to in the preceding paragraph for computing the year-end reserve in the case of deferred maternity hospitalization benefits for employees. Obtain for policies providing these benefits, all employee maternity claims where the employee, or former employee entered the hospital during the first nine months of the current year. Divide this total by the "in force" at the mid-point of the last nine months of the previous year. (The "in force" on a particular policy would be the product of the number of insured employees and the applicable daily hospital benefit.) The resulting ratio would be applied to the "in force" at the mid-point of the last nine months of the current year to obtain the required reserve. Only policies providing the benefits described would be used in the computation. Of course, the procedure should be varied as circumstances require.

It is intended that this reserve should be set up on the assumption that all insurance under policies containing an extension of benefits will be terminated on the statement date. The reserve should not be limited to the payments which the Company would expect to make under the extension of benefits clause in the year following the statement date.

Attach to the annual statement a description of the methods used in computing this reserve for each type of coverage for which a reserve is held.

PART 3—LOSSES PAID AND INCURRED—PAGE 8

Any changes in non ledger reinsurance recoverable on paid losses should be included in Column 3.

PART 3A—UNPAID LOSSES AND LOSS ADJUSTMENT EXPENSES—PAGE 9

Column 1—Adjusted or in Process of Adjustment. Include all losses which have been reported in any way to the Home Office of the company on or before December 31 of the current year. Provision for losses of the current year or prior years, if any, reported after that date would be made in Column 4 as Incurred But Not Reported.

Column 4—Incurred But Not Reported. Except where inapplicable, the reserve included in this column should be based on past experience, modified to reflect current conditions, such as changes in exposure, claim frequency or severity. Any known reinsurance recoverable on such losses may be deducted.

Make no deduction in Columns 1 or 4 for anticipated salvage or subrogation recoveries.

Column 5—Line 11 to agree with Sch. P, Part 1C Total, Col. 9.
  Line 16 to agree with Sch. P, Part 1D Total, Col. 9.
  Line 17 to agree with Sch. P, Part 1B Total, Col. 9.
  Line 19 to agree with Sch. P, Part 1A Total, Col. 9.

Column 6—Line 11 to agree with Sch. P, Part 1C Total, Col. 10.
  Line 16 to agree with Sch. P, Part 1D Total, Col. 10.
  Line 17 to agree with Sch. P, Part 1B Total, Col. 10.
  Line 19 to agree with Sch. P, Part 1A Total, Col. 10.

FOOTNOTE (a)—See Instructions for Footnote (b) under Part 2B.

ITEM 1—BONDS

The amount appearing in Column 4 must be the amortized or market value in accordance with the recommendations of the Committee on Valuation of Securities of the N. A. I. C. The amount needed to bring the book value to this value should be entered in Column 2 or 3.

Exclude: Interest due and accrued (include in Item 14).

ITEM 2—STOCKS

The amount appearing in Column 4 must be the market value in accordance with the recommendations of the Committee on Valuation of Securities of the N. A. I. C. The amount needed to bring the book value to this market value should be entered in Column 2 or 3.

ITEM 3—MORTGAGE LOANS ON REAL ESTATE

Include: Foreclosed liens subject to redemptions.

Exclude: Interest due and accrued (include in Item 14).

ITEM 4—REAL ESTATE

The amount appearing in Column 4 for properties occupied by the Company (home office real estate) shall not exceed actual cost, plus capitalized improvements, less normal depreciation. This formula shall apply whether the property is held directly or indirectly by the Company.

Exclude: Income due and accrued (include in Item 14).

ITEM 5—COLLATERAL LOANS

Exclude: Interest due and accrued (include in Item 14).

ITEM 6b—CASH ON DEPOSIT (Schedule N)

(In compiling Schedule N enter depository balances not on interest December 31st before those on interest and show subfooting of each class.)

Include: In Column 3 the excess of deposits in suspended depositories over the estimated amount recoverable.

ITEM 8—AGENTS' BALANCES OR UNCOLLECTED PREMIUMS

Column 4 of both Lines 8.1 and 8.2 consists of uncollected premiums less commissions and dividends applicable thereto and should equal direct balances plus reinsurance assumed balances (authorized and unauthorized) minus the over three months non-admitted portion.

In determining the over three months non-admitted portion of reinsurance assumed balances, do not include amounts due from a ceding insurer (a) to the extent the assuming insurer maintains unearned premium and loss reserves as to the ceding insurer, under normal principles of offset accounting, or, (b) where the ceding insurer is licensed and in good standing in the state of the assuming insurer's domicile.

In the case of Accident and Health premiums due and unpaid, include in Column 3 due and unpaid premiums effective prior to October 1 and, on other than group, any premiums in excess of one periodic premium due and unpaid in the case of premiums payable more frequently than quarterly.

ITEM 11—REINSURANCE RECOVERABLE ON LOSS PAYMENTS

Include: Amounts recoverable on losses paid by the ceding company. Reinsurance recoverable on unpaid losses should be treated as a deduction from the reserve liability therefor.

ITEM 12—FEDERAL INCOME TAX RECOVERABLE

Federal Income Tax Recoverable should be reported on Line 12 of Exhibit 1 and should include only those amounts previously reported in Exhibit 3, Line 14, of the current and prior years' annual statements.

In the case of an insurer that is a party to a consolidated tax return with one or more affiliates, the caption for Federal Income Tax Recoverable should reflect the source of the recoverable such as "Federal Income Tax Recoverable—Parent".

Insurers may recognize intercompany transactions arising from income tax allocations among companies participating in a consolidated tax return provided the following conditions are met:

1. There is a written agreement describing the method of allocation and the manner in which intercompany balances will be settled, and

2. Such agreement requires that any intercompany balance will be settled within a reasonable time following the filing of the consolidated tax return, and

3. Such agreement complies with regulations promulgated by the Internal Revenue Service, and

4. Any receivables arising out of such allocation must meet the criteria for admitted assets as prescribed by the domiciliary state of the insurer, and

5. Liabilities which offset the related intercompany receivables are established by other companies participating in the consolidated tax return.

ITEM 13—

Include: Enter in this line with the caption "Electronic Data Processing Equipment" the value of any electronic data processing equipment carried at an admitted asset value permitted by law, ruling or regulation. Any such value should be reported in Item 13, Page 2, and captioned "Electronic Data Processing Equipment".

Exclude: Under no circumstances should computer software other than operating system software be considered as an asset, either admitted or non-admitted.

ITEM 15—EQUIPMENT, FURNITURE AND SUPPLIES

Exclude: Any electronic data processing equipment which is carried at an admitted asset value permitted by law, ruling or regulation.

ITEM 26.2—PREMIUMS, AGENTS' BALANCES AND INSTALLMENTS BOOKED BUT DEFERRED AND NOT YET DUE

This item should include all future installments on all policies for which one or more installments are over three months past due.

EXHIBIT 3—RECONCILIATION OF LEDGER ASSETS—PAGE 12

Profit and Loss items must be itemized and should be entered gross in both increases and decreases.

ITEM 12 (g)—(Write-in)

Premiums for life insurance on employees (less $................... increase in cash values).

NOTE: If the cash values on such policies are **not** carried on the ledger, no deduction would be made in this item for the increase during the year in such values. Use this item only where the Company is beneficiary.

8a. The following information with regard to stock options should be furnished and analogous information should be supplied for warrants or rights:

1. A brief description of the terms of each option arrangement including:

    (a) the title and amount of securities subject to option;

    (b) the year or years during which the options were granted; and

    (c) the year or years during which the optionees became, or will become, entitled to exercise the options.

2. A statement of:

    (a) the number of shares under option at the end of the statement year, and the option price and the fair value thereof, per share and in total, at the dates the options were granted;

    (b) the number of shares with respect to which options became exercisable during the year, and the option price and fair value thereof, per share and in total, at the dates the options became exercisable;

    (c) the number of shares with respect to which options were exercised during the year, and the option price and fair value thereof, per share and in total, at the dates the options were exercised.

    Options to buy stock are deemed to be granted on the date that a designated number of shares are assigned to a specific individual, notwithstanding the stipulation at that time that such shares are not exercisable until certain attached conditions are met, such as those relating to persistency of insurance produced by the optionee or his continuance in employment for a period of years.

The required information may be summarized as appropriate with respect to each of these categories. The above information should be supplied whether the stock involved relates to the Company, the parent of the company, a subsidiary of the company, or an affiliated corporation. The information should be shown separately for (1) agents and brokers and (2) employees and others.

22. The information to be reported on all such transactions during the year must include, but not necessarily be limited to, the following items for each such transaction:

    (1) Dates of transaction—securities delivered on................ securities returned on ....

    (2) Complete description of securities involved ....

    (3) Number of shares or amount of bond or other security ....

    (4) Market value on date securities were delivered $............

    (5) Market value on date securities were returned $............

    (6) Collateral value held $............

    (7) Form of collateral ....

    (8) Collateral held by ....
    (name and address)

    (9) Names and addresses of all other persons involved in transaction ....

SCHEDULE F—PART 1A—SECTION 1—CEDED REINSURANCE AS OF DECEMBER 31, CURRENT YEAR—PAGE 32

List names and location of all reinsurers and list amounts of reinsurance in the appropriate columns. Where the total amount of unauthorized alien reinsurance premiums in force, other than with Underwriters at Lloyd's of London, constitutes less than 5 per cent of the total reinsurance premiums in force and where the total amount of losses recoverable from such unauthorized alien reinsurers, as reported in Columns 1 and 2, is less than 5 per cent of the total amount of such losses recoverable from all reinsurers, these amounts may be bulked and reported in a one-line entry only, captioned "Other Unauthorized Alien Reinsurers". When this method of reporting is used, the names of all alien reinsurers, other than Underwriters at Lloyd's of London, shall be reported in a separate schedule to be furnished to each Department not later than June 1st. Where reinsurance is ceded to an alien pool, list the names of the individual reinsurers and their home office locations, together with the amounts of reinsurance ceded to each reinsurer, or submit, not later than June 1, a schedule listing the name, home office location and share of each participant in each pooling agreement.

The unearned premium shown in Column 4 should be computed accurately for each authorized and unauthorized reinsurer.

Where a large number of reinsuring companies is involved, the following method will be acceptable:

1. The unearned premium reserve should be calculated accurately for each unauthorized reinsurer and totaled.

2. The total unearned premium reserve for all authorized and unauthorized companies (combined) should be calculated accurately.

3. A ratio should be computed by subtracting (1) from (2) above and then dividing the difference by total premiums in force for authorized companies.

4. The application of this ratio, as derived in (3), to the premiums in force of each authorized company gives the amount to be entered in Column 4.

A modification would be necessary in the case of portfolio reinsurance.

The inclusion of the foregoing method in the Instructions is not intended to prevent the use of other approximate methods which produce reliable results.

SCHEDULE F—PART 1A—SECTION 2—ASSUMED REINSURANCE AS OF DECEMBER 31, CURRENT YEAR—PAGE 32

Reinsureds for whom the total of the amounts in Columns 1, 2 and 4 is less than $50,000.00 may be combined and shown on one line identified as "Reinsureds for whom the total of Columns 1, 2 and 4 is less than $50,000.00". Reinsurance assumed from pools or syndicates may be reported in the name of the pool or syndicate instead of in the names of the insurers which ceded the reinsurance to the pool or syndicate.

SCHEDULE F—PART 2—FUNDS WITHHELD ON ACCOUNT OF REINSURANCE IN UNAUTHORIZED COMPANIES AS OF DECEMBER 31, CURRENT YEAR—PAGE 33

Segregate Unearned Premiums (Col. 1), Paid and Unpaid Losses Recoverable (Col. 2), Deposits by and Funds withheld from Reinsurers (Col. 4) and Miscellaneous Balances (Col. 5) on an individual contract basis. It is necessary in the case of Underwriters at Lloyd's of London to make the segregation by individual contract since there are different parties of interest under each agreement.

SCHEDULE H—ACCIDENT AND HEALTH EXHIBIT—PAGE 35

COLUMN 4—COLLECTIVELY RENEWABLE

Include amounts pertaining to policies which are made available to groups of persons under a plan sponsored by an employer, or an association or a union or affiliated associations or unions or a group of individuals supplying materials to a central point of collection or handling a common product or commodity, under which the insurer has agreed with respect to such policies that renewal will not be refused, subject to any specified age limit, while the insured remains a member of the group specified in the agreement unless the insurer simultaneously refuses renewal to all other policies in the same group. A sponsored plan shall not include any arrangement where an insurer's customary individual policies are made available without special underwriting considerations and where the employer's participation is limited to arranging for salary allotment premium payments with or without contribution by the employer. Such plans are sometimes referred to as payroll budget or salary allotment plans. A sponsored plan may be administered by an agent or trustee.

Include amounts pertaining to policies issued by a company or group of companies under a plan, other than a group insurance plan, authorized by special legislation for the exclusive benefit of the aged through mass enrollment.

Include amounts pertaining to policies issued under mass enrollment procedures to older people, such as those age 65 and over, in some geographic region or regions under which the insurer has agreed with respect to such policies that renewal will not be refused unless the insurer simultaneously refuses renewal to all other policies specified in the agreement.

COLUMN 5—NON-CANCELLABLE

Include amounts pertaining to policies which are guaranteed renewable for life or to a specified age, such as 60 or 65, at guaranteed premium rates.

COLUMN 6—GUARANTEED RENEWABLE

Include amounts pertaining to policies which are guaranteed renewable for life or to a specified age, such as 60 or 65, but under which the insurer reserves the right to change the scale of premium rates.

COLUMN 7—NON-RENEWABLE FOR STATED REASONS ONLY

Include amounts pertaining to policies in which the insurer has reserved the right to cancel or refuse renewal for one or more stated reasons, but has agreed implicitly or explicitly that, prior to a specified time or age, it will not cancel or decline renewal solely because of deterioration of health after issue.

COLUMN 9—ALL OTHER

Include any other Accident and Health coverages not specially required in other columns.

PART 1—PREMIUMS IN FORCE

Except for Lines 8 and 9, this part should be reported on a gross instead of on a net basis as regards reinsurance. Initial Premiums Written and Unpaid ("Unplaced Premiums") at December 31 are excluded from these items.

LINES 1, 7, 8 AND 9—IN FORCE

Include for each Policy paid for and in force one periodic premium (monthly, quarterly, semi-annual, annual or longer period) on the payment basis in effect at the end of the year. Policies on which premiums are paid in advance should be included for only the same periodic premium in force as in force policies on which premiums are not paid in advance.

LINES 2 AND 6—PREMIUMS PAID IN ADVANCE, DECEMBER 31

These differ from amounts in Line 11, which are on net basis as to reinsurance ceded and include the increase in active life reserve.

LINE 3—PREMIUMS WRITTEN OR RENEWED DURING YEAR

Lines 10c + 10d

LINE 4—EXCESS OF ORIGINAL PREMIUMS OVER REINSURANCE ASSUMED

When reinsurance is assumed at a date subsequent to the beginning of the direct policy period, there should be entered in this line the excess of the premiums which would have been received had reinsurance been effective on the effective date of the direct Insurance over the premium actually included in Line 10b in respect of the policy.

LINE 7—IN FORCE AT END OF YEAR

Lines 1 + 2 + 3 + 4 — 5 — 6

LINE 9—NET PREMIUMS IN FORCE

Lines 7 — 8

RECONCILIATION OF PART 1 OF SCHEDULE H WITH
FIRE AND CASUALTY ANNUAL STATEMENT BLANK

LINE 1—PREMIUMS IN FORCE, DECEMBER 31, PREVIOUS YEAR

Column 2 of Schedule H should agree with Line 14 of Column 5 of Part 2A less Line 14 of Column 5 of Part 2B of the previous Annual Statement. The total of Columns 3 to 9 inclusive of Schedule H should agree with Line 15 of Column 5 of Part 2A less Line 15 of Column 5 of Part 2B of the previous Annual Statement.

LINE 2—PREMIUMS PAID IN ADVANCE, DECEMBER 31, PREVIOUS YEAR

Column 2 of Schedule H should agree with Line 14 of Column 5 of Part 2B of the previous Annual Statement. The total of Columns 3 to 9 inclusive of Schedule H should agree with Line 15 of Column 5 of Part 2B of the previous Annual Statement.

LINE 3—PREMIUMS WRITTEN OR RENEWED DURING YEAR

Column 2 of Schedule H should agree with Line 14 of Column 2 of Part 2A. The total of Columns 3 to 9 inclusive of Schedule H should agree with Line 15 of Column 2 of Part 2A.

LINE 4—EXCESS OF ORIGINAL PREMIUMS OVER REINSURANCE ASSUMED

Column 2 of Schedule H should agree with Line 14 of Column 3 of Part 2A. The sum of Columns 3 to 9 inclusive of Schedule H should agree with Line 15 of Column 3 of Part 2A.

LINE 5—EXPIRATIONS AND EXCESS OF ORIGINAL PREMIUMS OVER RETURN PREMIUMS ON CANCELLATIONS

Column 2 of Schedule H should agree with Line 14 of Column 4

of Part 2A. The sum of Columns 3 to 9 inclusive of Schedule H should agree with Line 15 of Column 4 of Part 2A.

LINE 6—PREMIUMS PAID IN ADVANCE, DECEMBER 31, CURRENT YEAR

Column 2 of Schedule H should agree with Line 14 of Column 5 of Part 2B. The sum of Columns 3 to 9 inclusive of Schedule H should agree with Line 15 of Column 5 of Part 2B.

LINE 7—PREMIUMS IN FORCE, DECEMBER 31, CURRENT YEAR

Column 2 of Schedule H should agree with Line 14 of Column 5 of Part 2A less Line 14 of Column 5 of Part 2B. The total of Columns 3 to 9 inclusive of Schedule H should agree with Line 15 of Column 5 of Part 2A less Line 15 of Column 5 of Part 2B.

LINE 8—REINSURANCE PREMIUMS IN FORCE

Column 2 of Schedule H should agree with Line 14 of Column 6 of Part 2A. The sum of Columns 3 to 9 inclusive of Schedule H should agree with Line 15 of Column 6 of Part 2A.

LINE 9—NET PREMIUMS IN FORCE, DECEMBER 31, CURRENT YEAR

Column 2 of Schedule H should agree with Line 14 of Column 7 of Part 2A less Line 14 of Column 5 of Part 2B. The total of Columns 3 to 9 inclusive of Schedule H should agree with Line 15 of Column 7 of Part 2A less Line 15 of Column 5 of Part 2B.

NOTE: The advance premiums entering into the reconciliation of Lines 1 and 2 of Schedule H should be on a gross basis before deduction of reinsurance ceded, and the amounts in Column 5 of Part 2B may require adjustment for this.

RECONCILIATION OF PART 2 OF SCHEDULE H WITH FIRE AND CASUALTY
ANNUAL STATEMENT BLANK AND INSURANCE EXPENSE EXHIBIT

LINE 10—PREMIUMS WRITTEN

Column 2 of Schedule H should agree with Line 14 of Part 2C. The total of Columns 3 to 9 inclusive of Schedule H should agree with Line 15 of Part 2C.

LINE 11—INCREASE IN ADVANCE PREMIUMS AND ACTIVE LIFE RESERVES

Column 2 of Schedule H should agree with Line 14, Column 3 less Column 2, of Part 2. The total of Columns 3 to 9 inclusive of Schedule H should agree with Line 15, Column 3 less Column 2 of Part 2.

LINE 12—PREMIUMS EARNED

Net premiums earned in Column 2 of Schedule H should agree with Line 14 of Column 4 of Part 2. The total of net premiums earned in Columns 3 to 9 inclusive of Schedule H should agree with Line 15 of Column 4 of Part 2.

LINE 13—BENEFITS OF CURRENT YEAR

Column 2 of Schedule H should agree with Line 14 of Column 7 of Part 3 less any corresponding Increase in Claim Reserves included in Line 14 of Schedule H. The total of Columns 3 to 9 inclusive of Schedule H should agree with Line 15 of Column 7 of Part 3 less any corresponding Increase in Claim Reserves included in Line 14 of Schedule H.

LINE 14—INCREASE IN CLAIM RESERVES

Should agree appropriately with the net of Line 6 of Part 3B of Schedule H for current year less corresponding amount for previous year.

LINE 15—INCURRED CLAIMS

This is the sum of Lines 13 and 14 of Schedule H.

LINE 16—COMMISSIONS

Net commissions in Column 2 of Schedule H should agree with Line 6 of Column 14 of Part II of the Insurance Expense Exhibit. The total of Net Commissions in Columns 3 to 9 inclusive of Schedule H should agree with Line 6 of Column 15 of Part II of the Insurance Expense Exhibit.

LINE 17—GENERAL INSURANCE EXPENSE

Column 2 of Schedule H should agree with the sum of Lines 5, 7 and 10 of Column 14 of Part II of the Insurance Expense Exhibit. The total of Columns 3 to 9 inclusive of Schedule H should agree with the sum of Lines 5, 7 and 10 of Column 15 of Part II of the Insurance Expense Exhibit.

LINE 18—TAXES, LICENSES AND FEES

Column 2 of Schedule H should agree with Line 11 of Column 14 of Part II of the Insurance Expense Exhibit. The total of Columns 3 to 9 inclusive of Schedule H should agree with Line 11 of Column 15 of Part II of the Insurance Expense Exhibit.

LINE 19—TOTAL EXPENSES INCURRED

Sum of Lines 16, 17 and 18 of Schedule H.

LINE 20—GAIN FROM UNDERWRITING BEFORE DIVIDENDS

Line 12(d) less the sum of Lines 15d and 19 of Schedule H.

LINE 21—DIVIDENDS TO POLICYHOLDERS

Column 2 of Schedule H should agree with Line 14 of Column 14 of Part II of the Insurance Expense Exhibit. The total of Columns 3 to 9 inclusive of Schedule H should agree with Line 14 of Column 15 of Part II of the Insurance Expense Exhibit.

LINE 22—GAIN FROM UNDERWRITING AFTER DIVIDENDS

Line 20 less Line 21 of Schedule H.

A—ACTIVE LIFE RESERVE

LINE 2—ADDITIONAL RESERVES

A reserve must be carried in this line for any policy which provides a guarantee of renewability. The standards adopted by the N.A.I.C. in December, 1964, are acceptable bases for such additional reserves. A company which wishes to enter the entire active life reserve (other than the reserves required for Line 3) in a single sum may enter such amount in Line 2, with appropriate change of captions of Lines 1 and 2.

LINE 7—TOTALS (NET)

Column 2 of Schedule H should agree with Line 14, Column 7 less Column 5 of Part 2B. The total of Columns 3 to 9 inclusive of Schedule H should agree with Line 15, Column 7 less Column 5 of Part 2B.

B—CLAIM RESERVE

LINE 1—PRESENT VALUE OF AMOUNTS NOT YET DUE ON CLAIMS

Column 2 of Schedule H should include that portion of Line 14, Columns 1 and 4, of Part 3A which relates to unaccrued benefits on a gross basis. The total of Columns 3 to 9 inclusive of Schedule H should include that portion of Line 15, Columns 1 and 4, of Part 3A which relates to unaccrued benefits on a gross basis.

LINE 2—RESERVE FOR FUTURE CONTINGENT BENEFITS (DEFERRED MATERNITY AND OTHER SIMILAR BENEFITS)

No entry is needed for Line 2 of Claim Reserve if reserve is included in Line 3 of Active Life Reserve of Schedule H.

LINE 5—REINSURANCE

Include Reinsurance Ceded relating to gross amounts of Claim Reserve shown in Lines 1 and 2 of Schedule H.

INSTRUCTIONS

For Completing Accident and Health Policy Experience Exhibit

FOREWORD

Titles of the various items and lines are in general self-explanatory and as such constitute instructions. Specific further instructions are prescribed for items and lines about which there might be some question as to content. Any entry for which no specific instruction has been given should be made in a manner consistent with related items and lines covered by specific instructions.

GENERAL

1. The name of the company must be clearly shown at the top of each page or pages.

2. The actual blank form of the Exhibit furnished by this Department should be considered by a company as a guide in reporting its own figures as the spaces for each classification are in most instances too small to permit its use directly, and it is unlikely that a company would have items to report in each of the classifications. For those classifications for which a company has nothing to report the classification heading need not be shown on its report. The form should show each Section A, B, C, D and E and if there are no data in one of these sections, the word "none" should be inserted. Where necessary, one or more pages should be used with the size and general arrangement to be consistent with the sample blank.

3. This Exhibit should not include any data pertaining to double indemnity, waiver of premiums and other disability benefits embodied in life contracts.

4. Include membership or policy fees, if any, with Premiums Earned. (Col. 3)

5. Experience for classifications under Sections A and B need not be reported by policy form.

6. Policy forms issued on the Industrial Debit Basis (premiums payable weekly) which are included under Section C should be identi-

fied by placing the designation (I) to the left of the Name of the Policy.

7. A company may separate first year business and renewal business for any classification by using two lines for each form. Show first year business on top line and place the designation (F) to the right of the loss ratio. Show the renewal business on next line and place the designation (R) to the right of the loss ratio.

8. Experience under Schedule Form Policy (except Non-Cancellable and Guaranteed Renewable) should be reported for each combination of coverages issued under the forms. The experience for individual combinations of coverage with a premium volume less than 5% of the total for the Schedule Form Policy may be merged and reported on a single line.

9. Experience on a form not currently being issued need not be reported separately unless premiums on such policy form exceed 5% of total premiums, excluding premiums for group insurance. The combined data on all policy forms not reported separately should be included under the proper classification and identified under the second column as "Forms Not Currently Being Issued". If experience is reported separately on any form not currently issued, insert an asterisk (*) before the name of the policy form in the second column.

10. The "Totals" at the bottom of the Exhibit should agree with Column 1 of the appropriate lines of Schedule H.

DEFINITIONS

The classifications under each Section C, D, and E are the same classifications used for Columns 4 to 9 inclusive in Schedule H. The definitions of Collectively Renewable, Non-cancellable, Guaranteed Renewable, and Non-renewable for Stated Reasons Only are shown in the instructions for Schedule H. Other definitions are as follows:

1. Conversions—Include data on individual policies which have been converted without evidence of insurability from either Group or from another individual policy. Do not include data on policies which have been changed as a result of an increase or decrease in coverage or other similar change.

2. Premiums $7.50 or Less Per Person Annually—Include data on policy forms which average having an annual premium of $7.50 or less. Where a policy covers a contingency for a period of coverage less than a year, the premium for that period is to be considered as the annual premium.

3. Mass Underwriting Basis—This sub-classification of the Collectively Renewable classification under Section C pertains to (1) policies issued by a company or a group of companies under a plan, other than a group insurance plan, authorized by special legislation for the exclusive benefit of the aged through mass enrollment and to (2) policies issued under mass enrollment procedures to older people, such as those age 65 and over, in some geographic region or regions under which the insured have agreed with respect to such policies that renewal will not be refused unless the insurer simultaneously refuses renewal to all other policies specified in the agreement. Data on policies classified as Collectively Renewable but not meeting the above definition of Mass Underwriting Basis should be placed in the "other" sub-classification.

4. Mixed Benefits—Where a Policy Form provides both Medical Expense Benefits and Loss of Time Benefits, as well as other benefits and 50% or more of the premium is for one of these classifications, the data should be placed in such classification.

5. Mixed Renewal Provision—Where a Policy Form is Guaranteed Renewable or Non-cancellable up to some age, such as age 65 and, thereafter renewable at the option of the company, the data should be placed in the original classification.

6. "C—Hospital, Medical and Surgical Policies"—Include in this section data on policies providing Hospital, Medical and Surgical benefits as well as data on policies commonly referred to as Major Medical, Comprehensive Catastrophe, Hospital Indemnity, Nursing Home Benefits, Dental Expense and Blanket Accident Medical Expense.

7. "D—Loss of Time Policies"—Include in this section data on policies providing monthly or weekly income benefits for disability arising from sickness and/or accident. Policies providing limited benefits, for example, where benefits are payable only in the event of injury in a public conveyance should be placed in Section E. Include in Section D data on policy forms that provide Overhead Expense Benefits and Mortgage Disability Income Benefits.

8. "E—All Other Policies"—Include in this section all policy forms not belonging in Sections A, B, C, or D. Policy Forms belonging in this section are those which provide benefits specifically for cancer, dread disease, specified diseases, travel protection, accidental death, accidental death and dismemberment, student accident, trip insurance, etc.. where not included in Section A in the classification "Premiums $7.50 or Less Per Person Annually"

Medicare Fiscal Intermediaries act as administrative agents for the Social Security Administration on a reimbursement basis. In general, accounting activity in connection with Medicare should be handled such that the financial results reflected in the various statements and exhibits of the Annual Statement of those companies acting as Medicare Fiscal Intermediaries under such contracts are on a comparable basis to those of any other insurers. The following instructions should be applied for the particular transactions specified.

ASSETS—PAGE 2

Any excess of cash disbursements over cash received from the Social Security Administration and credited to Intermediaries' general accounts should be reported as a miscellaneous ledger asset.

Any amount in a bank account established under Medicare or similar programs should be excluded from assets.

LIABILITIES—PAGE 3

Any excess of cash received from the Social Security Administration over cash disbursements should be reported as a miscellaneous ledger liability.

PART 4—PAGE 10

Intermediaries' administrative expense reimbursements should be credited to the individual accounts, such as salaries, rent, travel, etc. In other words, each line in this part should be reported on a net after reimbursement basis. Reimbursement for minor indirect expenses allocated to the Medicare operation may be credited in total in Line 21—Miscellaneous.

EXHIBIT 1—PAGE 11
EQUIPMENT, FURNITURE AND SUPPLIES

Company-owned equipment, furniture and supplies used in connection with Medicare operations should be reported as provided in the instruction for Item 15 of this exhibit.

INSTRUCTIONS

For completing Consolidated Annual Statement for Affiliated Fire and Casualty Insurers

GENERAL

1. Every group of affiliated insurers which includes more than one fire and casualty insurer shall complete a consolidated annual statement and insurance expense exhibit for all affiliated fire and casualty insurers. Include United States branches of alien insurers and alien insurers owned, directly or indirectly, in whole or in part, by a United States insurer. Other affiliated alien insurers may be excluded.

2. The blank to be used is the NAIC annual statement blank for fire and casualty insurers and the instructions therefor subject to the additional instructions included herein.

3. Wherever the word "company" appears in the blank it should be construed to mean "company and its consolidated affiliates".

4. On the cover and on Page 1 print "Consolidated" above "Annual Statement" and in the space for the name of the insurer show the name of the principal fire and casualty insurer of the group followed by "and its affiliated fire and casualty insurers: "
Include the names of all affiliated fire and casualty insurers.

5. Date of filing: On or before April 1.

6. Appropriate changes may be made in the jurat on Page 1.

ASSETS—PAGE 2 AND EXHIBIT 1

Eliminate all amounts receivable or recoverable from consolidated affiliates. Make compensating adjustments in liabilities on Page 3. Eliminate mortgage loans to consolidated affiliates. Make compensating adjustments in the net amount of real estate. Eliminate collateral loans to consolidated affiliates. Make compensating reductions in liabilities for borrowed money on Page 3.

LIABILITIES—PAGE 3

Write in on Line 24 an item for minority interests, if there are any.

REINSURANCE—PAGES 6, 7, 8, 9, 10 AND SCHEDULES F AND H

Eliminate reinsurance ceded and assumed among consolidated affiliates.

SCHEDULE D

Eliminate all bonds and stocks of consolidated affiliates. Make compensating adjustments in liabilities, surplus and other funds on Page 3.

OMITTED INFORMATION

The following information may be omitted:
The General Interrogatories, the Special Deposit Schedule, the Schedule of All Other Deposits, Schedules A, B, BA and C, Schedule

D except for the Summary and the detail for parents, subsidiaries and affiliates, Schedule F except for the totals and subtotals for Parts 1A and 1B, Schedules M, N and X.